T0331876

Object-oriented Programming with Smalltalk

Series Editor
Imad Saleh

Object-oriented Programming with Smalltalk

Harald Wertz

First published 2015 in Great Britain and the United States by ISTE Press Ltd and Elsevier Ltd

ISTE Press Ltd
27-37 St George's Road
London SW19 4EU
UK

www.iste.co.uk

Elsevier Ltd
The Boulevard, Langford Lane
Kidlington, Oxford, OX5 1GB
UK

www.elsevier.com

Notices

Knowledge and best practice in this field are constantly changing. As new research and experience broaden our understanding, changes in research methods, professional practices, or medical treatment may become necessary.

Practitioners and researchers must always rely on their own experience and knowledge in evaluating and using any information, methods, compounds, or experiments described herein. In using such information or methods they should be mindful of their own safety and the safety of others, including parties for whom they have a professional responsibility.

To the fullest extent of the law, neither the Publisher nor the authors, contributors, or editors, assume any liability for any injury and/or damage to persons or property as a matter of products liability, negligence or otherwise, or from any use or operation of any methods, products, instructions, or ideas contained in the material herein.

For information on all our publications visit our website at http://store.elsevier.com/

British Library Cataloguing-in-Publication Data
A CIP record for this book is available from the British Library
Library of Congress Cataloging in Publication Data
A catalog record for this book is available from the Library of Congress
ISBN 978-1-78548-016-4

Printed and bound in the UK and US

Contents

Preface

In order to learn how to program objects, we must first get to know them. For this, we need to know the programming. This results in an infernal loop which can make learning an object-oriented language very painful.

With its intuitive presentation of topics, this book provides a way out of this loop. Being based on mini- and life-sized projects, it offers the support needed for acquiring the foundations and the know-how of object-oriented programming in an easy and, hopefully, stimulating way.

It represents a summary of a decade of teaching an introductory course on object-oriented programming. After this course, a student would have solid general programming foundations and the ability to design, develop and implement his own object-oriented programming projects. We use the language SMALLTALK through its dialect SQUEAK, chosen because of the pure object presentation, the power of its environment, the notable amount of sample programs available (the whole SQUEAK system is written in the SQUEAK language) and ultimately its *open-source* nature on all platforms. Effectively, SQUEAK works identically on computers of all types and operating systems, ranging from Windows, Apple-OS, Linux or others, to even mobile devices.

With the exception of Chapter 3, each chapter is organized as a course accompanied with tutorials and practical exercises. The contents of this book cannot be fully absorbed without the tutorials and without solving the practical problems. In this case, the ability to *solve the problems* translates into the ability to *design and implement* programs.

The *course* parts of this book are Chapters 1–6.

The *tutorials* are all in Appendix 1.

In order to learn, you must practise. It is true that to best learn a foreign language, you have to live where this language is *practiced* on a daily basis. The same applies for learning a programming language, where you have to "live" in the system using this specific language. Chapter 1 explains how to acquire a copy of the SQUEAK system suitable for creating a place where you can "live" a life of object-oriented programming. Using the SQUEAK system while reading this book is essential for understanding the text.

This constant use of the SQUEAK system provides the practical exercises which become crucial throughout the chapters all the way to Appendix 1. These are not discussed in this book and are the responsibility of the readers.

How can you do this? At first, you must familiarize yourself with the wonderfully distinct SQUEAK interface by interactively exploring and "playing" with it.

Then upon encountering a SMALLTALK expression that does not seem explicit, a computer check is needed. Even if it seems clear, verify it on your computer.

After reading each exercise description, stop and take the time to solve and implement it. The solution will not work right away. Have no fear, correcting and improving programs is part of a programmer's daily routine, so it is worth getting used to it when taking your first steps in programming. It is important to go beyond the simple framework of the exercise, as there is more than one possible solution. Finding several solutions is always more educational than finding just one. After enough practice, programming becomes a pleasant activity, and even a passionate one. The more time you spend on it, the faster you will become a good programmer. Only after finding your own solutions, are you encouraged to examine the solutions proposed in Appendix 1. *All* exercises in this book have a solution illustrated in the book. These solutions, these *tutorials*, make up an *integral* part of the chapter in which these exercises have been proposed. Continuing reading becomes impossible without previously studying and implementing the solutions. Often, we will tackle concepts, notions or additional techniques necessary for understanding the subsequent text. The alternation between reading courses and consulting the exercise solutions, created by separating the course materials and the exercise solutions, in a way reflects the need for personal research from the beginning.

Throughout this book, we have tried to present new features, new techniques and new concepts in a context where their use would be necessary, thus facilitating their understanding. Moreover, throughout the chapters, these same concepts, techniques and functionalities will reappear in various situations. This should improve the understanding of these concepts.

This book is divided into three parts. The first part, composed of Chapters 1–4, presents the foundations for object-oriented programming and SMALLTALK. It familiarizes the readers with the concepts such as class and instance, message passing, as well as static and dynamic inheritance. We also explore the most important SMALLTALK classes with their most used methods. More precisely, the first chapter presents the SQUEAK system and the second chapter introduces, in an intuitive manner, object-oriented programming. After a brief presentation of the software architecture and the heritage mechanisms in Chapter 3, the very long Chapter 4 goes through a complete tour of the syntax and grammar aspects of SMALLTALK.

From Chapter 5, we enter the second part, which will deepen the understanding of programming techniques learned in the first part using examples of complete SQUEAK programs. This introduces graphical user interface (GUI) programming for developing a set of programs for producing line drawings.

Chapter 6 presents the fundamental mechanism of *dependencies* by programming several calculators.

To make the most out of this book around which the course is structured, our advice is to begin with the first three chapters and then possibly some sections of Chapter 4. Then, continue with those in the second part that addresses programming in the Logo style and L-systems (visualizing drawings is much more appealing than examining dull strings of characters), the use of dependencies and the process coordination.

Chapter 4 then serves as a *vade mecum* for explaining and deepening the understanding of classes and methods encountered while developing the programs.

If this book has created the *desire* for you to program objects in SQUEAK, it has served its role perfectly.

Happy reading and happy compiling!

Program source

The programs found in the second part of this book are available on my Website www.ai.univ-paris8.fr/~hw. After downloading, you should place them in the directory where you keep your SQUEAK programs. Then, just open the File List and load them (using the load them button) into your SQUEAK image.

Acknowledgements

This book could not have been written without the help of my colleagues, friends and students. I want to thank everyone, particularly Pierre Audibert who discovered a countless number of shells and helped with my "Germanic" style text; Françoise

Balmas read the text in an attempt to understand it and thus was able to identify faults from an explanatory and educational perspective; Vincent Boyer for carefully reading and correcting my graphical programming vocabulary; Christian Fer, Julien Dervaux, Hubert Dupont and Serge Stinckwich all worked as additional correctors and each of them brought notable improvements; Jo Arditty and Marc Riesacher who helped me to find the appropriate words when I did not have more than foreign phrases in my head; Stephane Ducasse who asked me some great questions and whose relevant criticisms led me to actually rewrite parts of the text. Patrick Greussay, Jean-François Perrot, Gilles Bernard and Jym Feat have all proved their friendship to me and have inspired me throughout my CS career: through their discussions, courses and criticisms.

Of course, this book would have never been possible without the continuous questioning from my students and without their enthusiasm for object-oriented programming.

Like any book that develops in parallel with a course, its content is strongly influenced by the media used. My first object-oriented programming course was based on the system called LITTLESMALLTALK developed by Timothy Budd. His influence can be felt throughout this book. We thank him for making available a SMALLTALK microsystem that made it possible to easily understand its functioning *and* its implementation, and was compatible with the small machines that we had available at that time.

The idea of the calculators in Chapter 7 belongs to Philippe Krief, who used the programming of such calculators in his course on Smalltalk within our CS department.

Of course, the vast resources found on the Internet equally contributed to the content of this book. In particular, the Websites on the SQUEAK language http://www.squeak.org/ and http://minnow.cc.gatech.edu/Squeak, which any reader should consult regularly.

And a thank you also goes out to Fares Belhadj who graciously provided me with the wonderful image of the palm tree at the end of section A.8.

Harald WERTZ
September 2015

Introduction

All programs manipulate a certain number of *objects* (numbers, trees, lists, tables, objects, etc.). These *programmatic objects* correspond, more or less, to the *imaginary objects* which the programmer has in his head and which are representations of the real world or the world of computations, one as real as the other.

The power of object-oriented programming lies in proposing a definition of the programmatic objects that allows "pasting" them close to the imaginary objects.

Note that we must distinguish between the two meanings of the word *object*: in the technical sense of object-oriented programming (defined further) and the ordinary sense: objects of discourse. The charm of object-oriented programming lies exactly in the simplicity in which one passes from one to the other[1].

I.1. Everything is an object

– The fundamental idea of object-oriented programming is to systematically consider complex entities which, for each of the "beings" appearing in the program, regroup *the data structure* that describes them with the procedures that allow their manipulation. These entities are naturally called the *objects* of the program. The structure of each of these entities is specified by a *class*: it can be said that the object is an *instance* of its class.

– We can overlook the role of the class and only consider the object, without questioning its origins. Then, we talk of *actors* [AGH 97] rather than objects. The *frames* [MIN 85] form a particular variety of actors, complicated to meet the needs of

1 This passage does not necessarily go both ways: passing from languages to programs is always feasible in practice; the inverse, however, is less assured because of many poorly understood *syntax* questions related to programming languages.

artifical intelligence. The class/instance distinction and the explicit use of classes is essential when talking about object-oriented programming.

– We could also have talked of *types* instead of classes; this essentially comes down to tradition. However, an important distinction must be made regarding the nature of classes: are they objects just like the rest or are they essentially different from other objects? The tradition of describing types, including *abstract types*, assumes that types are not objects. In contrast, object-oriented programming *stricto sensu* assumes that classes are objects: *everything is an object.*

– Object-oriented programming systematically functions in two levels: class definitions (defining the behavior shared by the instances) and instances creation (defining what distinguishes different instances from one another), while traditional programming restricts and obscures this process by imposing the separation of data and procedures. This intellectual mechanism is not new, we practise it constantly. Mathematics and the structuralist thinking have accustomed us to the approach in two stages: "Let's call that thing an object that is ... that has ... Clearly thing is an object, etc." In short, this is to define what we will speak about before speaking about it effectively.

Object-oriented programming is meant to provide particular methods of carrying out this intellectual approach, allowing us to write *as we think*.

It is the possibility of directly using prevalent intellectual resources that makes object-oriented programming so powerful – and motivates its success. It allows less skilled programmers to tackle more difficult problems, solve them in less time and produce higher quality programs.

In conclusion, object-oriented programming is basically programming in a natural way.

I.2. Object-oriented languages

Any language proposing the object-oriented programming style can proclaim itself an "object-oriented language". Currently, there is a very large number of object-oriented languages. Here is a tentative classification:

1) The amazing ancestor from which all have descended (see Figure I.1) is *Simula-67* [DAH 67], itself derived from *Algol-60*, [PER 59] and [NAU 63]. All the essentials are there, including the object manual. As the name indicates, this language was created for complex process simulation applications.

Simula can be seen as an extension of Algol-60 with added concepts of class (in a more complex form than the current concept) and instance. These concepts were introduced precisely for *conveniently* simulating the real world. Simula also contains a powerful co-routine mechanism, which (almost) disappeared with its successors.

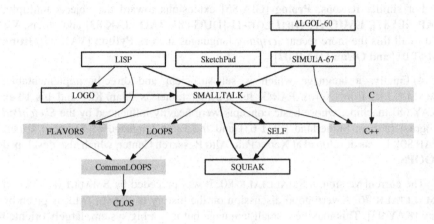

Figure I.1. *The* SQUEAK *family tree*

2) Classic imperative language extensions have been emerging since approximately 1983, when the fashion of pursuing object-oriented programming began to spread under the influence of SMALLTALK [GOL 83, GOL 84] and **Flavors** [CAN 82]. For example, the language **C** [KER 88] served as the basis for developing the languages **C++** [STR 87] and **Objective C** [COX 87], and **Pascal** [JEN 75] was used to develop **Object Pascal**, [JAC 87] and [SCH 86]. Currently, object extensions exist for everyone in all imperative languages, for example: *object-oriented Forth* [POU 87], *Object Fortran* [REE 91] or *Object-Oriented Cobol* [CHA 96].

You can regard these as simplified versions of Simula, built on different substrates. Their users are mainly in the field of Software Engineering. These languages are more abstract type languages than object-oriented languages, and should be compared with **CLU** [LIS 77] and **ADA** [DOD 83].

3) There are also **LISP** [MCC 62] extensions. There is a whole series: **Flavors** [MOO 80] from the Lisp Symbolics machine, **LOOPS** [BOB 86] of Xerox PARC and Interlisp, **CEYX** [HUL 83] and **ALCYONE** [HUL 85] from Le_Lisp, **KOOL**, [ALB 84] and [ALB 88], developed by Bull in Le_Lisp, **ObjVlisp** [BRI 87] as an extension of Vlisp, **CLOS**, the COMMONLISP OBJECT SYSTEM [BOB 88], and many others (new ones are developed on a daily basis).

This level of activity is due to the fact that object-oriented programming has acclimatized well in Lisp due to the incredible plasticity of the language and its "cultural" position as the main language of artificial intelligence. Indeed, these systems are very often based on complex artificial intelligence software for knowledge representation and the development of expert systems.

For similar reasons, **Prolog** [GIA 85] extensions toward the objects multiply: **LAP** [ILI 87], **EMICAT**, **OBJLLOG-II** [DUG 88], **TAO** [TAK 83] and others. We add to all this the more recent *scripting* languages such as **Python** [VAN 95], **Ruby** [MAT 01] and **OCaml** [LER 07].

4) Finally, a language which is self-sufficient and directly implementable: SMALLTALK, from Xerox PARC. Its spiritual father is Alan Kay and his Flex [KAY 68] machine, whose basic concepts were heavily influenced by the *SketchPad* program of Ivan Sutherland [SUT 63] and the **Logo** language of Seymour Papert [PAP 80]. It was developed at Xerox Palo Alto Research Center, which also developed **LOOPS**.

The current version is SMALLTALK-80. It was preceded by SMALLTALK-72 and SMALLTALK-76. A very good discussion on the history of SMALLTALK is given by Kay [KAY 93]. This may be a small language but it is a big system, largely oriented toward the management of a bit-mapped screen. Initially, SMALLTALK was only available for Xerox (1108, 1186) machines, on SUN and the Tektronix 4404 and 4406 computers. Since then versions have appeared for almost all computers and all operating systems. There is even a version for the Sony Playstation.

SMALLTALK has had a profound influence on the development of oriented programming, offering its most accomplished example, and (across Apple's MacIntosh, developed by members of the original SMALLTALK team) on all modern computing. Its conceptual simplicity and the richness of its environment amply justify its study, even if one has no plans to use it later.

Smaller versions have also been developed, for example: SMALLTALK-V by Digitalk or Little Smalltalk [BUD 88] by Timothy Budd. The latter is particularly useful for familiarizing yourself with the implementation of interpreters of object-oriented languages. However, let us consider the last in the SMALLTALK family: SQUEAK [ING 97]. It was developed by a team centered around the original developers of SMALLTALK, mainly Alan Kay, Dan Ingalls, Scott Wallace, Ted Kaehler, Jon Maloney, Andreas Raab and Michael Rueger.

It integrates the latest developments in man/machine interfaces and resimplifies the SMALLTALK virtual machine, which, nevertheless, had aged. It is distributed under an Open Source license (have a look at www.squeak.org) and runs on almost all computers. It is through this language that we will discuss object-oriented programming in this text.

PART 1

The Basics of SMALLTALK Programming

A Brief Tour of SQUEAK

We begin by giving a brief scenario for the use of SQUEAK. However, in order for us to truly experience it, we must first acquire an interpreter[1] of this wonderful language. In order to do this, we simply have to proceed to the download page of the Website www.squeak.org to download the necessary files. Currently, there are versions for Windows, OS X and Linux. For installation, follow their advice on installation.

Once the system has been installed, you should run SQUEAK. On Windows, this can be done by clicking the SQUEAK icon and then choosing your *image*, on Unix you activate it with the command "squeak squeak.image" from the directory containing the three files *squeak.image, squeak.changes, SqueakV?.sources* (in place of the question mark, there should be the version number). These three files are described in the table in Figure 1.1.

Once SQUEAK has been launched, you should see a screen similar to that in Figure 1.2.

When you work in SQUEAK, everything you do is done through this screen. SQUEAK is a complete system with its own editors, browsers, debuggers, etc. You will even have a tool for sending and receiving email, `celeste`, and another one called `scamper`, which provides us with the basics for browsing the Internet.

---

1 Without going into technical details, the question whether Smalltalk is an interpreter or not depends on our *interpretation* of the term. If we use the definition that an interpreter allows us to run programs *without* first using an explicit compilation phase, in that case SQUEAK is an interpreter. If, on the other hand, we consider that any acceptance of a Smalltalk method is actually a compilation of the method to the language of the *bytecode interpreter* of the Smalltalk virtual machine, in that sense we could say that we are dealing with a compiler and not an interpreter. For now, in these early pages, let us consider that this language is interpreted.

virtual machine	This file (in unix is the executable file `squeak`, in Windows is the file `squeak.exe`) containing the motor behind SMALLTALK: mainly the interpreter, memory management module and primitive methods
virtual image	This file whose original version is called "squeak.image" contains the editors, compilers, debuggers, the file management system, the process management system.
file *sources*	Contain the sources, written in SMALLTALK, for the SQUEAK system itself
file *changes*	Contain the history of all your additions and modifications, permitting to retrieve previous states

Figure 1.1. *The most important* SMALLTALK *files*

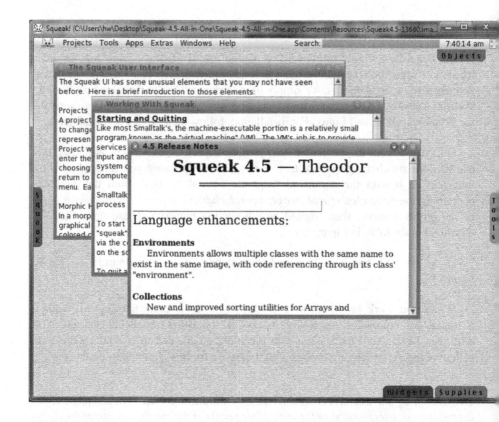

Figure 1.2. *Squeak (version 4.5) start screen*

Figure 1.3. *Main menu*

This window is your interface with the SQUEAK system and the rest of the world. For now, the first thing to do is construct a private virtual *image* in which you will be able to do whatever you want, and which will guarantee you are always able to find the original image, if you were to get completely lost. In order to do this, place your mouse anywhere in the SQUEAK window, outside of any subwindows, and click on the left button, this should bring up the main menu shown in Figure 1.3.

Figure 1.4. *A name for the image*

Choose *save as. . .* , and then in the window *New File Name?* (see Figure 1.4), which opens automatically, give a name of your choice (such as myImage.image), and then from that moment on, you will be working in your own image, and not the initial image distributed with SQUEAK. Then in the same menu, choose *save* or, when you want to quit, *save and quit*, you will save a personal image, accessible through the name that you have chosen (myImage.image in the example here), and usable in any subsequent SQUEAK launch.

Finally, we can begin to explore SQUEAK.

1.1. The first contact

On the start screen (Figure 1.2 page 4), the border of the SMALLTALK window is decorated with small colored rectangles: these are the *"flaps"*. By default, there is a flap called Squeak in the middle left of the window called Tools, and in the middle right, and at the bottom of the window there are, from left to right, the flaps Widgets and Supplies. All these flaps, if activated (by the click of the left mouse button), give access to a set of SQUEAK tools[2]. Figure 1.5, page 7, shows the content of the flap "Supplies". In order to activate any of its tools, simply select it (always with the left mouse button[3]) and pull it out of the flap (keeping the button pressed and by moving the mouse to the inside of the SQUEAK window).

---

2 To disable a flap, it is enough to simply click once more on the flap icon.

3 SMALLTALK-80, the ancestor of SQUEAK, assumed that the user had a mouse with three buttons in red, yellow and blue. The red button was used for *selecting* objects, the yellow button was used for *manipulating* inside a window and the blue button was used to manipulate the window itself. In order not to repeat ourselves so much, here are some basic mouse manipulations:

– with a mouse that has three buttons: the left button makes the selection, in SMALLTALK we call the button the *red button*. The middle button gives the contextual menu of the currently pointed window pane, this corresponds to the yellow button. The button on the right, for manipulating the current window (or subwindow), is called the *blue button*;

Figure 1.5. *The graphic object flap (Supplies)*

If we activate the tool `Workspace` of the flap `Tools`, we obtain a window similar to the one in Figure 1.6. In this window, we can enter code, select it and run it. Thus, if we enter in it:

$$7 + 4$$

and then select in the shortcut menu `print it`, SQUEAK will respond quite naturally with 11. Note that instead of selecting "`print it`" in the shortcut menu, we could type *Alt+p* (by pressing) "Alt" at the same time as "p"[4].

Note also that the expression "7 + 4" is read as: ask object 7 what it gets if we send it the message "+" with the argument "4".

Or even clearer: "the object 7 responds to the transmission of the message + with argument 4 by returning the object 11". We should also note that all the objects 7, 4 and 11 are integers, more precisely: small integers.

In short, in SMALLTALK, a calculation is always done by sending messages to objects and objects receiving messages respond by sending a response object to the initiator of the message. We will return to this fundamental aspect of object-oriented programming later. For now, recall that in SMALLTALK *everything* is an object and that the objects communicate between themselves by *transmitting messages*.

We can surely agree: this first program, 7 + 4, is a very minimalist one. Let us try another one and by using "`do it`" ("Alt+d") on the expression:

$$\texttt{Display restoreAfter: [Pen example]}$$

which will draw on our SQUEAK screen a beautiful spiral as can be seen in Figure 1.7.

– on a PC, a mouse has two buttons: the middle button and yellow button, the shortcut menu can be obtained by *Ctrl+left click* and the blue button can be obtained by *Ctrl+right click*;

– on a Macintosh with a mouse that has one button: the simple click gives the selection, *Option+click* gives the shortcut menu and *command+click* gives the window menu.

4 Many menu entries can be obtained simply by the combinations of the "Ctrl" or "Alt" keys and a letter, like in this case, "print it" which can be obtained using "Alt+p". Appendix 2 gives a list of these abbreviations.

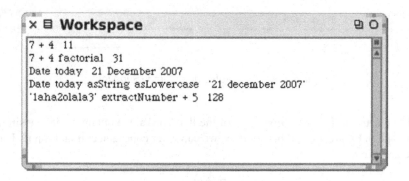

Figure 1.6. *A* Workspace *window*

Once more: `Display restoreAfter: [Pen example]` is the writing in SMALLTALK for transmitting to the `Display` object, the SQUEAK screen, the message `restoreAfter:` with the argument `[Pen example]`, which itself is a transmission of the message `example` to the object `Pen`. Remember this: all SMALLTALK calculations are the results of the transmission of a message, possibly with or without arguments. The message `example` does not have an argument. This is a unary message. On the other hand, the message `restoreAfter:`[5] has one argument (syntactically indicated by the colon). Here it is, in brackets, the SMALLTALK code corresponding to the transmission of the message `example` to the object `Pen`.

Note also that the action "`do it`" does the same thing as "`print it`", which means: it calculates, it evaluates the selected expression, but unlike "`print it`", it does not print the value of the transmission returned to the emitter (in this case, the returned value would be a `Display` object).

A final note on this example: "Display" and "Pen" begin with a capital letter. In SMALLTALK, which is case sensitive, this means that those words describe classes – objects that are classses or objects known to the whole SMALLTALK SYSTEM. A *class* is a specific and important object in SMALLTALK. A class *describes* a structure and it is the only object type which is capable of creating other objects upon demand (in general with the message `new`). It is almost like an *object mold*. Since in SMALLTALK everything is an object, at least now we know where they come from: they are created by objects of the class type. The objects that a class can create are called *instances*

---

5 `restoreAfter:` asks SQUEAK to *restore* the restore the screen to its state prior to the command given as an argument to restoreAfter. This restoration takes place after the user clicks a mouse button. In our example, the restoration effect of the screen will result in the disappearance of the drawing.

of a class. The classes themselves are instances of other classes: their *meta-class*. We will return to these concepts in the following chapters. For now, let us remember that:

– everything is an object;

– every object is an instance of a class;

– thus all messages are transmitted to an instance of a class.

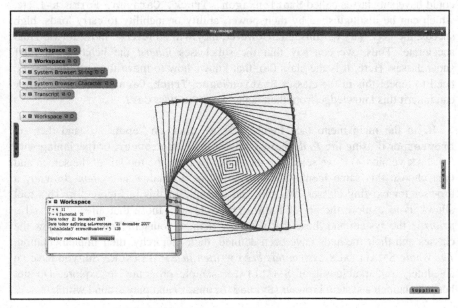

Figure 1.7. *The* Pen *example effect*

In its current version, the SQUEAK system puts approximately 3500 already existing classes at our disposal. We can always add new ones, defined so as to suit our needs. It is this activity of defining new classes that will be the main activity of a SMALLTALK programmer. But what is a class?

For now, let us say that they are the mold for producing instances and that this mold must define the characteristics determining the specificity of each instance (we can say that it must define the *instance variables*) and that it must define the specific messages that each of the instances can understand (we can say that it must define its *methods*). Thus, if in a program, we need to model cars, we will probably distinguish each car by its power, color, size, etc. These are the *instance variables* and each car will have its specific values associated with these instance variables. However, all cars will know how to move forward, reverse, accelerate, etc. These are the defined methods of the *Car* class, and all the specific cars (each instance of the Car class) can look into their class on how to accelerate, reverse, move forward, etc. We say that instances use, *a priori*, the methods defined in their own class. But, this is not all. Since a program will likely contain many different classes, and since, in any case, the SQUEAK system provides us with a notable number of classes, these are organized hierarchically in a tree structure, similar to classification systems, which always handle concepts organized in tree-like structures. Thus, we will be speaking not only about classes, but also about subclasses and superclasses. For example, the class Car could have subclasses called StationWagon, Truck, Caravan, Formula-1, etc. which can be distinguished by their power, ability or inability to carry loads, high speeds, the necessary permits, etc. However, they will all reverse, move forward and accelerate. Thus, we can say that the subclasses *inherit* the behavior of their superclasses. Here, it is the class Car that knows how to move forward, there is no need to repeat this in the classes StationWagon, Truck, Caravan, Bus, etc. They can inherit this knowledge from their superclass (the class Car).

If, in the main menu (see Figure 1.3) we click on "open..." and then on browser, or if using the *Tools* flap we import the icon browser, or (beginning with SQUEAK version 4) if we select the menu tools from the top left of the screen and then choose this same icon[6], SQUEAK gives us a window, a *System Browser*, a browser for existing classes. We show an example of this in Figure 1.8. This tool allows us to explore the set of SMALLTALK classes: those that already existed *a priori* in the system and those that you have defined yourself. You can see how the classes and their methods have been defined, their hierarchy, their implementation. *The whole SMALLTALK system has been written in SMALLTALK!* So, you have an absolutely remarkable set of SMALLTALK sample programs to explore. Do not hesitate, launch a system browser (System Browser) and play around with it.

The system browser consists of a first row of subwindows which describe, from left to right:

– *Categories*: SMALLTALK classes are grouped into categories based on the designer's ideas for these classes. A category is something conceptual and does not correspond to a particular class hierarchical organization level. Very often, project classes are grouped in a single category named after the project. The category window (see Figure 1.9, menu page 12) gives the opportunity to look for classes conceptually related. In our example, Figure 1.8, page 11, it was the Kernel-Numbers category that, when selected, made the set of classes related to this category appear in the "classes" subwindow.

---

6 Yes, SQUEAK gives you multiple ways to access the same tools. The method you use depends on the context in which you are in, and, after becoming an expert in object-oriented programming, your style of work. For now, let us explore these different methods and familiarize ourselves with the environment.

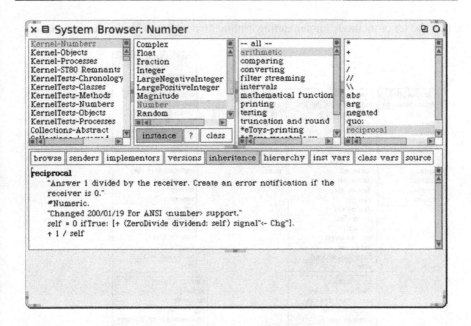

Figure 1.8. *System browser focused on the Number class*

– *Classes*: in this drop-down menu, we find sets of classes belonging to a particular category. Just click on the name of the desired class for its definition to appear in the large window below the first row. Below the class drop-down menu, there are three additional buttons: *instance, ?, class*.

The button "?" gives the relevant commentary pertaining to the class currently being viewed. The buttons "instance" and "class" indicate in the two following windows what messages can be sent to *instances* of a class or what messages can be sent to the *class itself*. In our example, Figure 1.8, it is the Number class and the button "instance" that has been selected, and has led to the set of existing instance protocols related to this class being displayed in the subwindow titled "protocols".

– *Protocols*: similarly   to categories, which conceptually regroup classes, protocols allow us to conceptually regroup methods. Often, we will see a protocol for *testing, printing* or *private*. As the names indicate, the protocol "testing" groups the methods that return either true or false, the protocol "printing" groups the methods for printing the instances of the class and the protocol "private" groups the methods that should only be known by instances of this class and should not be accessible outside of this class.

– *Methods*: in this drop-down menu, we find the names of the methods (the selectors) grouped together under the chosen protocol. In our example, Figure 1.8, this is the set of methods implementing arithmetic operations for the Number class.

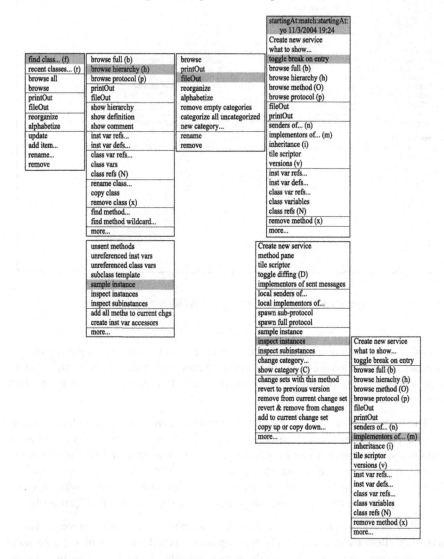

Figure 1.9. *The menus in the first row of the subwindows of the system browser, from left to right: categories (1 menu), classes (2 menus), protocols (1 menu) and methods (3 menus)*

Below this row, there are (in the current version) nine buttons which allow us (from left to right) to open another browser on the current selection, on all the methods that contain the selector of the currently selected method in a transmission (the *transmitters* of this message), on all the classes which implement the chosen selector, on all the different existing versions of the selection, on the set of methods with the same name and the indications on the means of inheritance, on the hierarchy of the selected class, on all accesses to the selected instance or class variable; and, finally, the last button determines the display manner of what is shown on the large window for the code.

We are left with only the most important and the largest subwindow: the one that contains the SMALLTALK code for the item, often the selected method. This subwindow contains an editor and all the capabilities of the Workspace window. Any code that is shown here can be edited, saved or evaluated. For the change to come into effect, we must choose to accept in the contextual menu (or simply by typing "Alt+s").

1.2. Important points

Let us summarize what we already learned about objects, messages, transmissions and expressions:

1) SMALLTALK uniformly manipulates objects, which can be very simple, such as numbers and characters, or very complicated, such as collections, processes and graphic screens.

These objects work by receiving messages and adopting for each message the appropriate behavior, which is described in the objects, class. The couple "*receiver object, message*" constitutes a transmission.

The elementary act of programming in SMALLTALK is the execution of a transmission, similar to the "evaluation of a form" in LISP and the "resolution of a goal" in Prolog.

These transmissions can either give a value (an object) as the result (functions) or operate the edge effects on the environment (procedures). We can compose them in a variety of ways, including placing them in a sequence.

2) We can assign an object as a value to a variable. The assignment *is not* a transmission because we are interested in the variable name, while a transmission would require the object to be its value.

Finally, we can call an *expression* any composition of variables, constants and transmissions, which results in an object as the value.

3) An object is characterized by its *state* and *behavior*.

The behavior depends on the state and the state can be modified by the behavior, according to the laws that are defined in the object *class*.

4) We will formalize the *object state* by the *values* of a set of variables (like in physics), and the behavior by a set of *procedures* or *functions*.

The variables in question appear – of course – in the procedure texts, which ensures the bidirectional link between the state and behavior.

According to the most common SMALLTALK terminology, the variables are called *instance variables*. Similarly, we call *methods* the procedures or functions defining the behavior of the object.

5) The list of instance variable names (but not their values) and the method catalog belong to the object class.

The *object itself* (the instance) consists of the list of values of its instance variables that characterize its current state, and the *indication* (the address) of its class.

6) Therefore, the execution of one of these procedures, realizing the behavior of the object, only requires that we know the procedure to run and its arguments: these elements constitute the *message* sent to the object that should produce, in response, the said behavior.

7) A message is composed of a *selector*, identifying the procedure in the catalog of methods (its name corresponding to the class), and the *arguments* transmitted.

Upon receiving the message, the object aquires of its class the method matching the selector, and then executes the corresponding code giving the instance variables occuring in code the values determined by the objects current state. This version should result in the expected behavior.

1.3. Exercises

The solutions can be found on page 341:

1) As shown in Figure 1.11, open a Workspace and enter any text, such as the following: This text is the first text entered in SQUEAK. Select a part of the text and then open the contextual menu and try the commands copy, paste, cut, undo on the text. Try the same commands without opening the shortcut menu using only the keyboard commands "Alt+c","Alt+v", "Alt+x" and "Alt+z" (see Appendix 2, 501–504). You should also try the command do again (either using the contextual menu or with the key combination "Alt+j"). To do this, select the second word of the text (the word text), enter the word test and then give the command do again.

2) Open a system browser, and:

   – search for the Integer class;

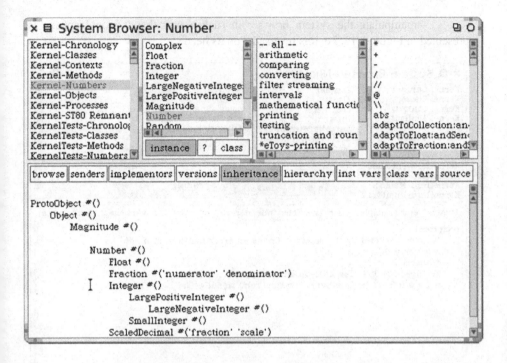

Figure 1.10. *A system browser showing the hierarchy*
of the Number *class*

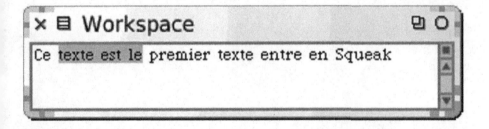

Figure 1.11. *A* Workspace *with a selected part of the text*

– display the class hierrachy of the Integer class;

– search the method + of the Integer class;

– search *all* the methods + (all the implementations of a method called +);

– search for all the methods using the selector + (that send the message +);

– manipulate the system browser in such a way that it would appear as presented in Figure 1.12, i.e. it is reversed, "on its head".

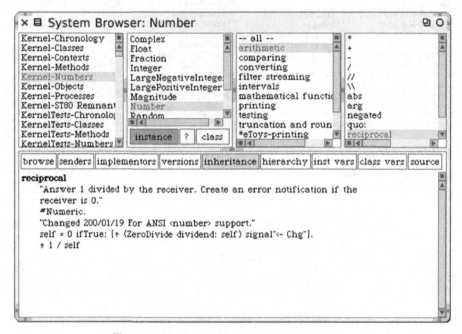

Figure 1.12. *An upside-down system browser*

2

The First Program

After having been introduceed to SMALLTALK and its specific incarnation SQUEAK, as well as being given a first glimpse of the system interface, let us build our own first small program: a microworld filled with several specific animals. Our world will have dogs, penguins, whales, parrots, etc. Some of these animals should know how to make sounds (for example, the parrots and dogs), some should know how to fly (e.g. parrots), others should know how to swim and live in the water. Naturally, we should be able to ask them to carry out particular actions: for example, we should be able to ask a particular dog to stop barking, or we should be able to teach new vocabulary to our favorite parrot.

2.1. Defining new classes

How can we do all of this in SMALLTALK? As we mentioned before, the main act of programming in SMALLTALK is the definition of new classes with methods and the creation of specific instances which will activate these methods.

Since we want to create a world filled with animals, it seems only natural to want to recreate, at least in part, the hierarchy of the animal classification as given in a phylogenetic tree. Figure 2.1 shows a part of such a tree. In order to recreate this hierarchy in SMALLTALK, we need to create an Animal class, which could serve as a subclass of the Object class, and allow us to then add subclasses and sub-subclasses corresponding to each of the nodes in the presented hierarchy.

Let us proceed. In order to create a subclass of an existing class – for example, the Object class – just open the class browser, click on any category and fill the template in the code window, describing the subclass that you want to create. Figure 2.2 shows such a browser with its template.

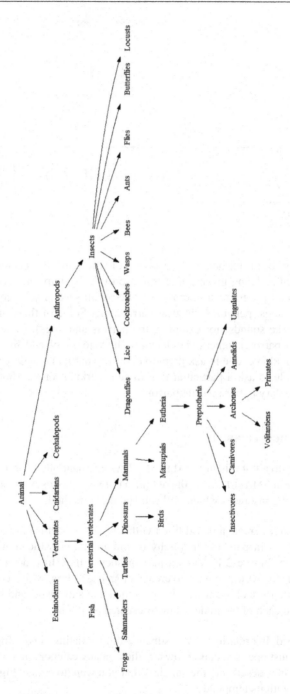

Figure 2.1. *An excerpt from a phylogenetic tree*

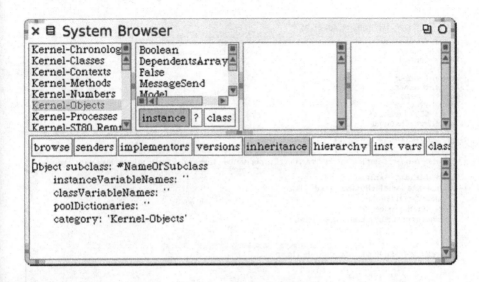

Figure 2.2. *A template for creating subclasses within the* Object *class*

```
Object subclass: #NameOfSubclass instance
            VariableNames: ''
            classVariableNames: ''
            poolDictionaries: ''
            category: 'Kernel-Objects'
```

So, to create an Animal class, just replace the name of the default subclass, the template NameOfSubclass, with the new class name, Animal in the case, insert the names of the instance variables which distinguish one instance of a class from another (one animal from another), and replace the category Kernel-Objects with the category name under which we would like to find the different animal classes. For now, let us assume that we want to create a new category called Smalltalk-Animal-Course and that at minimum any animal should have a name[1], which gives us:

---

1 We will return later to the entries classVariables and poolDictionaries. For now, it is sufficient to know that in order to create a new class, we have to send to the superclass the message:
subclass:instanceVariableNames:classVariableNames:poolDictionaries: category:

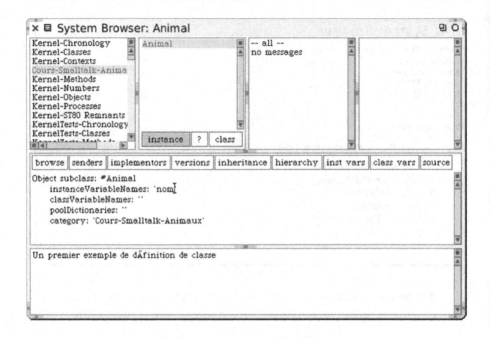

Figure 2.3. *The class browser after the creation of the* Animal *class*

```
Object subclass: #Animal
            instanceVariableNames: 'name'
            classVariableNames: ''
            poolDictionaries: ''
            category: 'Smalltalk-Animal-Course'
```

Just open the contextual menu in this window, click accept (or as shown in Appendix 2, just type the characters "Alt+s"), and SQUEAK will understand that from now Animal is a new class, which will naturally be added to the set of existing classes. SQUEAK will also understand that this class will be accessible through the category Smalltalk-Animal-Course. The browser should then take the shape of Figure 2.3.

Note that the Animal class has been defined in a manner where each instance has an instance variable, name, since every animal has a name and it will be this name which will distinguish one Animal instance from another.

We must also note that we have written the first letter of the name of the class as a capital letter: Animal. In SMALLTALK, it is good practice to capitalize the class names, class variables and pool-dictionaries, and conversely to start instance variables with a small character. This allows the readers to immediately recognize whether the item belongs to an instance (written with a small letter) or to a class (it is capitalized). We must remember that we also write programs for them to be read by other programmers.

This is, of course, the same way that we define the various subclasses that we will need. Thus,

```
Animal subclass: #Mammal
            instanceVariableNames: ''
            classVariableNames: ''
            poolDictionaries: ''
            category: 'Smalltalk-Animal-Course'
```

creates the Mammal class that will inherit the Animal class instance variable name and the methods that we will add later.

If we define the whale, bird, parrot, dog and penguin classes in the same way:

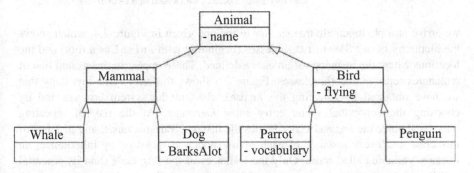

Figure 2.4. *Our simplified phylogenetic tree*

```
Mammal subclass: #Whale
            instanceVariableNames: ''
            classVariableNames: ''
            poolDictionaries: ''
            category: 'Smalltalk-Animal-Course'

Mammal subclass: #Dog
            instanceVariableNames: 'barkALot'
            classVariableNames: ''
            poolDictionaries: ''
            category: 'Smalltalk-Animal-Course'
```

```
Animal subclass: #Bird
                instanceVariableNames: 'flying'
                classVariableNames:''
                poolDictionaries: ''
                category: 'Smalltalk-Animal-Course'

Bird subclass: #Parrot
                instanceVariableNames: 'vocabulary'
                classVariableNames: ''
                poolDictionaries:''
                category: 'Smalltalk-Animal-Course'


Bird subclass: #Penguin
                instanceVariableNames: ''
                classVariableNames: ''
                poolDictionaries: ''
                category: 'Smalltalk-Animal-Course'
```

we arrive at a phylogenetic tree similar to the one given in Figure 2.4, which shows the hierarchy of our SMALLTALK classes (beginning with Animal as a root) and the locations where the instance variables are defined. These appear in the second line of rectangles representing the classes. Figure 2.5 shows this very same hierarchy that we have obtained by selecting the Animal class in the system browser and by choosing the contextual menu entry *show hierarchy*. At the risk of repeating ourselves: since the Animal class defines the instance variable name, any instance of this class *and* every instance of each of its subclasses possess, by inheritance, an instance variable called name. Only the instances of the Dog class (and its potential subclasses) possess the instance variable barkALot, and only the instances of the Bird class and its subclasses Penguin and Parrot possess an instance variable called flying. Thus, every parrot is defined by its three instance variables: name, flying and vocabulary; the latter being defined in the Parrot class.

2.2. Defining new methods

Once these classes are defined, we need to give the know-how to the instances.

First, we must note that we have created the Animal class exclusively so we have a superclass for all the animal classes that we would want to create in the future. We have no intentions of creating instances of this class. What would be an instance of the Animal class? A dog? A whale? What? It is like in the phylogenetic tree: the different *abstract* classes, such as "vertebrates", "mammals" and "Eutheria", only exist in order to group the set of characteristics shared between all the subclasses. If we move along the tree from top to bottom, it goes from general to more specific: all animals have DNA, having DNA is a property that is defined at the level of the Animal abstract class. Only mammals nurse their young, thus this is a characteristic which is defined at the mammal class level and shared among all of its possible subclasses, from marsupials to ungulates, dogs, primates or even the representatives of homo sapiens class. The classification is *de facto* a factorization of the properties and the know-how common to the class and all its subclasses.

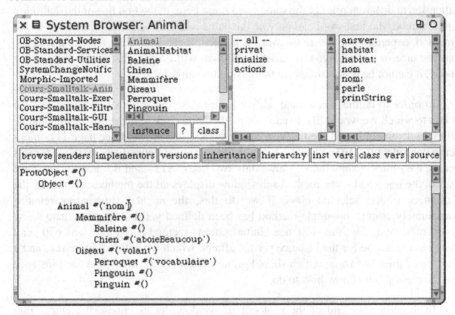

Figure 2.5. *The hierarchy tree of the* Animal *class*

Since our animals all share the property of having a name, throughout the instance variable name defined in the Animal abstract class, that all animals must possess is the ability to respond with their name, should it be asked. This know-how will be defined in the Animal class by the name method, as follows:

```
name
    "respond with the value of the instance variable name"
    name
```

Explanation: the first line gives the name of the method; the name, which will be the selector that can be used in the transmissions requesting the recipient's name. The second line is the comment for the readers of this end of program. Anything that is enclosed between two quote marks is a comment and is ignored by SMALLTALK (but not by us). The third line is the body of the method. The body describes what the recipient should do, if we were to send him the message name, the name of the method. Here, the only instruction "^name" is to run. The sign "^"[2] tells the receiver to return to the sender, the initiator of the transmission and therefore the sender of the message name, the value of the expression that follows this sign. What follows is the name of the instance variable, name; in short, the method name dictates that when someone asks you your name, you answer them with your name. You must pay attention to different roles of the same word name here. In the first line of the definition of a method, the first word can only be the name of a new selector. In the body of the method, depending on where the word is located, it can be used to refer to a selector, an instance or another type of variable (but, we will discuss that later). Here in the body, it cannot be a selector, since there is no transmission[3].

In order to define a new method, we have to use the system browser, select the class to which we would like to add this method and click in the *protocol* subwindow (the third subwindow in the first row of windows of the browser, see page 11). In our case, we select the Animal class. Since we have not yet defined any methods for this class, the *protocol* subwindow shows only two lines -all- and no messages. If we select the line -all-, the method subwindow displays all the methods defined by the instances of the selected class. If we do this, the *method* subwindow remains desperately empty: no single method has been defined yet. Let us first create a few *protocols*: one for the instance initialization methods, which we will call initialize; one for the instance private affairs, which we will call private; and a last one called actions, which should group the different actions that each instance of the class should know how to do.

In the context menu of the protocol subwindow, let us choose the entry "new category..." and then choose in the new menu, which will appear, the entry "new...". In the small window that will open, we will give the name of our new protocol, private for example, click on accept and we should see in the *protocol* subwindow the new protocol name added next to the already existing ones, or replacing the line no messages, if no method had been previously defined in the selected class. All this looks very complicated. In practice, it is very simple to do. It is the detailed description of actions to be followed that gives the impression of complexity.

We will repeat these operations in order to add the protocols initialize and actions. This way, we will have three protocols for the instances of this class. If we

---

2 This sign is displayed in some versions of SMALLTALK as an *up arrow* (↑).

3 Recall that a transmission involves at least two things: a receiver and a selector. Syntactically, there is no receiver here.

now click on the protocol `private`, the main subwindow should display a template for writing a method, as follows:

```
message selector and argument names
            "comment stating purpose of message"

            | temporary variable names |
            statements
```

It gives the most general form of the definition of a method. Since this template is selected (highlighted), it is sufficient to write the method that we defined previously. We must not forget to finish off with the keys "Alt+s" in order to tell SMALLTALK that we would like it to *accept* this definition. Finally, we have defined the first method, name, and we have placed it well into the `private` protocol. Figure 2.6 shows the browser after all these operations.

We will carry on with our small program. In order for an animal to be able to give us its name, we must first baptize it and give it a name. Giving a name to an animal gives a (new) value to its instance variable name. Clearly, this must also be a method defined at the level of the `Animal` class. We will add it to the `initialize` protocol, as follows:

```
name: aString
      "change the name of the animal in aString"
      name := aString
```

Explanation: the selector of this method is called name:. Note that the sign ":" is part of the word. This sign indicates to SMALLTALK that the selector we are currently defining requires an argument when used in a transmission[4].

For reference, we will give this argument the name aString. aString is the name of a parameter which, in the body, refers to the argument given upon transmission of the message. The aString name of this parameter was chosen to indicate that the argument should be a string of characters.

---

4 In the case when the selector name is written without the ":" sign, we are talking about a *unary* selector. Any transmission using it will be reduced to a simple <receiver selector> pair. If the name of the selector has one or more ':' signs, we are talking about a *keyword*. Any transmission using this will be a tuple in the form <receiver xxxx: argument1 yyyy: argument2 ...>, where xxxx: is the part of the selector up to the first ":" sign, followed by the first argument, yyyy: is the part of the selector beginning *after* the first parameter and going up to the second ":" sign, which will be followed by the second argument, etc. Remember the selector `subclass:instanceVariableNames:classVariableNames:poolDictionaries: category:` (see page 19) which took five arguments, one after each ":" sign.

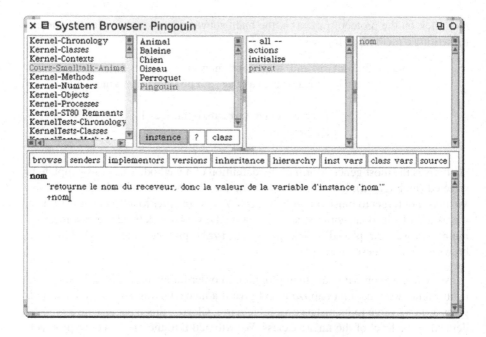

Figure 2.6. *The system browser after creating the method* name

Similarly, as when we first defined a method, the second line is a brief comment indicating the role of this method. And, just like in the previous method, the body is reduced to a single expression. Here, it is an *assignment*. The ":=" sign[5] is the sign of assignment, indicating that the variable on the left side of the sign receives a new value, which is the value of the expression on the right side of the sign. It is here that the instance variable name receives its new value, the value of the parameter aString, thus the value given to the argument during the transmission of this message name:. Note that this method does not use the *return* sign (^); therefore does not explicitly indicate the value that should be returned to the sender. In such a case, SMALLTALK returns, by default, the receiver of the message, indicating that the message was well received and everything demanded was done correctly. Finally, we will add a method to the actions protocol, by giving every animal the ability to speak, i.e. to respond with something when asked to say something. Of course none of the animals yet know how to speak. This is exactly what we will want to put in the unary talk method, as follows:

---

5 In some SMALLTALKS, assignments can also be written with the ← sign which can be obtained on the keyboard with the *underline* key (_).

```
talk
    "a message saying that the animal does not know how to talk"
    self answer: 'I do not know how to talk'
```

Once you have entered this method and clicked "Alt+s" (or choosen accept in the contextual menu), a window should appear saying that you are using an unknown selector: answer:.[6]. SMALLTALK is right: as we have not yet defined a method with the name answer:. The window in question also gives you a choice of known selectors, resembling the name that you have given. The first of these names is the name of the selector that SMALLTALK could not recognize. This is help from SMALLTALK. Whenever you enter something which the machine does not know, it informs you about it and proposes similar writings, in case you made a mistake. Here, we chose to write answer: intentionally; so, let us *confirm* and click the selector which SMALLTALK thinks that you might have written by mistake, answer:. Let us consider this method in a bit more detail. Its body says:

$$\text{self answer: '......'}$$

We send a message to self. Who is it? self is a reserved word in SMALLTALK. It is a *pseudo-variable* (see section 2.7, page 46). self is a way of being able to refer to the receiver of this message. Do you remember? We have said that the fundamental act of object-oriented programming is message transmission. A transmission always involves a receiver and a message (possibly with arguments). From time to time, it is necessary to know the receiver of a message when we are writing a method. This is simply because the method tells the receiver what it should do, and it may be necessary to tell it to do more than has been said. For this, it is good to know the receiver. But the same message can be sent to many objects, each of them considered the correct receiver of this message. In order to be able to address each of these individually, SMALLTALK provides us with this pseudo-variable self, which will be understood by each receiver as designating itself. This is a bit like if we said *you*. Who is "you"? Probably every person that we have said "you" to is designated by the same word. This is where the method body says several things, such as "if you would be asked to talk, send yourself the message answer: with the argument 'I do not know how to talk'", or, even simpler, "if you are asked to talk, answer: *I do not know how to talk*". This is something that regularly happens to us, when we are in a country where the inhabitants use a language that is unknown to us. Now all that is left for us to do is to teach the animals how to respond, how to answer:. Here is the last instance method that we will add to the initialize protocol of the Animal class:

---

6 The exact message is unknown selector, please confirm, correct or cancel.

```
answer: aString
     "print the class and the name of the animal in question
     followed by the argument aString"
Transcript show:
     (self class asString , ' ' ,
     self name , ': ' , aString);
     cr
```

Although it is slightly longer than the three other methods that we have written, it is not really difficult to understand. The Transcript is similar to a Workspace: a specific window which we can open by either using the entry open... in the main menu, or by importing it through the Tools flap, or simply by sending the unary message open to the Transcript object[7]. In general, this window is used to display system messages and, by extension, to the SMALLTALK programmer this serves as the screen which displays his or her own messages. The Transcript is an alpha-numeric window, which means that it is a window that only displays ordinary characters, letters and numbers. To display a string of characters in the transcript, simply send the message show: with an argument consisting of the string of characters that you would like to display.

Here is the famous program C *Hello World*:

```
\#include <stdio.h>
void main(int argc, char **argv){
   printf("Hello World\n")
   }
```

It is written in SMALLTALK simply as:

```
Transcript show:  'Hello World'
```

and if we want the output to be terminated by a *carriage return*, a *break*, we must, similarly as in C, specify:

```
\#include <stdio.h>
void main(int argc, char **argv){
   printf("Hello World\n")
   }
```

---

7 To do this, enter the line: "Transcript open" in Workspace followed by "Alt+d" or by selecting the entry do it in the main menu.

by sending the message cr in Transcript. This can be done by putting in a sequence the two transmissions as folows:

```
Transcript show: 'Hello World'.
Transcript cr
```

where the two transmissions are separated by a point, or by a *cascade*, as shown:

```
. Transcript show: 'Hello World'; cr
```

A cascade in SMALLTALK is a compact way of sending several messages to the *same* receiver. The general form of it is:

$$receiver\ message_1;\ message_2;\ \dots;\ message_n$$

The character ";" separates the different messages, which are all, one after the other, being sent to the same receiver. Thus, in our example of *Hello World*, Transcript first receives the message show: with its argument, and afterward it receives the message cr. The receiver deals such a cascade by executing the messages one after the other and returning the value of the last transmission.

Now that we know that the method answer: only prints a message in the Transcript window, let us look at the string of characters that it displays. Let us analyze the expression:

```
(self class asString , ' ' , self name , ': ' , aString)
```

This message is obviously quite complex, otherwise it would not be in parenthesis. We must note that here, as elsewhere, the parenthesis serve to group sets of things which we would like to see as a *single* entity. Indeed, the expression in parenthesis is followed by a semi-colon. This is part of the first message of this cascade of messages sent to the Transcript. Clearly, this is the argument for the selector show:, the string of characters to be displayed. Note that in SMALLTALK, the delimiter of a string of characters is the apostrophe character (').

This string of characters is composed of five parts: the result of the transmission self class asString, the string consisting of a space character (' '), the result of the transmission self name, the string of characters ': ' and the argument value of answer:, "aString". We know that these are the five parts that make up the string of characters to be displayed, as they are separated by the character "," (comma). This character is the name of a binary selector that can be sent to a string of characters and which takes another string of characters as an argument. The receiver returns a new string of characters resulting from the concatenation of the strings: the *receiver* and the *argument*. If, like in the previous example, we have four occurrences of the concatenation selector (,), this takes a general form:

$$string_1 , string_2 , string_3 , \ldots, string_n$$

It behaves as if we had written:

$$((\ldots((string_1 , string_2) , string_3) , \ldots) , string_n)$$

Thus: $string_1$ is the first receiver of the message "," with the argument $string_2$, which delivers a $result_1$ string, which will receive the message "," with the argument $string_3$, which delivers a $result_2$ string, which will receive the message "," with the argument ... until $result_{n-2}$, which is the result of the concatenation of all the strings of characters from $string_1$ to $string_{n-1}$, which will receive the message "," with the argument $string_n$, which will finally result in a string of characters representing the concatenation of all the strings given as arguments in all these transmissions. Clearly, *the result of a transmission can become the receiver of another transmission.*

Let us keep in mind the possibility that the receivers of a message, themselves, can be the result of previous transmissions, so these are calculated receivers, appearing in a dynamic and temporary manner during the execution of a program.

Now, let us have a closer look at the different parts of the string to be displayed in the `Transcript`. The beginning of this string is the string resulting from the transmission.

```
self class asString
```

We already know the receiver `self`: it will be the same object as the one which receives the message `answer:`, any instance of the animal class or one of its subclasses. In Chapter 1, we said that an instance is composed of the values of its instance variables *and* a pointer to its class. The message `class` asks an instance to return the class to which this instance belongs to the sender. So, it is a class that receives the message `asString`. The message `asString` is implemented in the `Object` class and only sends the message `printString` to the receiver of the message `asString`. `printString`, which is defined in many classes[8], asks the receiver to kindly give a representation of itself as a string of characters. Here, the transmission `self class asString` is reduced to the same thing as the transmission `self class printString`, which will then deliver the name of the class in the form of a string of characters.

---

8 Open a system browser, search for a method that uses `printString` and click on the tab `implementors`. In the dropdown menu that opens, click on `printString`. This will open a browser on all the definitions of this method.

The second part, ' ', is just the string of characters composed of the single character "*space*".

The third part self name once more sends a message to self[9], the receiver of the message answer:. It returns a string of characters consisting of the name of the receiver animal. This sends the message name that was defined previously.

The fourth part is the string of characters ':   ' as it is, and the last part is the value of the parameter aString of the method answer:. The only transmission of the message answer: that we are familiar with at the moment with is the one in the talk method where the argument is clearly a string of characters, the string 'I do not know how to talk'.

It is probably time to test, ever so slightly, the program that we have written so far. Let us proceed.

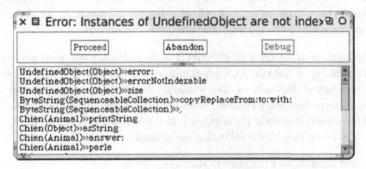

Figure 2.7. *A reduced error-indicating window*

2.3. Program test

To test our small program, we begin by opening a Workspace window and, since we know that the program should display the text in the Transcript, a Transcript window. We interact with our SQUEAK system through Workspace, our program communicates with us through the Transcript.

---

9 Are you beginning to see how useful this pseudo-variable self can be?

Afterward, we will have to create at least one animal, for example a dog. When creating the instances of a given class, it is sufficient to send the message new to the class. Thus, the transmission:

Dog new

returns a new instance of the class Dog. If we want the dog to talk, it should be enough to send the message talk to this new instance of the class Dog. Let us enter in the Workspace the line

Dog new talk

and select "Alt+d" to carry out do it – this is faster than opening a contextual menu and selecting the button do it. Unfortunately, it does not work – or rather it works too well. The result of these two transmissions, corresponding to the selectors new and talk, will be the appearance of a new window titled: Error: Instances of UndefinedObject are not indexable[10]. Figure 2.7 on page 31 showing this window at first seems to be incomprehensible.

The indication of an error is effectively a bit unintelligible with our still very limited knowledge of SMALLTALK programming. Let us examine it anyway. In the window just below the title of the window, the error message, we see a row consisting of three buttons: proceed, abandon and debug. We will select the button debug. This should transform the window into the new window shown in Figure 2.8, page 33, which begins with the following set of lines:

```
UndefinedObject(Object)>>error:
UndefinedObject(Object)>>errorNotIndexable
UndefinedObject(Object)>>size
String(SequenceableCollection)>>,
Dog(Animal)>>answer:
Dog(Animal)>>talk
...
```

Whenever you have an error, SQUEAK offers an incredibly powerful window like this one. Indeed, these lines give an *exact* description of the state of the SQUEAK machine[11]. They allow you to explore this state, to return to previous states, to modify the state, to stop or restart the calculation, taking into account the changes that you may have made.

---

10 Do not worry if you do not get this error. That means that you are most likely working with a newer version of SQUEAK than version 3.9, which is the version that I used while writing this chapter. The information given later on "how to interact with error windows" are nevertheless very important to know.

11 This is a misnomer: nevertheless, we regularly speak of the SQUEAK *machine*, since this software can be regarded as a simulation of a computer and it effectively behaves as a computer,

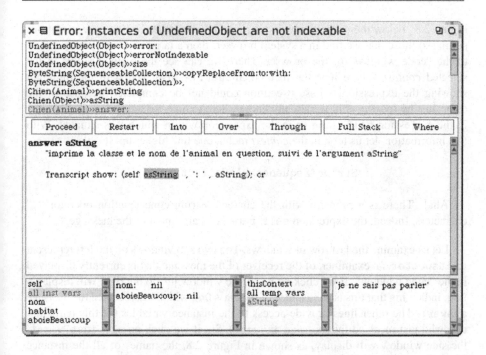

Figure 2.8. *A full-size error-indicating window*

These indications seem opaque. And yet, they are clear. This is why if you encounter such a window, ignore the lines that mean nothing to you and do not refer to something you know. Here you can ignore the lines beginning with UndefinedObject (we do not know what this is at the moment). Keep going until you come across a line that contains something that you know. Here is the first line of such a type:

Dog(Animal)≫answer:

Indeed, we know the class Dog, its superclass Animal and the method answer:. A line of this type gives a computation *context*. It can be read as:

> An instance of the Dog class received the message answer: and the method that it is currently executing is defined in the Animal class.

This will cause the answer: method to appear in the large sub-window that was empty until now. Before continuing, let us examine the different subwindows of

---

a machine with all its features, including interruption handling, device drivers, and personal machine language, to name just a few.

Figure 2.8: below the *context* subwindow, we first see an area with a row of buttons similar to those that we find in a system browser; then a large window corresponding to the "code window" of the browser. There we can see the method active in the selected *context* – here it is the method answer: – displayed with the highlight showing the expression, whose execution could not be completed because of the error. Just by *looking* at it, we already know where to look for the source of the error: in the expression self name or in the expression within which it is situated. With this information, let us look in the *context* menu, one line higher up. It says:

```
String(SequenceableCollection)≫,
```

Aha! There is a problem with the character-string concatenation operator " , " characters. Indeed, the expression self name is an argument of the message " , ".

Let us examine the last row of windows. The two subwindows on the left represent an inspector, an examiner, of the receiver of the message that is currently displayed in the "code window". If we click on self, the window just to the right will display a Dog, indicating that this is an instance of the class Dog which has received the message answer:. The other lines provide access to the instance variables (of this particular dog who just received the message answer:). So, if we click on all inst vars[12] the side window will display, as shown in Figure 2.8, the names of all the instance variables with their values *at the moment* when the error occurred:

```
name: nil
barkALot: nil
```

Indeed, all instances of the Dog class have two instance variables: the variable barkALot, defined within the Dog class, and the variable name, inherited from its superclass, Animal. The values of these two variables are nil. In SMALLTALK, nil is the name for something that is not defined. This is the one and only instance of the UndefinedObject class. This is why the error window announces to us that there is a problem with the instances of UndefinedObject: we did not give a name to the instance of the Dog class we just created. SMALLTALK says then, quite correctly, that the name of this Dog is not yet defined. The value of the instance variable name is thus nil. All variables upon creation are given the value nil. Since we are sending the message talk to this instance of Dog, and since the corresponding method sends the message answer: to this very same instance of the Dog class, and, finally, since in the method answer: we concatenate the string of characters resulting from the transmission self name to the string 'Dog' (the name of the class of the instance that received this message), SMALLTALK tells us that it cannot do such a concatenation, as nil is not a string of characters (but only the single and unique instance of the class UndefinedObject). We can thus conclude that we have forgotten to give our

---

12 This is an abbreviation of *all instance variables*.

dog a name. Then, let us leave this window, simply by closing it, and try the following transmissions:

Dog new name: 'Droopy'; talk

which transmits to the class Dog the message new, which creates a new instance of the class Dog, to which we will send the message name: with the string of characters 'Droopy' as argument[13], which gives the instance variable name of our dog the value Droopy, and in a *cascade* sends the message talk to the very same instance of Dog. As previously, this causes the transmission of the message answer: with the argument 'I do not know how to talk' to this same instance of the Dog class. The difference with the previous situation resides in the fact that now when in the method answer: the message name is sent to our dog, the method name returns the string of characters 'Droopy' (and not the object nil anymore), and there is no longer a problem with the concatenation. We should see the following text appear in the Transcript:

Dog Droopy: I do not know how to talk

We have managed to *run* our first SMALLTALK program until the end.

Before continuing to develop our program, take another look at the error window in Figure 2.8 on page 33. In the inspector part (the last row of subwindows), we have only examined the inspection part related to the receiver of the message (the two windows on the left). The two subwindows on the right allow us to inspect the context corresponding to the line selected in the subwindow displaying all the active contexts (the highest subwindow). This inspector is organized in the same way as the receiver inspector: the window on the left gives the list of items to be examined the window on the right provides the information requested. Thus, selecting the line thisContext leads to the current context of Dog(Animal)>>answer: being displayed; this is just a copy of the line selected in the context window. The selection of the following line, all temp vars[14], displays in the subwindow on the right, the list of all temporary variables with their values in this context, i.e. at the moment of calculation where SQUEAK was in the method answer: and tried to concatenate the object nil to the string of characters 'Dog'.

Here, there is only one temporary variable: the variable aString which is the variable parameter of the method answer:. Very correctly, SQUEAK displays:

aString: 'I do not know how to talk'

---

13 Naturally, it is the famous dog Droopy who is well known to Tex Avery fans.
14 This abbreviation stands for *all temporary variables*.

where the string `'I do not know how to talk'` is effectively the argument that we gave to `answer:` in the method `talk`. Do you see? An error indication is something that helps us to browse the program. It allows us to observe and examine the different stages of the computation that might have caused the error. Although at first it seems incomprehensible, do not dispose of it. Search for the *contexts* corresponding to your program, your classes, methods and variables. In most cases, when using such windows you will be able to find the reason(s) of the error(s) a lot faster than by just re-examining the code. The error indication is a positive thing: it is always a moment of discovery and deep understanding. Each time an error occurs you will discover a little more about how SMALLTALK functions and you will understand your own program a bit better. Through exploring these error windows, SQUEAK allows you to really learn from your errors[15].

2.4. Adding methods to subclasses of the Animal class

Until now, all our methods have been located in the `Animal` class. All the animals, therefore, have the same behavior. Should we ask an instance of the `Parrot` or `Whale` class to talk, they would all uniformly reply `I do not know how to talk`. Thus, the activation of the transmission:

`Parrot new name: 'Polly'; talk`

results in the `Transcript` displaying

`Parrot Polly:  I do not know how to talk`

---

15 This is the reason why IT professionals instead of talking about an *error* talk about a *bug*. Originally, this word comes from an accidental failure of the computer Mark-2, which was still operating with cathode ray tubes and where the reason for the failure was the accumulation of dead insects, burned by the heat of the cathode ray tube, between the tube and the contact plate, thereby cutting off the power supply to the tube. It was only after a few days that the researchers found the *bugs* (to see the photo of the first bug, take a look in [WIK 06b]). Since then, IT professionals have spent a lot of time searching their programs for *bugs*, the elements responsible for malfunctions. Statistics tell us that during the construction of a program, approximately 5% of time is used to write novel code and the rest of the time is devoted to changing this newly written code in order to eliminate *bugs*, which are introduced due to errors in the specifications, in the design or simply in the code writing phase. So, do not ever be depressed when the program does not work as you would like it to. Instead be happy. This is a new opportunity to *search for the bug*. And if you are really under the impression that your program works, go ahead, and deliberately introduce a bug; you will be surprised how much you can learn by *debugging* the program.

and the transmission:

> Whale new name: 'Moby'; talk

results in the display of

> Whale Moby: I do not know how to talk

This is rather boring behavior. Let us begin by rendering the behavior of the Parrots slightly more specific, and, since we all know that some parrots can learn to talk, we will give them the necessary knowledge to do just that.

For this, we return to our system browser, select the Parrot class and begin to create the protocols initialize and actions, in the same way that we did for the Animal class (see page 24).

Since we added the instance variable vocabulary to our Parrot class, this variable should contain at any given time the vocabulary of each of the parrots. We thus need an initialization method for this variable. Let us call it vocabulary: and put it in the initialize protocol. We also need a method to tell the parrots how to talk. The second method will naturally be called talk and we will put it in the actions protocol of the Parrot class. Here are the two methods (do not forget to accept them using the "Alt+s" combination):

```
vocabulary: aString
    "teach the parrot new vocabulary"
    vocabulary := aString
talk
    "make the parrot talk with its vocabulary"
    self answer: vocabulary
```

We will test the behavior of the parrots. To do this, create a parrot, give him a name and a vocabulary and ask him to tell us something. For example, if we enter the following expression in the Workspace:

```
Parrot new name: 'Polly';
vocabulary: 'Screatch@\#!? Go away';
talk
```

and carry out doIt (keys "Alt+d") on this expression, the following line will appear in the Transcript:

> Parrot Polly: Screatch#!?   Go away

We were able to create at least one animal who knows how to say something other than "I do not know how to talk"!

How has SMALLTALK proceeded? First, with the expression Parrot new, we have created an instance of the Parrot class. To this instance we have then sent the message name: with the string 'Polly' as an argument. The instance of the Parrot class that we had to create searched in its class the method corresponding to the selector name:. As it did not find any by this name, it searched in its superclass Bird. This class does not contain any method of this name either – it does not contain any method. Our instance continued to search for such a method in its superclass of its superclass, the Animal class. Finally, it found the method with that name (that selector):

```
name: aString
     "change the name of the animal in aString"
     name := aString
```

saying to assign *its* instance variable a new value, the value of the argument which the received transmission contained, the string of characters 'Polly'. From this moment onward, we can talk about this particular instance of the Parrot class as the parrot Polly. We say that the instances of the Parrot class *inherited* the method name: from the Animal class.

We must note that to find the method corresponding to a message selector, an instance begins to search for the selector in its class, and, if it cannot be found, it *goes* up the tree of its superclasses until it finds a corresponding method. It is this method that will be executed. If it cannot find such a method anywhere – the search would end in the Object class – SMALLTALK would send the message doesNotUnderstand: to the instance, with the selector, whose implementation couldn't be found in the tree of superclasses, as an argument. This would normally result in an error. Note also that the occurrence of an instance variable name in a method *always* refers to the instance variable of the *receiver* of the message – regardless of the class in which the method is in.

We continue to analyze our transmission:

```
Parrot new name: 'Polly';
   vocabulary: 'Screatch@\#!? Go away';
     talk
```

After the transmission Parrot new name: 'Polly', it continues, in a *cascade* – indicated by the semicolon character – by sending our parrot named Polly the message vocabulary: with the string of characters 'Screatch#!? Go away'.

Polly then, finding this method in its own class, can execute it immediately and thus give a new value to its instance variable vocabulary. Currently, Polly distinguishes itself from all the other instances of the Parrot class by its name *and* by its vocabulary – in short, as we said in the introduction, by the values of its instance variables.

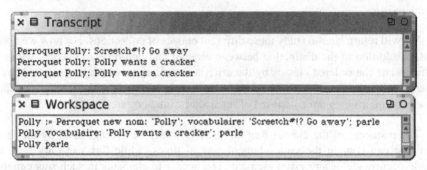

Figure 2.9. *A Transcript and a Workspace showing an interaction with a parrot*

Figure 2.9 shows a Workspace with an example of three successive transmissions to a parrot named Polly and the results of these transmissions in the Transcript. In this example, we have kept a new instance of the Parrot class in the *global* variable Polly, in order to send several messages, one after the other. For each of these lines of the Workspace, we have launched "doIt" with the keys "Alt+d"[16].

As we can see in the Transcript, our parrot lacks a bit of intelligence: every time it learns a new piece of vocabulary, it forgets what it already knew prior to this learning phase. Let us imagine that parrots could acquire a vocabulary of more than one phrase, and that, when asked to talk, they could respond with a random phrase from this vocabulary.

2.5. Modification of Parrot behavior

We will modify the behavior of our parrots, so that they will be able to have a vocabulary of several phrases. For that, clearly, the instance variable vocabulary cannot be a simple string of characters; it should be a structure, where each of the parrots can collect different phrases that he knows. For such cases – when it becomes necessary to be able to keep a *collection* of things accessible through a single unique name – SMALLTALK has a whole set of classes, all subclass of the class

---

16 If we wanted to run the set of these transmissions with a single doIt, of course, we should separate the different transmissions with dots or construct a long cascade.

`Collection`. There are classes of all types: classes with ordered elements, these are all the subclasses of the `SequenceableCollection` class; classes with unordered elements, these are mainly the `Dictionary`, `Bag` and `Set` classes; collections whose elements are indexed by integers, these are the subclasses of `ArrayedCollection`, etc. Figure 2.10 (adapted from [GOL 83] p. 148) gives their hierarchy and main characteristics.

We will return later to study these different classes of collections. For now we note that, in addition to the distinction between ordered and non-ordered classes, we can differentiate the ordered classes by the criteria according to which they are ordered, internal or external criteria, by the way we access the elements and – finally – by the *type* of elements they are composed of: characters, integers, etc.

The instances of the classes `Bag` and `Set` can only be distinguished by the fact that `Bag` can contain the same element several times, while `Set` can only have a single occurrence of any given element. The access to elements in such sets cannot be finely controlled, that is to say there is no option to search for a specific element in such a collection. Since we want a parrot to arbitrarily choose one of the phrases known to him when he has to say something, these two classes are not good candidates for implementing a vocabulary. So, we have to choose a class where we could easily access an arbitrary element and where choosing this element would not be too complicated. In such cases, a subclass of the `ArrayedCollection` is necessary, since the elements are accessible using keywords and since the keywords can be numbers, integers, we can talk about the first, second, ..., n-th element. Knowing that the numbers in SMALLTALK know how to respond to many requests (messages), and knowing that enumeration is a relatively simple activity, we will choose the class `Array`[17] (*array*) for representing our set of phrases.

Let us suppose then that our parrots are moderately intelligent and their vocabulary does not exceed 100 phrases. In this case, each instance of `Parrot` should have an instance of `Array` of 100 elements. The message `vocabulary:` should no longer change the value of the instance variable `vocabulary`, but add the new vocabulary as an additional sentence to the already existing vocabulary – it should, therefore, take the next available index of the `vocabulary` array and add the new phrase.

---

17 The class `Array` allows us to create similar structures to the indexable structures in other languages. For example, if the declaration C: `char **vocabulary[100]` creates an array of 100 entries for strings of characters, indexable from 0 to 99, in SMALLTALK the creation of an instance of the `Array` class using `Array new:    100` delivers a array of 100 elements, indexable from 1 to 100, with *a* difference in size: the objects that can be stored in a SMALLTALK array are not of a particular type: they can be strings of characters and/or numbers and/or pointers to classes or instances and/or ..., while in C all the objects must be of the type given in the declaration.

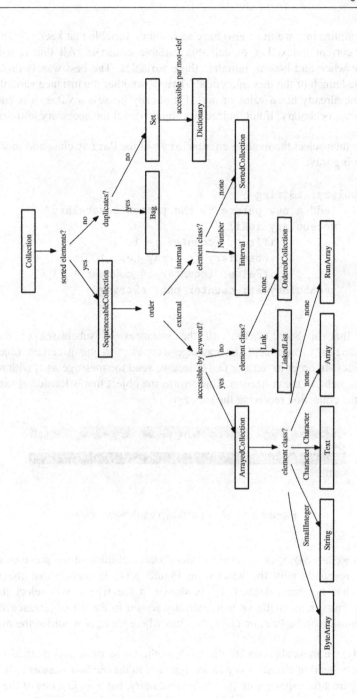

Figure 2.10. *The hierarchy of the Collection class*

This implies that we must also have an instance variable that keeps us up-to-date with the current index. Let us call this variable `counter`. All that remain is to determine when and how to initialize these variables. The best way is probably to look at the launch of the message `vocabulary:`, whether the instance variable of the same name already has a value or not. If it already possess a value, it is enough to add the new vocabulary; if not, indeed, we should do all the necessary initializations.

Let us then select the method `vocabulary:` of the `Parrot` class and modify it in the following way:

```
vocabulary: aString
        "add a new phrase to the parrot vocabulary"
        vocabulary isNil
                ifTrue: [counter := 1.
                vocabulary := Array new: 100]
                ifFalse: [counter := counter + 1].
        vocabulary at: counter put: aString
```

Note that in SMALLTALK, *all* the instances of subclasses of the class `indexedCollection` accept the message `at:put:` to *put* a certain object *at* a certain index. In order to retrieve this object we send the message `at:`, with an index as the argument, to the collection. This returns the object that is located at (`at:`), this index in the collection receiving the message.

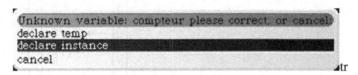

Figure 2.11. *The* unknown variable *window*

When we ask SQUEAK to *accept* ("Alt+s") the definition of the previous method, SQUEAK responds with the window in Figure 2.11, indicating that the variable `counter` has not been defined. If, as shown in the figure, you select the entry `declare instance`, SQUEAK automatically adds it to the list of instance variables in the definition of the `Parrot` class, the class where we have modified the method.

Clearly, we must also modify the `talk` method, otherwise this method will give the whole collection `vocabulary` as an argument to the method `answer:`. We do not want the parrot to respond with its whole vocabulary, but with just one of the phrases that it knows. Moreover, we would like this phrase to be chosen at random.

SQUEAK provides us with a class that allows us to generate random numbers in the interval [0,1]. This class is called Random and it is a subclass of the class Object. It creates an instance of a random number generator with the message new and each of these instances knows how to respond to the message next, which delivers a new random number. If we truly want every instance of Parrot to know how to respond with a randomly chosen phrase from its vocabulary, each instance should also have such a random number generator.

We once again modify our vocabulary: initialization method to give an initial value of a random instance variable. This new version can be written as follows:

```
vocabulary: aString
        "add a new phrase to the vocabulary of the parrot"
        vocabulary isNil
                ifTrue: [counter := 1.
                        random := Random new.
                        vocabulary := Array new: 100]
                ifFalse: [counter := counter + 1].
        vocabulary at: counter put: aString
```

Of course, as before, SQUEAK will ask us how to interpret this new variable random, and, as before, we will choose the option declare instance so that SQUEAK will add this variable to the set of instance variables of the Parrot class. Let us also write a method that would give us access to this variable[18]:

```
random
        "return the value of the random instance variable"
        random
```

The new version of the talk method will be:

```
talk
        "give a random vocabulary phrase to the parrot"
        self answer:
                (vocabulary at:
                        self random next * 100 \\ counter
                                                truncated + 1)
```

---

18 In SMALLTALK, it is a good practice to define two methods for each instance variable: one that allows us to access it and usually has the same name as the instance variable (as we did in the Animal class for the instance variable name) and one that allows us to modify this variable. Normally, this method also has the same name as the instance variable but with the ":" sign at the end for indicating that this method takes an argument – the new value of the instance variable.

Naturally, as in the previous version of the `talk` method, this method only sends `self`, the message `answer:` to the receiver. It is just the argument that is slightly more complex. Instead of only giving the instance variable `vocabulary`, now it must return a random element from the `vocabulary` array. Let us look in some detail at how this is done. Recall the transmission that calculates the index:

```
(self random next {*} 100 \\  counter) truncated + 1
```

This transmission begins by sending the message `random` to the receiver, an instance in `Parrot` class, which responds with the value the `random` instance variable `random:` a random number generator[19] an instance of the `Random` class. In response to the message `next`, any generator, and – *a fortiori* – any instance of the `Random` class generates a new element which is sent back to the message sender. At this point, the transmission `self random next` returns a new random number in the range [0,1]. As an example, let us assume that it is the number 0.453201. What we want is to calculate a valid *index* for an array that can have a maximum of 100 elements. Sending the message * with the argument 100 to this number returns the product of 100 times this number. Here it is thus the number 45.3201. It is not bad, it is a number between 1 and 100, thus a number in the interval of possible indices in our array. The problem that we have at the moment is that we have only `counter` of valid elements in our `vocabulary` array, since the instance variable `counter` contains the number of phrases that the message-receiving parrot has learned. The message \\ with the argument `counter` asks the receiver to return the remainder of the division of the receiver by the argument. Here, we assume that the `counter` value is 2, which would mean that the remainder of the division of 45.3201 by 2 would be equal to approximately 1.3201. *Voila*, we have a value between 1 and 2, the only two possible indices in our hypothesis. Sadly, 1.3201 is not a legal index of an array. The indices have to be integers. This is not a problem. If we send 1.3201, the result of the message transmissions sent up to now, the message `truncated`, the receiver, 1.3201, will return its whole number part, this is to say: 1. Since the method `truncated` always rounds a real number to the nearest whole number, and since \\, with the argument *arg* delivers a number between 0 and *arg* − 1, let us add 1 to the result obtained. All this ensures that we get a number between 1 and *arg*. This is achieved with the last transmission which consists of sending the result obtained so far, the integer 1, the message + with the integer 1 as an argument, which returns the integer resulting from the sum of 1 and 1, thus 2.

---

[19] To see the generator programming in more detail, look at Chapter 8 in the excellent book written by Timothy Budd [BUD 88].

We will return to arithmetic messages in Chapter 4. Here, we just schematically summarize what we have just done:

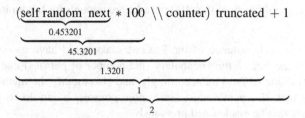

Figure 2.12 shows a Transcript and a Workspace where we have tested the new methods of the Parrot class. In this Workspace, we have already created a parrot called Polly. Then, we taught it a vocabulary of three phrases and asked it six times to say something. In the Transcript, we can see that Polly has learned these three phrases and gives us a randomly selected one every time we ask it to talk.

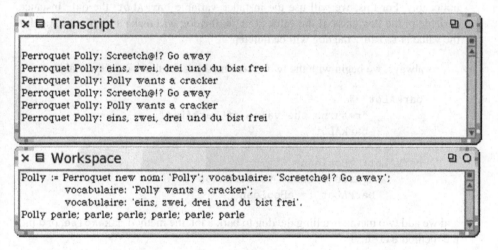

Figure 2.12. *A test of the methods of the* Parrot *class*

2.6. Exercises

The solutions can be found on page 254.

1) The method vocabulary:, every time that it is evaluated, adds a new phrase to the collection of phrases that the parrot knows. This can be a problem, if we teach the parrot more than 100 phrases, since the array containing the phrases is limited to 100

elements and the transmission vocabulary at: counter put: aString would then produce an error when trying to add a 101-th phrase. Modify the method in such a way that none of the parrots could learn more than a maximum of 100 phrases. If you try to teach him more, he should answer that 100 phrases are enough for his limited intelligence.

2) We can imagine that each instance of the Parrot class could have its own intelligence, measured by the size of the vocabulary (the number of phrases) that it can learn. Modify the definition of Parrot accordingly, and also modify the method vocabulary: in a way that, if a parrot must learn more phrases, it can do so by forgetting a random phrase that he has learned previously.

2.7. self **and** super

Let us continue our small program by adding several methods to the instances of the Dog class. We will distinguish between dogs that bark a lot – who make a lot of noise – and the others, the better behaved ones, who limit themselves to "woof" less noticeably. For this, we will use the instance variable barkALot, the only instance variable of the Dog class. If the value is true, the dog will make a lot of noise, and if the value is false[20] the dog will be quieter.

As always, we begin with the two access methods for this instance variable:

```
barkALot
          "returns the value of barkALot"
          barkALot

barkALot: aBoolean
          "gives a value to barkALot"
          barkALot := aBoolean
```

and we add two methods telling the dog to bark a lot, the method makeNoise, or a bit, the method silence.

Here, they are[21]:

---

20 true and false are the only instances of the classes True and False, respectively. We will return to these classes in Chapter 4.

21 If you want to have an apostrophe in a string of characters, SMALLTALK asks that they be doubled in order to be taken into account. This is necessary for distinguishing an apostrophe at the "end of a string" and an apostrophe in the string. In the French version of this book, we apply this rule in the method silence further on. However, this is a noteworthy concept to remember. We will return to the syntax of the string of characters in more detail in section 4.3.3, page 65 and afterward.

```
makeNoise
        "change the status of the dog to a noisy dog"
        self barkALot: true.
        self answer: 'I will bark a lot'

silence
        "change the status of the dog to a quiet dog"
        self barkALot: false.
        self answer: 'I do not bark a lot'
```

Here, we teach the dogs to bark:

```
bark

        "make the dog bark"
        self barkALot
        ifTrue: [self answer: 'bow wow, bow wow, bow wow']
        ifFalse: [self answer: 'woof']
```

Nevertheless, we would like to not increase beyond measure the commands that we can give to these animals. Clearly, all animals know how to talk: at the very least, they can say "I do not know how to talk", due to the talk method of the Animal class. All the Parrots know how to talk because of their vocabulary. But in the current status of our method definitions of the Dog class, if you ask a dog to talk, it will reply with the default answer given by all animals, saying "I do not know how to talk", although he knows how to bark. Let us write a talk method for the instances of the Dog class too. This should – *a priori* – make the dog receiving the message talk, bark. The barking manner of a dog depends on its instance variable barkALot; that is how we defined the method bark. So, what should a dog say, if the variable barkALot is not defined, that is to say we have not asked the dog to make noise (by sending him the message makeNoise) nor to rest silent (by sending him the message silence)?

One possibility is that such a dog does not know how to talk and therefore should, like all the animals who do not know how to talk, respond with "I do not know how to talk". Knowing that an undefined variable has an *undefined value* which is called nil in SMALLTALK, we then define the instance method talk for the class Dog:

```
talk
    "makes the dog bark or not"
    self barkALot isNil
        ifTrue: [self answer: 'I do not know how to talk']
        ifFalse: [self bark]
```

This is a beautiful definition: it tells the dog to indicate its inability to talk, if the instance variable barkALot is nil[22], otherwise it sends the dog receiving the message (self), the message bark, which knows how to distinguish between the values true and false of the variable barkALot.

What is inconvenient in this definition is that in the case where the instance variable is not defined, we are re-doing for dogs what all the animals that do not know how to speak do. In general, each time we write the same thing twice in the program, something is not right. We must find a better way to avoid this rewriting, a way to factor the code. Here is a second version of the talk method of the Dog class:

```
talk
      "makes the dog bark or not"
      self barkALot isNil
            ifTrue: [super talk]
            ifFalse: [self bark]
```

We have replaced sending the message answer: with self, the receiver of the message, by sending the message talk to super. What is super? Reply: super and self designate exactly the same object: the receiver of the message. Both of them are *pseudo-variables* used to refer, within methods, to the receiver of the message corresponding to the selector of the method (in our case here, the selector is talk). The difference between the two pseudo-variables is that self begins the search for the method in its own class, whereas super begins the search in its superclass. In our case, the transmission self bark tells the receiver dog to do what is said in the method with the name, or more precisely, the selector, bark, by looking for this method first in its own class Dog and searching upward in its superclasses only, if it does not find it in its own class. The transmission super talk tells the receiver dog to search for a method with the name talk starting from its superclass Mammal, and ignoring the method with that name in its own class. This guarantees that a dog responds well. When its variable barkALot is not defined, "I do not know how to talk", as it is said in the talk method of the Animal class, which is the first class in the chain of superclasses having the method talk.

If we create a dog with:

```
                  Lassie := Dog new: 'Lassie'
```

---

22 This is a misnomer: it would be more correct to say that "the variable is linked to a certain value". Sometimes, we also say that "a variable has a certain value" or even more compactly that "a variable is a certain value". But, let us remember that this is not a proper way of speaking.

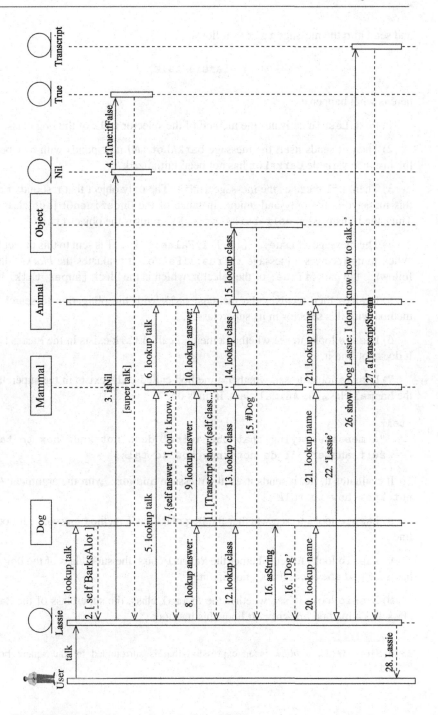

Figure 2.13. *Graphical representation of the transmission sequence*

and send him the message `talk` as follows:

`Lassie talk`

here is what happens:

1) First, `Lassie` activates the method of the selector `talk` of the `Dog` class.

2) Then, it sends itself the message `barkALot` and it responds with `nil` because the instance variable `barkALot` has not been initialized.

3) Then, `nil` receives the message `isNil`. The only object that responds `true` to this message is the only and unique instance of the `UndefinedObject` class, `nil`. Thus, the transmission `self barkALot isNil` returns the object `true`.

4) The message `ifTrue: [...] ifFalse: [...]` is sent to this object `true`. When `true` receives a message `ifTrue:ifFalse:` it evaluates the *block*[23] directly following the part `ifTrue:` of the selector, which is the block `[super talk]` here.

5) `Lassie` then receives the message `talk` with the obligation to search for a method with this selector in its superclasses.

6) `Lassie` looks to see whether a method called `talk` exists in the `Mammal` class. It does not find it.

7) `Lassie` looks to see whether a method called `talk` exists in the superclass of the `Mammal` class, the `Animal` class. It finds one:

```
talk
    "a message saying that the animal does not know how to talk"
    self answer: 'I do not know how to talk'
```

It evaluates it, i.e. it sends itself the message `answer:` with the argument `'I do not know how to talk'`.

8) `Lassie` looks to see whether the `Dog` class has a method `answer:`. It does not find it.

9) `Lassie` looks to see whether the `Mammal` class, the superclass of the `Dog` class, has a method `answer:`. It does not find it.

10) `Lassie` looks to see whether the `Animal` class, the superclass of the `Mammal` class, has a method `answer:`. It finds this method:

---

23 In SMALLTALK, a *block* is an expression that is surrounded by the square brackets "[" and "]".

```
answer: aString
        "prints the class and the name of the animal in
                question followed by the argument aString"

        Transcript show:
        (self class asString , ' ' ,
                self name , ': ' , aString);
        cr
```

It evaluates it by sending the Transcript the message show: after evaluating the argument.

11) Lassie sends itself the message class.

12) It looks in the Dog class, to see whether such a method exists there. It does not find it.

13) It looks in its superclass Mammal, to see whether such a method exists there. It does not find it.

14) It looks in its super-super-class Animal, to see whether such a method exists there. It does not find it.

15) It looks in its super-super-super-class Object, to see whether such a method exists there. It exists there and it returns a pointer to the class to which Lassie belongs.

16) Dog receives the message asString. This transmission returns the string of characters 'Dog'.

17) The string of characters 'Dog' receives the concatenation message ",", with the argument ' ' which returns the string of characters 'Dog '.

18) The string of characters 'Dog ' receives the concatenation message ",", with the argument self name.

19) Lassie sends itself the message name.

20) It looks in the Dog class, to see whether such a method exists there. It does not find it.

21) It looks in its superclass Mammal, to see whether such a method exists there. It does not find it.

22) It looks in its super-super-class Animal, to see whether such a method exists there. Yes, it does. It sends the string of characters 'Lassie', the value of its instance variable name.

23) The string of characters 'Dog' can finally respond to the message ",", with the string of characters 'Dog Lassie'.

24) This string of characters receives the message ",", with the argument ': ' which results in the string 'Dog Lassie: '

25) This string of characters receives the message ",", with the parameter of the method `answer:` as the argument. This is the string `'I do not know how to talk'`.

26) `Transcript` receives the message `show:` with the string of characters `'Dog Lassie:    I do not know how to talk'` as the argument. The result of this transmission is the display of this string of characters in the `Transcript` window.

27) `Transcript` receives, in cascade, the message `cr`. The result of this transmission is the display of a "carriage return" in the `Transcript`.

28) `Lassie` has reached the end of the `talk` method. Since none of the expressions told it what to return to the sender, `Lassie` returns itself (any method whose evaluation finishes out of reach of the ' ^ ' sign, returns the receiver of the message). *Voila*, that is it. After this very detailed description, do you see what the mechanisms of message sending are?

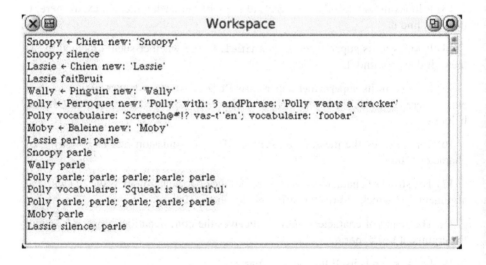

Figure 2.14. *A test of our program*

Figure 2.13, on page 49, graphically shows the sequence of these transmissions and their returns. To facilitate the reading of this figure: class instances are represented by circles with a vertical line below them, classes itself are represented as rectangles with vertical lines underneath[24]. The names of the instances are written in the circles and the names of the classes are written in the rectangles. An open arrow pointing to the right corresponds to the sending of the message marked on the arrow pointing toward

---

24 In UML, *Unified Modeling Language* [FOW 97], such objects are known by the name *lifelines*. The lifelines and such graphical representations are called *sequence diagrams*.

the target object. A closed arrow pointing to the right labeled *lookup xxx* corresponds to the search for the method *xxx*[25]. The returns, either of a *lookup* or a transmission of a message, are represented by dashed arrows. For an ordinary return, this arrow is labeled by the return value. For a method search, the label shows, between brackets, the next transmission to be performed. The temporal order is from top to bottom. This figure is limited to the transmissions concerning objects: classes and instances, users. We have also included the objects `nil`, `true` and `Transcript`.

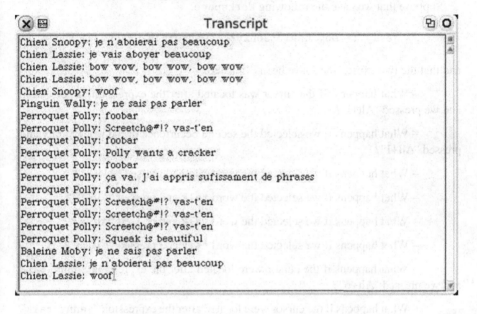

Figure 2.15. *The test result of Figure 2.14*

Note that if, in the method `talk` of the Dog class, we had written `self talk` instead of `super talk`, the execution of the method `talk` would never end, it would *loop*, since the dog receiveing the message `talk` initially would be instructed to do whatever results from sending the message `talk` to itself, which, in turn, would result in the sending of the message `talk` to itself, . . . and so on endlessly.

Figure 2.14 shows an interaction with our program through a SQUEAK `Workspace`. In it, we use all the methods that we have defined so far, including those that were given as exercises. Figure 2.15 gives the results in a `Transcript`.

---

25 In general, this method search is not represented in the UML sequence diagrams since it does not directly concern the application or the model but the details of the program execution.

2.8. Exercises

The solutions can be found on page 256.

1) You have started to program and operate the SQUEAK user interface. Further on are some simple questions on SQUEAK commands that you should know at the moment.

Suppose that we have the following Workspace:

```
jenny := Dog new: 'Jenny'. jenny talk
```

and that the two expressions have been evaluated:

– What happens, if the cursor was located after the expression jenny talk and we pressed "Alt+i"?

– What happens if we selected the second occurrence of the word jenny and pressed "Alt+I"?

– What happens if we selected the word Dog and pressed "Alt+b"?

– What happens if we selected the word talk and pressed "Alt+E"?

– What happens if we selected the word talk and pressed "Alt+n"?

– What happens if we selected the word talk and pressed "Alt+m"?

– What happens if the cursor were located after the expression jenny talk and we pressed "Alt+o"?

– What happens if the cursor were located after the expression "jenny talk" and we pressed "Alt+w"? And, if this "Alt+w" was followed by pressing "Alt+z", what happens then?

– What happens if we selected the word talk and pressed "Alt+x"? And if it was followed by "Alt+v"?

– What happens if the cursor was located after the word talk and we pressed "Shift+←" + "Shift+←" + "Shift+←" ?

– What happens if the cursor was located after the word talk and we pressed "Ctrl+←" + "Ctrl+←" + "Ctrl+←" ?

– If we selected the expression "Dog new: 'Jenny'" and pressed "Alt+("? what would happen? And if it was followed by a second "Alt+("?

2) Study the following definitions of the three classes One, Two and Three (graphically represented in Figure 2.16) and reply to the question underneath:

```
Object subclass: #One
        instanceVariableNames: ''
        classVariableNames: ''
        poolDictionaries: ''
        category: 'Smalltalk-Course-Exercises'
```

with the instance method a:

```
a
        ^1
```

The class Two:

```
One subclass: #Two
        instanceVariableNames: ''
        classVariableNames: ''
        poolDictionaries: ''
        category: 'Smalltalk-Course-Exercises'
```

with the two following instance methods:

```
a
        ^2
```

```
b
        ^super a
```

Finally, the class Three:

```
Two subclass: #Three
        instanceVariableNames: ''
        classVariableNames: ''
        poolDictionaries: ''
        category: 'Smalltalk-Course-Exercises'
```

with the following four instance methods:

```
a
        ^3
```

```
b
        ^self a
```

```
c
        ^super b
```

d

       ^super a

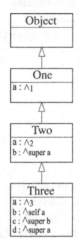

Figure 2.16. *The hierarchy of the three classes* One, Two *and* Three

If we have the three variables one, two and three, what will the Transcript display upon execution of the following program?

```
one := One new.
two := Two new.
three := Three new.
Transcript show: one a; cr;
          show: two a; cr;
          show: two b; cr;
          show: three b; cr;
          show: three c; cr;
          show: three d; cr
```

3) For now, we can create various animals, dogs and parrots, that know how to talk, or whales and penguins, that do not know how to do anything (since we have not added methods to these two animal classes). Where do these animals live? Currently, they exist but we do not know where. It would be good to put them in their habitats: with us in the house, in the Atlantic, in the Arctic, etc.

To do this, create a class AnimalHabitat which must understand the message add:, which takes an animal as the argument and whose effect would be that the animal would from that moment onward live in the receiver habitat. Naturally, several animals can share the same habitat. The habitat should know the animals that live in it. Each animal should also know where it lives. Therefore, a habitat should have a name, such as AtHome or Atlantic.

For the collection of animals in a habitat, use an instance of the class Set, the class of non-ordered *sets*. It is created by sending the message new to Set. To add an item to Set just send the message add: with the item to be added to the set as the argument. Conversely, to remove an element from the set, send the message remove: with the item to be removed as the argument. Good luck.

4) (Open project) In reality, our animals do not know how to do too many things at the moment. They know how to talk and they can, due to the solution to the previous exercise, live in a habitat. Continue to develop this animal microworld. All the evolutionary directions of this program are possible. For example, you can give form and color to the animals; you can move them from one place to another; you can make the animals meet. At the moment, the animals are born (using the message new) but an animal could also die, possibly upon encountering another animal capable of eating it, or simply by starvation due to not being able to find enough food for lengthy periods. You could have male and female animals, whose encounters could result in new animals of the same species being born and assigned a name chosen by their parents. The animals could live in a group and moving one of them could then lead to the movement of all the other animals in the group. The birds could fly and you could graphically display their flight (see the magnificent program by Reynolds [REY 87], presented at the *Computer Graphics* conference in 1987). Go ahead, design your own project and try to implement it. There is no better way to explore a new programming language than by the realization, development, modification and evolution of your own personal project.

3

Architecture and Inheritance

During the construction of our first SMALLTALK program, implementing a set of animals, we have intuitively learned quite a lot about object-oriented programming in general, and SMALLTALK and SQUEAK programming in particular.

In this short chapter, we interpret and formalize a few notions of static and dynamic *inheritance* and method *activation*. We also touch upon issues related to software architectures.

3.1. SMALLTALK software architecture

The set of predefined classes of an object system represents a real *world construction*. This construction is not complete, each system user contributes and it should be seen as a dynamic process, which takes place over time.

From this point of view, the best approach seems to be to move from general to specific, in other words, to acquire specifics from other more general cases. In terms of defining classes, this approach translates into: *for constructing a new class (which is more specific), we add variables and methods to one or more of the existing classes, which are more general.* This is what we did in our program: we built the Animal class based on the Object class by adding the instance variables name and habitat, and, in addition to access methods and modification of these instance variables, defining the methods speak, answer: and printString. Then, we built the subclasses of the Animal class: the Mammal class and the Bird class. The Mammal class did not have variables or methods added to it, perhaps to indicate that the animal *world* is not yet finished. Finally, we created the Parrot class as a subclass of the Bird class by adding a set of instance variables (vocabulary, counter and random and maxVocabulary) and by redefining the speak method. Clearly, the Parrot class is more specific than the Bird class, which is more specific than the Animal class, which is more specific than the Object class, which is the most general class of the SQUEAK system. This process of going from general to more specific, by adding classes, is at the core of object-oriented programming[1]. The new class *inherits* the old, it is a *subclass*, while the former is its *superclass*. This term *superclass* is justified by the fact that the set of instance variables of the subclass includes the instance variables of its superclasses.

As shown in Figure 3.1, superclasses describe behaviour shared by all its subclasses. Subclasses specialize the behaviour of their superclasses.

The link between the superclass and the subclasses can be represented by an acyclic graph (this is an ordered relation), called the system *inheritance graph*. In SMALLTALK systems, this graph is always a *tree*. We have seen the subclass tree of the Collection class in the previous chapter (Figure 2.10). The inheritance tree has a beginning, a unique *root*, the only class that does not have a superclass and is often called Object and in SQUEAK it is called ProtoObject. The class that is at the root of the tree gathers all the common attributes shared within all the objects of the system. Notably, it is in this class (in SQUEAK, a part is covered by the ProtoObject class and another part by the Object class) where all the definitions, related to methods associated with selectors of messages understood by all objects, error treatments, etc., can be found.

---

1 In comparison, in traditional imperative programming using procedural programming languages, for example in C [KER 88] or Pascal [JEN 75], a program is characterized as the establishment of a functional relationship of a set of activities. Ideally, these activities are organized in *modules*, independent functional units. Each module has a interface for communicating with other modules and each module knows the other modules through these interfaces. There does not exist an initial world which evolves through programming. On the contrary (possibly with the exception of libraries), every single program begins to create a new world, which risks being isolated from the other existing worlds. Of course, the idea of organizing groups of programs into *modules* was done with the potential of program *reutilization*. Unfortunately, their closed, isolated and overspecialized nature and, more importantly, the lack of a well-documented and indexed repository renders this reutilization obsolete.

In "philosophical" terms, the main difference between the software architectures in object-oriented languages and imperative languages lies in the fact that imperative languages aim to reuse activities, "as is", one imports "black boxes". In object oriented languages one does not reutilize neither the "black boxes", nor the code. We reuse the existing by adding new properties and capabilities. We *modify* the existing world gradually and *non-locally*: it is not *one* interface which we use or adapt for new reasons, these are *multiple* classes which we refine, specialize and complete.

This difference is due to completely opposite views on programming when comparing imperative programmers and object-oriented programmers: if the first one conceives a program as an interaction between *actions* which act on inert data, the second one sees it as an interaction between *objects*, active and responsible data.

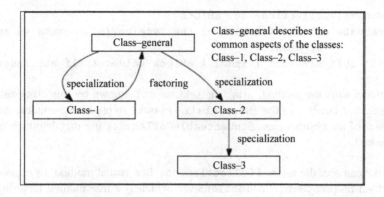

Figure 3.1. *Inheritance, factoring and specialization*

In SQUEAK, the Object and ProtoObject classes are the most important *abstract classes* of the system; they have many *virtual methods*. By *abstract class*, we mean that a class exists mainly for *factoring* and regrouping the common behaviors of its subclasses. An abstract class is not expected to have its own *instances*. It exists to generate subclasses. In our animal program, the abstract classes are Animal, Mammal and Bird.

A *virtual method* is a method which is declared but not defined within a class. For example, the Collection abstract class implements the famous method do:, understood by all its subclasses, such as[2]:

```
Collection>>do: aBlock
        "evaluate aBlock with each of the receiver's
              elements as the argument"
        self subclassResponsibility
```

which says that although the selector method do: exists for all instances of all subclasses of the Collection class, the definition of the corresponding method will be the responsibility of the subclasses: subclassResponsibility[3]. Indeed, the SequenceableCollection class, for example, which is an abstract subclass of the abstract class Collections and superclass of the very concrete Array, implements the method do: as:

---

2 We use the notation *className≫methodName* for designing the method *methodName* defined in the class *className*.

3 Note that the method subclassResponsibility is part of the messages that every single object should understand and is defined in the Object class.

```
SequenceableCollection>>do: aBlock
    "evaluate aBlock with each of the receiver's elements as an
        argument"
    1 to: self size do: [:index | aBlock value: (self at: index)]
```

It implements the method, using the selector at: known by this class, as well as the selector to:do: of the Interval class in order to produce the index. All the subclasses of the abstract class SequenceableCollection use this definition of the do: method.

As we can see, the method Collection»do: is a virtual method, as opposed to the method SequenceableCollection»do: which is a true method factoring the behavior of the set of its subclasses: the class Array, for example, does not have a custom implementation of this method, and it inherits this method from its superclass.

3.2. Static and dynamic inheritance

Once the principle of inheritance has been established, it is important to know exactly *how* it will be realized, since the use, that we can make of it, strongly depends on this concrete realization.

SMALLTALK delivers two types of inheritance: static inheritance and dynamic inheritance:

– *Static* inheritance of variables:

The instance variables of the superclass are added to those which are declared in the subclass immediately as they are defined. Each instance of a subclass thus *physically* possesses the complete collection of all the specific variables *and* the instance variables of all its superclasses.

This characteristic can be easily verified by *inspecting* an instance of a class.

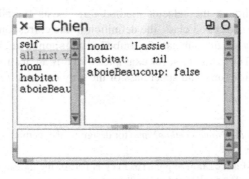

Figure 3.2. *The inspection window of the dog* Lassie

Figure 3.2 shows such an inspection of the dog Lassie. It is obtained by selecting the object Lassie, and entering the characters "Alt+i" (or by selecting in the contextual menu (see page 6) the button inspect). This *inspector* portrays that Lassie has three instance variables: the variables name and habitat, inherited from the Animal class, and the variable barksALot which is defined in the Dog class.

A consequence of choosing static inheritance is that two variables cannot have the same name, and that when defining a class, you must know the names of variables of all its superclasses in order to avoid homonyms. Moreover, the SQUEAK system ensures that, in case this is forgotten, the programmer knows that the name is reserved by alerting that it has already been defined in a superclass. It even tells us in which superclass it has been defined in.

– *Dynamic* inheritance of methods:

Unlike static inheritance, the collection of method texts of the superclass in dynamic inheritance is not recopied at the subclass level. These texts are accessible from the subclass at the time of transmission. They will be shared among the subclasses. The mechanism of a transmission can be specified as follows: knowing the receiver, and thus also the class, the SMALLTALK interpreter searches for the message selector within the class. If one is found, it applies the corresponding method. Otherwise, it will search, going up the inheritance tree in the superclass, and eventually in the superclass of the superclass, etc., until it finds the selector or until it arrives to the root of the tree. In the latter case, if the selector still cannot be found, an error is triggered (doesNotUnderstand: *selector*).

We see that this dynamic inheritance process gives a very different result from static inheritance: nothing prevents certain methods of the subclass to have the *same* names (selectors) as the methods in the superclasses. The ambiguity is resolved by the path order: it is the first encountered method in the path ascending the inheritance tree which is adopted, in this case that of the subclasses. Figure 3.3 shows the path of the inheritance tree during the search, activation and return of the methods for evaluating the transmission Lassie talk.

This is not by accident; it is the same basic programming technique: it is a current practice to *redefine* a method, which already exists in the superclass, at the subclass level to better adapt to instances in the subclass, which are, in general, more specific or more complex than the instances of the superclass. Previously, we saw an extreme example with two definitions of the method do:. We have practiced with them in our program with the method talk, which as defined in the Animal class:

```
Animal>>talk
    "a message saying that the animal cannot speak"
    "self answer: 'I cannot speak'"
```

gives the default behavior of an animal: *a priori*, no animal knew how to speak.

And, we have redefined it in the Dog class:

```
Dog>>talk
    "make the dog talk by barking or not"
    self barkALot isNil
            ifTrue: [super talk]
            ifFalse: [self bark]
```

which, in the case where the instance variable barkALot is not defined, explicitly directs, with the pseudo-variable super, the research of the talk method in order to activate a more general version than that implemented in the Dog class.

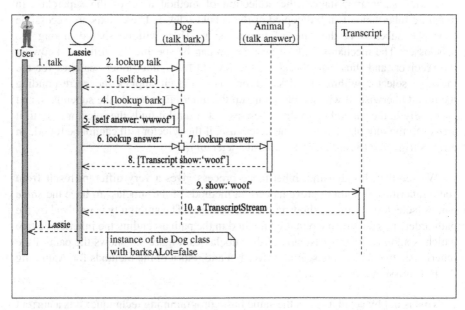

Figure 3.3. *Activation of the method* talk *in the receiver class*

Figure 3.4 shows the path of the heritage tree for this case in the evaluation of the transmission Lassie talk[4].

---

4 Recall that *lookup* means to *research a method*, the ordinary arrows correspond to the sending of messages, the dashed arrows correspond to returns, the start of an arrow is the issuer and the arrival of an arrow is the recipient message.

Finally, we have also redefined the method `talk` in the `Parrot` class:

```
Parrot>>talk
   "give random sentence of the vocabulary"
   self answer:
            (vocabulary at: self random)
```

Although this method has been defined three times, once in each class, there is no ambiguity in deciding which of the three methods must be activated: during the search of the adequate message, each animal chooses the first method encountered.

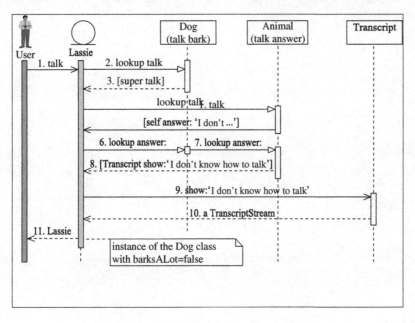

Figure 3.4. *Activation of the method* `talk` *in a superclass*

In this context, also recall our redefinition of `printString`, a method which is defined in the `Object` class for the whole SMALLTALK system and which we have adapted to the specific needs of the `Animal` class.

Some Elements of SQUEAK
Syntax and Grammar

After these rather intuitive first approaches on programming in SMALLTALK, let us try to give a description of syntax and grammar restrictions that any SMALLTALK programmer must follow. Fortunately, there aren't many and the majority have already been presented in the previous chapter. They will be thoroughly discussed and formalized in this chapter.

4.1. Pseudo-variables

Identifiers and variable names whose value the programmer cannot explicitly change, neither by assignments nor by using them as parameters, are called *pseudo-variables* in SMALLTALK. These variables, that either yield the same value every time they are evaluated, regardless of the context of the evaluation – those are the pseudo-variables nil, true and false – or change their values dynamically according to the context, are the pseudo-variables self, super and thisContext. Therefore, there are only six pseudo-variables in SMALLTALK and all of them have just been presented above: nil, true, false, self, super and thisContext.

4.1.1. *The pseudo-variable* nil

nil is the single one instance of the UndefinedObject class. It is the default value of instance variables. nil means the non-existence of explicit value associated with an object. In other words, it is the SMALLTALK name for the *undefined value* of other programming languages. nil as an *undefined value* indicator was already encountered in section 2.3 when the dispatch of Dog new speaks yielded an error, since the instance variable name had not received a value yet. It was also encountered in the definition of the method `vocabulary`: via the selector `isNil` (section 2.5) that precisely assesses whether a specific instance variable is already associated with a value or not. This is yet another beauty of SMALLTALK: the method `isNil` is defined in exactly two classes of SQUEAK. Once in `UndefinedObject` class as

```
UndefinedObject>>isNil
    ^true
```

and the other in the `ProtoObject` class as

```
ProtoObject>>isNil
    ^false
```

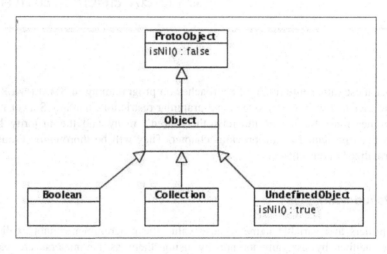

Figure 4.1. *A snippet of the beginning of the tree of* `Smalltalk` *classes with the two locations where a method* `isNil` *is defined. The* `UndefinedObject` *class has no subclass*

Thus, the `nil` object, single one instance of the `UndefinedObject` class, will answer `true` (i.e *yes*) if it were asked whether it is equal to `nil`. Any other object will answer to that same question with a resounding `false` (i.e. *no*). In fact, every object different from `nil` that is not an instance of the `UndefinedObject` class inherits the method defined in the root class of the inheritance tree, `ProtoObject` (see Figure 4.1).

4.1.2. *Pseudo-variables* `true` and `false`

The `Object` class has a subclass named `Boolean`. It is an *abstract* class, therefore, a class that factors out behaviors common to the instances of its subclasses but does not have it own instances. Its two subclasses are the `True` and `False` classes. These are thus the classes of the *true* objects and the *false* objects. Following the propositional logic, the *Boolean* logic[1], there only exists one true "object" and only one false "object": *true* and *false*. SMALLTALK follows this tradition: theTrue class has only one instance, it is the `true` object. Likewise, the `False` class has only one instance, the `false` object.

What is the purpose of these two instances? Naturally, they are used to provide answers to questions that ask whether something is *true* or *false*. And when do we need to determine whether something is true or false? When there is a need to choose between two alternatives. For instance, the sentence "if it's raining, then I take my umbrella" mainly says: "Is it raining? If the answer is yes (it is *true* that it rains) then I take my umbrella (if not, I leave it at home)". In SMALLTALK, this possibility to choose between two alternatives is implemented with the two classes `True` and `False` that describe what their instances, `true` and `false`, respectively, should do if they are the receiver of a selection message between alternatives. The simplest selection mechanism is as follows:

If *sth is true* then do *alternative true* otherwise do *alternative false*

This sentence can be translated in the object-oriented thinking as:

> *what is the truth value of sth*
> if true *do alternative true*
> if false *do alternative false*

where "*what is the truth value of sth*" corresponds to any receiver whose only thing of interests is to know whether the value of this receiver is `true` or `false`[2]. For instance, it is exactly what has been done intuitively in the method `barks` of the Dog class presented previously and that is reproduced as follows:

---

1 The *Boolean* adjective is derived from the name of the English mathematician and logician of the 19th Century Boole. In his major work, *An investigation of the Laws of Thought* [BOO 72], published in 1872, he was the first to completely formalize the propositional logic, only using the operators *and*, *or* and *not*, and implementing an entire algebra theory for its exploitation. Even today, not only do we speak of *Boolean logic*, but also of the *Boolean algebra* and *Boolean search* methods. The common point of these disciplines is that they only require these three operators. Then, in the first half of the 20th Century, some 70 years later, Claude Shannon recognized the connection between these logical operators and electromechanical relay circuits [SHA 37], thus laying the foundations of modern computing.
2 This receiver can obviously be the result of a computation, the return of a message transmission.

```
Chien>>barks
    "make the dog barks"
    self barksALot
        ifTrue: [self answer: 'bow wow, bow wow, bow wow']
        ifFalse: [self answer: 'woof']
```

where we can easily recognize the correspondence between *what is the truth value of sth* and self barksALot, between *do alternative true* and ifTrue: [self answer: 'bow wow, bow ...'] and between *do alternative false* and ifFalse: [self answer: 'woof'].

Let us recall that the variable barksALot would either have the true value or the false value. It is, therefore, one of those two *pseudo-variables* that receives the message ifTrue:ifFalse:, which itself is defined in the True class as follows:

```
True>>ifTrue: trueBlock ifFalse: falseBlock
    "anwers the trueBlock value"
    ^trueBlock value
```

A method for this same selector ifTrue:ifFalse: is also implemented in the False class as follows:

```
False>>ifTrue: trueBlock ifFalse: falseBlock
    "answers the falseBlock value"
    ^falseBlock value
```

Let us recall that a *block* is a SMALLTALK expression (and its *context*) waiting to be evaluated. Any *block* provides as an answer to the reception of the message value the result of its evaluation[3].

Both methods ifTrue:ifFalse: state, if the true object receives this message, then, without hesitation, it returns the value of the true block (the value of the parameter trueBlock), otherwise, if it is the false object that receives this message, then, with as little hesitation, it returns the value of false block (the value of the parameter falseBlock). The true object knows it is true just as the false object knows it is false.

We have just seen how to build *control structures*[4] in SMALLTALK. While control structures are primitive instructions in most conventional programming languages, those are messages like any others in SMALLTALK: any control structure can even be

---

3 The behavior of the blocks was described in the solutions to the exercises 2.8 from pages 357 onward.

4 By *control structure* we mean expressions of a programming language that influence the sequence of execution of expressions.

written in SMALLTALK itself[5]. It is the research methods in the inheritance tree that enable us to distinguish between the different cases. In other words, the different cases materialize in the structure of the inheritance tree, or yet: the difference materializes in belonging to different classes. Naturally, if we only want to distinguish between two cases, only two separate classes are required. And if we want to rebuild Boolean expressions, we only need to have a True class, describing what to do in case an object is *true*, and a False class, describing the behavior to exhibit when an object is *false*[6].

In order to use this ifTrue:ifFalse: message anywhere in the system, we only need to ensure that the receiver of this message is always an expression that can be evaluated as true or false, exactly as we did in our message barks.

We can easily write a control structure that only chooses one alternative using this method ifTrue:ifFalse: – ifTrue:, which determines what there is to do when the receiver object is true, and another, ifFalse:, which will indicate the activity to be executed when the receiver object is false. In order to avoid writing this method twice, in the True class and in the False class, we will add its definition in the abstract superclass of these two classes, the Boolean class, thus factoring out the behavior common to both classes. Here is a way to define these two methods:

```
ifTrue: trueBlock
        "answers the trueBlock value
        if the receiver is true, otherwise nil"
        self ifTrue: trueBlock ifFalse: [nil]
```

and

```
ifFalse: falseBlock
        "answers the falseBlock value
        if the receiver is false, otherwise nil"
        self ifTrue: [nil] ifFalse: falseBlock
```

---

5 The fact that control structures can be written in the same language is also possible in other interpreted languages, as in Lisp [MCC 62], for instance. However, they still generally require a basic primitive selection (such as the function if in Lisp) and they introduce specific function or procedure types in order to distinguish between functions or procedures that evaluate their arguments and those that do not evaluate them. This latter feature is also present in SMALLTALK: blocks are indeed special structures which *delay* the evaluation of expressions they contain.

6 There is clearly a relationship with the *data driven function invocation* ([SAN 77] and [SAN 78]) from Lisp and other functional languages. However, a (mini-)interpreter should be built in those languages in order to access them. In SMALLTALK, this is the basic foundation of the virtual machine.

Therefore, all the work will be delegated to the `ifTrue:ifFalse:` methods of the `True` and `False` classes.

However, let us open a class browser and admire the methods of the `True`, `False` and `Boolean` classes. These are very simple and wonderful examples about programming in SMALLTALK[7].

4.1.3. *Pseudo-variables* `self` and `super`

We have already described in detail in the previous chapter these two pseudo-variables. Let us just recall that as a receiver of a message, `self` and `super` refer to the same object, the receiver of the message corresponding to the method within which they are used. The difference between these two pseudo-variables is that if a message is sent to `self`, the search for the method corresponding to the selector will start in the class of the object designated by this pseudo-variable. On the contrary, if a message is sent to `super`, the search for the method will start in the superclass of the class that contains the method that is being executed or less clear but more formal: the superclass of the class that contains the method or that contains this message transmission to `super`.

4.1.4. *Pseudo-variable* `thisContext`

As opposed to other pseudo-variables, which are used constantly in every SQUEAK program, the pseudo-variable `thisContext` is rarely used in ordinary programs. This pseudo-variable gives access to the operation of the *virtual machine* SQUEAK. It contains at all times a pointer to the *execution stack*. Specifically, through this pseudo-variable, we can access the current *context* of the execution[8].

The pseudo-variable `thisContext` was encountered in the error window in Figure 2.8. In fact, `thisContext` is used primarily in programs contributing to the development of SQUEAK: error handling routines, utilities for visualizing the

---

7 Note that the designers of SQUEAK have decided to implement the methods `ifTrue:` and `ifFalse:` in the `True` and `False` classes, renouncing to the possible factoring. This is due to efficiency reasons.

8 SQUEAK distinguishes two contexts: the context of a method, an instance of the `MethodContext` class, and the context of a block, an instance of the `BlockContext` class. A `MethodContext` contains the receiver and the sender of the currently active method, a pointer to the method itself, the linkages of the method's arguments and naturally a pointer to the execution stack. A `BlockContext` is very similar and contains an extra pointer to the context in which this block was created, mainly in order to share values with this other context. For "lispians" (people who are used to program in Lisp): a *block* is the same as a *closure* in Lisp.

execution, inspectors, etc. For now, we can live perfectly happy in the environment SQUEAK without really having to use this variable. It was mentioned here just to note its existence.

Let us recall that which we, SQUEAK programmers, cannot change the value of nil, self, super, true, false   and   thisContext   are   the   only pseudo-variables of the SQUEAK system.

4.2. Comments and identifiers

4.2.1. *Comments*

Every programming language allows us to insert comments while writing code. These are free-form texts that will be read by the human programmer but ignored by the interpreter or compiler of the language. In SMALLTALK, comments are written between double quotes (") and may contain any character except the double quote character itself. For example:

```
"this is a comment"
"this too"
"and this: '&'=}@^\'|[({' too"
```

are one line comments. Since one can include any character (except the double quotes), one can insert as many "*new line*" characters as one wants. A comment can also span multiple lines, as shown below:

```
"A comment
on
three lines"
```

If we really want to, we can also include double quotes. This can be done by doubling each occurrence of that character. Thus, the line below is a comment, quite useless, but syntactically correct:

```
"This is a comment with ""double quotes"""
```

Comments were used in the writing of our methods. In fact, it is good practice to start a method with a short comment indicating the purpose of the method.

4.2.2. *Identifiers*

Identifiers are variables, selectors and classes names. Their writing is subject to some simple rules:

1) Identifiers are case sensitive: the identifiers `Smalltalk` and `smalltalk` are two separate identifiers.

2) An identifier starts (almost) always with a letter. The exceptions to this rule are the identifiers corresponding to the selectors of arithmetic operators ($+$, $-$, $*$, $/$, etc.), the selectors of some logical operators ($\&$, $|$, $==>$), the comparison selectors ($<$, $>$, etc.), the concatenation selector of two collections (,). In short, the exceptions are mainly the *binary* selectors. The rest of the identifier generally contains letters and digits. Whenever possible, it is recommended not to include non-alphanumeric characters, as they often render reading more difficult.

3) By convention, compound identifiers are written as a sequence of several words such that the first character is in lowercase and each following word starts with a capital letter[9], as, for instance, in the writing of the following identifiers:

```
sumOfSides
barksALot
suspendedContext
```

4) Identifiers naming global variables, such as `Transcript`, and class variables are written by convention with an initial capital letter. Let us note that class names are also global variables and are thus written with an initial capital letter too. For instance: `Animal`, `Dog`, `Integer`, `SortedCollection`, `SystemDictionary` or `UndefinedObject`.

The set of global variables is accessible through the global variable `Smalltalk`[10]. Figure 4.2 shows an inspector window opened on this variable. The global variable `Smalltalk` itself can be recognized along with our dog `Snoopy` that had been declared as a global variable.

---

9 The convention can vary from one language to another. Thus, in `Pascal` or C, the style is to separate the different words composing an identifier by *underscore* (_), providing for the same identifiers: `sum_of_sides`, `barks_a_lot`, `suspended_context`. In my opinion, this one-character writing has less esthetics. Anyway, there is no constraint: they are conventions. For SMALLTALK, however, let us keep in mind that the *entire* SMALLTALK system is written following this convention.

10 Note the writing with capital letters.

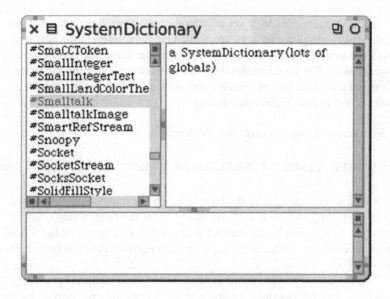

Figure 4.2. *An inspector on the global variable* Smalltalk

4.3. Literals

Literals, or *constant expressions*, are expressions that are evaluated during compilation. In this section, we distinguish objects that cannot be altered, these are the *numbers*, *characters* and *symbols*, and special collections that can be created during compilation *constant arrays* and *strings*.

4.3.1. Numbers

SQUEAK distinguishes, like any other programming language, between different types of numbers. For integers, SQUEAK distinguishes between *small integers*, instances of the SmallInteger class, which are numbers in the range $[-2^{30}, 2^{30} - 1]$[11], and all other integers, which are instances of the LargePositiveInteger or the LargeNegativeInteger class[12]. The Integer class is an abstract class factoring out the knowledge common to these three classes. The distinction between the *small* integers and the others is primarily an efficiency

---

11 It is therefore the interval $[-1073741824, 1073741823]$.

12 No limitation is imposed on the size of the instances of the LargePositiveInteger and LargNegativeInteger classes.

matter: small integers possess a set of internal *primitive*[13] operators that are very powerful, greatly speeding up computations. The *large integers* do not have these primitives. However, the end user does not notice the difference between small and large integer since SQUEAK handles the automatic conversion from one to the other. Hereafter, we will only talk of integers and no longer distinguish according to the subclasses of the Integer class they belong to.

Three examples of integers are shown below:

$$153^{14}, 815915283247897734345611269596115894272000000000^{15}, 40585^{16}$$

SQUEAK allows us to specify the base in which the numbers are expressed. This is done by preceding the number by an indication of the base, a *radix*, followed by the character "r" and then by the number expressed in that base. The radix is always written in decimal (base 10). Thus, these same integers could have been written as follows:

2r10011001, 16r8EEAE81B84C7F27E080FDE64FF05254000000000, 10r40585

The first number here was expressed in binary, i.e. in base 2. The second number in hexadecimal, i.e. in base 16, and the last number in decimal, therefore in base 10. If no base is specified, SQUEAK assumes that the number was expressed in base 10. It is thus not necessary to specify this base.

SQUEAK also allows us to express numbers with an exponent. The exponent expresses by which power of the base the number should be multiplied in order to have the non-exponential representation of the number. The notation for an exponent is to add the character "e" after the number, followed by the value of the exponent. Thus, 10e2 is the same as $10 * 10^2$, therefore 1,000. Let us note that the base of the exponent is always the same as the one specified in the radix. Thus, 2r1010e2 is equal to the decimal value 40, since 2r1010 is 10 in base 10, and 2r1010e2 is $10 * 2^2$ (the base is 2, so the base of the exponent is also 2) and this indeed gives $10 * 4 = 40$.

---

13 A *primitive* is a method that is not written in SMALLTALK but it is directly part of the SQUEAK virtual machine.

14 Did you know that this number is the smallest integer greater than 1 which is equal to the sum of the cubes of its digits? Only three other such integers exist. Find them. (370, 371, 407)

15 Definitely not a *small* integer. What kind of number is it?

16 This is the larger of the two numbers equal to the sum of the factorial of their digits (in base 10 and apart from two trivial solutions 1 and 2), thus: 40585 =!4+!0+!5+!8+!5 or, in SQUEAK: 4 factorial + 0 factorial + (2 * 5 factorial) + 8 factorial. What is the other number with the same properties? The solution is on page 82.

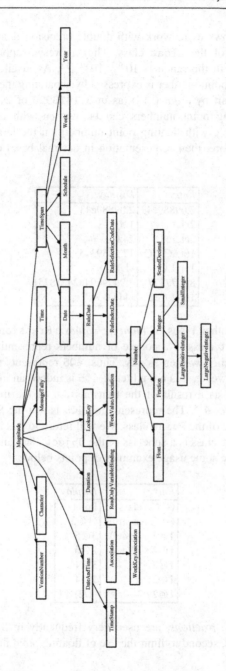

Figure 4.3. *The hierarchy of the* `Magnitude` *class*

SQUEAK also allows us to work with double precision floating point numbers. These are instances of the `Float` class. They represent approximations of *real* numbers and can be in the range $[-10^{307}, 10^{307}]$[17]. As in all other programming languages, a floating point number is expressed by separating the whole-number part from the fractional part by a *dot* ("`.`"), as in `3.1415926` or `2.7182`. Naturally, as with integers, floating point numbers can be written with exponents and/or in arbitrary bases. A table with floating point numbers on the left and how SQUEAK displays them (therefore, their representation in decimal base) on the right, can be seen below:

Entry	Display
2.09889e43	2.09889e43
2r1.1	1.5
2r1.1e4	24.0
16rAC.DC	172.859375
16r-1.C	-1.75
8r7.77777	7.999969482421875
16r-1.Ce2	-448.0

SQUEAK allows other types of *numeric values*: `Fractions` and `Points`. An instance of the `Point` class is a couple of numbers representing coordinates in a Euclidean plane which is written as *x*@*y*. Thus, `4@5` represents the coordinate point $x = 4$ and $y = 5$. However, it is not a literal: `4@5` is indeed an instance of the `Point` class; it was created as a result of the transmission of the message `@` with 5 as argument to the integer `4`[18]. The representation `4@5` is just the SMALLTALK way of displaying an instance of the `Point` class. We will return to this later on. For now, let us note that the `Point` class is a subclass of the `Object` class and not of the `Number` class and let us admire some usage examples of points below:

Entry	Display
(1@2) class	Point
(1@2) asString	'1@2'
1@2 + (2@3)	3@5
1@2 * (2@3)	2@6
1@2 + 2	3@4
1@2 * 2	2@4
1@2 / 2	(1/2)@1

Rational numbers, *fractions*, are used very frequently in SMALLTALK, first to avoid rounding errors, second to limit the use of floating point numbers. Like points,

---

17 It is said that they are *double precision* floating point numbers. The single precision floating point numbers allow only numbers in the range $[-10^{38}, 10^{38}]$.

18 Please take a look at the definition of the message "`@`" in the abstract class `Number`.

fractions are not *literals*: they are obtained by sending the message "/" to an integer. This message creates an integer if the integer receiver is a multiple of the integer that was passed as argument, for instance, in the transmission 8/2 that returns the integer 4. It creates an instance of the Fraction class if the receiver, the *numerator* is not a multiple of the argument, the *denominator*, as, for instance, in the dispatch 8/5 returning the fraction (8/5). It is as if SMALLTALK *was delaying* the evaluation of the division until the evaluation becomes necessary. Below are some usage examples of fractions:

Entry	Display
1 / 13 + (12 / 13)	1
1/3 + (1/4)	(7/12)
1/3 * (1/4)	(1/12)
1/3 / (1/4)	(4/3)
24 / 10 + (2/5)	(14/5)
24 / 10 + 2 / 5	(22/25)
1.0 / 3 + (1/4)	0.583333333333333
(1/3) sin	0.327194696796152

4.3.2. Characters

SMALLTALK provides access to all the 256 extended ASCII characters[19]. A character is an instance of the Character class being itself a subclass of the abstract class Magnitude[20]. An instance of the Character class is written by preceding the character with the sign "$". For instance, $a is a reference to the instance a of the Character class. Some of the messages that a character understands are:

– asciiValue, which returns the integer value corresponding to the receiver character in the ASCII code;

– isAlphaNumeric, which returns true if the character is a letter or number;

– isAlphabetic[21], which tests if the receiver is a letter;

– isDigit, which test if the recipient is a digit;

– isUppercase and isLowercase which tests if the receiver is, respectively, a letter written in upper case or lower case;

---

19 ASCII, an acronym standing for American Standard Code for Information Interchange, is currently the most used code to represent characters. The table of corresponding ASCII codes and characters is given in Figure 4.4.

20 Let us note that Magnitude is also on the superclass of the Number class. Thus, the Number class factors out the knowledge common to numbers, while the Magnitude class factors out the knowledge of any thing having a *size* as feature, so things that can be numerically compared. Figure 4.3 shows the tree of subclasses of this Magnitude class.

21 The selector isLetter is a synonym and does exactly the same thing.

– the comparison operators =, < and >, respectively, tests if the recipient is equal, lower or higher than the argument;

– and like any SMALLTALK object, the message `asString` that returns a string consisting of the receiver character of the message.

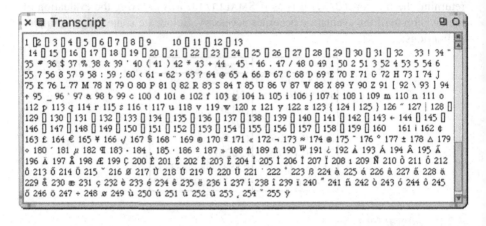

Figure 4.4. *The table of ASCII characters*

Moreover, let us add the method `asCharacter` that any instance of the `Integer` class understands and returns the character corresponding to the ASCII code of the receiver. This message is obviously meaningful only if the receiver integer is in the range $[0, 255]$. Below are some examples regarding characters[22]:

Transmission	Result
$I asciiValue	73
45 asCharacter	$-
$- asciiValue	45
($A asciiValue + 32) asCharacter	$a
$a asUppercase	$A
$A < $a	true

---

22 Let us note that the characters that are complex to print (or write) can be obtained by the following transmission to the `Character` class: `backspace` for the character "backspace", `cr` for the character "carriage return", `delete` for the character "delete", `escape` for the character "escape", `lf` for the character "line feed", `space` for the character "space" and `tab` for the character "tab".

Finally, let us note that the ASCII table given in the `Transcript` of Figure 4.4 was obtained by the following transmission:

```
1 to: 255 do:
    [:i | Transcript
            show: i;
            show: ' ',
            i asCharacter asString, ' ']
```

Note that the first 32 characters do not have printable representations: they are reserved characters, *control* characters.

4.3.3. Strings

Strings have already been encountered multiple times. Let us just recall that a string is any sequence of characters enclosed by single quote characters (`'`). If we wish to include the delimiter character of strings, the single quote, it must be doubled, as in `Transcript show: 'Jean said: ''Hello'''` which will be displayed `Jean said: 'Hello'` in the `Transcript`. Any other character, including the *new line* character is allowed[23]. Strings are instances of the `String` class. The simplest instance is the string `' '`, i.e. the empty string. The `String` class, as subclass `ArrayedCollection`, understands, in addition to its own messages, the majority of messages from other collections, and – above all – the concatenation message of two collections: the message "`,`". Below are some examples of message transmissions to strings and the result of their evaluation (preceded by the character "⤳"):

---

[23] Let us note that the character "line feed" can be written as the *backslash* character within a string *IF* the message `withCRs`, is sent to the this string which will have the following effect: the receiver will replace any occurrence of the *backslash* by a "line feed" character. Thus, the transmission

                    `Transcript show: '\foo\bar\foobar\'`

will display in the `Transcript` the string

                        `\foo\bar\foobar\`

while the transmission

                    `Transcript show: '\foo\bar\foobar\' withCRs`

will have as effect the display of the string

    foo
    bar
    foobar

in the `Transcript` windows.

– computation of the size of a string:

    'foobar' size ⤳ 6

– another size computation; please note that the two single quotes only count as one character:

    'Jean said: ''hello''' size ⤳ 20

– transformation of every character to upper case:

    'Squeak' asUppercase ⤳ 'SQUEAK'

– search for the first occurrence of a string of digits and its conversion into an integer:

    'a32b' asInteger ⤳ 32

    'a32b34c' asInteger ⤳ 32

– extraction of all the digits of a string and transformation of the obtained string of digits:

    'a1b45c' extractNumber ⤳ 145[24]

– extraction of all alphabetic characters in a string:

    'a32b34c' onlyLetters ⤳ 'abc'

– conversion of a string into a number:

    '32.45' asNumber ⤳ 32.45

– arithmetic operations on strings composed of digits:

    '123' + '3' ⤳ '126'

    '123' / '3' ⤳ '41'

---

24 145 is the smaller of the two numbers equal to the sum of the factorial of their digits (see footnote 16 on page 76).

```
'124' / '3' ~> '(124/3)'
```

– extraction, into an array, of all the sub-strings separated by «separators» (ASCII character: 9, 10, 12, 13, 32)[25] :

```
'Jean said: ''hello''' substrings
```

```
~> #('Jean' 'said:' '''hello''')
```

– computation of the index of the first occurrence of a character:

```
'Jean said: ''hello''' indexOf:  $h ~> 15
```

– computation of the nth character:

```
'Jean said: ''hello''' at:   15 ~> $h
```

– substitution of the nth character with another:

```
'Jean said: ''hello''' at:  15 put:  $H ; yourself[26]
```

```
~> 'Jean said: ''Hello'''
```

– lexicographical comparison between two strings:

```
'Jean' < 'Jeannette' ~> true
```

– search of all the sub-strings separated by one character (here the character $a):

```
'Jean said: ''hello''' findTokens:   'a'
```

```
~> an OrderedCollection('Je' 'n s' 'aid: ''hello''')
```

– search of all the sub-strings separated by a set of characters (here the characters $a and $e):

---

25 ASCII code 9 corresponds to the *tab* character, 10 to the *line feed*, 12 to the *form feed*, 13 to the *carriage return* and 32 to the *space* character.

26 We will get back to the message **yourself** at the end of this list of examples.

```
'aha, you''wont''take off immediately' findTokens:   'ae'
```

⤳ an OrderedCollection('h' ', you'wont' 't' 'k'''' 'off imm'
'di' 't' 'ly')

– substitution of {1}, {2}, etc., with the first, second, etc., element of the argument[27]:

```
Transcript show:

  ('{2} we are the {1}'

    format:  {Date today . 'Today'})
```

was displaying on the 18 May 2005 in theTranscript:

```
'Today we are the 18 May 2005
```

Structural comparisons

Any instance of the String class also understands the match: message. This is a message which allows us to check if a string corresponds to the structural description of the receiver of this message. For this type of comparison, two characters have a special meaning: the character # and the character *. Where the receiver contains a character #, the argument can contain any character, and where the receiver string contains a character *, the argument can contain between 0 and n characters. It is a type of comparison where we assert that the argument contains all the common characters in the same order as the receiver, optionally separated by any single character (specified in the receiver by the character #), or a string of any characters specified in the receiver by the character *. Here are some simple usage examples of this message[28]:

```
'foo' match:   'foo' ⤳ true
'fo#' match:   'foo' ⤳ true
'#o' match:    'foo' ⤳ false
```

---

27 The transmission Date today returns the current date. The braces enclosing this dispatch and the string 'today' define the two elements array #('18 May 2005' 'today'). This is a *brace* array. Such arrays are covered in section 4.3.5.2.

28 This method corresponds to the *pattern matching* operation well known in artificial intelligence programs (see [WER 89] and also [KNU 67] for related algorithmic problems), except that this pattern-matching is limited to strings. The receiver can then be considered as the *pattern*, the model, and the argument should match the given model for the comparison to succeed.

```
         '*o' match:   'foo'  ⤳ true
'f#r' match:   'foobar' ⤳ false
'f*r' match:   'foobar' ⤳ true
            equality test:
   'Jean' copy = 'Jean' ⤳ true
            identity test:
   'Jean' copy == 'Jean' ⤳ false
```

An equality test checks the structural equality between two objects. An identity test checks whether the two objects are physically the same. The string 'Jean' is indeed *structurally* equal to any *other* string 'Jean' (both strings are composed of the same sequence of characters). On the contrary, there is *a priori* no reason that two strings refer to the same physical object[29].

Please open a class browser on the String class and examine the different methods. For a better understanding, as always, just build some usage examples and test them.

Let us note that in the example:

```
'Jean said: ''hello''' at:  15 put:  $H ; yourself
```

The cascade ends with the selector yourself. Although it slightly looks like self and super, yourself is not a pseudo-variable. A pseudo-variable can be the receiver of a message. yourself *is* a message defined in the Object class. It is used when we want a transmission to return the receiver.

In our example, the message at:put: that returns the second argument (the character $H), the cascading containing yourself forces the return of the receiver of this message, which is clearly the string 'Jean said: ''hello'''. Because this string was *physically* altered by the message at:put: in the string 'Jean said: ''Hello''', it is this last string that is returned by yourself. The pseudo-variable self cannot be used here since it refers to the receiver of the method selector in which this self has an occurrence. Here, we are not in a method[30].

---

29 For lispians (people who know how to program in Lisp): it is the same difference as the one between the functions equal and eq.

30 Naturally, the message yourself does nothing but return the receiver of the message, therefore self. Just look at its definition. It is given here as it is in the Object class in SQUEAK:

```
yourself
    "return self"
```

This is almost a provocation: the method has no body. It, therefore, uses the SMALLTALK mechanism that returns the receiver of the message if no other return is specified. It is by embedding yourself in a *real* method that allows us to return self. If you get to appreciate the beauty of this implementation of yourself and the implementation of ifTrue:ifFalse: (see page 70), you have already understood a good half of what should be known in order to understand SMALLTALK.

Everything is very simple: every time we want to be sure that a transmission returns the receiver of this transmission, it can be guaranteed by cascading the dispatch with the message yourself.

4.3.4. *Symbols*

Any sequence of characters, either a string or an identifier, preceded by the character # is a symbol. Thus, #'a string' and #AString are symbols. Symbols are instances of the Symbol class, a subclass of the String class.

Symbols are distinguished from regular strings in that they are *unique*, i.e in a SMALLTALK system there cannot exist, at any time, two different symbols with the same name. In other words: two occurrences of the same symbol name denote the same instance of the Symbol class. On the contrary, if we have two occurrences of a string composed of the same sequence of characters, we cannot *a priori* know whether the two strings are the same or just equal, whether they refer to the same instance of the String class or not.

In order to illustrate this uniqueness of symbols, we should know that any string understands the message asSymbol that builds a symbol consisting of the same sequence of characters as the receiver string of this message. If the message asSymbol was dispatched to two distinct instances of the String class, composed of the same sequence of characters, the result will be a single and *same* symbol. Figure 4.5 graphically shows the results from two strings, both composed of characters $b, $a and $r, and whose answer to the message asSymbol yields the *same* symbol #bar.

The selector used to test the equality is "=". Two strings composed of the same characters sequence are equal. For instance, the dispatch 'foo' = 'foo' always returns true. Naturally, both symbols of the same name, since they are one single symbol, are equal too. Therefore, #foo = #foo also always returns true.

The SQUEAK selector for testing the identity between two objects is "==". Two symbols of the same name are always identical; and #foo == #foo always returns true. On the contrary, although the string 'foo' and the string 'foo' copy are equal strings, they are guaranteed not to be identical and 'foo' == 'foo' copy always returns false.

In SMALLTALK, *identity* always means: *same instance*. Except for symbols, it is not always easy to know if two objects are identical. Thus, two small integers (instances of the SmallInteger class) that are equal (for efficiency reasons in the implementation of SMALLTALK) are always identical. On the contrary, there is no reason that the fraction (1/4) is identical to another occurrence of the fraction (1/4).

The programmer can ensure the identity, if he himself controls *pointers* redirection. Thus:

$$(1/4) == (1/4)$$

returns false. But, the evaluation of the expression:

$$|x\ y|\ x\ :=\ 1/4.\ y\ :=\ x.\ x\ ==\ y^{31}$$

returns true, since the variables x and y denote (are linked to) the same instance of the Fraction class.

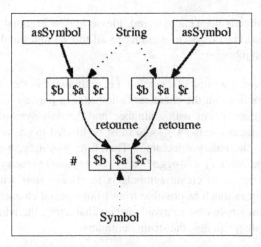

Figure 4.5. *The creation of a* Symbol *from two instances of the* String *class using the* asSymbol *message*

SMALLTALK needs this uniqueness feature of symbols since it uses them for the class names: if there were two different classes of the same name, how SMALLTALK would know it, and we, readers of SMALLTALK programs, would we know which class is targeted at a certain time? The method selectors are also symbols. Thus, #+, our selector for performing additions on various objects, is a unique symbol for a similar reason to that of symbols representing class names: in order to inherit a

31 Recall that the expression | a | declares the temporary variable a. We will formally revisit this in section 4.4.1.

method from one of its superclasses, it is necessary that each class containing this selector represents it by an identical symbol, it greatly accelerates its research. That is another explanation of the following line of code:

$$(x < y) \text{ ifTrue: } [...] \text{ ifFalse: } [...]$$

the message selector is the symbol#ifTrue:ifFalse:, i.e. the concatenation of the constant parts of all the transmissions of that type[32]. Naturally, still for the same reasons, the receiver object can be either true – one and single instance of the True class – or false – one and single instance of the False class. At least these two classes must understand the *same* selector. If it is the same symbol, there is not much research to do in order to find the associated method.

Symbols have already been encountered. Please look at Figure 4.2 which showed a snippet of the Smalltalk system dictionary: all the variables and classes that can be found there are symbols.

Note that the *regular* writing of a symbol, i.e. without using the strings delimiters, imposes some restrictions on the characters allowed. For parsing reasons, a symbol, let us say *regular*, cannot start with a number, and the only symbols that start with allowed special characters «:+-/*\~<=>@ must be limited to one or two characters. They correspond to the binary selectors[33]. Therefore, #4oeufs, #" or #!aha! are not symbols. On the contrary #'4eggs', #'"' or #'!aha!' are symbols. The best strategy when one needs to create symbols is to always start with an alphabetic character and refrain as much as possible from using special characters. In very rare cases where it seems impossible to avoid special characters, the whole name can be enclosed with two single quotes, the string delimiters.

4.3.5. *Arrays*

Both strings and symbols are object sequences: sequences of instances of the Character class. Although there are many ways for strings or symbols manipulation, neither one nor the other can be used to represent a sequence of other objects, a sequence of numbers for instance. It thus appears necessary to have at our disposal other objects that can contain objects, in which other types of objects than characters can also be placed. The simplest SMALLTALK object allowing this is the *array*. It is also called array in most of the other programming languages. An instance of the Array class is an object with a fixed number of "cells", where each cell can be assigned any object (see Figure 4.6).

---

32 It can be noted that the SMALLTALK speech is very similar to Finno-Ugric linguistic structures: by agglutination.

33 Nevertheless, SQUEAK prohibits (always for parsing reasons) the symbol #−−.

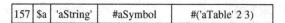

Figure 4.6. *An instance of the* Array *class with five cells*

4.3.5.1. *Array constants*

The easiest way to define an array, an instance of theArray class, is to write it in the form #($element_1$ $element_2$ ...). The array in Figure 4.6 can be written as:

#(157 $a 'aString' #aSymbol #('anArray' 2 3))

where the first cell is occupied by the Integer 157, the second cell is occupied by the Character $a, the third cell is occupied by the String 'aString', the fourth cell is occupied by a Symbol #aSymbol and the last, the fifth, cell is occupied by an Array #('anArray' 2 3)[34].

In order to ease the writing of such arrays, SQUEAK allows us to omit the # sign within the parentheses. Our example array in Figure 4.6 can, therefore, also be written as:

#(157 $a 'aString' aSymbol ('anArray' 2 3))

As questions can be asked to any SMALLTALK object, we can also transmit requests to arrays. Thus, in order to ask the size of an array, transmitting the message size is sufficient, as for a string or a symbol. Finding out which object is located in a certain cell of an array can be done by sending the message at: to the array, as for strings and symbols. The argument of at: will be the index of the cell. Note that SMALLTALK assigns to the first element the index 1 (and not 0 as the C language for instance). Therefore, the last element has the (size) for index. Some examples of messages that any array can understand are given in the following:

---

34 Since the idea of aggregating things in an array is fundamental in programming, the majority of other programming languages also provide arrays. However, in most of these other languages, things that can be placed in an array must be of the same type. Thus, arrays of integer or real numbers, of process, of characters, etc., can be found. This restriction does not exist in SMALLTALK: cells can contain any type of objects, as we have seen in our array example. Once again, another highly pleasant SMALLTALK feature.

Nevertheless, it is necessary to have arrays that only consist of elements of the same type as with strings. In SMALLTALK, those are thus subclasses of the Array class or subclass of the ArrayedCollection class which is the superclass of both of the Array class and the String class.

`#(1 foo 'bar' (2 3.0)) size`	$\leadsto$ 4 – *computes the size*
`#(1 foo 'bar' (2 3.0)) at:  3`	$\leadsto$ 'bar' – *returns the 3th cell*
`#(1 foo 'bar' 2) includes:  #foo`	$\leadsto$ true – *presence test* of an element
`#(1 $a 2 $a 3) occurencesOf:  $a`	$\leadsto$ 2 – *computation of the number of occurrences*
`#(1 2 3) reverse`	$\leadsto$ #(3 2 1) – *yields an array with the receiver elements in reverse order*
`#(1 2 3) copyWith:  $F`	$\leadsto$ #(1 2 3 $F) – *yields a copy of the receiver array with the argument appended at the end*
`#(3 1 3 2 3) copyWithout:  3`	$\leadsto$ #(1 2) – *yields a copy of the receiver without occurrences of the argument*

In the following, we will see more selectors of the `Array` class. Let us immediately note that many selectors understood by an array are also understood by the instances of the subclasses of the `Collection` class.

Arrays that are created as described above only contain objects known at time of writing. This is the reason for the name *constant arrays*. Expressions whose *values* should be associated with a cell cannot be placed there. Therefore, although 1 + 2 is a SMALLTALK expression whose value is the integer 3, writing #(1 + 3) creates an instance of `Array` with three cells, containing the `Integer` 1, the `Symbol` #+ and the `Integer` 3, respectively. No element of such an array is the result of a transmission or a computation.

4.3.5.2. *Brace arrays*

If we still need to write an array with elements whose value should be computed, a first solution is to add them explicitly using the message `at:put:`. Therefore, if we assume the variable `variable` known by SQUEAK, the expression:

```
variable := #(1 'placeholder' $a) at:  2 put:  6 factorial;
                                  yourself
```

will put in the variable `variable` the array #(1 720 $a). The second element has been replaced by !6 which has indeed been computed[35]. We get the same result with the following expression:

```
variable := Array with:  1 with:  6 factorial with:  $a
```

---

[35] Please note the *cascade* with `yourself`. It is necessary here to assign to the variable `variable` the value of the altered receiver and not the integer 720, the return value of this transmission of the message `at:put:`.

or with the following expression:

```
(variable := Array new: 3) at: 1 put: 1;
                           at: 2 put: 6 factorial;
                           at: 3 put: $a;
                           yourself
```

This latter version uses the instance creation method of the Array class: new:. The argument of the message new: is the size of the array. The expression Array new: 3 therefore creates an array of three cells. The rest of the above expression, a cascade, assigns the desired value to each of the cells.

The previous version uses the selector with:with:with:. The corresponding method creates a three cells array. It then assigns the first argument of with:with:with: to the first cell the second argument to the second cell, and the third argument to the third cell. All collections understand this instance creation message with the initialization of cells. There are six versions of this message:

with: that creates a one element collection;

with:with: that creates a two elements collection;

with:with:with: that creates a three elements collection;

with:with:with:with: 4 elements;

with:with:with:with:with: 5 elements;

with:with:with:with:with:with: 6 elements.

If one needs to create an array with more elements, the only solution is to create the array with the messages new: and at:put:.

SQUEAK provides a more compact way to write arrays with elements that are computed using *brace arrays*. The elements of such an array are the values of the corresponding expressions. The expressions are separated by dots. Our array example can then be simply written as:

```
variable := {1 . 6 factorial . $a}
```

Below are some other examples of *brace* arrays:

```
{1 + 2}                              ↝ #(3)
{1. 2.5. 3. 4}                       ↝ #(1 2.5 3 4)
{(1 2 3) . variable}                 ↝ #(#(1 2 3) #(1 720 $a))
{100 factorial / 99 factorial        ↝ #(100 'view?')
. 'view?'}
```
however:
```
{10@10 . 100@100}                    ↝ {10@10 . 100@100}
```

4.3.5.3. *Digression: the inspector and the explorer*

Before continuing with the arrays, let's introduce an indispensable tool for any SMALLTALK programmer: the inspector. It is used to *inspect*, examine, modify, etc., SMALLTALK objects. It can be launched by selecting in a Workspace the object to be inspected, a variable or an array declaration for instance, and then either selecting the "inspect it" entry from the context menu or typing the keys "Alt+i". It can also be explicitly launched by performing a "do it" action on an expression, such as:

```
{1 . #(2 3 4) . 6 factorial} inspect
```

After such an action, an inspector like the one shown in Figure 4.7 will open. The title of the inspector window shows the name of the class whose instance is the inspected object. Here an array is inspected, it is therefore an instance of the Array class. The rest of the window is divided into three panes. The first provides a menu on different aspects of the object being examined: first on the object itself, self, then on all of its instance variables, then an input on each of the instance variables (if there are) or, as it is the case here, on the different parts composing the object. The entries for an instance of a subclass of ArrayedCollection are the indexes of the collection. Here we inspect the array #(1 #(2 3 4) 720), a three-element array. We thus have an entry for the indexes 1, 2 and 3. The right pane provides information on the selected entry in this menu. If we select the entry self, we get the inspector shown in Figure 4.8.

The third pane, on the bottom, is an ordinary Workspace focused on the inspected object, that is in thisWorkspace, self refers to the inspected object. One can freely evaluate here any transmission: it will be taken into account by *all* the SQUEAK environment.

In order to check this, let's choose the second element of the array (by clicking on the entry 2 in the menu). This will then display the array#(2 3 4). With the entry 2 selected, let's choose inspect from the context menu. This opens a second inspector, this time on the array #(2 3 4). Aha! We can therefore inspect each element of the inspected object (and so on, recursively). If we position the cursor in the Workspace pane of this second inspector, and if we activate here the transmission:

```
self at: 2 put: 11 factorial
```

the effect will be immediately shown in the *two* inspectors. In fact, if one changes a sub-array, the entire array is changed too. Figure 4.9 shows the two inspectors immediately after the modification of the array of to second inspector.

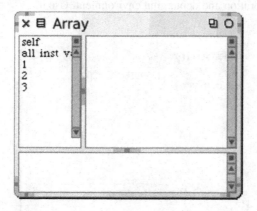

Figure 4.7. *An inspector on a three-element array*

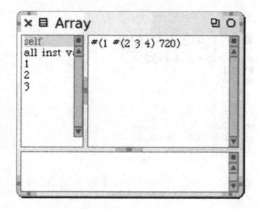

Figure 4.8. *The inspector showing* self

An inspector as an error handling pane has already been encountered (see Figure 2.8 which shows a SQUEAK debugger window). There, it was just used to visualize the state of the instance variables, and the state of the computation at the time an error was encountered. We know now that an inspector can also be used to change the state of variables, data structures, etc. An inspector (and the debugger window) is an extremely powerful tool. Let's thus open an inspector, look at its context menu and "play" with. Also, try to write a method containing an error, then run a transmission that uses it, then use the debugger in order to correct the method and then pursue the computation from where it was interrupted by the error. A major strength of SMALLTALK, in general, and of SQUEAK in particular, is the associated development, exploration and debugging environment. Use it!

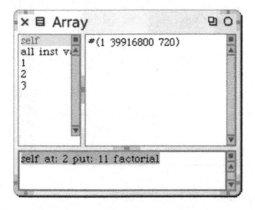

Figure 4.9. *Effect of the dispatch self at: 2 put: 11 factorial*

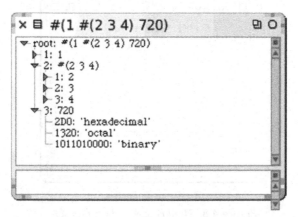

Figure 4.10. *An object explorer focused on an array*

If instead of activating the expression:

```
{1 . #(2 3 4) . 6 factorial} inspect
```

we had activated the expression:

```
{1 . #(2 3 4) . 6 factorial} explore
```

we would have obtained the *object an explorer* of the Figure 4.10. Such an explorer is like an inspector, except that the window title does not give the class of the explored object, it gives the object itself. Below there is a window showing an *outline* of the object: a tree structure in which the triangles pointing to the right indicate structures that can be explored by "opening" the triangle with a simple mouse click. Selecting an item in this outline allows, through the context menu, to open an ordinary inspector on the selected object. Let's note that an inspector allows to find the class of an object, which the explorer does not allow. The last window of an `explorer` is a `Workspace` as in an `inspector`.

4.3.5.4. *Back to the arrays*

Now that we know the arrays, let's look at some other messages that instances of the `Array` class understand. If one wants to know the messages that the instances of a certain class understand, a class browser can be opened on that class. For instance, we can evaluate (with a "`do it`" action or "Alt+d") the expression:

```
Array browse
```

in order to open a browser on the `Array` class. Unfortunately, this is not sufficient, as no methods that the class *inherits* from its superclasses are seen. In order to see *all* the methods that the instances of a class understand, a *protocol browser* should be launched. Such browser is obtained from a class browser by selecting the class of interest and typing the keys "Alt+p" or by selecting from the context menu entry `browse protocol`. Figure 4.11 shows such a browser on the `Array` class. There is indeed *all* the vocabulary that an array can understand: both the methods inherited from the superclasses and those implemented in the class.

Such a browser is divided into four panes and two rows of buttons:

1) on the top left, a window for the protocols;

2) on the top right, a window for methods located in the chosen protocol. For each method selector, SQUEAK provides in parentheses the first class implementing this method, by going up in the class hierarchy;

3) below the two protocols and methods windows is a horizontal window providing additional information on the selected object: comments, the number of implementors of a method, etc.;

4) finally, at the bottom, like for any browser, a window to display the source code of the selected method.

This window is separated from the other by *two* rows of buttons: a first one identical to that found in any class browser, and a second, specific to the protocol browser, especially allowing to easily restrict the number of superclasses included in the methods presentation. For instance, if we open a protocol browser on the `Array` class and we choose the `ProtoObject` class as the last superclass to include, all the vocabulary understood by the instances of the `Array` class can be browsed. On the contrary, if we choose the `SequenceableCollection` class, only the vocabulary (the selectors) implemented in classes `Array`, `ArrayedCollection` and `SequenceableCollection` will be shown.

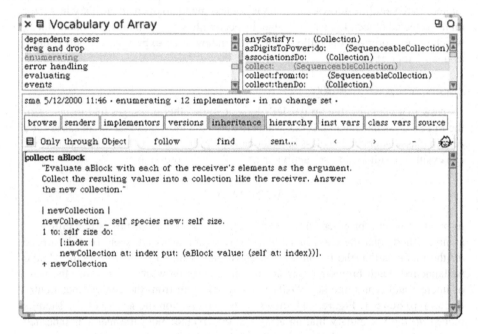

Figure 4.11. *A protocol browser*

But let's come back to our arrays. Below, some message transmission examples to arrays. In order to simplify the writing, let's suppose that a variable, named x has been initialized as:

```
x := #(1 -2 3 5 ($h $a $r $a $l $d) 'and a string')
```

and has this same value during each example.

– x size ↝ 6:

the size of the array. The message size is understood by all the collections. We will subsequently use, instead of the *array* word, the name of the class whose instances (or instances of its subclasses) understand the message.

– x first ↝ 1:

the first element of the receiver SequenceableCollection. Following the convention stated above, first is understood by all sequential collections. For the ArrayedCollections, this is equivalent to x at: 1. There are also the methods second, third, fourth, fifth, sixth, seventh, eighth and ninth, which, respectively, compute the 2nd, 3rd, 4th, ..., up to the 9th element of any SequenceableCollection.

– x last ↝ 'and a string':

the last element of the receiver SequenceableCollection. Equivalent to x at: x size

– x indexOf: #($h $a $r $a $l $d) ↝ 5:

the index of the element given as an argument in the receiver SequenceableCollection. If the argument is not part of the array, indexOf: returns the index 0, such as the dispatch: x indexOf: $a which returns 0. Why[36]?

– x replaceFrom: 3 to: 6: with: #(1 2 3 4) ↝ #(1 -2 1 2 3 4):

physically replaces the 3rd, 4th, 5th and 6th element of the receiver SequenceableCollection with the elements of the SequenceableCollection given as the 3rd argument.

– (x at: 5) replaceAll: $a with: $A ↝ #($h $A $r $A $l $d):

yields the receiver SequenceableCollection with all occurrences of the first argument that have been physically replaced by the second argument.

– x atAllPut: 1 ↝ #(1 1 1 1 1 1):

replaces all the elements of the SequenceableCollection x with the value of the argument.

---

36 Since the variable x is associated with the array #(1 -2 3 5 ($h $a $r $a $l $d) 'and a string'), the character $a is not an element of this array. It is only an element of the subarray #($h $a $r $a $l $d).

− x copyFrom: 3 to: 5 ⤳ #(3 5 #($h $a $r $a $1 $d)):

creation of a new SequenceableCollection composed of elements of indices from 3 to 5 of the receiver SequenceableCollection.

− (x at: 5) copyWithout: $a ⤳ #($h $r $1 $d):

copies the receiver SequenceableCollection by removing all occurrences of the argument.

− x copyWith: 1 ⤳ #(1 -2 3 5 ($h $a $r $a $1 $d) 'and a string' 1):

copies the receiver SequenceableCollection with the argument as an additional and last element.

− x findFirst: [:var| var < 0] ⤳ 2:

the block given argument is evaluated with each of the elements of the receiver collection as an argument. Returns the index of the first element for which the evaluation of the block yields true.

There is also the message findLast: which returns the index of the last element satisfying the condition of the argument block.

4.3.5.5. *Iterators*

− x do: [:var | Transcript show: var; cr] ⤳ #(1 -2 3 5 ($h $a $r $a $1 $d) 'and a string'):

returns the receiver collection, after evaluating the argument block with each of the elements of the receiver as argument. Here, each of the receiver elements is displayed in the Transcript.

There is also the message reverseDo: which traverses the collection in reverse, from the last to the first element.

− x detect: [:var | var isCollection] ⤳ #($h $a $r $a $1 $d):

searches for the first element of an array satisfying the block given as argument. Here, detect: returns the first element that is an instance of one of the subclasses of the Collection class.

Please do have a look at all the selectors starting with is in the Object class, in the testing protocol: all the tests of object types are there. They all return false. Do you see why[37]?

– x select: [:var | var isNumber] ⤳ #(1 -2 3 5): returns an instance of the receiver class containing *all* the elements satisfying the block given in argument. Here, select: returns an array containing all the elements of the receiver that are numbers.

– x reject: [:var | var isNumber] ⤳ #(#($h $a $r $a $l $d) 'and a string'):

returns an instance of the receiver class containing all the elements that do not satisfy the block given in argument. Here, reject: returns an array containing all the elements of the receiver that are not numbers.

– x collect: [:var | var isNumber] ⤳ #(true true true true false false)

returns an arry containing the results of the evaluation of the block given in argument for each of the elements of the receiver.

The solution to a problem often involves applying an operation to all the elements of a collection and returning a single result. For example, if we have an array that only contains numbers, we could be required to compute the sum of these numbers. This can be done with the following expression:

```
| sum |
sum := 0.
#(1 2 3 4 5) do: [:e | sum := ^sum + e].
sum
```

which returns 15, the sum of the elements of the receiver. A more compact way of computing the same can be achieved by using the selector inject:into::

```
#(1 2 3 4 5) inject: 0 into: [:sum :e | sum + e]
```

---

37 For example, the method isNumber asks the receiver if it is a number. Clearly, only the instances of the Float, Fraction, Integer, LargePositiveInteger, LargeNegativeInteger, SmallInteger and ScaledDecimal classes are numbers. All these classes are subclasses of the Number class. It is, therefore, in the Number class that the method isNumber can also be found which returns true. Thus, the instances of these classes inherit from this method and can all answer true to this question.

The instances of any other classes inherit from the method of the Object class and therefore positively answer false: they are not instances of one of the subclasses of the Number class.

The action performed by this message is to iterate over the elements of the collection, and to pass one element after the other, in each iteration, to the second variable of the argument block, e, while the first variable, sum, is, at the beginning assigned the value 0, the first argument of inject:into:. During the iterations, the first variable will always be linked to the value of the block obtained in the previous iteration. For a better understanding, nothing is clearer than observing the implementation of inject:into: exactly as it is given in the Collection class:

```
inject: thisValue into: binaryBlock
    | nextValue |
    nextValue := thisValue.
    self do: [:each |
            nextValue :=
                binaryBlock value: nextValue value: each].
    ^nextValue
```

Here are three additional usage examples of the message inject:into::

– #(1 -2 3 -4 5) inject: Float infinity into:[:m :e | m min: e] ⤳ -4:

computes the minimum of a set, represented as an array, of numbers. The dispatch Float infinity returns an object that is considered numerically higher than any number handled by SQUEAK;

– 'foobar' inject: '' into: [:a :b| a, 'A', b asString]:

⤳ 'AfAoAoAbAaAr'

yields the string where "A" is inserted before each letter of the receiver string;

– 'gppcbs' inject: 'Gives: '   into: [:a :b | a, (b asInteger - 1) asCharacter asString] ⤳ 'Gives: foobar':

returns a string beginning with 'Give:' followed by a string where each character in the receiver string has been replaced by the character lexicographically inferior, i.e. $b has been replaced by $a, $c by $b, etc.

Finally, let us note that the operator ",", which has already been encountered as a binary concatenation selector of two strings, also allows us to concatenate two arrays. Thus, the transmission:

#(1 2 3) , #($c $b $a)

yields the new array #(1 2 3 $c $b $a).

4.3.6. *Exercises*

Solutions can be found on page 359.

All the exercises in this section assume that you first find an answer (on paper), and then, only after providing an answer, open a Workspace and check each of your answers.

1) Exercises on numbers. For each of the transmissions below, give the answer that SQUEAK would give if you evaluated it in a Workspace:

1.1. 16rFF	1.19. 12 squared
1.2. 10/2	1.20. 12 odd
1.3. 11/3	1.21. 1.2 odd
1.4. 2e5	1.22. (11/3) ceiling
1.5. 1+2	1.23. (11/3) negated ceiling
1.6. 1+2; yourself	1.24. 4 asFloat
1.7. 8r55	1.25. 4 asFraction
1.8. 8r55e2	1.26. 4.0 asFraction
1.9. 2.5 asInteger	1.27. 5 between: 1 and: 10
1.10. 2.5 truncated	1.28. (1/3) = 0.3333333333
1.11. -2.5 truncated	1.29. (1/3) = 0.3333333333
1.12. 2.5 rounded	1.30. 1 + 3 * 4
1.13. 2r1010.1010	1.31. (1@6) + (1@5)
1.14. 2 + 1.0	1.32. (3.8@7.3) rounded
1.15. 5 factorial	1.33. (3@6) + 5
1.16. 1/12 + (1/6)	1.34. (3@6) \\ 5
1.17. 1/12 + 1/6	1.35. 144 sqrt
1.18. 1 / 4 / 3	

2) Exercises on characters. By following the same directive as in exercise 1, give the results of the evaluation of the expressions below:

2.1. $W asLowercase

2.2. $e isVowel

2.3. $r asInteger

2.4. $t < $$

2.5. $z isAlphabetic

2.6. $2 isAlphabetic

2.7. $2 isDigit

2.8. $a asUppercase

2.9. $f between: $A and: $z

2.10. $f between: $a and: $Z

2.11. $f = $f

2.12. ($f asInteger + 1) asCharacter

2.13. $a asciiValue

2.14. 32 asCharacter isSeparator

3) Exercises on arrays:

3.1. What are the results of the following transmissions?

   i. #((((1 2 3) 4) 5) first first first

   ii. #(-1 2 -3 4) detect: [:x | x > 0]

   iii. #(-1 2 -3 4) select: [:x | x > 0]

   iv. #(1 ($a $b) 2) at: (#(1 ($a $b) 2) indexOf: #($a $b))

   v. #(1 2 3 (1 2 3) 2 3 (2 3) 3 (3)) copyWithout: 3

   vi. #(1 2 3) raisedTo: 3

   vii. #(1 2 3) * #(4 5 6)

   viii. #(1 2 3) raisedTo: #(4 5 6)

   ix. #(me you his her ours yours their) reject: [:ele | ele size > 2]

3.2. Write the methods that implement the given selectors.

For instance, the selector collect: (see page 99) is implemented in the SequenceableCollection class (almost) as:

```
collect: aBlock
    |newCollection |
    newCollection := self class new: (self size).
    1 to: self size do:
        [:index |
            newCollection at: index
                          put: (aBlock value:
                                (self at: index))].
    ^newCollection
```

i. The method `middle` which yields the element that is in the middle of a `SequenceableCollection`.

ii. The method `swap:with:` which takes as arguments two indices i and j, and swaps the ith and the jth element of the receiver.

iii. The method `negated` which can be sent to a collection of numbers and returns a copy of this collection with the reverse sign of each of its elements.

iv. The method `concat:` which returns a `SequenceableCollection` composed of elements of the receiver followed by the elements of the collection given as argument.

v. The method `inject:into:` which takes as the second argument a two parameters block. It dispatches an element after the other from the receiver `Collection` to the second parameter of the block. The first parameter of this block should receive during the first activation of this block the first argument of `inject:into:` and the result of the previous evaluation of the second argument block during subsequent activations. Thus, the dispatch:

```
#(1 2 3 4 5) inject: 0 into: [:s :e | s + e]
```

should return the sum of the elements of the receiver array: 15.

vi. The method `copy`, which yields a new instance of the receiver `SequenceableCollection` containing the same elements in the same order.

vii. The method `copyWithFirst:` which takes as argument any object and returns a copy of the receiver `SequencableCollection` with the argument at the first index.

viii. The method `select:` which returns a new instance of the receiver `Collection` that only contains those elements of the receiver for which the argument block returns `true`.

ix. The method `anySatisfy:` that should return `true` if it exists at least one element in the receiver `Collection` satisfying the block given as argument and `false` otherwise.

x. The method `allSatisfy:` that should return `false` if it exists at least one element in the receiver `Collection` that does not satisfy the block given as argument, and `true` otherwise.

xi. The method `before:` that should return the element that is located before the argument in the `SequenceableCollection`.

xii. The method `atAll:` which takes as argument an array of indices and returns an array with the elements in the positions given in the array of indices.

xiii. And why not a method `atAll:put:` which receives two arguments: an array of indices and an object, and puts at each position corresponding to the indices given in the array of indices the object given in the second argument.

xiv. While we are at it, let's complicate things a little and also write a method `atAll:putAll:`. This method takes two arguments: an array of indices and an object collection. It replaces each of the objects indexed in the array of indices receiver collection by the corresponding object of the object collection.

For instance, the dispatch:

```
#(1 2 3 4 5 6 7) atAll: #(1 3 5 7)
                 putAll: #(\$a \$b \$c \$d);
    yourself
```

should return the array #($a 2 $b 4 $c 6 $d): each index^{ith} element of the receiver SequenceableCollection is replaced by the index^{ith} element of the second argument.

4) Translate each of the following problems into a SMALLTALK expression:

4.1. Transform the lowercase character "w" into the uppercase character "W".

4.2. What is the product of 3.14 with the sum of the square root of 64 and 2?

4.3. Is the character "b" higher than the character "E"?

4.4. If the cube of 3 is an even number then output in the Transcript the word "even", otherwise output the word "odd".

4.5. Is the character "O" a vowel?

4.6. Is the character corresponding to the ASCII code of the sum of 47 and 50 a vowel?

4.7. If we have only a quarter of cake and we want to share it among five friends, each can eat a share of what size?

4.8. Remove all the digits from the string 1a2b3c4d500e.

4.9. At which position is the character "É" in the string 'Boum ! Boum ! Le roi O et la reine É Sont assis sur leurs trônes'[38]?

4.10. Write down all the vowels of a text in capital letters, that is to say: replace all the vowels of a text with the same vowel written in upper case.

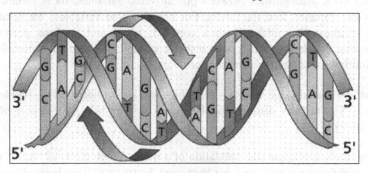

Figure 4.12. *A graphical representation of an extract of a DNA molecule*

4.11. A DNA molecule is a structure composed of two chains of nucleotides. Figure 4.12 shows a graphical representation of it. There are only four nucleotides, named A (for adenine), G (for guanine), C (for cytosine) and T (for thymine). Both chains are *complementary*, that is to say, if they are placed one next to the other, where a chain has an adenine nucleotide, the other must have the thymine nucleotide. The same property holds between cytosine and guanine. Thus, the double chain below:

```
T - G - C - T - A - A - C
A - C - G - A - T - T - G
```

could represent an extract of a DNA molecule. Write a SMALLTALK expression that checks whether two strings of nucleotides can form a DNA molecule.

4.4. Variables

In any program progress, it may prove necessary to keep intermediate results in order to reuse them in subsequent computations. This is particularly useful if these intermediate results should be used in several places. This backup of computation results is performed in SMALLTALK, as in any other programming language, using *variables*. A SMALLTALK variable can hold *any* SMALLTALK object, and messages can be sent to this object by sending a message to the variable holding the object. As

---

38 *Les gens de lettres* by Charles Cros [CRO 08].

opposed to other programming languages, SMALLTALK does not distinguish between the *types* that a variable can keep. Nevertheless, before using a variable, a name must be assigned to it, it must be declared.

SMALLTALK distinguishes between private value variables, local variables and shared value variables and the others. For private value variables, we distinguish between *temporary variables* (with a context), block and methods *parameters*, named *instance variables* (this type of instance variable has been encountered in our class definitions) and *indexed instance variables*.

Regarding shared value variables (variables that are written with the first letter in uppercase), SMALLTALK distinguishes between *class variables*, *global variables* and *pool variables*.

During the compilation (the validation of a method with the keys "Alt+s"), if an unknown variable, i.e. undeclared, has been used, SQUEAK will ask how this unknown variable should be declared. If the variable begins with a lowercase character, SQUEAK will open a window (see Figure 4.13) suggesting to declare it either as a temporary variable, as an instance variable or replace it with a pseudo-variable or some specific values, such as nil, false or true.

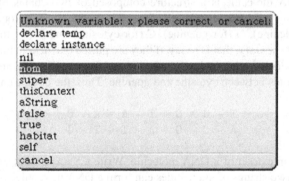

Figure 4.13. *Menu for the declaration of an undefined variable* x

On the contrary, if the name of the variable begins with an uppercase character, SQUEAK will suggest to declare it as a global variable or class variable, or to consider the writing of this unknown thing as a reference to a class not yet defined, or even to replace the occurrence of this name by a global variable already known by SQUEAK and whose name contains that name as a subpart. Figure 4.14 shows an interaction with SQUEAK when an unknown variable X is encountered.

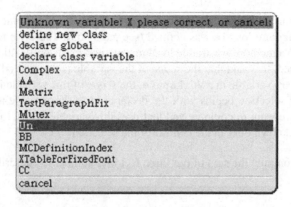

Figure 4.14. *Menu for the declaration of an undefined variable* X

4.4.1. *Temporary variables*

When we are working in a Workspace, it can often happen that we need a variable to temporarily keep intermediate values. For example, if we want to compute the sum of three successive factorial numbers $!n$, $!(n + 1)$ and $!(n + 2)$, we can write, for instance:

$$100 \text{ factorial } + 101 \text{ factorial } + 102 \text{ factorial}$$

But this writing is not very elegant: mostly because we compute the factorial of 100 three times. What we need is to compute the factorial of 100, keep it somewhere, for example in the temporary variable n to perform the sum of n with the product of n and 101, while keeping this new result in the same variable. Finally, add to the last obtained result the product of the new value n and 102. It can be clearly seen that in this way we save the computation of 201 multiplications[39]. In order to declare a *temporary variable*, we write it between vertical bars ("|"), as in the expression "| x |", which declares the existence of the temporary variable x. This variable that has just been declared has no value. It is, therefore, initialized to nil (the SMALLTALK undefined value). This declaration does nothing more than tell SMALLTALK that from now on, the name x can be used to refer to a variable, to which values can be assigned and whose value can be accessed. Let us reiterate: in contrast to other programming languages such as Ada [DOD 83] or C [KER 88], the SMALLTALK variables are not typed: any variable can take values of any type, either collections, numbers, bit-mapped displays or processes. A value is just a pointer to the *object* representing the value, and, of course, all pointers are of the same type (the *pointer to an object* type).

---

39 The computation of factorial 100 factorial and the computation of 101 factorial

Temporary variables of a particular type have already been encountered when the method asUppercaseVowels was defined (see page 365). There we have defined a *variable local* to a method. A variable local to a method exists only within the method where it is defined. It is said that the *scope* of the variable is the method's body. If we define a *temporary* variable in a Workspace, the *scope* of this variable is the selected expression. The selection begins with the declaration of the variable and ends with the expression we want to compute and that uses this variable. Thus, to reiterate: the variable will be known only in the *context* of the selection.

In order to compute the sum of our three factorial numbers as described above:

```
| n |
(n := 100 factorial) + (n := n * 101) + (n * 102)
```

the two lines should be selected and then "Alt+p" should be typed in order to see the result[40].

Let us note that this expression uses twice the fact that the assignment is an expression that returns the new value given to the variable. That is the value of the expression at the right of the sign ":=".

Naturally, if we need to declare more than one, listing these variables between the two vertical bars is sufficient. Thus,

```
| x y |
```

declares the two temporary variables x and y.

4.4.2. Method parameters

Throughout our definitions of methods, we have encountered some method parameters. Therefore, we are not going to return to this, except to recall that these parameters are defined in the header of the method and can be identified by the ":" character that precedes them, or, more precisely: that ends the words preceding them. Thus, in the header:

```
newMethod: firstParameter with: secondParameter
```

---

40 The result of this expression is the number "97 0965 9454 7879 4964 5003 9888 1060 5987 5190 5408 9338 2262 6389 7592 4119 6365 8439 1032 9564 0419 9542 6991 2079 3241 6250 1834 7316 8286 4359 8084 5330 9343 7905 3056 0000 0000 0000 0000 0000 0000".

both parameters, firstParameter and secondParameter are variables local to the body of the method newMethod:with: and receive values during a transmission that uses this method. Thus, the transmission:

```
foo newMethod:  1 with:  {3 * 4. 16 sqrt}
```

will have the following effect: the foo object will activate its method newMethod:with: by binding, respectively, the variable firstParameter to the integer 1, the instance 1 of the Integer class, and the variable secondParameter to the array #(12 4), instance of the Array class, during the execution of the method's body. Naturally, these two variables are known only within the method, in the method's *context*: they are *private* to the method newMethod:with:.

4.4.3. *Block parameters*

First and foremost, let us recall that a block is a piece of program that can be executed by sending the message value if the block has no parameters or by the message value: if the block has *one* parameter; if the block has two parameters by the message value:value:, and so on up to four parameters where we use the message value:value:value:value:. As for the method parameters, which are defined at the start of a method, the block parameters are defined at the beginning of a block and can be identified by the ":" character that precedes them. For instance, the block:

```
[:x :y | x squared + y squared]
```

declares two block parameters, the variables x and y. The character "|" syntactically indicates the end of the declaration of the series of parameters. In the body, each of these two variables receives the message squared. The objects associated with these variables are, therefore, the ones receiving this message. Thus,

```
[:x :y | x squared + y squared] value:  4 value:  5
```

is the activation of the block where the integer 4 will be the value of the first parameter, x, and the integer 5 will be the value of the second parameter, y. Then, everything will be as if we had written:

```
4 squared + 5 squared
```

This block, defining the program $x^2 + y^2$, computes after the reception of the message value: 4 value: 5, the expression $4^2 + 5^2$ and returns the integer 41.

As we have already seen, in the solutions to the exercises, on page 366, a block can also declare *temporary* variables. This requires enclosing, as with any declaration of temporary variables, their declaration between two vertical bars. If the block contains some parameters, the declaration of the temporary variables must follow the declaration of the parameters. The block:

```
[:x :y | | temp | temp := x squared + y squared. temp squared]
```

has two parameters, variables x and y, and a temporary variable, temp. All these three variables are private to that block. In more technical terms, we say that these three variables are private to the context of this block, to its BlockContext. You have probably notice it, this block computes $(x^2 + y^2)^2$. If we send it the message value: 4 value: 5, it will return $(4^2 + 5^2)^2$, therefore 41^2, therefore 1681[41].

Here is another little SQUEAK program using a temporary variable and a block with one parameter:

```
| block |
block := [:anInteger | anInteger <= 1
            ifTrue: [1]
            ifFalse: [anInteger * (block value: anInteger - 1)]].
block value: 12
```

What does this program compute?

Just wait. Find the answer by yourself. Do not immediately look up the solution below.

This program clearly shows that a block is nothing more than a piece of program. Here, we keep the block, the piece of program:

```
[anInteger| anInteger <= 1
        ifTrue: [1]
        ifFalse: [anInteger * (bloc value: anInteger - 1)]].
```

---

41 1681 is one of several years when the city of Strasbourg was changing countries of affiliation. That year, Strasbourg became French. Some other such dates, when it was alternating affiliation between Germany or France, are 1871, 1919, 1940 and 1945. 1681 is also the year of the publication of the *Discourse on Universal History* from Jacques-Benigne Bossuet.

in the temporary variable named block[42]. Then, we send the message value: 12 to this variable, so to the block that is its value. The integer 12 will, therefore, be the value associated with anInteger, the block parameter. The block's body asks this variable if its value is the integer 1. This is clearly not the case, its value is 12. anInteger, therefore, answers false, which will receive the message ifTrue:ifFalse: and, as we have seen, will send the message value to the argument block of ifFalse: as below.

```
[anInteger * (block value:  anInteger - 1)] value
```

which sends to the parameter anInteger, therefore the integer 12, the message

```
* (block value:  anInteger - 1)
```

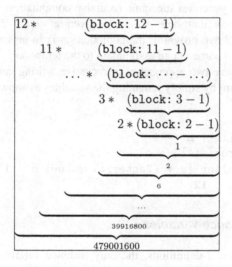

Figure 4.15. *Outline of the* bloc value: 12 *stack trace*

The argument of the message * is the result of the expression value: anInteger - 1, so the result of the transmission of the integer 11 to this same block that we are currently executing. This time the argument is one less than the previous argument of the dispatch of the message value:. Clearly, we will compute the product 12*11*10*. These successive computations of a product will stop when the block's parameter anInteger will be bound to the integer 1, since in this case the block simply returns 1. This block, therefore, computes the product of all the integers between the first

---

42 The binary message <= ask the receiver whether it is less than or equal to the argument.

value of anInteger (in our example: 12) and 1. It *recursively* computes, as outlined graphically in Figure 4.15, the factorial of its argument.

This program, therefore, computes the same as the transmission

12 factorial

Let us note that the method factorial can also be defined as:

```
factorial
  ^self <= 1
    ifTrue: [1]
    ifFalse: [self * (self - 1) factorial]
```

which approximately generates the same recursive computation as the block above. The only difference is that here we have given a *name*, factorial, to the computation. In the above program, the computation is in an anonymous block, to which we have given a name via an assignment to the temporary variable block. The similarity between these two approaches of recursive writing can be clearly seen if we rewrite our program by simply renaming the variables as shown below[43]:

```
| factorial |
factorial := [:n | n <= 1
          ifTrue: [1]
          ifFalse: [n * (factorial value: n - 1)]].
factorial value: 12
```

4.4.4. *Named instance variables*

Throughout our class definitions, the only instance variables we created were named instance variables. They were created during the definition of classes, using the second parameter, the parameter instanceVariableNames:[44], as (see page 20) in:

---

43 By the way, let us note the remarkable resemblance of the syntax of this definition with the procedure definitions as they were performed in Algol [PER 59].

44 This is a misnomer: here, we use the term *parameter* to abstractly name the argument following the keyword instanceVariableNames:. If you look at the implementation of this method in the Class class, you will see that the parameter is called f. In the absence of the source code of the implementation, let us stick with the convention by naming the keyword preceding the parameter that parameter itself.

```
Object subclass: #Animal
    instanceVariableNames: 'name habitat'
    classVariableNames: ''
    poolDictionaries: ''
    category: 'Course-Smalltalk-Animals'
```

where we have created two named instance variables: name and habitat. Each instance of the Animal class and its subclasses, therefore, has values corresponding to these two variables, which are accessible by their names and which are private to each of these instances. If, as we did, the subclass Dog has an instance variable barksALot, each instance of the Dog will then have access to three instance variables: name and habitat, defined in the superclass Animal and the latter, barksALot, defined in its own class. Thus, the instance Lassie of the Dog class, which lives AtHome and barksALot, can be visualized as shown in Figure 4.16.

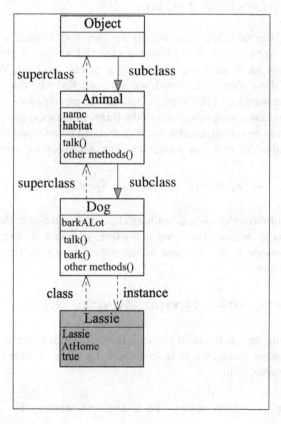

Figure 4.16. *Relationships between class, subclass and instance*

We have already widely talked about this type of variables that we will not return to it in more detail. If you still have some issues with the notion of named instance variable, please reread sections 1.2, 2.1 and 2.2.

4.4.5. Indexed instance variables

This is something that can appear strange at first glance: an indexed instance variable. It is a variable with no name, nevertheless accessible and, moreover it can be *indexed*.

Let us start with the end: it can be *indexed* means there are multiple values in a specific order, accessible via numerical keys: 1, 2, 3, etc. The numerical keys are named *indexes*. We will talk of the first element in this collection, it has index 1, the second element which has index 2 and so on.

There is nothing new. We have already encountered it when we used arrays, instances of the `Array` class. The messages `at:` and `at:put:` give access to an element and allow us to alter one element in a precise position. We did not ask ourselves where these objects are stored, we were satisfied with the explanation that the creation of an instance of the `Array` class, via the message `new:`, by passing the size of the array as argument, or *via* one of the forms of the message `with:`, with the various elements as argument, creates an array that can be accessed afterward by the name of the variable the array was assigned to. For instance, the expression:

```
Array with:  $a with:  $b with:  $c
```

creates an array of three elements, containing characters a, b and c. However, there is no way to access it: because the name is missing, it cannot be referred to, unless, eventually, a message is directly sent to the object during its creation, as in the following expression:

```
(Array with:  $a with:  $b with:  $c) at:  3
```

which successfully returns the third element. But out of this expression, the array is once again no longer accessible. In order to give it a name, it must be explicitly be assigned to a variable, as in:

```
x := Array with:  $a with:  $b with:  $c.
```

It will only be through this variable that the elements of the array will be accessible for any subsequent access or alteration operation.

In contrast to the instances of other classes, which always have a fixed size, determined by the number of named instance variables that the class has, the instances of the Array class have an arbitrary size, determined when they are created. These are instances with *variable size*. By analogy with the named instance variables, we then speak of indexed instance variables.

Such indexed instances variables are used, in the SQUEAK system itself, in (almost) all the subclasses of the abstract class ArrayedCollection and they are created when defining the subclasses using one of the following three messages[45]:

```
variableSubclass:instanceVariableNames:
    classVariableNames:poolDictionaries:category:

variableByteSubclass:instanceVariableNames:
    classVariableNames:poolDictionaries:category:

variableWordSubclass:instanceVariableNames:
    classVariableNames:poolDictionaries:category:
```

The difference between these three selectors is that the first one, beginning with variableSubclass:, creates indexed collections of arbitrary objects (numbers, collections, instances of whatever class), while the second one, beginning with variableByteSubclass:, creates indexed collections which can only contain byte-sized objects (like characters or small numbers) and the third, beginning with variableWordSubclass:, can only contain objects requiring word-sized objects (machine instructions for example). The latter two parameters are optimizations for the operation of the SQUEAK interpreter and compiler and we are not going to delve into it.

Let us create a subclass of ArrayedCollection with indexed instance variables just to illustrate it:

```
ArrayedCollection variableSubclass: #Test
    instanceVariableNames: ''
    classVariableNames: ''
    poolDictionaries: ''
    category: 'Course-Smalltalk'
```

This class inherits all the methods from the ArrayedCollection class, therefore, also its creation and access methods. Figure 4.17 shows a Workspace where we test the behavior of an instance of this class. In order to facilitate reading, we have inserted here the sign "->" between a transmission and its result, the value it returns.

---

45 Here, the SQUEAK syntax is different from that of other implementations of SMALLTALK, such as SMALLTALK-80 [GOL 83], or VisualWorks [VIS 05], etc.

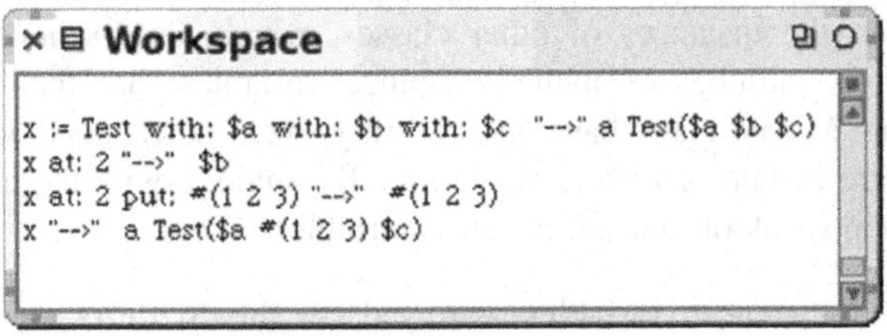

```
× ⊟ Workspace                                              ⊒ ○

x := Test with: $a with: $b with: $c  "-->" a Test($a $b $c)
x at: 2 "-->" $b
x at: 2 put: #(1 2 3) "-->"  #(1 2 3)
x "-->" a Test($a #(1 2 3) $c)
```

Figure 4.17. *Some interactions with an instance of the* Test *class*

On the contrary, if we had defined our class with the ordinary creation message of subclasses, as in:

```
ArrayedCollection subclass: #Test1
    instanceVariableNames: ''
    classVariableNames: ''
    poolDictionaries: ''
    category: 'Cours-Smalltalk'
```

then, already during the creation of an instance using the following example transmission:

```
Test1 with:  $a with:  $b with:  $c
```

SQUEAK would have answered with an error message stating that this class does not know any indexed instance variable or rather, that an instance of the Test1 class cannot be of variable size. Figure 4.18 shows such an error window.

These additional approaches for creating classes have been given for reasons of completeness. It is very rare for a SMALLTALK programmer to need them. He would normally rather use already existing instances of classes with indexed instance variables, subclasses of the ArrayedCollection class, such as the classes Array, a variableSubclass:, and String, a variableByteSubclass:.

4.4.6. *Global variables*

Regarding private variables: so far we know that they are variables that are only accessible to a very specific set of objects. Therefore, a temporary variable is unknown outside its scope: if it is a temporary variable defined in a method, it is only known in that method, or if it is a temporary variable defined in a block, it is only known within that block. This implies that there may be several temporary variables of the same name in a given program. If the method foo declares a temporary variable x, there is no relationship between it and the temporary variable with the name x of the method bar, even if the methods foo and bar are located in the same class. It is as if a variable named x was born during the activation of these methods and it would disappear right after the exit of the method[46]. The same happens for the instance variables: if the Animal class has an instance variable called name, *all* the instances of the Animal class – or of one of its subclasses – will have an instance variable of the same appellation name. Each of these variables is unique to each of the instances, just as each name, each weight, each height of a person is specific to a person – even if someone else has the same name, same weight and same size. If my friend Patrick decided suddenly to grow a few inches, it does not mean that the other Patrick I know, the other people, will also change height. The variables that had been seen so far are effectively variables (referring to values) private to the object for/within which they were declared.

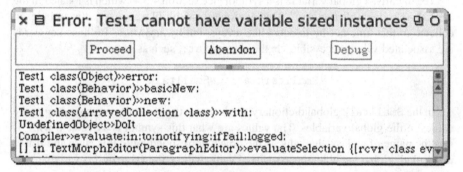

Figure 4.18. *An error window due to the absence of indexed instance variables*

Global variables are entirely different. There can only be a single global variable Foo in a SQUEAK or SMALLTALK system[47]. It will be the *same* global variable Foo that every objects accesses, and if an object decides to change the value of this variable, the value will be changed for everyone: any object that accesses this variable will have access to this new value. It is truly all the objects that have the right to access *and* to alter a global variable.

We can consider the alteration of a global variable as an information on the alteration of something that is instantly transmitted to all living objects[48]. It is messy,

---

46 We, computer scientists, then talk of the *lifetime* of a variable.

47 Note the writing in capital letter.

48 We will return later on other ways a SQUEAK object has for dispatching information about its change to other objects.

since no control nor security can be linked to a global variable. It is dangerous, since any object, no matter how insignificant it may be, can alter its value and therefore influence the behavior of the rest of the world. However, it is extremely useful if we need specific information to be publicly available to everyone, to all objects. It is also extremely useful for information that should be shared by all objects.

Clearly, the SQUEAK programmer would very rarely need to use global variables. On the contrary, the SQUEAK system itself constantly utilizes it, since a lot of objects of the SMALLTALK system must be known to all. This is especially important for class definitions. Naturally, every class must be known to any other object, otherwise new instances of those classes could not be created: the classes are indeed part of the global variables.

Technically, a global variable is a symbol (see section 4.3.4) which is located in the Smalltalk global *dictionary*[49]. This dictionary is a bit like an array, it is an indexed collection, this time not by integers like arrays, but by *keywords*. To those keywords are associated values accessible via the message at:, such as in:

```
Smalltalk at:  #Smalltalk
```

In the Smalltalk global dictionary, the keys are the symbols corresponding to the names of the global variables. The values are what this symbol is associated with: if it is the name of a class, the value is the object corresponding to this class and if it is a "regular" global variable, the associated value will be the value of this variable.

In order to create a global variable Foo, it is sufficient to add the symbol #Foo and its new value to the Smalltalk dictionary, as in the following expression:

```
Smalltalk at:  #Foo put:  'I am a global variable'
```

From this moment, the variable Foo is globally accessible to any SQUEAK object. Thus, if we execute the transmission

```
Foo size
```

SQUEAK will answer the number of characters in the string associated with this global variable (there are 28 characters).

In order to destroy a global variable, it is sufficient to remove the corresponding key from the Smalltalk dictionary. This can be done with the message, known by any instance of the Dictionary class, removeKey:, as in:

---

49 Since this Smalltalk is *global*, the symbol #Smalltalk should also be in this dictionary. How beautiful are recursive data structures.

```
Smalltalk removeKey:  #Foo
```

which destroys the entry #Foo from Smalltalk dictionary[50].

The message includesKey:, also understood by any dictionary, can be used to find out whether a global variable exists. Thus, the transmission:

```
Smalltalk includesKey:  #Foo
```

returns true if the global variable Foo exists and false otherwise.

Once again: as far as possible, please avoid using global variables. If one really needs to share variables, please use either *class variables* or *'pool' dictionaries*. These two types of variables are described below.

4.4.7. Class variables

The *class variables* are global variables in a class and its subclasses. They are declared during the definition of a class with the parameter classVariableNames:. For example, the definition of the Character class of SQUEAK is:

```
Magnitude subclass: #Character
    instanceVariableNames: ''
    classVariableNames: 'CharacterTable
                         ClassificationTable
                         LetterBits
                         LowercaseBit
                         UppercaseBit'
    poolDictionaries: ''
    category: 'Collections-Text
```

This class defines five class variables, the arguments of the parameter classVariableNames:. These variables are accessible to the same class and also to any instance of this class and its possible subclasses, so to any character. Outside of the class and its subclasses, the class variables are unknown and their access yields an *undefined variable* error. The *scope* of such a variable is, therefore, considerably more limited than that of a *global variable*: only the class and instances of the class (and the subclasses and instances of the subclasses of the class), in which a class variable is defined, can access and alter its class variables.

---

50 As during the use of the rm command of Unix (file removal command), think carefully before removing a key from the Smalltalk dictionary. Inadvertent use of this operation can have highly regrettable consequences.

For example, let us reconsider our `Test` class defined above and let us assume that no instance of the class should have more than 10 elements. Knowing that the creation methods with the variants of the message `with:` are limited to creating instances with up to six elements, we do not need to modify this set of methods. The only creation method that is likely to yield instances of arbitrary size is the method `new:`. We can redefine it, as a *class method*, in the `Test` class as:

```
new: n
    n > 10
        ifTrue: [self error: 'too many elements']
        ifFalse: [super new: n]
```

and, from the compilation of this method, if we want to create an instance of the `Test` class with more than 10 elements, the sending of the message `error:`[51] will naturally be triggered and no instance will be created.

If we decide later that we can only admit instances having less than 16 elements, we can modify this method, replacing the integer 10 by the integer 15 and recompile the method. This is not very elegant, especially if the decision is the result of a computation and the modification should be automatic. In this case, it would probably be easier to add a class variable named `MaxNumberOfElements` for instance, to the definition of our `Test` class:

```
ArrayedCollection variableSubclass: #Test
    instanceVariableNames: ''
    classVariableNames: 'MaxNumberOfElements'
    poolDictionaries: ''
    category: 'Course-Smalltalk'
```

and initialize it to the desired value with a transmission using the method below[52]:

```
maxNumberOfElements: n
    MaxNumberOfElements := n
```

Then, the above method `new:` should be replaced by:

---

51 The method `error:` is a method defined in the `Object` class creating a new instance of error, which then opens an error window, a "debugger" window, with the message given as argument.

52 If `maxNumberOfElements` is a class method, it should then be activated like `Test maxNumberOfElements: 15`. If this is an instance method, the same message could just be sent to an instance of the `Test` class. The choice is yours according to your preferences.

```
new: n
    n > MaxNumberOfElements
    ifTrue: [self error: 'too many elements']
    ifFalse: [super new: n]
```

Thus, every time you decide another maximum number of elements, you only need to change the value of the class variable MaxNumberOfElements with this new number and it is not necessary to recompile the method new:.

The above example was a possible use of a class variable. We could have, as we have indicated, done the same thing without using this type of variable, without using a shared variable: which is certainly a less elegant way but just as effective.

Let us suppose that we had wanted it to never be more instances than the maximal number of elements they may contain. How can this be done without using a shared variable? In order to resolve this issue, we should save a memory of every creation of an instance and we should not allow any subsequent creation after MaxNumberOfElements creations[53].

Let us then start by creating an additional class variable named NumberOfInstances:

```
ArrayedCollection variableSubclass: #Test
    instanceVariableNames: ''
    classVariableNames: 'MaxNumberOfElements
                         NumberOfInstances'
    poolDictionaries: ''
    category: 'Course-Smalltalk'
```

which will contain at any time the number of instances that have been created with this method new: specific to the Test class. We must evidently also modify this method new: so that it satisfies these new constraints: it is necessary that it checks that both the new instances do not contain too many elements and that the total number of instances does not exceed the allowed number of elements. In the process, let us also implement the initialization of the class variable NumberOfInstances in this new method new:. It is:

---

53 Here, we do not take into account the creation of instances with the variants of the method with:. If we want to ensure that the methods with:, with:with:, etc., are not used for instance creation of the Test class, they should be redefined in the Test class as follows:

```
with: argument
    self error: ['Prohibited Method. Use new:'].
```

```
new: n
    n >= MaxNumberOfElements
        ifTrue: [self error: 'too many elements'].
    NumberOfInstances == nil
        ifTrue: [NumberOfInstances := 1].
    NumberOfInstances := NumberOfInstances + 1.
    ^super new: n
```

Note the use of the pseudo-variable super in both our definitions of new:. In both cases, it is used to ask SQUEAK to launch its "true" instances creation procedures after our verification operations have been performed.

4.4.8. Pool variables

Finally, the last type of shared variables that SMALLTALK provides are the pool variables.

As has already been seen, SMALLTALK groups all the global variables in the Smalltalk pool. This pool is a *dictionary* known to everyone. Any shared variable is part of such a pool.

Therefore, any class then gives access to at least two "pools": a first one, that is shared by all classes, is our famous Smalltalk pool that contains as keys all the global variables, and a second one, accessible only to its instances and to the instances of its subclasses, containing as keys all of its class variables.

It may happen that a pool to be shared between several classes is needed. For example, the codes of the ASCII characters that are difficult to represent, such as the characters 'carriage return', 'line feed', 'tab', 'space' and 'backspace', are saved in a dictionary of the Text class, in the dictionary TextConstants. Since these ASCII codes must be accessible to all the relevant classes processing texts and strings, the dictionary TextConstants is declared as a pool variable of the Text class and in other classes requiring access to these variables[54].

Figure 4.19 shows a snippet of the inspector open on this pool variable TextConstants. We can recognize the keys CrLf corresponding to the character "carriage-return-line-feed", clearly a character that is difficult to represent, and it can be seen that the character corresponding to the ASCII code of <Ctrl+A> (code ASCII 212) is represented as $'. CrLf and CtrlA are then variables declared in this pool.

---

54 The inheritance of pool variables is standard in SQUEAK. In other versions of SMALLTALK, there is no automatic inheritance of pool variables but only an explicit sharing.

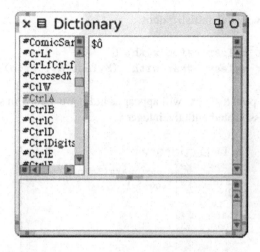

Figure 4.19. *An inspector on the pool variable* `TextConstants`

As example, let us add to our `Test` class the pool variable `MyTest`:

```
ArrayedCollection variableSubclass: #Test
    instanceVariableNames: ''
    classVariableNames: 'MaxNumberOfElements'
    poolDictionaries: 'MyTest'
    category: 'Course-Smalltalk'
```

During the compilation of this definition, SMALLTALK opens a window informing us that the pool variable `MyTest` does not yet exist and proposes to create it automatically. Clearly, this means that a pool variable can be declared in several classes; otherwise how could it already exist? In fact, if we want to declare a pool variable of the same name in the `Test1` class, this window will no longer appear, thus assuring us that we are indeed referring to the same pool variable, that it will be shared between these two classes.

In order to initialize our variable `MyTest`, let us create a class method `myTest:with:` in the `Test` class, which does nothing but send the message `at:put:` to our pool variable, thus adding an additional entry to the dictionary `MyTest`:

```
myTest: aSymbol with: aValue
    MyTest at: aSymbol put: aValue.
    ^MyTest
```

After the following two initializations:

```
Test myTest: #foo with: 5.
Test myTest: #bar with: (MyTest at: #foo)
```

our dictionary, our pool MyTest, will appear as in Figure 4.20 with symbol #foo and the symbol #bar associated with the integer 5.

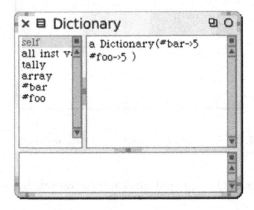

Figure 4.20. *An inspector on MyTest after initialization*

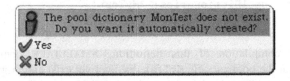

Figure 4.21. *Information on the non-existence of a pool variable*

In order to check if the pool variable MyTest of the Test class and the one of the Test1 class are indeed the same variables, let us add the instance method myTest: to the Test1 class which should search for the value associated with the argument in MyTest:

```
myTest: aSymbol
    ^MyTest at: aSymbol
```

Figure 4.22 shows a Workspace with some transmissions of both these methods myTest:with: and myTest:. The variable pool of the Test class is clearly shared with the Test1 class.

In order to not mislead the readers, let us immediately admit that we cheated a little bit. Here is why: pool variables are indeed *dictionaries*, instanced of the Dictionary class. During their creation, with the parameter poolDictionaries:, SQUEAK creates an instance of this class. The name given to this dictionary, the name specified as an argument (or one of the arguments) of poolDictionaries:, is automatically added to the Smalltalk dictionary, which contains the names of all *global* variables. So, the pool variable – automatically – becomes a global variable, therefore, a variable that is accessible to everyone, at any object of a SQUEAK system. Technically, it is, therefore, wrong to state that the pool variables are known only in the classes where they were declared as such: they are known, accessed and altered by all objects alive at a certain time in the SQUEAK. The sharing limitation to the classes that declare a specific variable as pool variable is only in our interpretation, our programmer discipline. As SQUEAK programmers, we hold to this discipline. And we can have some degree of confidence (but not more) that this variable will be in fact shared by these classes that declare them in their pool variables set, since no honest SMALLTALK programmer will look in the Smalltalk dictionary for global variables that he could "squate" for its own needs. Programming, all programming, is a highly disciplined activity, and any good programmer submits to the discipline of his programming language.

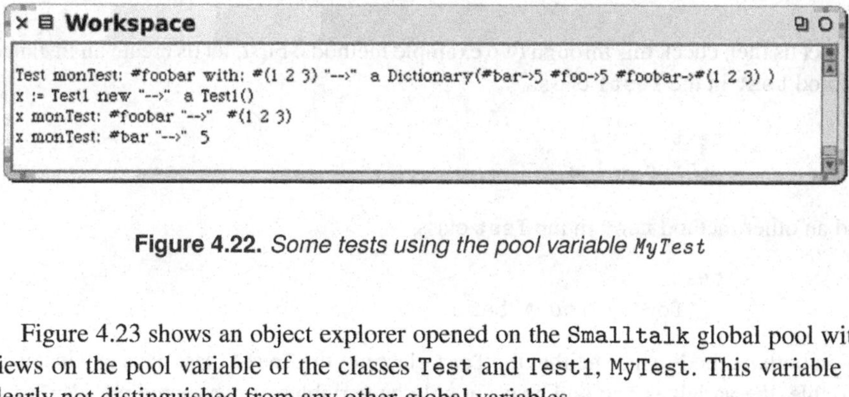

```
x ☐ Workspace                                                   ▣ O

Test monTest: #foobar with: #(1 2 3) "-->" a Dictionary(#bar->5 #foo->5 #foobar->#(1 2 3) )
x := Test1 new "-->" a Test1()
x monTest: #foobar "-->" #(1 2 3)
x monTest: #bar "-->" 5
```

Figure 4.22. *Some tests using the pool variable MyTest*

Figure 4.23 shows an object explorer opened on the Smalltalk global pool with views on the pool variable of the classes Test and Test1, MyTest. This variable is clearly not distinguished from any other global variables.

All this makes it a bit skeptical. Why then distinguish between global variables and pool variables? In order to answer this question, let us recall that the keys of the Smalltalk global pool are *symbols* corresponding to the names of the global variables. Every pool, so also our pool MyTest, contains associations between some variables and their values. Thus, the keys of Mytest, #foo, #bar and #foobar correspond to the variables foo, bar and foobar, and these *variables* and their associated values are the ones which are known only among the classes that share the pool MyTest, i.e. in the classes Test and, after having transformed the Test1 class into a subclass of Test, Test1. Thus, the proper use of pool variables is to consider the initialization of these variables as the declaration of variables to be shared among classes that share that specific pool. And we do not access the global variable pool itself, as we have done previously, but only the variables in the pool.

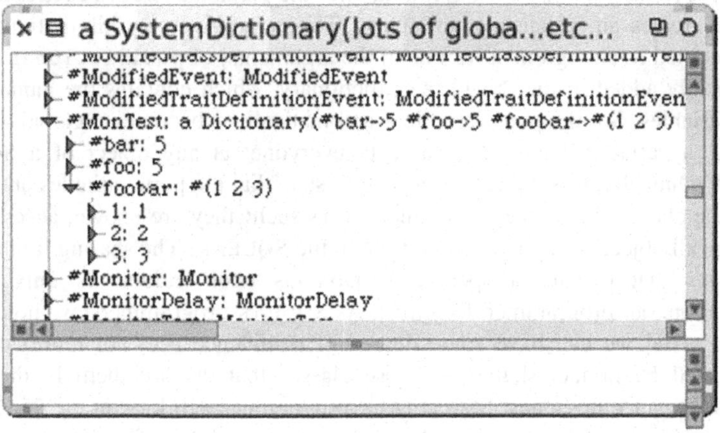

```
× ⊟ a SystemDictionary(lots of globa...etc...  ⊡ O
   ▼ MUUIIICUUIGSSDEIIIIIUUIIEVEII. MUUIIICUUIGSSDEIIIIUUIIEVEII
 ▶ #ModifiedEvent: ModifiedEvent
 ▶ #ModifiedTraitDefinitionEvent: ModifiedTraitDefinitionEven
 ▼ #MonTest: a Dictionary(#bar->5 #foo->5 #foobar->#(1 2 3)
    ▶ #bar: 5
    ▶ #foo: 5
    ▼ #foobar: #(1 2 3)
       ▶ 1: 1
       ▶ 2: 2
       ▶ 3: 3
 ▶ #Monitor: Monitor
 ▶ #MonitorDelay: MonitorDelay
   ▼ #i....i. . . . . . . .  . . . . . .
```

Figure 4.23. *An explorer of the* Smalltalk *dictionary showing the pool* MyTest

Let us then check this through two example methods. First, let us create an instance method `test` in the `Test1` class:

```
test
    ^foo + bar
```

and an other method `test` in the `Test` class

```
test
    ^foo := foo * bar
```

In both methods, since neither the `Test` class nor the `Test1` class have any instance variable, the variables `foo` and `bar` can only be variables of our shared pool `MyTest`. Each of these methods has, therefore, access to the same variables[55].

If we assume that our pool variable `MyTest` contains the following dictionary:

---

55 In SQUEAK, there is a kind of precedence when the same variable name is used for two different types of variables. If we have both a global variable `foo` and a pool variable of the same name, the pool variable *hides* the global variable. We say a variable x hides a variable y when the existence of x renders y inaccessible. An instance variable hides all other variables of the same name. Moreover, it is not advisable to give instance variables names of a pool. The latter variables would be totally be useless, since they would be completely hidden, and therefore inaccessible.

#bar -> 5 #foo -> 5

and that the variable x contains an instance of the Test class and the variable y an instance of the Test1 class, the transmission "y test" then returns 10, the sum the values of foo and bar. Figure 4.24 shows a series of transmissions of the messages test and their results.

To summarize: the instance variables represent the current state of an object. Temporary variables represent transient states that are necessary for carrying out an activity, a computation. Temporary variables are normally associated with an execution of a method; they are created when a message triggers the execution of the method and they are eliminated when the method finishes by returning a value. The other types of variables can be accessed by more than one object, i.e. they are shared. Most of the shared variables in the SMALLTALK system are either class variables or global variables. Shared variable names are written with an initial capital letter, as opposed to private variables. The value of a shared variable is independent of the instance using the method in which it is located. The value of a private variable depends on the instance using the method in which it is located, that is to say, it depends on the instance that receives the message. Shared variables are organized into pools. Variables in the Smalltalk pool are accessible to any object, i.e. they are global variables. Each class features a pool for its class variables, which are accessible only to instances of the class and its subclasses. In addition to these two "pools" that each class already has, a class can have other "pools" declared in the parameter poolDictionaries:. Every class declaring a poolDictionary of the same name has access to the variables of this same pool. Those are variables shared by a subset of objects.

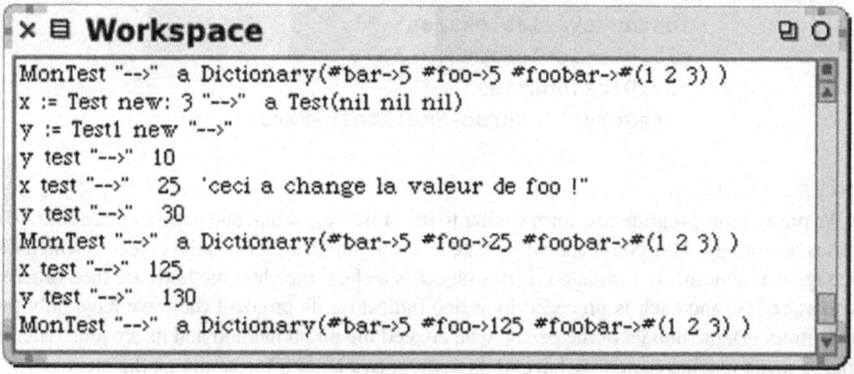

```
× 目  Workspace                                              🔲 O
MonTest "-->" a Dictionary(#bar->5 #foo->5 #foobar->#(1 2 3) )
x := Test new: 3 "-->" a Test(nil nil nil)
y := Test1 new "-->"
y test "-->" 10
x test "-->"  25  'ceci a change la valeur de foo !'
y test "-->"  30
MonTest "-->" a Dictionary(#bar->5 #foo->25 #foobar->#(1 2 3) )
x test "-->" 125
y test "-->"  130
MonTest "-->" a Dictionary(#bar->5 #foo->125 #foobar->#(1 2 3) )
```

Figure 4.24. *A series of transmissions (commented) using the variables of the pool MyTest*

4.4.9. *Exercises*

Solutions for the following exercises can be found on page 376.

A program comprehension exercise adapted from [BÜC 39].

Attentively study the definitions of classes A, B and C below[56]:

```
Object subclass: #A
        instanceVariableNames: 'a b'
        classVariableNames: ''
        poolDictionaries: ''
        category: 'Course-Smalltalk-Exercises'

A methodsFor: 'test'
a
        ^a - 2

a: aNumber
        a := aNumber

b
        ^ b - 1

b: aNumber
        b := aNumber

A subclass: #B
        instanceVariableNames: ''
        classVariableNames: ''
        poolDictionaries: ''
        category: 'Course-Smalltalk-Exercises'
```

---

56 We present this program in a form similar to the presentation that one gets if a `printOut` of a class is performed. This command will create a "html" file that presents the object to which the message was sent nicely formatted. If this object is a class, the class methods are then ordered by `protocols`, and each is preceded by a line indicating its protocol (here we have only the `test` protocol), the initials of the person who created the initial method and its creation date. In order to make reading easier, we have omitted these two latter information on the methods.
A `printOut` can be obtained from a class browser by choosing from the menu of the pane corresponding to the object to be displayed the `printOut` entry. If instead of simply displaying the object we want to save it in a file that can be loaded later on, the `fileOut` entry of the same menu should be used.

```
B methodsFor: 'test'
a
    | x |
    ^super a <= 0
        ifTrue:[1]
        ifFalse:[x := B new.
                 x a: super a.
                 x a + 1]


A subclass: #C
        instanceVariableNames: ''
        classVariableNames: ''
        poolDictionaries: ''
        category: 'Course-Smalltalk-Exercises'


C methodsFor: 'test'
b
        | c |
      ^ super b = 0
            ifTrue: [1]
            ifFalse: [c := C new.
                      c b: super b.
                      c b + super b + 1]
```

For the following questions, try to first find a solution *without* writing the program and *without* running it on the machine. Only once the solutions have been found that you can implement the classes and check your answers.

1) Give the sequence, transmission by transmission, of the execution of the expression:

B new a: 3; a

2) What is the result of the SMALLTALK expression below?

```
| b |
(1 to: 10) collect: [:i |
    b := B new.
    b a: i.
    b a]
```

3) Can you simplify the method a of class B so that it contains only one reference to super?

4) Can you simplify the method b of class C so that it no longer contains any reference to super?

5) And what is the result of the SMALLTALK expression below?

```
| c |
(1 to: 10) collect: [:i |
  c := C new.
  c b: i.
  c b]
```

6) In a more descriptive way, more mathematically, what do the methods a of class B and b of class C compute?

7) What will be the result of the previous question if we change the method b of class C in:

```
b
    | c |
  ^ super b = 0
            ifTrue: [1]
            ifFalse: [c := C new.
                  c b: super b.
                  c b * super b + 1]
```

8) How should the method a of class B be changed so that it computes the integer division by three of the value of the instance variable a (rounded to the next whole number if a is not a multiple of 3)?

9) Modify the method a of class B from the previous exercise so that it yields the result of the integer division by three of the instance variable a rounded to the *previous* whole number.

10) How should the method b of class C be changed so that it computes the factorial of the value of the instance variable b?

11) Perform all the changes in the definitions of classes A and/or B and/or C that should be done and write the necessary methods in order to add, at each *new* computation of b, the result into a dictionary and, in order not to reactivate method b, if the result is already in the dictionary it should be sufficient to return this cached result.

12) Also apply the *caching* technique of the previous exercise to the method a of class B.

4.5. Messages

It should be known by now: any SMALLTALK computation is done through messages sending[57] and a message is always sent to a *receiver*, which can be an object or the result of another message sending or any expression. We call the message sending a transmission (of a message).

SMALLTALK provides three types of message sending, three types of selectors[58]: *unary*, *binary* and *keyword* based messages. The distinction is made on the syntax, it is manifested in the way messages are written.

4.5.1. *Unary messages*

Unary messages are messages that do not admit any arguments. They follow the syntactic pattern:

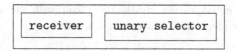

The *unary selector* is simply the name of a method. The only existing restrictions on the writing of that name, of that selector, are: it must be composed of a sequence of regular characters that does not contain the sign ":" and must comply with the restrictions imposed by the writing of identifiers (see section 4.2.2). The first method that we wrote, the method name (see section 2.2), was compliant with this rule, it is therefore a *unary message*; let us repeat it, a message with no arguments.

---

57 Let us restrict this statement slightly: some syntactic elements do not correspond to messages:

1) As has already been seen, the explicit return of a method, with the operator "∧" or "↑", is not the transmission of a message.

2) Also, the assignment sign ":=" or "←" is an operator and not a selector.

3) Regarding the writing of SMALLTALK programs, the syntactic signs for grouping: (and), [and], the separator character between two transmissions: ".", the character signaling a parameter: ":" and the declaration delimiter character of temporary variables: | are clearly not involved in the transmissions of messages. They are used only during the syntax parsing phase of SMALLTALK code sources.

58 We will talk of *messages* when we are referring to transmissions and we will talk of *selectors* when we are referring to the instance that has received a message and that should find the message selectors in the methods dictionary of its class or its superclasses. Both terms refer to the same object viewed from different angles.

Some examples of unary messages are:

Dispatch	Return value	Comment
45 sin	0.850903524534118	computation of the sine
15 sqrt	3.872983346207417	square root
'Squeak' size	6	collection size
(1/5) negated	(-1/5)	0 − receiver
10 asString	'10'	conversion
'Squeak' asLowercase	'squeak'	transformation to lowercase
(1 to: 12 by: 3) last	10	*why?*
56 odd	false	odd number?
Float halfPi	1.570796326794897	constant $\frac{\pi}{2}$
(5@5) degrees	45.0	angle
Pen example	Pen	see page 7
Date today	30 August 2005	today's date
'Date' inspect	a SystemWindow	inspection of an object
Random new next	0.1578134536546717	*two* unary messages

All these unary messages are clearly compliant with the writing rule that is imposed and with the aforementioned syntactic scheme.

The answer to the question *why* the transmission (1 to: 12 by: 3) last returns the integer 10, in the table above, can be found in the footnote[59].

4.5.2. *Binary messages*

Binary messages are provided by SQUEAK mainly to facilitate the reading of programs containing logical and arithmetic expressions. These are messages that require exactly *one* argument and whose name is composed of *one* or *two* characters, to be chosen from the following characters set: +, -, /, &, =, >, <, ~, , (the character "comma") and @[60].

Binary messages should comply with the following syntax diagram:

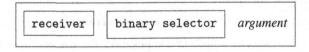

receiver | binary selector | *argument*

---

59 (1 to: 12 by: 3) creates an interval starting with 1 and consisting of the numbers obtained by taking a step of 3. The second element of this interval is $1 + 3$, so 4, the next is $4 + 3$, 7, the next $7 + 3$, so 10, the next number would be $10 + 3$, so 13. But 13 is greater than the limit, 12, of the interval. The integer 10 is therefore the last element of this interval. The unary message last indeed requests the last element of a sorted collection.

60 With an exception: "−−", the combination of two characters "minus", is excluded from it for syntax parsing reasons.

Some examples of binary messages existing in SQUEAK are given below:

Dispatch	Return value	Comment
8 + (5/4)	(37/4)	the arithmetic sum
(1 to: 3) + 10	(11 to: 13)	creation of an interval
Float pi >= 3	true	$\pi \geq 3$?
Float pi		
Float e:	0.423310825130748	remainder of the division $\frac{\pi}{e}$
(24/125) * 125	24	multiplication
(1 < 2) & (2 > 3)	false	the *and* logical operator
8 // 3	2	the integer division
2r1010 ≫ 1	5	a right shift
16 ≪ 2	64	two left shifts
$c == $c	true	characters identity
76 ~= 75	true	the $\neq$ operator
#(1 2 3) , #(a b c)	#(1 2 3 #a #b #c)	the concatenation

In this list of examples, we have given binary messages already existing in the SQUEAK system. Other binary messages can obviously be defined, all that is necessary is that their writing properly follows the writing rules that have been mentioned above. Therefore, if in our class A of the previous exercise (see section 4.4.9), we want to have a message !! which returns the value associated with the instance variable a incremented by the value of the single argument that this binary method accepts, adding the following method to this class is sufficient:

```
!! aNumber
    ^ a + aNumber
```

Note that we chose an identifier consisting of only two characters and that these two characters are included in the set of possible characters for building binary messages. The writing is indeed compliant with that of binary operators. This method can then be normally used like any other binary message, as shown in the set of transmissions and return values below:

Dispatch	Return value	Comment
X := A new	an A	creation of an instance
X a: 3	an A	initialization of a
X !! 10	13	a+10

Digression 1

These binary messages are compromises – quite troublesome ones – between SMALLTALK and non object-oriented languages that are more familiar to programmers. By introducing a particular type of message, the *binary message* type,

SMALLTALK designers wanted to ease the writing and reading of portions of code corresponding to operations commonly expressed with infix operators. Everyone learns to write arithmetic expressions, such as $a * x + b$, because the other possible writings, like the writing using a postfix notation[61], is considered more difficult to manage.

Then, under the pretext of facilitating the writing of arithmetic or logical expressions, SMALLTALK wanted to keep, in the context of object-oriented programming and thus programming via messages sending, this writing standard. But at what cost: restrictions on the number of characters that can compose the selector of a binary message, restrictions on the characters allowed in its writing (with the additional absurd restriction mentioned in the footnote 60 on page 132) and, as we will see in the next section, restrictions imported from the writing of keywords to the keyword messages.

Perhaps, we should return to a writing of messages using only unary messages (messages *without* argument) and keyword messages. We will return to this lack of elegance of the SMALLTALK grammar and syntax in the next section.

4.5.3. Keyword messages

The keyword messages represent the writing of messages in *total accord* with SMALLTALK logic. This is the most general version for writing them. They require at least *one* argument and their method names, their selectors, must have the sign "`:`". They should comply with the syntax diagram below:

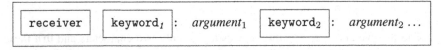

where $keyword_1 : keyword_2 : \ldots$ is the name of the selector, the name of the method that implements the corresponding activities.

The character "`:`" precedes any argument. Therefore, there are as many occurrences of that character as there are arguments. Thus, if we have a two arguments message, it will be written as:

receiver $firstPartOfTheName:$ $argument_1$ $secondPartOfTheName:$ $argument_2$

---

61 These other notations, introduced mainly by the Austrian/Polish logician Jan Lukasiewicz [LUK 29], are commonly called *Polish prefix* if the binary operator precedes its arguments (e.g. "$(x + 3) * (y + 2)$" is translated to Polish prefix as "$* + x\,3 + y\,2$"), *Polish postfix* if the binary operator follows its arguments (the same expression "$(x + 3) * (y + 2)$" is written in Polish postfix as "$x\,3 + y\,2 + *$", popularized by Hewlett-Packard scientific calculators). Finally, via a kind of misnomer, the expression "$(x + 3) * (y + 2)$" is called *Polish infix*. Let's note that neither the prefix notation, nor in postfix, require parentheses!

and the message name is firstPartOfTheName:secondPartOfTheName: – the characters ":" included.

A lot of such selectors have already been encountered in this chapter. For instance, the selectors:

```
inject:into:
swap:with:
with:do:
```

are all keyword selectors. All these selectors contain two occurrences of the character ":", so they take two arguments, each of which must come after each of these characters ":".

This message form is clearly the most common form in SMALLTALK programs. The unary and keyword messages also represent the most intrinsic form of message to object-oriented programming. Conceptually, it is simple: if the message has no arguments, there is no occurrence of the character ":" in the corresponding selector of the message, otherwise, there are as many ":" as there are arguments.

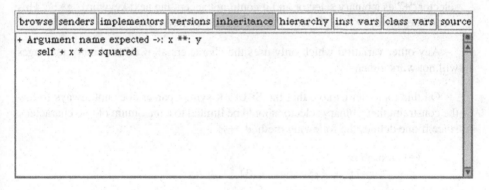

Figure 4.25. *The creation of a keyword "+:" is impossible*

Digression 2

This nice simplicity, with only two rules:

– the number of occurrences of the character ":" throughout any selector corresponds to the number of parameters of the method that implements the activity corresponding to this selector;

– any character except characters having a syntactic role (., [,], ;, " and :) can be used to form the different keywords, which can furthermore be composed of any number of characters;

is unfortunately undermined by the existence of binary selectors. Not only because, as stated above, the number of characters of binary selectors is limited to 2, but also because SMALLTALK prohibits the definition of keyword messages composed exclusively of characters reserved to binary selectors. Thus, if we wish, for example, to define a method +:**:, computing "$self + argument_1 \times (argument_2)^2$", as:

```
+: aNumber **: anotherNumber
    ^ self + aNumber * anotherNumber squared
```

SMALLTALK will refuse the compilation of this method, as shown in Figure 4.25 under the pretext that after the sign "+" it expects not a sign ":" but an argument.

Naturally, if you try the following alternative:

```
+ aNumber **:   anotherNumber
```

this does not work either, since now SMALLTALK will very correctly interpret the selector "+" as a binary selector and it could not accept the next keyword "**:". This second keyword, **:, is obviously also a prohibited keyword.

Any other variation which only uses the characters allowed for binary messages will not work either.

On this topic, let us note that the SQUEAK syntax parser does not always follow the constraint that a binary selector should be limited to a maximum of two characters, since if one defines the following method +++:

```
+++ aNumber
    ^ self + (aNumber * 3)
```

Not only does SQUEAK compile without any problem, but it can be used afterward such as any other binary message – although it is composed of more than two characters. This is not very nice, but we can indeed define binary selectors composed of an arbitrary number of the *same* character (except the character "–", for the reasons given in the footnote 60 on page 132).

This is really not nice.

Pending a redesign of SQUEAK syntax, let us forget all that and keep in mind that we cannot use keywords exclusively composed of characters reserved for writing binary messages. This is also why we have said, see section 4.2.2, that an identifier should begin with a letter, an alphabetic character.

4.5.4. *Message composition*

Now that we know the different types of messages (unary message, binary message and keyword message), let us look at the rules that determine the order of evaluation, the order of computation, during their compositions.

In arithmetic, it is said that multiplication and division operators have precedence over addition and subtraction operators. Thus, the expression:

$$x + a^2 \times y + b^2 \tag{4.1}$$

may be parenthesized as:

$$x + ((a^2) \times y) + (b^2) \tag{4.2}$$

Both expressions compute exactly the same thing. This shows that the raising to power operation takes precedence over both the multiplication and addition, and that the multiplication has precedence over the addition. We can order the precedence of these three operations, from the highest to the lowest as:

$$raising to power \succ multiplication \succ addition$$

This precedence expresses the order of computation: in our example, before being able to compute the sum of the three terms x, $a^2 \times y$ and b^2, we clearly need to compute the value of the product to $a^2 \times y$ and the square of b. In order to compute the product, we must first compute the square of a. All this is obvious – in computer science terms we say that the precedence determines the evaluation order of arithmetic subexpressions. It is this precedence of operators that allows us the economy of parentheses in expression [4.1]. If we truly do not remember the order of precedence or if we want to change it, we can always force it by adding parentheses to the expression. Thus, the parenthesized expression below clearly changes the precedence, the order of computation of subexpressions, and its results are different from those of expression [4.1] and [4.2][62].

$$(x + a^2) \times (y + b^2) \tag{4.3}$$

The same occurs in SMALLTALK: each message type has its own precedence that determines in which order the messages should be evaluated if an expression contains more than one message. The order of precedence of SQUEAK message types is given below:

---

62 However, let's recall that if we had used a *Polish prefix* or *postfix*, this ambiguity would no longer exist.

> *unary message* ≻ *binary message* ≻ *keyword message*

Hence, the expression:

```
#(1 2 3) at:  5 // 2 put:  5 factorial
```

places, in the second position (the evaluation of the transmission 5 // 2 returns the integer 2) of the receiver array, the integer 120 (the evaluation of 5 factorial returns 120): the keyword message at:put: has a priority order lower than the binary message // and the unary message factorial. And, if we write:

```
#(1 2 3) at:  5 // 2 put:  5 factorial / 4 factorial
```

it will naturally lead to the substitution of the second element of the array with the integer 5, the result of the division 120, the factorial of 5, by 24, the factorial of 4.

Below are three additional examples of the messages composition:

Dispatch	Return value
'Hello World' size squared	121
#(1 2 3 4 5) findFirst: [:e | e > 8 sqrt]	3
'Hello' , 'World' reverse copyWithout: $1	'HeodroW'

Carefully examine these examples! They show that the evaluation proceeds strictly from left to right. Thus, in the last example, the order of evaluation is:

1) The string 'Hello' receives the concatenation message "," with 'World' reverse as argument.

2) Because of the precedence of unary messages over binary messages, SQUEAK first proceeds with the evaluation of the argument, which returns the reversed argument string: 'dlroW'.

3) Now, because of precedence of binary operators over keyword operators, SQUEAK can proceed with the computation of the concatenation. The return value is the string 'HellodlroW'.

4) Finally, this string 'HellodlroW' receives the keyword message copyWithout: with the character $1 as argument, which returns the final result, the string 'HeodroW'.

If, in the second example, we do not want to find the first element that is larger than the square root of the integer 8, but the element that is larger than $1 + \sqrt{8}$, we cannot write:

```
e > 1 + 8 sqrt
```

since that expression first checks if e is greater than 1 and then sends to the result of this test the binary message + with 8 sqrt as the argument. But this makes no sense: the result of a test can only be true or false and these two objects do not know the message +. Simply put, this means that SMALLTALK proceeds strictly from left to right when evaluating compound messages having the same precedence. We have to *force* the precedence with the proper parentheses in order to solve this issue:

$$e > (1 + 8\ sqrt)$$

We conclude that the parenthesized messages have the highest priority over any message type, which leads to the precedence order below:

> *parenthesized ≻ unary ≻ binary ≻ keyword messages*

This order of precedence and the highly strict discipline to proceed with the evaluation of an expression, always from left to right, are the only rules that SQUEAK applies when evaluating a transmission containing several messages. There is no other, and above all, there is not, as in other programming languages (and as in mathematics), precedences between arithmetic or logical operators. Thus, as it has already been seen, the dispatch:

$$1 * 2 + 3 * 4$$

does not return 14 but the integer 20, the result of a strict evaluation from left to right, as in:

$$((1 * 2) + 3) * 4$$

So let us also keep in mind that:

> *Any binary message has the same precedence, even if it corresponds to an arithmetic or logical operator.*

As a conclusion to the presentation of keywords messages, let us note that the parentheses ((and)) and the square brackets ([and]) delimit *regions* of text, of source code. The square brackets delimit the blocks and the parentheses delimit the expressions. A selector of a keyword message is, within a given region, the longest sequence of words that ends with the character ":". This sequence stops either at the end of the region or at the encounter of a character "." or a character ";". Thus, in the example below:

```
#(1 2 3) at: ('hello' indexOf: $e)
         put: ((1 to: 10) inject: 0 into: [:s :e | s + e])
```

there are five distinct regions:

1) the region formed by the whole expression;

2) ('hello' indexOf: $e);

3) ((1 to: 10) inject: 0 into: [:s :e | s + e]) the latter being composed of two regions:

4) (1 to: 10);

5) [:s :e | s + e].

So, there are four keywords messages: at:put:, indexOf:, to: and inject:into:. If we had not put parentheses, as in:

```
#(1 2 3) at: 'hello' indexOf: $e
         put: 1 to: 10 inject: 0 into: [:s :e | s + e]
```

we would have a single keyword message:

```
at:indexOf:put:to:inject:into:
```

taking five arguments. Clearly, this selector (not defined) is the longest sequence of words ending with the character ":" of the main region of this expression.

4.5.5. Expression sequences

In order to place more transmissions and/or assignments in sequence, it is sufficient to separate them by the *expression separator* character: the dot (.). During the evaluation of an expression sequence, SQUEAK evaluates, from left to right and from top to bottom, each expression one after another, and the returned value is the value of the last expression[63]. The values of the other expressions are ignored. Thus, if we evaluate the following expression sequences in a Workspace:

```
| dict |
(1 to: 5) with: #(one two three four five)
         do: [:key :value |
               dict at: key put: value.
               dict at: value put: key].
    dict
```

---

[63] Naturally, if the body of a *method* consists of an expression sequence, the return value obtained after evaluating the method is either the value of the expression (or of the expression sequence) according to the sign *return*, the character "^" or ↑, or the receiver of the message implemented by this method.

we obtain as a result the value of the last expression. Here it is the expression `dict`, it is thus the value of the temporary variable `dict` that will be returned as value. Having selected the expression sequence, if we perform a `print it`, with the keys "Alt+p", we obtain:

```
a Dictionary(1->#one 2->#two 3->#three 4->#four
            5->#five #five->5 #two->2 #four->4
            #three->3 #one->1)
```

Note that the expression sequence above consists of two phrases preceded by the declaration of a temporary variable. This declaration is not an expression (it is neither a message transmission, nor an assignment), that is why it is not separated by the dot character of the following expressions. The separator character for the declarations of temporary variable is the vertical bar, the character " | ". Let us note also that the second expression is reduced to an identifier: `dict`, the name of the temporary variable. As in every expression, the name of a variable is just a reference to the value that has been assigned to it. The result is indeed the value associated with the temporary variable `dict` after the evaluation of the first expression of the sequence.

Note that the argument block of the parameter `do:` is itself also a sequence of two instructions, preceded by the declaration of the two block parameters.

4.5.6. Cascaded messages

Cascades have been discuessed multiple times, beginning in section 2.2. Here, we will return to it, very briefly, and only for reasons of completeness: when we talk of various ways of sending messages, we also need to recall the value of cascades.

A *cascade* is a compact way of sending multiple messages to the *same* object. It allows us to transform a sequence of transmissions all having the same receiver into a single expression. It follows the following scheme:

```
receiver expression   message₁; message₂; message₃; ...
```

and is therefore mainly a syntax simplification in the writing of programs. Thus, since in the *sequence* of expressions:

```
Transcript show: 'Often, '.
Transcript show: 'to have fun, ' , 'the men of the crew'.
Transcript cr.
Transcript show: 'Take albatrosses, vast ...'.
Transcript cr
```

each transmission has the same recipient, `Transcript`, we can transform this sequence into the following *cascade*:

```
Transcript show: 'Often, ';
           show: 'to have fun, ' , 'the men of the crew';
           cr;
           show: 'Take albatrosses, vast ...';
           cr
```

which outputs exactly the same thing in the transcript[64], but whose writing is more compact. Naturally, the receiver object of the these cascaded messages can be the result of other transmissions, as it has been done in exercise 1 of section 4.4.9, when we have written:

$$B \ new \ a: \ 3; \ a$$

Here, the receiver of the message a: with 3 as argument and of the message a is the new instance of class B created with the expression B new.

4.5.7. *Primitives*

In principle, a computer understands only programs written directly in its "machine" language, that is programs directly "wired" in the processor. In this language is written a program allowing us to read and interpret programs written in the assembler language. The assembler language is nothing more than a written representation of instructions of the wired microcode[65]. In this assembler language are written other programs allowing us to either interpret programs written in other languages, or to translate programs written in these other languages to the assembler language. It may be that in these other languages are written programs allowing us to translate or interpret programs also written in other languages. In every computer, there are layers and layers of such translators and/or interpreters.

We, computer scientists, then distinguish between compiled languages and interpreted languages. In a compiled language such as Fortran [ELL 94], Pascal [JEN 75], C [KER 88] and C++ [STR 87], we always proceed in two stages: first, a compiler compiles the program, then the compiled program is executed. To compile a program is to translate the program in another language, it is often another language closer to the machine, such as an assembler language. It may be, as illustrated in

---

64 Yes, this is the beginning of the third poem of *Evil flowers* from Charles Baudelaire. To read more, please check [BAU 80] (from the second edition dated of 1861).

65 Moreover, the program translating programs written in assembler into the microcode is also called *assembler*.

Figure 4.26, that a whole chain of compilers is needed to arrive at a program that the machine can run, an executable program. For example, many compilers of so-called *high level* languages translate the program into C and then that generated C program needs to also be compiled in order to obtain an executable program[66].

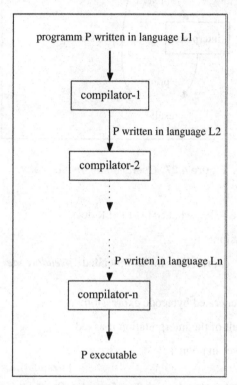

Figure 4.26. *A compilation chain*

An interpreter is quite another thing: it reads a program, or *an expression* (and the data on which the program is supposed to process), and directly *interprets* it in order to compute a result. So, there is no translation at all, just an immediate understanding. It is as if the interpreter was a computer whose machine language was the language that is interpreted. Figure 4.27 shows its operation diagram.

The best-known interpreter languages are Lisp [MCC 62] and, of course, SMALL-TALK.

---

66 For instance, this is the case of the `Eiffel` language [MEY 86] whose compiler generates a program written in the C language, which should then be compiled by one of the standard C compilers in order to obtain an executable program.

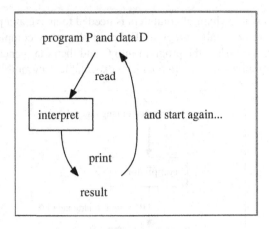

Figure 4.27. *Operation of an interpreter*

In fact (see Figure 4.28), what SMALLTALK does is to:

1) read an expression;

2) compile this expression in a so-called *pseudo-code* language, named *bytecode*[67];

3) interpret the generated bytecode expression;

4) output the result of the interpretation if asked;

5) finally, start over in point 1.

Let us repeat: SMALLTALK, and therefore also SQUEAK, is an interpreter that translates SMALLTALK expressions first in a pseudo-code, the bytecode, and it is the bytecode expression which is then interpreted by a bytecode interpreter[68]. All this activity is performed by the SMALLTALK *virtual machine* (see page 4). Like any computer, this virtual machine implements a set of machine instructions. In

---

67 It is the effect of the `accept` command or "Alt+s"

68 This translation or compilation from the SMALLTALK, code to the bytecode allows:

1) to write almost all of the SMALLTALK system in SMALLTALK itself;

2) to easily apply the SMALLTALK system to new machines. For this, "small" bytecode interpreter, the rest is just a copy of the SMALLTALK code to this new machine. This is also what allows a full compatibility of SMALLTALK programs and of *image* files from one machine to another. It is not SMALLTALK that changes with the change of machine, it is just the kernel of the *bytecode* interpreter.

SMALLTALK we can directly have access to these instructions through special commands that are called *primitives*.

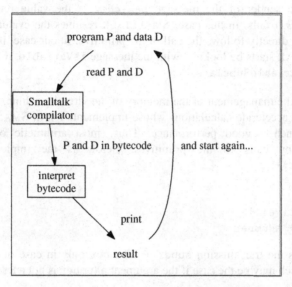

Figure 4.28. *Operation of a Smalltalk interpreter*

We now know that the whole SMALLTALK system is written in SMALLTALK. We also know that in SMALLTALK *everything* is an object and every computation is done by the execution of methods in response to message transmissions. This is absolutely valid, *except* for a small number of messages that cannot be written in SMALLTALK itself, since, for instance, they must impact the inner state of the interpreter, so the virtual machine. A typical case of such a message is represented by the method new, which should create a new object, so reserved, somewhere in the memory of the interpreter, enough space for this new object.

In fact, if we examine the message transmissions generated by sending a message new to a class, it can be noticed that they end (almost) always with the message basicNew. Below, a snippet from the implementation of this message in the Behavior class:

```
basicNew
    <primitive: 70>
    self isVariable ifTrue: [^ self basicNew: 0].
    ...
```

The instruction <primitive: 70> directly refers to the implementation in the virtual machine of the message new. new is the 70th primitive. The activation of such a primitive interrupts the message transmission mechanism, which only resumes when the execution of the code associated with this primitive is completed. The value returned to the sender of the message basicNew is the value returned by the primitive *unless* it fails. In this case, SMALLTALK resumes the evaluation with the expression that directly follows the call of the primitive. In our case, if the primitive 70 fails, SQUEAK starts by looking, with the message isVariable, if the receiver is a variable, a variableSubclass.

Except for the management of the memory of the virtual machine, primitives are mainly used to accelerate calculations whose implementation in SMALLTALK could not achieve such a good performance. Thus, most arithmetic operations are implemented by calls to the primitives. Below is the implementation of SmallInteger»+:

```
+ aNumber
     <primitive: 1>
     super + aNumber
```

which activates the transmission super + aNumber only in case of failure of the primitive – which may be the case if the argument aNumber is not a SmallInteger.

We give in Appendix 4 the primitives list[69], but, in this book we will never write a program using such primitives. On the contrary, if later on we want, for example, SQUEAK to be able to recognize a new device, it may well be that we have to use primitives, or define its own primitives. It is quite possible: a primitive writing manual is available on the www.squeak.org documentation page [POP 98].

4.6. Control structure

As we know, SMALLTALK does not require special instructions, with their own syntax, for control or conditional expressions structures: keyword messages with blocks, closures, as arguments are sufficient to construct all the desired control structures. In this section we will present the most common structures.

4.6.1. *Conditional control structures*

In the section 4.1.2, we have already thoroughly analyzed the implementation of conditional structure of the four messages, ifTrue:ifFalse:, ifFalse:ifTrue:,

---

69 We will limit ourselves to the *numbered* primitives. SQUEAK also provides a *named* primitive mechanism. These are primitives that can be added to the system without recompiling the kernel.

ifTrue: and ifFalse: in the Boolean class, and its two subclasses, True and False. We will, therefore, not return to it except for a brief reminder on their behavior:

1) *booleanExpression*   ifTrue: *blockTrue*   ifFalse: *blockFalse*   and *booleanExpression* ifFalse: *blockFalse* ifTrue: *blockTrue* return the value of *blockTrue* if the value of the receiver, therefore, of *booleanExpression*, is true. Otherwise, if the value of the receiver is false, both expressions return *blockFalse*'s value.

2) *booleanExpression* ifTrue: *blockTrue* returns nil if the receiver *booleanExpression* is evaluated by giving the value false, otherwise, if the evaluation of the receiver gives the value true, the returned value is *blockTrue*'s value.

3) *booleanExpression* ifFalse: *blocFalse* returns the value of *blockFalse* if the evaluation of the receiver gives the value false, otherwise the returned value is nil.

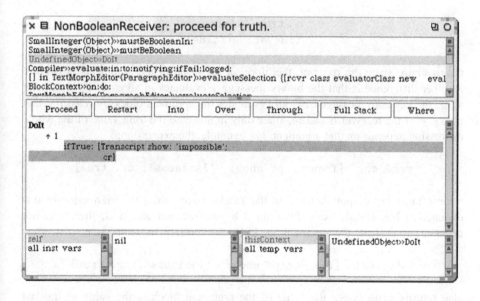

Figure 4.29. *Error indication after the dispatch of the message* ifTrue: *to a non-Boolean receiver*

Let us recall that *blockTrue* and *blockFalse* are blocks with no argument and that the receiver, *booleanExpression*, must always be evaluated either to true or to false. Otherwise, as shown in Figure 4.29, if we send one of these messages to a non-Boolean receiver, as in:

```
1 ifTrue:  [Transcript show:  'impossible'; cr]
```

SQUEAK will display an error window stating that the receiver is not a Boolean expression[70]. The *BooleanExpression* part may naturally also be a composition of Boolean expressions. In order to combine such expressions, SQUEAK provides the boolean selectors |, or:, &, and:, not, xor:, ==> and eqv:.

The selectors | and or: represent the logical operation *or*, the disjunction that we have already encountered in the solutions to exercises. Let us recall that the logical operation:

A or B

returns true if at least one of the arguments *A* or *B* is true. The difference between the binary message | and the keyword message or: first lies on the fact that or: takes as argument a block (with no argument) and | takes as argument a Boolean expression. Thus, the following two expressions:

```
true | false
true or:  [false]
```

return true, since the receiver, therefore, at least one of the arguments is (true). Another difference is that the binary message | evaluates in all cases its argument, while the keyword message or: only evaluates the argument block *if necessary*, that is to say: if the receiver is false, since only in this case the truth value of the whole expression depends on that argument. For example, the expression:

```
true or:  [Transcript show:  'laziness'; cr. true]
```

returns true but outputs nothing in the Transcript, since the truth value of this disjunction has already been determined by the receiver and it is, therefore, not necessary to evaluate the argument block. On the contrary, the expression:

```
false or:  [Transcript show:  'laziness'; cr. true]
```

also returns true (since the value of the argument block is the value of the last expression of the expression sequence composing the block), but it also outputs in

---

70 This error indication is somewhat strange: normally, SQUEAK should answer something like "ifTrue: message not found", since the message ifTrue: is neither defined in the SmallInteger, class, nor in any of its superclasses. Let us take this as an indication that SQUEAK compiles these messages in a *very* optimized manner, leading in fact to not sending that message at all.

the Transcript the string "laziness", since the truth value of this disjunction can only be determined after the evaluation of the argument block.

If we evaluate the following expression:

```
true | [Transcript show: 'laziness'; cr. true] value
```

although the receiver already determines the truth value (true), SQUEAK outputs in the Transcript the string "laziness". The message or: is called a *lazy or* or a *lazy disjunction*, where *lazy* refers to the evaluation economy[71].

The binary message & and the keyword message and: represent the logical operator *and*, i.e. a conjunction. A conjunction:

$$A \ and \ B$$

is true only if the two arguments *A* and *B* are true. As for the disjunction operators, & always evaluates its argument, while and: only evaluates the argument if necessary, that is to say: if the receiver is true. If the receiver is false, we know that the whole conjunction is also false. and: is the *lazy and* or the *lazy conjunction*.

For completeness: the operator not is the negation or inversion operator, the transmission true not returns false and the dispatch false not returns true.

The message ==> is the logical implication. An implication is false, false in SMALLTALK, only if the receiver is true and the argument is false. For this message, the argument must be a block and it is implemented in the Boolean class as:

```
==> aBlock
    self not or: [aBlock value]
```

It is, therefore, a lazy implication.

Both remaining composition messages of Boolean expressions, eqv: and xor:, take a Boolean expression as an argument. Therefore, these are non-lazy messages. The message eqv: represents the logical equivalence operator, which in SMALLTALK corresponds to a simple test of identity between receiver and argument. The message xor: represents the exclusive disjunction operator, the *exclusive or*, the *either one or the other, but not both at the same time*. It returns true if the receiver and the argument are different. The implementation in the Boolean class of these two messages is:

---

71 Naturally, this *only if necessary* evaluation is entirely due to the fact that the argument is a block, and the value of a block is that block itself (or that context block).

```
eqv: booleanExpression
    self == booleanExpression

xor: booleanExpression
    (self == booleanExpression) not
```

4.6.2. Recursive control structures

Recursion is the nicest way of performing repetitions. Let us start with an example, a program that counts in reverse: from a certain integer to zero:

```
countdownTimer
    self < 0
        ifTrue: [Transcript cr; show: 'finished']
        ifFalse: [Transcript cr; show: c.
                 (self - 1) countdownTimer]
```

Figure 4.30 shows the `Transcript` after the transmission 5 `countdownTimer`. It can be clearly seen that the repetition is syntactically realized by the transmission of this same message not to the one that is being defined, `countdownTimer`, but to another receiver.

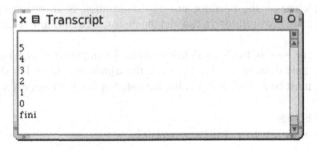

Figure 4.30. *Effect of the dispatch 5* `countdownTimer`

Every recursive definition follows the same principle, in three steps:

1) determine when there is nothing left to do. Here, it is the case if the receiver is less than zero;

2) perform the actual job during each repetition. Here, it is outputting of the value of the counter in the `Transcript`;

3) perform the same but with a new receiver, which results from the transformation of the current receiver. This transformation should be such that if it is repeated a finite number of times, a receiver satisfying point 1 will be reached.

If we track, follow step-by-step, the resulting actions of the transmission:

```
5 countdownTimer
```

we obtain the following series of actions:

1) The integer 5 receives the message countdownTimer.

2) Since 5 is not less than 0, SQUEAK outputs 5 in the Transcript and sends the message countdownTimer to the integer 4.

3) Since 4 is not less than 0, SQUEAK outputs 4 in the Transcript and sends the message countdownTimer to the integer 3.

4) Since 3 is not less than 0, SQUEAK outputs 3 in the Transcript and sends the message countdownTimer to the integer 2.

5) Since 2 is not less than 0, SQUEAK outputs 2 in the Transcript and sends the message countdownTimer to the integer 1.

6) Since 1 is not less than 0, SQUEAK outputs 1 in the Transcript and sends the message countdownTimer to the integer 0.

7) Since 0 is not less than 0, SQUEAK outputs 0 in the Transcript and sends the message countdownTimer to the integer -1.

8) Since -1 is less than 0, SQUEAK outputs the string finished and, because there is nothing more to do, SQUEAK returns the integer 5, the initial receiver of the message countdownTimer.

It is very simple: there is just a succession of transmissions, some using the same selector.

Let us then slightly change our program into the following version:

```
counts
    self <= 0
        ifTrue: []
        ifFalse: [(self - 1) counts].
    Transcript cr; show: self
```

which can be simplified as:

```
counts
    self > 0
        ifTrue: [(self - 1) counts].
    Transcript cr; show: self
```

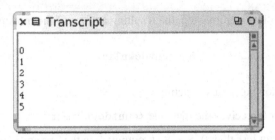

Figure 4.31. *The effect of the dispatch* 5 `counts`

Figure 4.31 shows the effect of the dispatch 5 `counts`.

What happened? Let us have a close look at this new method definition. Naturally, it is also a recursive method since it kicks off a transmission of `counts` within the definition of the method `counts`. Here, we have – in some way – *factored out* the outputs in the `Transcript`. But, this is not the main difference, since we could well have also factored out the outputs in the method `countdownTimer` as in the version below:

```
countdownTimerBis
    Transcript cr; show: self.
    self > 0
        ifTrue: [(self - 1) countdownTimerBis]
```

where the method `countdownTimerBis` almost behaves as the method `countdownTimer`[72].

The main difference can immediately be seen if we follow step-by-step the execution step of a dispatch. The stack trace of the execution of the dispatch 5 `counts` is thus given below:

1) The integer 5 receives the message `counts`.

2) Since 5 is greater than 0, SQUEAK sends the message `counts` to the integer 4. Let us remind ourselves that after the return of this transmission, the value of `self`, 5, should also be displayed in the `Transcript`.

3) Since 4 is greater than 0, SQUEAK sends the message `counts` to the integer 3. Let us remind ourselves that after the return of this transmission, the value of `self`, 4, should also be displayed in the `Transcript`.

---

72 The only difference is that `countdownTimer` outputs at the very end the chain `finished`, which the method `countdownTimerBis` does not do.

4) Since 3 is greater than 0, SQUEAK sends the message counts to the integer 2. Let us remind ourselves that after the return of this transmission, the value of self, 3, should also be displayed in the Transcript.

5) Since 2 is greater than 0, SQUEAK sends the message counts to the integer 1. Let us remind ourselves that after the return of this transmission, the value of self, 2, should also be displayed in the Transcript.

6) Since 1 is greater than 0, SQUEAK sends the message counts to the integer 0. Let us remind ourselves that after the return of this transmission, the value of self, 1, should also be displayed in the Transcript.

7) Since 0 is not greater than 0, SQUEAK exits from the expression ifTrue: with the value nil executes, in sequence, the next transmission, which results in the display of the value of self, 0, in the Transcript. SQUEAK has completed the transmission 0 counts.

8) SQUEAK can resume the transmission 1 counts with the display of the value self, 1, in the Transcript. SQUEAK has completed the transmission 1 counts.

9) SQUEAK can resume the transmission 2 counts with the display of the value self, 2, in the Transcript. SQUEAK has completed the transmission 2 counts.

10) SQUEAK can resume the transmission 3 counts with the display of the value self, 3, in the Transcript. SQUEAK has completed the transmission 3 counts.

11) SQUEAK can resume the transmission 4 counts with the display of the value self, 4, in the Transcript. SQUEAK has completed the transmission 4 counts.

12) SQUEAK can resume the transmission 5 counts with the display of the value self, 5, in the Transcript. SQUEAK has completed the transmission 5 counts. Since there is nothing more to do, SQUEAK ends by returning the value of self, therefore the integer 5.

The main difference between the method countdownTimer (and countdownTimerBis) and the method counts is that the former method performs all the computation as and when the successive recursive transmissions are sent, while the latter method uses the recursive messages to compute the data (the receivers) that will then, after their computation, be used again for other operations. It is as if the method countdownTimer was doing its job exclusively during the *descent* of the recursive transmissions and did nothing more during the returns of the transmissions, while the method counts is doing part of the computation during the descent and another during the returns, the ascent, of the recursive transmissions.

Graphically, these two recursive executions can be represented as in Figures 4.32 and 4.33.

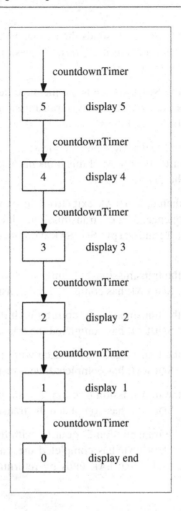

Figure 4.32. *Graphical stack trace of the execution of the dispatch 5* `countdownTimer`

Please carefully study both recursion types. Have you noticed that there is an inversion in the traversal? We will return to this later. For now, let us just admire the natural beauty and the computational power of this way of organizing repetitions, *loops*: as will be discussed below, any other type of repetition is defined trough procedures which are methods using either one of these two recursion approaches.

4.6.3. *Iterative control structures*

In this section we will look at iterative control structures on blocks, natural numbers and collections.

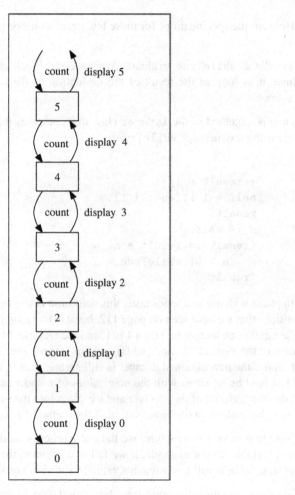

Figure 4.33. *Graphical stack trace of the execution of the dispatch* 5 `counts`

4.6.3.1. *Conditional structures on blocks*

We have just seen the usefulness of blocks to define conditional expressions to implement lazy evaluations and to define recursive procedures.

The `BlockContext` class also provides a set of methods allowing us to conditionally repeat a receiver block. In SQUEAK, these are the messages `whileTrue` and `whileTrue:`, its negative counterparts `whileFalse` and `whileFalse:`, also `doWhileFalse:`, `doWhileTrue:` and `repeat`.

Here are the specifications for those few iteration messages of the `BlockContext` class:

1) *aBlock* `whileTrue` evaluates the receiver block *aBlock* and continues to evaluate it as long as the result of the evaluation of the receiver block returns the value `true`.

Here is a method of the `Integer` class that computes the factorial of the receiver integer using the message `whileTrue`:

```
fact
    | result n |
    self < 1 ifTrue: [^1].
    result := 1.
    n := self.
    [result := result * n. n := n - 1.
        n > 0] whileTrue.
    ^result
```

In phase with my aesthetics taste, this definition is less beautiful than the recursive definitions that we have seen on page 112, but it is more simply computed. It says that the factorial of an integer less than 1 is 1, and the factorial of any other integer n is the product of the `result` obtained so far and this integer; then n should be decremented by 1, and if the new obtained number is still greater than 0, then the evaluation of the block should be *repeated* with the new values of n and `result`. Otherwise, `result` contains the factorial of the receiver and we can return the value of this variable as the result of the evaluation of the activation of the method `fact`.

Note that in such a structure, we have to explicitly modify the value of the loop control variable. In our example, if we fail to decrement the variable n, the loop will never stop, since n will never reach a value less than or equal to zero.

SQUEAK significantly optimizes the compilation of transmissions that use the message `whileTrue`. Here is the bytecode program[73] generated by the SQUEAK compiler for our method `fact`:

---

73 In order to see the bytecode program that SQUEAK generates for a method, just open a class browser, define here a method composed of only the expression you want to see how it compiles, compile this method (always with an "Alt+s" or the entry `accept` from the context menu) and then click on in the middle right button, where it is marked `source` and there select the entry `bytecode`.

```
 5 <70> self                      18 <68> popIntoTemp: 0
 6 <76> pushConstant: 1           19 <11> pushTemp: 1
 7 <B2> send: <                   20 <76> pushConstant: 1
 8 <99> jumpFalse: 11             21 <B1> send: -
 9 <76> pushConstant: 1           22 <69> popIntoTemp: 1
10 <7C> returnTop                 23 <11> pushTemp: 1
11 <76> pushConstant: 1           24 <75> pushConstant: 0
12 <68> popIntoTemp: 0            25 <B3> send: >
13 <70> self                      26 <99> jumpFalse: 29
14 <69> popIntoTemp: 1            27 <A3 F2> jumpTo: 15
15 <10> pushTemp: 0               29 <10> pushTemp: 0
16 <11> pushTemp: 1               30 <7C> returnTop
17 <B8> send: *
```

The evaluation part of the receiver block and the transmission of the iteration message whileTrue is between line 15 and line 27. It is clear that the optimization even fully eliminates the transmission of the message whileTrue: there is no line that activates a send:[74] with this message as an argument.

If SQUEAK was not providing the method whileTrue, we could have recursively defined it in the BlockContext class as:

```
whileTrue
        self value ifTrue: [self whileTrue]
```

2) *aBlock* whileTrue: *anotherBlock* evaluates the receiver block *aBlock* and, if this evaluation returns false, SQUEAK moves to the next transmission. On the contrary, if the evaluation returns true the argument block *anotherBlock* is also evaluated to then start over with the evaluation of the receiver block.

Using the message whileTrue: we can rewrite our method fact as:

```
fact
    | result n |
    self < 1 ifTrue: [^1]
    result := 1.
    n := self.
    [n > 0] whileTrue:
            [result := result * n. n := n - 1].
    ^result
```

---

74 send: is the bytecode instruction for sending the message given as argument. Thus, the instruction send: < from line 7 sends the message < to the object self, stacked in line 5, with the argument 1, stacked in line 6.

This second iterative writing is clearly easier to read. We can translate whileTrue: in: as long as the receiver block is true, compute *anotherBlock*. Like in the code using the selector whileTrue, we naturally must always ensure that the loop control variable is updated in such a way that the test receiver block is evaluated to false after a finite number of iterations. Otherwise, we will write infinite loops[75].

If SQUEAK had not already defined the method whileTrue:, we could have recursively redefined it in the BlockContext class as:

```
whileTrue: aBlock
    self value
        ifTrue: [aBlock value. self whileTrue: aBlock]
```

Please also note that SQUEAK compiles this version using whileTrue: in a sequence of bytecode instructions very similar to that obtained using whileTrue. As it can be seen below, the difference lies mainly in the order of the instructions:

```
 5 <70> self                  18 <AC 0A> jumpFalse: 30
 6 <76> pushConstant: 1       20 <10> pushTemp: 0
 7 <B2> send: <               21 <11> pushTemp: 1
 8 <99> jumpFalse: 11         22 <B8> send: *
 9 <76> pushConstant: 1       23 <68> popIntoTemp: 0
10 <7C> returnTop             24 <11> pushTemp: 1
11 <76> pushConstant: 1       25 <76> pushConstant: 1
12 <68> popIntoTemp: 0        26 <B1> send: -
13 <70> self                  27 <69> popIntoTemp: 1
14 <69> popIntoTemp: 1        28 <A3 F1> jumpTo: 15
15 <11> pushTemp: 1           30 <10> pushTemp: 0
16 <75> pushConstant: 0       31 <7C> returnTop
17 <B3> send: >
```

3) *aBlock* whileFalse and *aBlock* whileFalse: *anotherBlock* are, already by their names, clearly the counterparts of whileTrue and whileTrue:. The only difference is in the repetition condition: if whileTrue repeats the evaluation of a block as long as its evaluation returns true, whileFalse repeats the evaluation of a block as long as its evaluation returns false.

---

75 An infinite loop is inherently not always something undesirable. Many programs *should* be infinite, such as operating systems, interpreter (like our SQUEAK interpreter, whence a specific dispatch should be activated to exit), or programs that control industrial processes. It is just that, at our level, we want programs that complete after a fixed number of loops.

Our example method, fact, can be rewritten using these two selectors as:

```
fact
    | result n |
    self < 1 ifTrue: [^1]
    result := 1.
    n := self.
    [result := result * n. n := n - 1.
        n <= 0] whileFalse.
    ^result
```

and

```
fact
    | result n |
    self < 1 ifTrue: [^1]
    result := 1.
    n := self.
    [n <= 0] whileFalse:
            [result := result * n. n := n - 1].
    ^result
```

4) *aBlock* doWhileTrue: *aConditionalBlock*
aBlock doWhileFalse: *aConditionalBlock*
where doWhileTrue: evaluates the receiver block *aBlock* once, and then again as
many times as the evaluation of the block *aConditionalBlock* returns true, while
doWhileFalse: repeats the evaluation of the receiver block *aBlock* as long as the
evaluation of the block *aConditionalBlock* returns false.

All these methods are similar. The choice of one of them depends more on the way
we conceptualize the problem than the reflections on the performance or the efficiency
of the different methods.

Using the method doWhileTrue:, our method fact can be written as:

```
fact
    | result n |
    self < 1 ifTrue: [^1]
    result := 1.
    n := self.
    [result := result * n. n := n - 1]
        doWhileTrue: [n > 0].
    ^result
```

This method is compiled without optimization, i.e. without hiding the transmission of the method, as SQUEAK does for the four iteration methods above. For the interested readers, here is the bytecode generated by the SQUEAK compiler for our latest version of fact:

```
9  <70> self                       28 <11> pushTemp: 1
10 <76> pushConstant: 1            29 <76> pushConstant: 1
11 <B2> send: <                    30 <B1> send: -
12 <99> jumpFalse: 15              31 <81 41> storeIntoTemp: 1
13 <76> pushConstant: 1            33 <7D> blockReturn
14 <7C> returnTop                  34 <89> pushThisContext:
15 <76> pushConstant: 1            35 <75> pushConstant: 0
16 <68> popIntoTemp: 0             36 <C8> send: blockCopy:
17 <70> self                       37 <A4 04> jumpTo: 43
18 <69> popIntoTemp: 1             39 <11> pushTemp: 1
19 <89> pushThisContext:           40 <75> pushConstant: 0
20 <75> pushConstant: 0            41 <B3> send: >
21 <C8> send: blockCopy:           42 <7D> blockReturn
22 <A4 0A> jumpTo: 34              43 <E0> send: doWhileTrue:
24 <10> pushTemp: 0                44 <87> pop
25 <11> pushTemp: 1                45 <10> pushTemp: 0
26 <B8> send: *                    46 <7C> returnTop
27 <68> popIntoTemp: 0
```

Here is a good example of non-optimized code generation. Have you seen the sending of the message doWhileTrue: in line 43?

Naturally, the method doWhileFalse: is (still) the counterpart of doWhileTrue: with a reversal of the exit test. doWhileFalse: can be defined, in the BlockContext class as:

```
doWhileFalse: aConditionalBlock
    | result |
    [result := self value.
     aConditionalBlock value] whileFalse.
    ^result
```

5) *aBlock* repeat Finally, the last iteration method that SQUEAK provides for instances of the BlockContext class. This method is simply defined as:

```
repeat
    [self value. true] whileTrue.
```

Do you see what it does?

It computes the value of the receiver block *aBlock* and, since the value of the argument block for whileTrue is always true (since the last expression of the block is true), without being concerned at all about the result, it continues indefinitely to compute the value of the receiver block of the message repeat. This clearly appears to be an infinite loop. It is an infinite loop.

The only way to get out is that the receiver block *aBlock* contains an explicit exit instruction, the instruction "∧", as it is done in the following version of fact:

```
fact
    | result n |
    self < 1 ifTrue: [^1]
    result := 1.
    n := self.
    [result := result * n. n := n - 1.
        n > 0 ifFalse: [^result]] repeat.
```

4.6.3.2. *Enumerative structures on integers*

The Integer class defines a method allowing us to repeat a block a fixed number of times, this is the method timesRepeat:. The abstract class Number also provides a couple of methods allowing us to evaluate repeatedly an argument block. These are the two messages to:do: and to:by:do:. Let us thus examine each of these messages.

1) *integer* timesRepeat: *aBlock* evaluates the argument block *integer* times and returns the *integer* receiver. It is defined in the Integer class using the message whileTrue::

```
timesRepeat: aBlock
    | counter |
    counter := 1.
    [counter <= self]
        whileTrue:
            [aBlock value.
            counter := counter + 1]
```

Naturally, we could also have defined it more elegantly as[76]:

```
timesRepeat: aBlock
    self > 0
    ifTrue: [aBlock value.
            self - 1 timesRepeat: aBlock]
```

---

[76] Let us note that the bytecode programs generated for these two versions of timesRepeat are exactly of the same size. This is due to the beautiful optimization the compiler performs for the transmission of the message whileTrue:.

In order to see how this method can be used, here is an original version of our method fact `fact`:

```
fact
  | result n |
  self < 1 ifTrue: [^1]
  result := 1.
  n := self.
  self timesRepeat:
    [result := result * n. n := n - 1].
  ^result
```

2) *integer* `to:` *anotherInteger* `do:` *aBlockWith1Argument* evaluates the argument block *aBlockWith1Argument* for each of the numbers between *integer* and *anotherInteger*. For instance, the transmission:

```
1 to:  5 do:  [:e | Transcript cr; show:  e]
```

outputs in the `Transcript` the series of numbers 1, 2, 3, 4, 5, one number per line. The dispatch

```
(1 to:  5) do:  [:e | Transcript cr; show:  e]
```

outputs exactly the same, the sequence of integers from 1 to 5, but the effect is fundamentally different, since in this second version we send the message `do:` to the result of the transmission `1 to: 5`. The latter transmission creates an *interval*, an instance of the `Interval` class, which will then receive the message `do:`. We will return to it in the next section. For now let us just keep in mind that the message `to:` and the message `to:do:` are very different. In order to convince you of this difference, let us look at the bytecode generated for each of these expressions.

The method `to:do:` is implemented in the `Number` class as follows:

```
to: stop do: aBlock
  | nextValue |
  nextValue := self.
  [nextValue <= stop]
    whileTrue:
      [unBlock value: nextValue.
       nextValue := nextValue + 1]
```

Note that the receiver number should be less than the argument `stop` for a repetition to take place.

Our famous method `fact` computing the factorial of the receiver can be rewritten using the message `to:do:` as:

```
fact
    | result |
    self < 1 ifTrue: [^1]
    result := 1.
    1 to: self do:
    [:n | result := result * n]
    ^result
```

3) *initalNumber* to: *stopNumber* by: *step* do: *aBlockWith1Argument*
evaluates the block *aBlockWith1Argument* for each of the numbers obtained by
starting with *initalNumber* and incrementing this number by *step* until *stopNumber*
is reached. For example, the dispatch:

```
1 to: 5 by: 2 do: [:e | Transcript cr; show: e]
```

outputs in the Transcript the series of numbers 1, 3, 5, one number per line. And if
the argument of by:, *step*, is 3, then there will only be the display of number 1 and 4.
In a slightly heavier way, our function fact can, therefore, also be written as:

```
fact
    | result |
    self < 1 ifTrue: [^1]
    result := 1.
    1 to: self by: 1 do:
    [:n | result := result * n]
    ^result
```

What then does the method foo of the Integer class below computes[77]:

```
foo
    | r |
    r := 0.
    1 to: self by: 2 do: |:e| r := r + e].
    ^r
```

4.6.3.3. *Enumerative structures on collections*

Finally, all the subclasses of the Collection class provide the methods that
traverse it in order to allow the access to each of the elements. These are naturally
iterative methods, i.e. methods that iterate over all the elements of a given collection.
We have already seen the majority, either in Chapter 4 (see section 3.1), or in the
section where we presented the special collections that are the arrays, the instances of

---

[77] This expression naturally computes the sum of odd integers in the interval $[1, self]$ which is
equal to $\left(\frac{self}{2}\right)^2$.

the `Array` class (section 4.3.5.4 on page 95 onwards), or also in the solutions to the exercises (section A1.3 on page 351 onwards and on page 361 onwards). Let us also recall that we gave the full tree of subclasses of the `Collection` class on page 41. This is the moment to return to it if you no longer recall its subclasses, nor its messages `do:`, `reject:`, `collect:` or `inject:into:`.

Here, we will just recall what are the most important iterators traversing collections. These are the selectors `do:`, `with:do:`, `select:`, `reject:`, `collect:`, `detect:`, `detect:ifnone:` and `inject:into:`.

As usual, we will give the behavioral specification of the method, some examples and a possible SQUEAK implementation of the method. Each of these implementations can be seen in two ways: either as a prototype example of programming in SMALLTALK or as a *formal* specification of this same method. Personally, I consider a program written in a high-level abstraction language, and SMALLTALK is certainly one, always as a formal specification of the activity implemented by the program, resolutely enrolling myself in the operational semantics line of thought.

Digression 3

It is an old debate among computer scientists to determine the semantics of a program. Several schools of thought coexist and confront each other from time to time.

There are those who want to see computer science as a subdiscipline of mathematics, for instance see Edgar Dijkstra [DIJ 76] or Dana Scott [SCO 70]. Their aim is to understand the programs by abstracting the algorithms used to implement functionalities, in order to define them exclusively in terms of sets (tuples) transformed by pure and abstract *functions*. It is slightly the opposite of what had been done by Alonzo Church [CHU 41] who had completely abstracted the tuples of data by uniformly transforming everything in functions, algorithms. But, the idea that the functions (the functionalities performed by algorithms) would be independent of the ways by which they are calculated, although this is true for mathematical functions, can be very fragile in computer science. Even if it was true just for mechanical constraints.

Let it be said, a function in computer science field can exhibit unconventional behavior in mathematics, for instance the stack *overflows* or memory overflows (those famous "ill memory reference – core dumped" well known by every Unix programmer). The lattice theory presented by Scott is very beautiful, but I think it only works on idealized mathematical objects. Even Scott has noticed it, since he has said that his way of representing the program semantics is consistent with human understanding, but that the operational approach should not be ignored because, as he says, machines on which the designed programs must run are not able to work with such a level of abstraction. All the various mathematical theories on programs are categorized under the term *denotational semantic*.

Assuming that this beautiful idea to represent programs as mathematical entities that can be manipulated with proven mathematical methods has very serious limitations, we still have to present the other standard approach to the formalization of program semantics: the *operational semantics* which, in its simplest version, is the description of an interpreter – or an abstract machine, such as Peter Landin's SECD-machine [LAN 64] – for a specific language, followed by a set of rewriting (or state transitions [PLO 81]) rules describing the effect of each of the instructions (commands, procedures and functions) of the language we wish to formalize. The advantage of not describing abstract functions that realize the correspondence between the elements of a domain with the elements from another domain, but describing the computations performed for the realization of a function, of an instruction or a procedure, also allows us to include physical constraints, memory or structures size limitations. This then allows us to stay much closer to the actual computation, as it is performed by a computer. This may appear less elegant, but in any case it will be more in line with what we, programmers, do.

But let us return to our iterators:

1) *aCollection*   do: *aBlockWith1Argument*   evaluates   the   block *aBlockWith1Argument* for each of the elements of the collection *aCollection*.

This message do: is known to all collections, the sets (implemented by the classes Set and Bag) as well as the dictionaries (the Dictionary class), the arrayed collections (all subclasses of the ArrayedCollection class), the lists (LinkedList) and also the ordered or sorted collections (these are instances of the classes OrderedCollection and SortedCollection) and the intervals (instances of the Interval class).

This message has already been used in the AnimalHabitat class in order to display the set of animals living in a given habitat (see exercise 3 on page 357).

Here are some usage examples of this method:

– 'hello world' do: [:c | Transcript show: c asUppercase] sends the message do: to a string, an instance of the String class, with a block argument stating: display in upper case each of the characters that compose the receiver. This dispatch, therefor, outputs HELLO WORLD in the Transcript.

|s| s:=0. #(100 200 300 400 500) do: [:n | s := s+n]. s

the execution of this expression will take each of the elements of the receiver array and will add it to the local variable s. Since we have initialized the variable s to zero, this dispatch of do: therefore computes the sum of the receiver array elements. The result will be the value of s, the integer 1500:

```
|n| n:=0. 'hello' do: [:c | n:= n+1]. n
```

Clearly, this last expression computes the size of the receiver string of the message do: This is how is implemented the message size in the Collection class.

– |s| s:=0. (0 to: 500 by: 100) do: [:n| x := x+n]. s computes exactly the same as the second example above, therefore $\sum_{i=0}^{5} 100 * i$. If earlier we had used an array listing the different numbers whose sum we were computing, here the message to:by: creates an Interval that yields the different numbers as and when we need them in evaluating the argument block of the message do:. It is a version using much less memory space.

The message do: is defined in several subclasses of the Collection class. In the SequenceableCollection class, it is defined as:

```
do: aBlock
    1 to self size do:
        [:index| aBlock value: (self at: index)]
```

taking advantage of the message to:do: of the Number class that we saw in the previous section.

This same message is defined in the Interval class as:

```
do: aBlock
    | aValue |
    aValue := start.
    step < 0

            ifTrue: [[stop <= aValue]
                whileTrue:
                    [aBlock value: aValue.
                    aValue := aValue + step]]
            ifFalse: [[stop >= aValue]
                whileTrue:
                    [aBlock value: aValue.
                    aValue := aValue + step]]
```

In order to understand this method, let us know that every instance of the Interval class has three instance variables:

– start, which contains the first number of the interval. So, if we create the interval via the transmission 1 to: 5, the variable start will be equal to 1.

– stop, which will contain the last number of the interval. So, for the interval created above, the value of the variable stop will be 5.

– step, which will contain the increment by which we move from a number of the interval to the next. Also, for our example, interval 1 to: 5, the instance variable stop will have as value the integer 1, the default increment value. We have already seen that we can create intervals with arbitrary increment by using the message to: by:, as in 0 to: 500 by: 100 where the instance variable step is initialized to the integer 100.

Our method Interval»do:, therefore, very explicitly computes each of the elements of the interval: even if the interval is huge, with no space – except the one for the three instance variables – is required.

To finish our studies on the implementations of the message do:, let us examine the version of do: of the LinkedList class, a class that delivers linked structures, similar to the lists of Lisp [WER 89], as shown in Figure 4.34.

A LinkedList is composed of instances of the Link class, where each Link points to its successor, thus allowing us to go from one element, from one Link to the next. This pointer to the next Link is accessible by the unary message nextLink understood by any Link instance. In order to traverse this structure, it is, therefore, sufficient to know its beginning, its first Link, which is kept in the instance variable firstLink, and its last element, which is kept in the instance variable lastLink of each instance of the LinkedList (see Figure 4.34). Naturally, the transmission lastLink nextLink cannot answer with the next element: there is no more. In this case, the message nextLink returns nil. The method do: of the LinkedList class is then:

```
do: aBlock
    | aLink |
    aLink := firstLink.
    [aLink == nil] whileFalse:
        [aBlock value: aLink.
         aLink := aLink nextLink]
```

We have seen three very distinct implementations of the message do:: the first traverses the elements of a collection by accessing to the successive indices, the second traverses the elements by computing them and the third traverses them by following pointers from one element to the next. This is indeed normal since the structures of these three collections are very different. We, the developers of the SMALLTALK system, have great need of this knowledge; it allows us to evolve the system. But we, ordinary programmers in SMALLTALK, do not need to know it if all that interests us is to have at our disposal a message to traverse a collection. The fact that it is the *same* selector that allows the traversal of any collection would make it easy: no need to know the type of structure on which one works at a given time. Conceptually, it is the *traversal* that interests us, not its implementation.

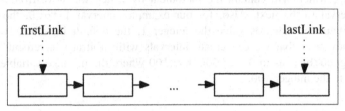

Figure 4.34. *Structure of a* `LinkedList`

This feature to be able to use the same name for computations that are computationally different but conceptually identical is a seductive force of object-oriented languages, and particularly of SMALLTALK[78].

2) *aCollection* `with:` *anotherCollection* `do:` *aBinaryBlock* In the initial SQUEAK system, this message is only recognized by the instances of the `SequenceableCollection`. It evaluates *aBinaryBlock* by traversing, in parallel, the collection receiver of the message and collection argument of `with:`, *anotherCollection*. These two collections must be of the same size.

Here is an usage example:

```
| str |
str := ''.
'Hello' with: 'World' do:
     [:x :y | str := str, x asString, y asString].
str
```

which returns the string `'HWeolrllod'` obtained by concatenating the first character of the receiver with the first character of the argument of `with:`, the second character

---

78 SMALLTALK differs from other object-oriented languages such as C++ [STR 87], for example, in that it dynamically determines - that is to say, when receiving the message - what procedure (which method) must be run. In other languages methods of the same name can be defined, but when using it the class of the receiver should be known and the class of the method to be activated should be explicitly mentioned. It's less beautiful.

of the receiver with the second character of the argument of with:, and so on, each time taking a character in each collection.

All this is easily understood if we look at the implementation of the method with:do: in the SequenceableCollection class:

```
with: otherCollection do: twoArgBlock
    otherCollection size = self size
        ifFalse:
        [self error:
            'collections must be the same size'].
    1 to: self size do:
        [:index |
        twoArgBlock value: (self at: index)
                value: (otherCollection at: index)]
```

This method begins by comparing the size of the two collections, the receiver and the first argument, to yield an error message, so to open a debugger window, if both have different sizes. Otherwise, for each of the indices of the receiver collection it sends to the argument do:, twoArgBlock, the element that is at the index-th position in the receiver collection, and the corresponding element in the argument collection.

Inspired by this example, we can easily write a method with:do: that traverses two *intervals* in parallel. For this, a method should just be added to the Interval class like the one given below. In fact, it follows the same algorithm: it takes a two arguments block receiving the corresponding elements of both intervals receiver and argument, if the intervals are of the same size.

Because we need to compute these successive elements, we need the initial element of the receiver collection, which is accessible via the instance variable start, and the initial element of the argument collection. The message first, sent to an interval, returns the contents of the instance variable start of the receiver interval. We also need the increment of both intervals for the receiver of the message with:do:. We directly have access to it in the variable step, and the message increment returns the contents of the variable step of the receiver. Then, in the argument block of do:. We can use these values to compute the next elements of both collections. So, here this method:

```
with: anInterval do: aBlock
    | aValue otherValue otherStep|
    self size = anInterval size
        ifFalse:
        [self error: 'intervals must be the same size'].
    aValue := start.
```

```
otherValue:= anInterval first.
otherStep:=anInterval increment.
step < 0
    ifTrue:
        [[stop <= aValue]
            whileTrue:
                [aBlock value: aValue value: otherValue.
                aValue := aValue + step.
                otherValue:= otherValue+otherStep]]
    ifFalse: [[stop >= aValue]
            whileTrue:
                [aBlock value: aValue value: otherValue.
                aValue := aValue + step.
                otherValue:= otherValue+otherStep]]
```

Armed with this method, we can then traverse two intervals in parallel like in the expression:

```
(1 to: 5) with: (6 to: 10)
        do: [:x :y|
            Transcript show: x + y; cr]
```

which outputs in the Transcript the sums of the elements of the interval (1 to: 5) and of the interval (6 to: 10), therefore, the integers 7, 9, 11, 13, 15, one number per line.

The definition of the method with:do: of the above Interval class can be made slightly easier, if we do not use instances of the Interval class but instances of its one and single subclass, the StreamInterval class.

What is a *stream*[79]? It is an object which yields as and when requested the successive elements that compose it. The most important messages that a *stream* understands are first, which yields the first element of a *stream*, and next which yields the next element. A *stream*, therefore, has a memory and always recalls the last item that it has yielded. This memory is materialized for the instances of StreamInterval class in the variable instance current. This variable is always associated with the last element generated. As we cannot return toward the waters that have sunk along a river, in a *stream* we cannot, normally, return to the elements that have already been generated by the *stream*.

The StreamInterval class, therefore, represents intervals behaving like *streams* yielding their elements through the messages first and next. We will return to this

---

79 The English word *stream* can mean *river* or, in computer science, *flow*.

notion of *stream* later on: it is particularly important in everything related to inputs/outputs of programs. For now, let us just examine the version of the method with:do: for the instances of these stream-intervals. Here it is:

```
with: anInterval do: aBlock
    | aValue otherValue |
    self size = anInterval size
        ifFalse:
            [self error: 'intervals must be the same size'].
    aValue := start.
    otherValue:= anInterval first.
    step < 0
        ifTrue: [[stop <= aValue]
            whileTrue:
                [aBlock value: aValue value: otherValue.
                aValue := self next.
                otherValue:= anInterval next]]

        ifFalse: [[stop >= aValue]
            whileTrue:
                [aBlock value: aValue value: otherValue.
                aValue := self next.
                otherValue:= anInterval next]]
```

Since the computation of the next element can be delegated to the same interval, we no longer need the temporary variable otherStep.

We can also start our intervals by a first additional element, which will be ignored thereafter. For instance, instead of defining an interval 1 to: 5 we could generate the interval 0 to: 5. If we had done that, we would no longer need a special treatment for the first item, so we can optimize our program using only the message next. This would give the new version, much more compact, as follows:

```
withOpt: anInterval do: aBlock
    self size = anInterval size
        ifFalse:
            [self error: 'intervals must be the same size'].
    step < 0
        ifTrue: [[actuel > stop]
            whileTrue:
                [aBlock value: self next
                        value: anInterval next]]
        ifFalse: [[actuel < stop]
```

```
whileTrue:
    [aBlock value: self next
           value: anInterval next]]
```

This is a considerably shorter version which, moreover, no longer uses any temporary variable.

All that remains to do is to find some methods to easily create instances of the StreamInterval class. This class already provides both methods from:to: and from:to:by:. Here is the latter method:

```
from: startInteger to: stopInteger by: stepInteger
    | aux |
    aux := self new
                setFrom: startInteger
                to: stopInteger
                by: stepInteger.
    aux actuel: startInteger.
    ^ aux
```

As for regular intervals, the message setFrom:to:by: initializes the three instance variables start, stop and step. The instance variable current is specific to the StreamInterval class and contains at any moment the last computed element, that is to say, the current element of the interval.

In order to create a StreamInterval that only uses the message next, in order to have access to its elements, only, we can add to the Number class the following method streamTo:

```
streamTo: stop
        "Answers a StreamInterval from the receiver to the
                argument, incrementing by 1"
        ^StreamInterval from: self - 1 to: stop by: 1
```

and *voila*.

If we want to create a StreamInterval of the same behavior but with a step different from 1, the following method Number≯streamTo:by: just needs to be defined:

```
streamTo: stop by: step
        "answers a StreamInterval from the receiver to the
                        argument stop, incrementing by step"
        ^StreamInterval from: self - step
                        to: stop
                        by: step
```

There is an additional traversal message for collections where elements are accessible via keys – so for all the collections except the sets (Set and Bag). It is the message keysAndValuesDo:. This message, sent to a collection, takes as argument a two-arguments block: the first will be linked to the key or the index of the current item, the second to the value corresponding to that key or index, hence to the element itself. It traverses the collection by evaluating this two-arguments block for each of the elements of the collection. For instance, the following expression outputs in the Transcript each vowel of the receiver string preceded by its index:

```
'Ceci est un exemple' keysAndValuesDo:
    [:key :value |
        value isVowel
            ifTrue:
                [Transcript cr; show: clef; tab; show: value]]
```

The result of this transmission is shown in Figure 4.35. This expression returns as the value of the receiver of the message keysAndValuesDo:, i.e. of the string Ceci est un exemple.

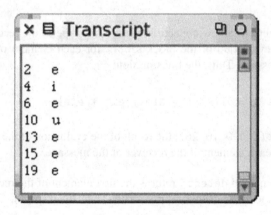

Figure 4.35. *The vowels of* Ceci est un exemple

3) *aCollection* select: *aBlock*
aCollection reject: *aBlock*
aCollection collect: *aBlock*
aCollection detect: *aBlock*
aCollection detect: *aBlock* ifNone: *blockException*

These are the most common collection traversal methods:

– select: returns a collection of the same type as the receiver containing only the elements of the receiver for which the evaluation of *aBlock* gives true. For example, the expression:

```
#(1 -2 3 -4 5) select: [:ele | ele > 0]
```

returns the new array #(1 3 5), the collection of positive elements of the receiver.

– reject: is the complement of select:, that is it returns a collection of the same type as the receiver containing only those elements for which the evaluation of block *aBlock* returns false. Thus, the transmission:

```
#(1 -2 3 -4 5) reject: [:ele | ele > 0]
```

returns the array #(-2 -4), the collection of the receiver elements that are not positive.

– collect: returns a new collection of the same type as the receiver containing the result of the evaluation of the block *aBlock* for each element of the collection receiver of the message. Thus, the transmission:

```
#(1 -2 3 -4 5) collect: [:ele | ele * ele]
```

returns the array #(1 4 9 16 25), the result of the evaluation of the block [:ele | ele * ele] for each element of the receiver of the message.

– Finally, the method detect: returns the first element of the receiver for which the evaluation of the block *aBlock* returns true. Thus, the dispatch:

```
#(1 -2 3 -4 5) detect: [:ele | ele < 0]
```

returns the element -2, the first element of the receiver array less than 0. If none of the elements of the receiver collection matched the condition of the block *aBlock*, SQUEAK stops the processing with an error message indicating that no object is part of the receiver collection.

If one does not want this interruption with an error, the programmer can use the method detect:ifNone: whose second argument, *blockException* explicitly states the value to return if no element matches the condition of the block *aBlock*. Thus, the transmission:

```
#(1 -2 3 -4 5) detect: [:ele | ele > 10]
```

will stop the processing with the error window (let us recall that this is an inspector.) given in Figure 4.36, while the transmission:

```
#(1 -2 3 -4 5) detect: [:ele | ele > 10] ifNone: [nil]
```

returns nil, the value of the block *blockException*. Let us note that the argument *blockException* must be a block without argument.

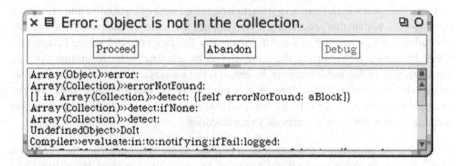

Figure 4.36. *Indication of absence of the searched element*

4.7. Exception handling

Exceptions are events interrupting the normal flow of execution of a program. We have already seen such situations of error that – indeed – interrupt the normal flow of a program. Errors are often thrown by the SMALLTALK virtual machine. However, they can also be intentionally caused by the program, for instance with the transmission of the message error: to any object[80]. This message, which can be sent to any SQUEAK object, does nothing but cause an error, or, as we prefer to say: it throws an exception of the *error* type.

In this section, we will give a brief overview of the methods that SQUEAK provides to adapt what happens during interruptions to our programmatic needs. First, let us note that in SMALLTALK *exceptions* are SMALLTALK *objects*, that can, like any other object, receive messages and answer to received messages. All exceptions correspond to one of the subclass of the abstract class Exception. Exceptions are classes.

---

80 For instance, look at the method newInstance on page 374.

Figure 4.37 on page 177 shows a snippet of the subclasses tree of the Exception class[81]. The most important subclasses can be recognized there: Error[82], with its arithmetic error handling subclass, the ArithmeticError class, the exception for programmed inspection, Halt and exceptions requiring a notification, Notification, with its subclass for warnings, Warning.

4.7.1. *Exceptions handling messages of the* Object *class*

Let us then start by messages throwing exceptions defined in the Object class.

The message error: with a string as argument, throws, as mentioned above, an Error exception which results in interrupting the current computation and opening a debugger in which the programmer can inspect the state of the variables and the execution stack, where he can rectify or modify the program and where he can exit either by completely aborting the computation or, eventually, by resuming with the consideration of his modifications. In general, the message error: is used in areas where the programmer can foresee the possibility of unanticipated data. In our example on page 374, we activate this exception when the nucleotide string contains a character that does not correspond to a nucleotide.

During the program's development, it is often desirable to interrupt the execution of a program in order to check the status of the computation (variable values) and then to resume the computation. To do this, SMALLTALK provides the message halt: which throws the Halt and whose effect is identical to the message error:. We use the message error: to handle errors due to a misuse of the program. error: handles user errors. On the contrary, the message halt: is used to find errors of the programmer, of the program developer. Upon completion of the program, it no longer contains halt: messages, since it should not contain any errors. For instance, we introduced a transmission of the message halt: in the method Integer»fact below:

```
fact
    | res n |
    self < 1
        ifTrue: [^ 1].
    res := 1.
    n := self.

    [self halt: 'in ', self asString, ' fact'.
     res := res * n.
     n := n - 1.
     n > 0] whileTrue.
    ^res
```

---

81 Tabs give the superclass/subclass relationships.
82 Figure 4.36 shows an instance of this exception.

```
Exception #('messageText' 'tag' 'signalContext'
          'handlerContext' 'outerContext')
  Abort #()
  Error #()
    ArithmeticError #()
      FloatingPointException #()
      ZeroDivide #('dividend')
    AttemptToWriteReadOnlyGlobal #()
    BlockCannotReturn #('result' 'deadHome')
    CRCError #()
    EndOfStream #()
    FTPConnectionException #()
    FileStreamException #('fileName')
      CannotDeleteFileException #()
      FileDoesNotExistException #('readOnly')
      FileExistsException #('fileClass')
    InvalidDirectoryError #('pathName')
    InvalidSocketStatusException #()
    MessageNotUnderstood #('message' 'receiver')
    NetworkError #()
      ConnectionClosed #()
      ConnectionRefused #('host' 'port')
      ConnectionTimedOut #()
      NameLookupFailure #('hostName')
      NoNetworkError #()
    NonBooleanReceiver #('object')
    ProtocolClientError #('protocolInstance')
      LoginFailedException #()
      POP3LoginError #()
      TelnetProtocolError #()
    RegexError #()
      RegexCompilationError #()
      RegexMatchingError #()
      RegexSyntaxError #()
  Halt #()
    AssertionFailure #()
    BreakPoint #()
  IllegalResumeAttempt #()
  Notification #()
    ExceptionAboutToReturn #()
    InMidstOfFileinNotification #()
    OutOfScopeNotification #()
    ParserRemovedUnusedTemps #()
    PickAFileToWriteNotification #()
    ProgressNotification #('amount' 'done' 'extra')
    ProgressTargetRequestNotification #()
    Warning #()
      Deprecation #()
  UnhandledError #('exception')
```

Figure 4.37. *Snippet of the hierarchy of the* `Exception` *class*

The execution of the transmission 3 fact is then interrupted with the display of the window in Figure 4.38, which clearly states that we are in a Halt type exception followed by the message we dispatched to this exception. It is substantially the same window as an error window and allows the same interactions: we can continue the computation by clicking on the Proceed button, with the Abandon button we can abandon, so stop, the computation and the Debug button allows to open a debugger. Figure 4.39 shows the debugger with its various panes. In the window of the execution stack, we have selected the method fact, which has led to the output in the code window of that methods definition, with the currently active message in reverse video.

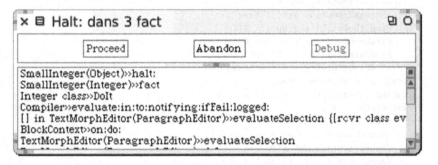

Figure 4.38. *A* Halt *exception window*

In the inspection window of the receiver of the message, we have selected self, the object designated by self, the integer 3, is then displayed on its right. Finally, in the inspection window of the specific context in which the execution currently is, the value of the pseudo-variable thisContext, we have selected the entry all temp vars, which then outputs all the temporary variables, res and n, as well as their values. In the inspection windows, we can inspect in more detail the different shown values, and by selecting inspect in the context menu; we can even change the values. Thus, if we choose the temporary variable n, and we change the value 3 to the value 1 (do not forget to persist this modification with an "Alt+s"), the remainder of the computation will be performed with this new value of n. If we edit the text of the method in the code window, for instance by removing the transmission of the message halt: to self (again, do not forget the "Alt+s"), the remainder of the program execution will occur with this modified method[83].

If instead of the selector halt:, we use the selector notify: we will obtain the windows in Figure 4.40.

---

83 Let us note that a method modification will be dispatched to any other window showing this method. In short: the modification is not local to the debugger, but is valid globally in the SMALLTALK system.

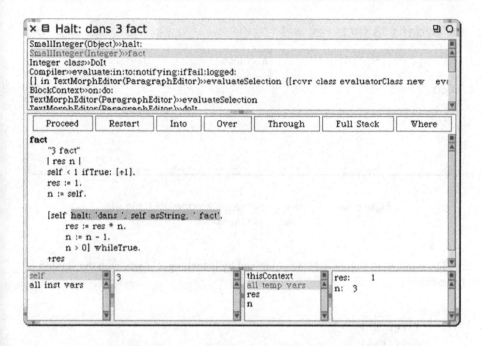

Figure 4.39. *A Halt exception window open via a debugger*

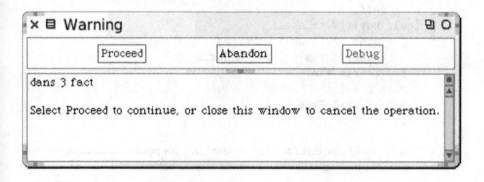

Figure 4.40. *A Warning exception window*

This is the same as a Halt window, except that the execution stack is not shown in the original window. It is replaced by the string given as an argument to notify:.

We could as well have used the selector notifyWithLabel:. In this case, the title of the window, Warning for notify:, will be the string given as an argument.

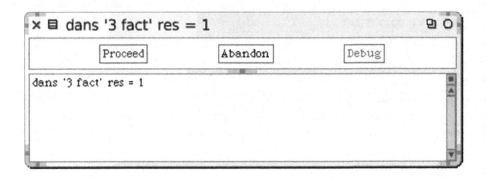

Figure 4.41. *A* `Warning` *exception window obtained with*
`notifyWithLabel:`

The window in Figure 4.41 was obtained by launching 3 `fact` with the version of fact below:

```
fact
    | res n |
    self <= 1
        ifTrue: [^ 1].
    res := 1.
    n := self.
    [self notifyWithLabel:
        'dans: ''', self asString,
        ' fact'' res =', res asString.
      res := res * n.
      n := n - 1.
      n > 1] whileTrue.
    ^res
```

If we want to make sure that `fact` is computed only for positive recipients, we can do this by using the message `assert:` as in the version below:

```
fact
    | res n |
    self assert: [self >= 0]
    self <= 1
        ifTrue: [^ 1].
    res := 1.
    n := self.
```

```
[ res := res * n.
  n := n - 1.
  n > 1] whileTrue.
 ^res
```

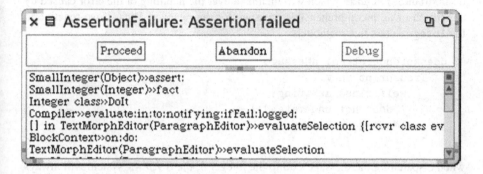

Figure 4.42. *An AssertionFailure exception window*

This message takes as argument a block without arguments and throws an AssertionFailure exception if the evaluation of the argument block returns false. This exception also opens a window giving access to a debugger. It is just the name of the window that changes as the Figure 4.42 obtained during the execution of the transmission -3 fact. We could have substantially obtained the same by writing:

```
self >= 0
   ifFalse:
      [self halt: 'AssertionFailure: Assertion failed']
```

instead and in place of

```
self assert: [self >= 0]
```

But, it is less elegant. The method assert: is yet another method for program development. While halt: and notify: activate the debugger whenever the exception is activated, assert: only activates it if the condition given as argument is not satisfied. It is an extremely useful method if we search for the source of a known error: it is not until the sought error is encountered that the debugger is activated and the stack and variables can be inspected.

There is also the message doesNotUnderstand:. Although a SMALLTALK programmer uses it only rarely, he will regularly face its effect. This message creates a MessageNotUnderstood exception which is activated when a message that is sent to an object, for which it is not defined. Figure 4.43 shows a MessageNotUndersood type window obtained after evaluation of the transmission 1 foo.

Naturally, for our own classes, we can always redefine such a method doesNotUnderstand: which will then take over the handling of the error caused by a dispatch of an incomprehensible message for the receiver. Thus, if we redefine in the Integer class this method as:

```
doesNotUnderstand: aMessage
    Transcript show:
        self class asString,
        ' does not understand ',
        aMessage asString.
    ^1
```

when dispatching the message foo to the integer 3, the SQUEAK system will always activate the message doesNotUnderstand:, but this will no longer be the method defined in the Object class, but that of the Integer class, closer in the classes tree. This will then result in the display of the string Smallinteger does not understand foo in the Transcript and the return of integer 1 as a result of any transmission of an undefined message to the receiver integer[84].

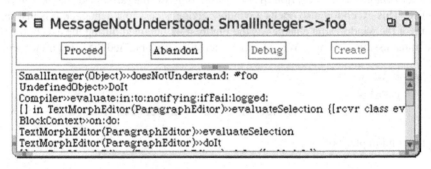

Figure 4.43. *A MessageNotUnderstood exception window*

To conclude this section and for completeness, let us note the two additional messages shouldNotImplement and subclassResponsibility are often encountered when exploring classes. The first method is used in subclasses for inherited methods that should not be implemented in this subclass. The second

---

84 This redefinition of doesNotUnderstand: in the Integer class is very dangerous because it hides *all* the dispatch errors containing an undefined selector. Use the redefinition of this method only after much thought, and only in your own classes, not in classes that SQUEAK provides immediately after its installation.

method is used to define *abstract* methods thus indicating to subclasses that they should define this method. If, for instance, we define the method Integer method Integer»foo as follows:

```
foo
    self subclassResponsibility
```

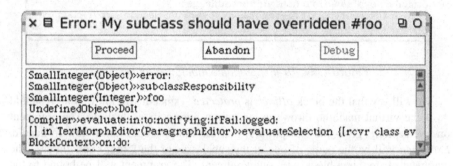

Figure 4.44. *A 'method not redefined' error window*

The message foo will still be unknown to SmallIntegers and the transmission

3 foo

will no longer result in a MessageNotUnderstood exception but in an Error exception as shown in Figure 4.44.

If we had defined Integer»foo as:

```
foo
    self shouldNotImplement
```

the error window obtained after the launch of 3 foo would be the one given in Figure 4.45.

4.7.2. *Exception handling messages for blocks*

The most common form of exception handling on blocks is realized with the message on:do:. Here is its usage template:

```
aBlock
    on: Exception
    do: [:exception | handler]
```

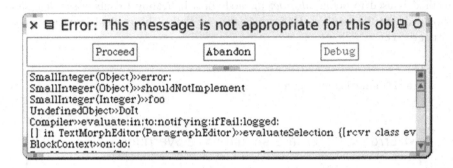

Figure 4.45. *An 'inappropriate method' error window*

We will say that the block *aBlock* is *protected* – since it will know what it should do if the virtual machine throws an exception during its evaluation. The argument on: *Exception*, gives the exception(s) that the block should know how to handle. *Exception* will be the name of one of the subclasses of the Exception class[85]. The argument of do: is a block with one argument. The argument will be bound to the caught exception. The block should indicate what to do in case of an activation of this *Exception*.

Let us take a simple example: if we evaluate the expression 1/0, SMALLTALK, as any mathematician who respects himself, will answer with an indication stating that the division by 0 is not defined. SMALLTALK, therefore, answers with the ZeroDivide exception as shown in Figure 4.46.

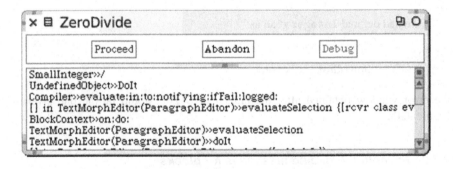

Figure 4.46. *A 'division by 0' error window*

---

85 Let us recall that exceptions are classes.

In the expression below, we catch this exception with the dispatch on:do:

```
[1 / 0]
    on: ZeroDivide
    do: [:exception | Float infinity]
```

So, when the exception ZeroDivide is thrown, it is caught by the handler that says not to stop the calculation, but simply return the infinity value, ∞, the result of the transmission Float infinity.

The return value of a transmission of the message on:do: to a block is either the block value if no exception is activated, or the return value of the *handler*. In our example above, the handler is the expression Float infinity, whose value is infinity, i.e. SQUEAK'S symbolic value for the infinite numerical value.

To be a little bit more concrete, let us put this definition into the method inverse of the Number class:

```
inverse
    ^[1 / self]
        on: ZeroDivide
        do: [:exception | Float infinity]
```

This method yields the inverse of the integer, except for the integer zero, where it yields the infinite value. Thus, the transmission 4 inverse returns the protected block evaluation value, so the fraction (1/4), and infinity, the value of the exception handler for the dispatch 0 inverse. In the latter case, in fact, a ZeroDivide exception will be activated.

If the exception occurs in a subexpression, such as in [1/0 + 100], we should explicitly say in the handler, with the message resume:, that we want to use the value of the handler in the computation of the protected block. Without it, the value of the whole dispatch on:do: will be the handler value in the case of an exception activation. resume: tells SQUEAK that we do not want to return the handler value as the value of the whole expression, but we want that value just for the expression that has generated the exception and to *resume*, so continue, the computation with this value.

Thus, the expression:

```
[1 / 0 + 100]
    on: ZeroDivide
    do: [:exception | 1]
```

returns the integer 1, the handler block value. On the contrary, the expression:

```
[1 / 0 + 100]
    on: ZeroDivide
    do: [:exception | exception resume: 1]
```

returns the integer 101, the sum of the handler's value 1 and the integer 100. The execution of the protected block has *resumed* where the exception occurred, using the value of handler instead of the undefined expression [1 / 0].

If, instead of ...on: ZeroDivide..., we had written ...on: Error..., the result would have been the same, since ZeroDivide is a subclass of Error (see the subclasses hierarchy of the Exception class on page 177) and since in on:do: an exception catches all its subexceptions. Thus, the expression

```
[1 / 0 + 100]
    on: Error
    do: [:exception | exception description]
```

successfully catches the ZeroDivide exception: it returns the string 'ZeroDivide'[86]. Thus, there is an inheritance mechanism in the exceptions handling.

Every block also understands the message ensure:, which takes as argument another block. ensure: guarantees that the argument block will always be executed, even if the evaluation of the receiver block generates an exception. Let us take, for example, the method Integer»testEnsure below:

```
testEnsure
    [1 / self + 100]
        ensure: [Transcript show: 'in block ensure']
```

If we launch this method with the transmission 0 testEnsure, the division by 0 causes a ZeroDivide exception to be thrown, which then opens a debugger window. If we choose to continue the calculation (by clicking on the Proceed button), the exception will return itself, so ZeroDivide, which will be the value of the evaluation of the block [1/self + 100]. The dispatch of the message ensure: to this same block then forces the evaluation of the argument block of this message, which will result in the display of the string 'In block ensure' in the Transcript. Since we have reached the end of the method testEnsure and since no return value has been specified, the value of self is then default return value.

If instead of Proceed we had chose the Abandon button that aborts the computation, the method would indeed have return no results – obviously, since the

---

[86] Every exception understands the message description. It returns the name of the exception as a string.

computation was interrupted – but, nevertheless, the argument block of ensure: would have been executed *before* the definitive abortion of the computation. The block ensure: is *guaranteed* to be evaluated after the exception handling. This is very useful if we want to ensure that independently of the occurrence of errors or other exceptions during the evaluation of a block, a number of actions (often these are cleaning up or previous states restoring actions) are performed.

Here is a second illustrative usage example of ensure:

```
[[1 / 0]
    ensure: [Transcript show: 'In block ensure'; cr]]
 on: ZeroDivide
 do: [:exception | Transcript show: 'In handler'; cr]
```

The evaluation of this expression displays in the Transcript:

```
In handler
In block ensure
```

first the result of the evaluation of the argument block do: followed by the result of the evaluation of the argument block ensure:.

4.7.3. *Messages understood by exceptions*

Up to now, we have used the argument :exception of the block on:do: only once by dispatching the message resume:. Naturally, exceptions also understand other messages. Here is the list of the most important messages that any exception understands:

– resume and resume: *anExpression*
: allows us to exit from the exception handler by continuing the computation where the exception was caused. The value of the erroneous expression is either nil, for resume, or, as we have seen it, the value of the argument *anExpression*, for resume: *anExpression*.

– return and return: *anExpression*
: terminates the evaluation of the block that caused the exception by returning either the value nil, for return, or the value of *anExpression*, for return: *anExpression*.

– retry
: re-evaluates the protected block. Warning, if nothing has changed since the exception was thrown, retry will create an infinite loop. Thus, the evaluation of the expression below:

```
[1 / 0 + 100]
    on: ZeroDivide
    do: [:exception | exception retry]
```

loops indefinitely. On the contrary, evaluating the following expression:

```
| x |
x := 0.
[1 / x + 100]
    on: ZeroDivide
    do: [:exception | x := 1/10000000000.
                      exception retry]
```

an expression where we change the value of the variable responsible for throwing exception, is indeed stopped and returns the integer 10000000100.

– retryUsing: *aBlock*

evaluates *aBlock* instead of the protected block. For instance, the expression:

```
[1 / 0 + 100]
    on: ZeroDivide
    do: [:exception |
        exception retryUsing: [1 / 100]]
```

returns the fraction (1/100), the value of the argument block of retryUsing:.

– resignalAs: *anException*

rethrows the exception as another exception *anException*. For example, the expression:

```
[1 / 0 + 100]
    on: ZeroDivide
    do: [:exception |
        exception resignalAs: BreakPoint]
```

transforms the ZeroDivide exception into a throw of the BreakPoint, exception, an exception that is subclass of the Halt class, which by default has the same effect as Halt.

4.7.4. *Multiple exceptions*

It may be that we want, in a message on:do:, to catch more than one exception. SQUEAK then provides two ways to specify all the exceptions to catch: either by separating the different exceptions with comma, as in the example below:

```
[1 / x + 100]
    on: ZeroDivide, Warning
    do: [:exception |
            Transcript show: exception description; cr.
            exception resume: 1/1000000]
```

or by constructing an *exception set*, i.e. an ExceptionSet, with the messages with:, with:with:, up to with:with:with:with:with:with:, or the message withAll:, that adds the elements of the argument collection to the recipient collection. Thus, the above example can also be written as follows:

```
| exc |
exc := ExceptionSet with: ZeroDivide with: Warning.
[1 / x + 100]
    on: exc
    do: [:exception |
            Transcript show: exception description; cr.
            exception resume: 1/1000000]
```

These two expressions catch both the ZeroDivide exceptions type and the Warning ones to apply there the same handler.

Let us note that there is no reason not to nest on:do:, such as in the expression below:

```
[[1 / 0]
    on: ZeroDivide
    do: [:exception |
            Transcript show:
                exception description , ' inner'; cr]]

        on: ZeroDivide
        do: [:exception |
                Transcript show:
                    exception description, ' outer'; cr]
```

Which of the two handlers will then be activated? The answer is simple – when an exception is thrown:

1) by starting with the code that caused the exception, let us search for the handler that is most inside, the one that is in the nearest expression;

2) let us continue to search in handlers that are more outside;

3) the first handler that specifies the exception that has occurred will be activated. All the other handlers will be ignored. Only if none of handlers surrounding the code that generated the exception applies, that is to say, no argument on: refers to the exception that has occurred, then the default behavior of the exception is activated.

According to this algorithm, the following example should, therefore, output in the Transcript the string 'ZeroDivide inner', since it is the first inner handler that handles the ZeroDivide exception. The outside one will always be ignored.

On the contrary, if we had written:

```
[[1 / 0]
    on: Halt
    do: [:exception |
            Transcript show:
                exception description , ' inner'; cr]]
      on: ZeroDivide
      do: [:exception |
              Transcript show:
                  exception description, ' outer'; cr]
```

naturally, the message 'ZeroDivide outer' would have been displayed in the Transcript, because now it is only the outer handler which considers the ZeroDivide exception and since ZeroDivide is not a subclass of the Halt class, the exception considered by the inner handler.

Finally, if we had written:

```
[[1 / 0]
    on: Halt
    do: [:exception |

            Transcript show:
                exception description , ' inner'; cr]]
      on: Notification
      do: [:exception |
              Transcript show:
                  exception description, ' outer'; cr]
```

since none of the handlers surrounding the code that generated the exception knows how to handle the ZeroDivide exception, it will be the default behavior of this exception to be thrown: as in Figure 4.46, a *division by 0* error window will open.

Up to now, the activation of our exceptions was controlled either explicitly by a message sent to any object – such as the messages halt, notify:, or assert: – or implicitly by the SQUEAK virtual machine – for instance, when an error has occurred, as in our famous division by zero. An additional way that can be used to throw exceptions is to send the message signal or signal: directly to one of the subclasses of the Exception class. Thus, the evaluation of the following expressions:

```
Warning signal: 'Hello world'.
Transcript show: '...the remainder'; cr
```

first displays the Warning window shown in Figure 4.47 and terminates the evaluation if we click on the Abandon button or, if we click on the Proceed button, displays the string '...the remainder' in the Transcript.

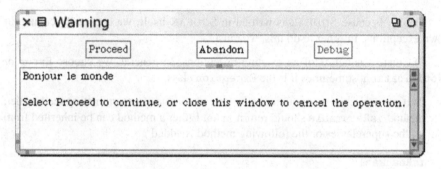

Figure 4.47. *A Warning window*

Let us recall that according to the algorithm that determines the choice of the handler to handle the exception, in the example above, the display of this Warning should be the default handler activation behavior, since no handler surrounds the expression Warning signal: '...' that has generated the exception. The default behaviors are determined in the methods defaultAction of various subclasses of the Exception class. In order to know the default behavior of exceptions, it is sufficient to explore these classes and to examine these methods.

For the most important exceptions, here are their default behavior:

– Notification: normally, throwing this exception does absolutely nothing: the computation continues as if nothing had happened. In order to change this behavior, those exceptions are surrounded by handlers, such as in:

```
[Notification signal. 1] on: Notification
  do: [Transcript show: 'make a clean sweep of the past'; cr]
```

whose evaluation returns the integer 1, the value of the protected block after the display in the Transcript, of the string 'make a clean sweep of the past'.

– Warning: opens a dialog window asking the user if he wants to continue or not, or if he wishes to open a debugger.

– Error: opens a debugger window.

4.7.5. *Define its own exceptions*

Finally, because SQUEAK is written in SQUEAK itself, we can easily create our own exceptions. In order to do this, we must:

1) Create a subclass of an existing exceptions. In general, we choose Error or Notification, sometimes it is the Exception class.

2) If we desire the computation to be able to resume after terminating the handler, the method isResumable should return true. Either a method can be inherited from one of the superclasses or the following method is added

```
isResumable
  ^true
```

to the new exception class.

3) If we do not want to inherit the default behavior of the class, the method defaultAction should be redefined.

We have seen that the default behavior of the Notification exception is to do nothing. If we want to have a notification whose default behavior is the display of a string in the Transcript, we can create a subclass the Notification class, let us called it MyNotification, as:

```
Notification subclass: #MyNotification
            instanceVariableNames: ''
            classVariableNames: ''
            poolDictionaries: ''
            category: 'MyExceptions'
```

From the compilation of this class definition, SQUEAK knows a new exception: the exception MyNotification. It behaves exactly as the Notification exception, since it inherits all of the methods from its superclasses. The Notification exception *can be resumed* – that is: its method isResumable returns true. The only specific thing we want from this exception is that it displays in the Transcript the message given as argument every time it is thrown. Let us then define a method MyNotification»defaultAction:

```
defaultAction
    Transcript show: self messageText; cr
```

The method messageText is defined in the abstract class Exception. It returns the text, the string, dispatched to the exception by the message signal:[87].

If we now define the method Integer»myNotice:

```
myNotice
    ^self < 0 ifTrue: [MyNotification signal: 'negative'.
                       0 - self]
             ifFalse: [self]
```

The transmission 1 myNotice returns the integer 1. The transmission -1 myNotice activates the MyNotification exception, which results in the display of 'negative' in the Transcript, and, since this exception *can be resumed*, it continues with the computation of 0 - -1 which then returns the integer 1.

What will the variant below then do?

```
myNotice
    ^self < 0 ifTrue:
             [[[MyNotification signal: 'negative'.
              0 - self]
              on: Notification
              do: [:exception |
                      Transcript show: '...viewed?'; cr.
                      exception resume]]
             ifFalse: [self]
```

Let us explain: naturally, in the case where the receiver is a number greater than or equal to zero, nothing changes. On the contrary, if the receiver is a negative number, let us say -1 as above, the MyNotification exception is activated. Since this activation

---

87 This is the value of the instance variable messageText specific to any instance of any subclass of the Exception class.

is surrounded by a handler, by the transmission of the message on:do:, it is no longer the default handler which is activated (the action specified in the defaultAction method), but this surrounding handler, that output the string '...viewed?'. The next transmission is exception resume that, therefore, resumes the computation of the protected block after the dispatch that has generated the exception, the expression MyNotification signal: 'negative'. The computation is thus resumed with the dispatch 0 - self, which yields, since the receiver is the integer -1, the integer 1.

Let us keep in mind that the default behavior is only realized if no other handler is present. It is really a default behavior in the absence of other handlers.

4.8. Exercises

The solutions for these exercises are found on page 390.

1) Exercises on collections:

   1) Give the results of the evaluation of the following expressions:

   i. 'cat' asSortedCollection

   ii. 'foobar' asBag

   iii. 'foobar' asSet

   iv. #(3 1 4 9) asSortedCollection

   v. #(3 1 4 9) asSortedCollection: [:x :y| x > y]

   vi. #(3 1 4 9) asSortedCollection: [:x :y| x < y]

   vii. a := OrderedCollection
           with: $a
           with: 'cat'
           with: 3.

   viii. By keeping the value of a of the above exercise, what is the value of a after the dispatch: a addAll: 'foobar'?

   2) In each of the exercises in this section, we assume that the variable data contains the OrderedCollection {3 1 4 9}. Give the state of the variable data after each of the following transmissions.

   i. data remove: 4

   ii. data remove: 5 ifAbsent: []

   iii. data removeAll:
                (OrderedCollection with: 1 with: 9)

iv. `data removeAllFoundIn:  #(1 6)`

v. `data removeAllSuchThat:  [:ele | ele > 3]`

2) Exercises on enumerative structures:

2.1. Write the method `String»getVowels` which yields the string composed of the sequence of vowels of the recipient. Examples:

```
'cat' → 'a'
'hello World' → 'eoo'
'Donaudampfschiffahrtsgesellschaftskapitaen'
              → 'oauaiaeeaaiae'
```

2.2. Write the method `Collection»pair` which returns a collection of the same type as the receiver containing all the even numbers of the receiver collection.

2.3. Write the method `Collection»pairSquared` which returns the collection of all the square of the even numbers of the receiver collection.

2.4. Write for the `String` class the method `numberOfVowels` which gives the number of vowels contained in the receiver string.

2.5. Write for the `String` class the method `numberOccurrences:` which takes as argument a character and yields as result the number of occurrences of that character in the receiver string.

2.6. Write the method `ArrayedCollection»times:` which returns a new array containing `times` times a copy of a receiver array.

Examples:

```
#(1 2 3 4) times:  3 → #(1 2 3 4 1 2 3 4 1 2 3 4)
'ha' times:  4 → 'hahahaha'
```

2.7. Write the method `Array»sum` which computes the sum of the numbers in the receiver array while displaying in the Transcript the intermediate results. For example, the dispatch:

$$\#(1\ 2\ 3\ 4)\ sum$$

should return the integer 10, the result of $1 + 2 + 3 + 4$, and display in the Transcript the series of the intermediate sums, so 1, 3 and 6.

2.8. By considering collections as sets, write for the Collection class the method intersection:, the method union: and the method difference: which, respectively, compute the intersection, union and the difference of two collections.

Examples:

```
#(1 2 3 4) union:  #(1 2 6 4) → #(1 2 3 4 6)
#(1 2 3 4) intersection:  #(1 2 6 4) → #(1 2 4)
#(1 2 3 4) difference:  #(1 2 6 4) → #(3 6)
```

2.9. What does the below method String»foo do?

```
foo
  Transcript show: 'character';
             tab;
             show: 'frequency';
             cr.

  self asBag sortedElements do:
      [:ele |
        Transcript
          show: ele key;
          tab; tab; tab;
          show: ele value;
          cr]
```

2.10. Let us return to our DNA chains covered in the exercise on page 105:

i. there is a simplified test to know whether there is a *risk* of being in the presence of a DNA chain, check that the sum of adenine and cytosine nucleotides is equal to the sum of guanine and thymine nucleotides. That is to decompose the two nucleotide chains in its nucleic constituents, to pour each nucleotide in a tube that contains only the same type of nucleotide, finally to count the nucleotides A and C, and the nucleotides G and T. Then, write the method String»simplifiedDNATest: that verifies the equality of the two sums.

ii. One of the problems of genetic engineering is the *amplification*, that is: the multiplication, of a "small" specific fragment of DNA[88]. This problem is particularly important if the fragment is hidden in a huge mass of other fragments.

Fortunately, there is a technique to solve this problem. It is known as the *polymerase chain reaction*, or by its acronym: PCR. It was discovered by Kary Mullis

---

88 In general, it is a fragment which encodes a particular gene.

in 1983 (why not read his marvellous book [MUL 98]) who won the 1993 Nobel Prize in chemistry for this (in partnership with Michael Smith, another biochemist). This technique has completely renewed molecular biology. It applies in areas as diverse as genetic engineering (for genetic sequencing), forensic analysis (for identifying or eliminating suspects by using traces of blood or other tiny traces), genomic analysis, archaeology and paleontology (the biologists were able, from extremely small quantities of DNA extracted from fossils of extinct species, to place these species in the phylogenetic tree) or clinical diagnosis (to determine, from a small set of DNA material, viral or bacteriological agents of an infection).

PCR is a process that is as accurate and efficient[89] as it is simple and elegant. Here is how it works:

Let us suppose that we want to amplify a DNA molecule α whose extremities composition is known. Let us call these extremities β and γ as shown below (X and Y can be any nucleotides; $\overline{X}$ is the nucleotide complementary to the nucleotide X):

$$\alpha : \quad \overbrace{\overline{XXXX}}^{\overline{\gamma}} \ldots \ldots \overbrace{\overline{YYYY}}^{\beta}$$

$$\underbrace{XXXX}_{\gamma} \ldots \ldots \underbrace{\overline{YYYY}}_{\overline{\beta}}$$

The amplification of the DNA chain α is then realized by repeating the basic cycle consisting of three steps : *denaturation, priming* and *extension*.

At the start, we prepare the solution containing the target molecule α, synthetic oligonucleotides[90], the *primers* complementary to β (β-primers) and γ (γ-primers), polymerases (enzymes allowing the assembling of DNA chains) that are resistant to heat and nucleotides. Then, come the three basic cycles:

   – Denaturation: in this phase, we heat the solution at very high temperatures (very near to the water boiling temperature) so that the hydrogen links, that bind

---

89 A PCR cycle takes only a few minutes. After 30 cycles, PCR generates approximately trillion copies of the original DNA chain.

90 *oligonucleotides* are just DNA or RNA molecules of very small size that consist of only a few nucleotides.

the two chains of nucleotides, are destroyed. Thus, the double chain α separates (is denatured) in a chain α_1 and α_2, as illustrated below:

$$\alpha : \quad \overline{XXXX} \ldots \ldots \overbrace{\overline{YYYY}}^{\beta}$$

$$\underbrace{\underline{XXXX}}_{\gamma} \ldots \ldots \overline{YYYY}$$

$$\Big\downarrow reheating$$

$$\alpha_1 : \overline{XXXX} \ldots \ldots \overbrace{\overline{YYYY}}^{\beta}$$

$$\alpha_2 : \underbrace{\underline{XXXX}}_{\gamma} \ldots \ldots \overline{YYYY}$$

– *Priming:* once both chains separated, we cool down (around 55 °C) so that the *primers* can bind[91] to their corresponding extremities: the β-primers to β and γ-primers to γ. The figure below illustrates this:

$$\alpha_1 : \overline{XXXX} \ldots \ldots \overbrace{\overline{YYYY}}^{\beta}$$

$$\alpha_2 : \underbrace{\underline{XXXX}}_{\gamma} \ldots \ldots \overline{YYYY}$$

$$\Big\downarrow cooling$$

$$\alpha_1 : \overline{XXXX} \ldots \ldots \overbrace{\dfrac{\overline{YYYY}}{\underline{\overline{YYYY}}}}^{\beta}_{\beta-primer}$$

$$\alpha_2 : \overbrace{\dfrac{\overline{XXXX}}{\underline{XXXX}}}^{\gamma-primer}_{\quad} \ldots \ldots \overline{YYYY}$$

– *Extension:* then, we reheat again the temperature (at 72 °C) so that the

---

91 This process is called *annealing* in genetics and physics.

polymerases, the enzymes, can extend the *primers* with the available nucleotides in the solution in order to produce two complementary DNA chains. These two chains are identical to the original α chain. Below, we schematize this process for the extension of the α_1 chain.

$$\alpha_1 : \overline{XXXX} \dots \dots _{\leftarrow} \begin{array}{c} \overset{\beta}{\overbrace{YYYY}} \\ \underline{YYYY} \\ \scriptstyle \beta-primer \end{array}$$

$$\downarrow polymerase$$

$$\alpha : \quad \overset{\overline{\gamma}}{\overbrace{XXXX}} \dots \dots \overset{\beta}{\overbrace{YYYY}}$$

$$\underset{\gamma}{\underbrace{XXXX}} \dots \dots \underset{\beta-primer}{\underbrace{\overline{YYYY}}}$$

And below for the chain α_2 :

$$\alpha_2 : \underset{\gamma}{\underbrace{\overset{\overbrace{XXXX}^{\gamma-primer}}{XXXX}}} \dots ^{\rightarrow} \dots \overline{YYYY}$$

$$\downarrow polymerase$$

$$\overset{\gamma-primer}{\overbrace{XXXX}} \dots \dots \overset{\beta}{\overbrace{YYYY}}$$

$$\alpha : \quad \underset{\gamma}{\underbrace{XXXX}} \dots \dots \underset{\beta}{\underbrace{\overline{YYYY}}}$$

If we repeat this cycle n times, we obtain 2^n copies of α[92].

Here is a small series of exercises:

  – Write a method allowing, from a DNA chain, to reconstruct a double DNA chain.

---

92 Naturally, this is a theoretical value, assuming a sufficient reserve of nucleotide and the availability of polymerases that are well resistant to heat, otherwise they might not survive the multiple reheatings. In general, such polymerases are isolated using thermophilic bacteria that live in hot springs at temperatures near the boiling point.

– Write a method for simulating a basic PCR cycle, that is to say, from a DNA molecule, of two complementary chains, it yields two copies of the original DNA molecule.

– Write a method allowing us to perform n iterations of the basic PCR cycle, that is to say, from a DNA molecule it yields, after n iterations, 2^n copies of the original DNA molecule.

PART 2

Programming in SQUEAK

Drawings Like in Logo

As we have seen at the beginning of this book (see Figure I.1), the design of SMALLTALK, and therefore of SQUEAK too, was influenced by the language *Logo*.

Logo is a programming language, developed by a team from MIT and BBN working with Seymour Papert[1] in the late 1960s. Papert was particularly interested in the use of computers by children in school environments. His conception of learning processes and programming as a mean for exploring new areas is wonderfully presented in [PAP 80]. A description of the use of Logo in French school environments can be found in [WER 80].

Logo is a language derived from Lisp (another ancestor of SQUEAK) where a robot named *turtle* can receive simple motion commands such as *move forward*, *move backward*, *turn right* and *turn left*. If the *turtle* is placed on a large sheet of paper, it may, with a retractable pencil, leave a trace of its movements.

To develop programs or algorithms in the Logo style, all we need is to identify ourselves as the turtle and describe the actions and movements to do in order to follow the path along the lines of the desired drawing. For example, if I want to draw a square with the Logo turtle, I start by analyzing my behavior when I move around the perimeter of a square. Clearly, this requires that I move forward a number n of steps, that I turn a 90 degree angle, that I still go forward the same number of steps, that I

---

1 To learn more about Seymour Papert and his thoughts on the use of computers in learning environments, go and take a look at his Website [PAP 05]. MIT stands for the Massuchessets Institute of Technology, an excellent technology university along the James River in Cambridge, just off Boston. BBN, an acronym for "Bolt, Beranek and Newman" is a technology "think tank" located, also in Cambridge, Massachusetts. BBN became known by its participation in the development of the ARPA network. The "leader" of the logo project at BBN was Wallace Feuerzeug.

turn 90 degrees again in the same direction, and that I repeat moving forward n steps and turning 90 degrees twice.

This results to the following eight commands in Logo:

```
move forward 100
right 90
move forward 100
right 90
move forward 100
right 90
move forward 100
right 90
```

or simply:

```
repeat 4
  move forward 100
  right 90
```

The execution of any of these programs draws a square of length 100 by the turtle, as shown in Figure 5.1. After finishing the drawing, the turtle is in exactly the same position as it was at the start.

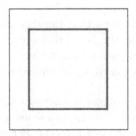

Figure 5.1. *The square drawn by Logo*

5.1. The Pen **class**

As not all users of SQUEAK have a robot able to move around and make drawings, SQUEAK provides a simulation of such robots in the Pen class: any instance of the

Pen understands the messages turn:[2] and go:[3]. Armed with these methods, we can translate the above Logo program in the following sequence of two expressions:

```
pen := Pen new.
4 timesRepeat: [pen go: 100; turn: 90]
```

If we write them in a Workspace and we perform a doIt on it, SQUEAK draws us a nice rectangle in the middle of the screen, as shown in the snippet of SQUEAK in Figure 5.2.

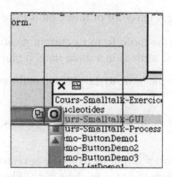

Figure 5.2. *The square drawn by* SQUEAK*'s* Pen

This drawing is displayed above our SQUEAK window and – moreover – it disappears only if we cover it, at least temporarily, with a SMALLTALK window[4]. To restore the screen after drawing something on it, we can encapsulate the expressions that generate the drawing in another expression which itself restores the screen after the display of the drawing. The following program does just that for our program that draws a square:

```
pen := Pen new.
Display restoreAfter:
    [4 timesRepeat: [pen go: 100; turn: 90]]
```

Display is the name of the SQUEAK screen. This is an instance of the DisplayScreen class, which is itself a subclass of the Form class. When our screen,

---

2 *turn* for Logo's *left* or *right*. If the argument of turn is a positive number n, the turtle turns n degrees to the right, if n is negative, it turns n degrees to the left.

3 The message go: with a positive integer n as the argument makes the turtle *move forward* n steps, and if the argument is negative, the turtle *moves backward* n steps.

4 That is to use the window as an eraser.

our `Display`, receives the message `restoreAfter:` with a block as the argument, after the evaluation of the argument block it waits for a mouse click to redraw the screen. The drawings generated in this way are fleeting.

Here are some additional messages for the instances of the `Pen` class:

– `down:` puts the turtle in a state such that it leaves a trace of all its movements: it is drawing;

– `up:` puts the turtle in a state such that it moves without drawing;

– `color:` *aColor* changes the color of future plots to be *aColor*;

– `goto:` *aPoint* moves the turtle from its current position to the new position at the coordinates *aPoint*. If the turtle is in a `down` state, it plots the movement;

– `place:` *aPoint* moves the turtle to the position at the coordinates *aPoint* without drawing this movement;

– `home` moves the turtle to its "home", the center of the drawing surface, without drawing the movement;

– `north` puts the turtle in a position such that the next movement will be performed toward the north, that is toward the top of the screen (like on maps produced in the northern hemisphere);

– `defaultNib:` *aNumber* tells the turtle to draw with a square tip black pencil of size *aNumber*;

– `roundNib:` *aNumber* tells the turtle to draw with a round tip black pencil of diameter *aNumber*;

– `squareNib:` *aNumber* tells the turtle to draw with a square tip black pencil of size *aNumber*;

– `fill:` *aBlockWith1Arg* `color:` *aColor* the evaluation of *aBlockWith1Arg* should generate a closed form that will be filled in with the color *aColor*.

Before even starting to program these SQUEAK "turtles", these instances of the Pen class, let us make the drawings less fleeting. For this, let us remember that a `Pen`, an instance of the `Pen` class, always draws on a *form*, an instance of the `Form` class or one of its subclasses. Thus, the transmission

`Pen new`

is just an abbreviation of the transmission

`Pen newOnForm:  Display`

SQUEAK's screen, the Display, is the default drawing canvas of any instance of the Pen class. However, we can draw on any canvas, any other *form*. A form is just a pixel array[5] used to hold images. The only special feature of the Display canvas is that SQUEAK already provides it and it is always available. We can create our own canvas by creating our own instances of the Form class. Such a canvas is defined by its size, its extent: and, possibly, its depth, its depth:, which indicates the number of colors each pixel can take[6]. By default, the depth is 1: the default canvas only allows drawing in black and white. In general, it is best to give the depth of the screen to your personal forms. Below is a transmission that creates a canvas of 300 by 300 pixels (it is big enough on a screen, but very small on a good printer as the real size of a pixel depends on its media) where each pixel can have the same number of colors as the screen:

```
Form extent:  300 @ 300 depth:  Display depth
```

This *form* can then be used as a drawing canvas for our turtle. To visualize it, all we need to do is to send it the message display, which displays the form at the top left of the screen, or the message displayAt:, which displays the form at the point given as the argument. Thus, the evaluation of the following transmission sequences[7]:

```
| form pen |
form := Form extent: 150 @ 150 depth: Display depth.
form fillColor: Color white.
pen := Pen newOnForm: form.
pen roundNib: 2;
     color: Color red.
pen home.
pen up.
pen goto: 25 @ 125.
pen down.
4
    timesRepeat: [pen  go: 100.
         pen turn: 90].
form displayAt: Display center - form center
```

displays, in the center of the screen, in a white square 150 by 150 pixels, the outline of a colored square that has sides of 100 pixels, as shown in Figure 5.1.

---

5 A *pixel* is the smallest element of a canvas where a color and an intensity can be individually associated with.

6 More precisely, by *depth* of a canvas we mean the number of bits required for the internal representation of a pixel. Increasing the number of bits obviously influences the number of colors available in the Canvas. For a black and white drawing, the depth is 1.

7 Note that we have intentionally used almost all the move commands that can be dispatched to a class instance Pen. The message fillColor: gives to a form the background color given as the argument.

Unfortunately, this drawing is still as fleeting as the others: it can neither be moved nor be covered *temporarily* by a less fleeting SQUEAK object. What we would like to have is drawing canvas that can be reduced, enlarged, moved, copied, etc., as regular SQUEAK windows.

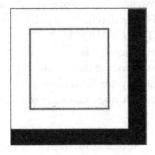

Figure 5.3. *The square drawn on a* Morph

In order to achieve this, we must transform the canvas in an object having the same characteristics as a window. We must transform it into a Morph, since in SQUEAK all windows are instances of either the Morph class itself, or one of its multiple subclasses specializing in various aspects of the graphical interface of SQUEAK. Without directly delving into a description of Morphs (we will return to this later), let us note that if we change the last line of our small program that draws a square:

```
form displayAt:  Display center - form center
```

into the line:

```
form asMorph openInWorld
```

the execution of the program will create an instance of the Morph class of size 150 by 150 pixels that contains the drawing of the square with 100 pixels sides, as shown in Figure 5.3 (the shadow on the right bottom indicates that this Morph has been selected). This drawing is then a true window, with the same halo, and therefore the same manipulation possibilities, as the one described in the solutions to the exercises in section 1.3 (page 344). We can then move, enlarge, rotate, or change the square's color, in short, apply there all the operations that can be applied to other instances of the Morph class that have already been encountered.

Finally, we are ready to write some Logo "like" programs. In order to give a first glimpse of the power of these instructions, five example mini-programs and the results of their execution are given below.

Admire the beauty of this geometry: it is based entirely on the analysis of our behavior when our own movement should lead to a specific figure[8]. This is a language to express choreographies. Please carefully analyze these examples, implement them, make them "run" and modify them in order to see what you can do.

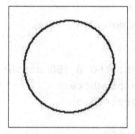

Figure 5.4. *A circle drawn with program 1*

Readers interested in Logo and this particularly constructivist version of Geometry can always read the excellent book by Hal Abelson and Andy diSessa [ABE 81] which presents in a captivating way "the turtle geometry": starting from the simulation of the growth of living organisms and the evolution of forms, through topology and multi-dimensional geometries. They end, always using (relatively) simple programs, with phenomena in curved spaces and the theory of general relativity.

Here is the remainder of our mini-programs:

1) First a program that draws a beautiful black circle[9]:

```
| form pen |
form := Form extent: 150 @ 150 depth: Display depth.
form fillColor: Color white.
pen := Pen newOnForm: form.
pen roundNib: 2;
    color: Color black.
```

---

8 Seymour Papert uses the term "body syntonicity" to describe this analogy between physical behavior experienced during a movement and algorithmic behavior of turtles during generation of the same displacement.

9 Note that the circle is obtained in terms of "body syntonicity", by moving forward one small step and turning 1 degree right. These two operations are repeated 360 times. Naturally, if you turn 1 degree 360 times, you have done a full circle. Question: is the angle of 1 degree the inner corner angle or the outer corner angle?

```
pen place: 20@75.
  360 timesRepeat:
    [pen go: 1;
       turn: 1].
form asMorph openInWorld
```

2) A program drawing an almost square spiral:

```
| form pen |
form := Form extent: 150 @ 150 depth: Display depth.
form fillColor: Color white.
pen := Pen newOnForm: form.
pen roundNib: 2;
    color: Color black.
pen home.
  1 to: 50 do:
    [:i |pen go: 2*i;
       turn: 89].
form asMorph openInWorld
```

Figure 5.5. *A rectangular spiral drawn with program 2*

3) The same program as the previous one, except that it enlarges at each iteration, with the message roundNib:, the width of the pencil tip, and therefore also the plot of the movement:

```
| form pen j |
form := Form extent: 150 @ 150 depth: Display depth.
form fillColor: Color white.
pen := Pen newOnForm: form.
j := 1.
pen roundNib: j;
    color: Color blue.
```

```
pen home.
1
   to: 50
   do: [:i |
      j := j + 0.08.
      pen go: i * 2;
          turn: 89;
          roundNib: j].
form asMorph openInWorld
```

Figure 5.6. *The spiral obtained with program 3*

4) In order to fill a drawing (closed) with a color, we use the message fill:color:. The first argument is a block describing the figure to be filled with the color given as the second argument. SQUEAK, like ourselves, can only fill closed figures, that is figures where the final point is the same as the starting point[10]. SQUEAK will inject a particular version[11] of the receiver of this message in the block argument, which is why we cannot use the turtle receiver of the message fill:color: inside the block: the turtle is accessible only through the block argument (in the program below, it is the argument :each).

So, here is a program drawing a colored star:

```
| form pen |
form := Form extent: 150 @ 150 depth: Display depth.
form fillColor: Color white.
pen := Pen newOnForm: form.
```

---

10 In topological terms, a closed drawing defines a *compact* space.

11 The particularity of this version, an instance of the PenPointRecorder class, is that it does not draw the lines of the movement, but it just registers the destination points in order to be able to then calculate the edges of the drawing. The method fill:color: acts as if it was executing the block twice: once in order to compute the borders and the other to effectively draw the figure.

```
pen roundNib: 2;
    color: Color black.
pen place: 50 @ 120.
pen
    fill: [:each | 5
            timesRepeat: [each go: 100;
                    turn: 144]]
    color: Color yellow.
form asMorph openInWorld
```

Figure 5.7. *A colored star obtained by program 4*

5) As a final example in this series of Logo-style mini-programs, here is a variant (where we have omitted the initialization parts identical to other programs) of program 2 which, instead of yielding a rectangular equiangular spiral, yields an equiangular spiral similar to those observed in seashell shapes (as in the famous *Nautilus*). What is, in geometric terms, the common point of these two programs, their fixed point?

```
| form pen dist |
...
pen place: 60 @ 90.
dist := 1.2.
200 timesRepeat: [pen go: (dist := dist * 1.03);
            turn: 13].
form asMorph openInWorld
```

5.2. Some fractals: recursive drawings

In his now classic work: "The Fractal Geometry of Nature" [MAN 77], Benoît Mandelbrot provides a set of recursive structure descriptions that are particularly well suited to replication by drawing techniques of the turtle. The fractals feature that most interests us here is self-similarity[12], that is: the feature that part of the drawing is similar to the entire drawing. The best-known example of such a self-similarity is probably the Koch curve, by the Swedish mathematician Helge von Koch, described (in a paper published in 1904) as "a continuous curve with no tangent obtained by an elementary geometric construction" [VAN 04], which can be obtained as follows:

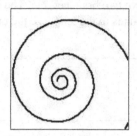

Figure 5.8. *An equiangular spiral obtained with program 5*

– *Level 0:* draw a line of length l.

– *Level 1:* slice the line into three equal parts of length $\frac{l}{3}$. Remove the middle part, duplicate it and replace the two parts in the middle such that the middle part forms an equilateral triangle open at the bottom, as in the first drawing in Figure 5.9.

– *Level 2:* the drawing obtained in the preceding level consists of four lines. For each of these lines, apply the operation of the previous point, that is slice each line into three equal parts of length $\frac{l}{9}$, remove the middle parts and replace them by two copies of length $\frac{l}{9}$ such that each middle part becomes an equilateral triangle open at the bottom, as in the second drawing in Figure 5.9.

– ...

– *Level n:* in the drawing obtained at level $n-1$, take each of the lines (of length $\frac{1}{3^{n-1}}$) that compose it and apply to each of them the operations of level 1. The last drawing in Figure 5.9 shows the curve obtained at level 5.

We will leave the implementation of the program drawing such a curve as an exercise (see page 411) and start with a program drawing stylish trees showing regular branchings: a regular binary tree, that is a tree where each branch yields two subbranches. The length of a subbranch is half the length of the original branch and each branch will be a straight line. Let us note the fundamentally recursive nature of this tree description: a branch consists of something (the trunk) and two subbranches

---

12 On this subject, also read the excellent book by Michael Barnsley [BAR 93] which presents these self-similar objects as fixed points of affine transformation sets.

(things having the same structure as a branch). This is exactly how we will write the method `tree1:` of the Number class. The receiver integer determines the number of branchings that we want: 0 corresponds to no branching (this is a simple vertical line, much like the Parisian trees in spring, after the roadworks services have pruned them), 1 corresponds to a trunk with two branches, 2 corresponds to a trunk with two branches which themselves have two branches, etc. The integer given as an argument to the method `tree1:` corresponds to the length of the original trunk.

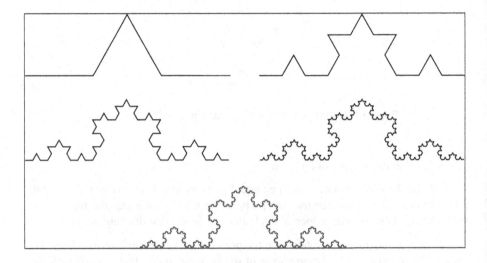

Figure 5.9. *The first few levels of the Koch curve (from top to bottom and left to right: level 1, 2, 3, 4 and 5)*

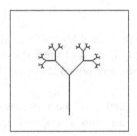

Figure 5.10. *A tree obtained by 6* `tree1:` *50*

Since this procedure will fundamentally be recursive, we will divide it into two methods: a first for the initializations, and a second to effectively draw the tree.

Here they are. First, the initialization method:

```
tree1: length
  | form pen |
  form := Form extent: 150 @ 150 depth: Display depth.
  form fillColor: Color white.
  pen := Pen newOnForm: form.
  pen roundNib: 1;
      color: Color black.
  pen home; down.
  pen place: 75 @ 130.
  self tree1a: length pen: pen.
  form asMorph openInWorld
```

This method sets up a Form of the desired size and background color, creates an instance of the Pen class acting on this form, positions that instance of Pen, this turtle, in the right place in the form in order to then ask the receiver integer to effectively draw the tree with the procedure tree1a:pen:, and upon completion of the drawing, it displays it as *morph*. It is very similar to what we did before.

Then the method preforming the drawing of the tree:

```
tree1a: length pen: pen
  self <= 0
    ifFalse: [pen go: length;
          turn: -45.
      self - 1 tree1a: length / 2 pen: pen.
      pen turn: 90.
      self - 1 tree1a: length / 2 pen: pen.
      pen turn: -45;
          go: 0 - length]
```

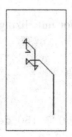

Figure 5.11. *The drawing obtained with* 4 *tree1:* *50 modified*

Somehow, the least obvious transmissions in this procedure `tree1a:pen:` are those of the last two lines:

```
pen turn: -45;
    go: 0 - length]
```

Here is why: the method draws only if the receiver is greater than 0. In this case, it makes the turtle move forward `length` steps, to turn 45 degrees left, in order to draw the left subtree (the branch(es) toward the left). When that is finished, it turns right 90 degrees (which is the same as if it had initially turned 45 degrees right) to draw the right subtree (the branch(es) toward the right). The drawings of the two subtrees are performed by the same procedure, `tree1a:pen:`. Therefore, the subbranches can themselves contain left and right subbranches – since our method always draws either one branch or a left branch *and* a right branch. The two lines below are then required to replace the turtle, after drawing the left subtree, in the *direction* it had before embarking on the drawing of this subtree (it is the dispatch `pen turn:   -45` which reverses the effect of the dispatches `pen turn:   -45` and `pen turn:   90` of the fourth and sixth line of the method) and regain its previous *position* with the transmission `pen go:   0 - length` which reverses the effect of the transmission `pen go:   length` of the third line.

In order to check this, readers are invited to observe the behavior of this method without these two lines. Figure 5.11 shows the drawing obtained by 4 `tree1:   50` using our method without these last two lines. Clearly, this is no longer a tree.

Naturally, the chances of encountering in nature a tree as regular as the one we draw with method `tree1:` are extremely reduced. Let us then try to make our trees slightly more natural by varying both the angles and the lengths of branches. Figure 5.12 shows a tree whose left branches are longer than the right branches. For this program, we then have a method to draw a left branch and another to draw a right branch. The method `node:angle:pen:` (inspired by a similar program in [ABE 81]) is used to prepare the next level of branchings. So, here are our four methods:

The first method is responsible for initializing the canvas and launching the tree drawing:

```
tree2: length angle: angle
    "7 tree2: 10 angle: 20"
    | form pen |
    form := Form extent: 150 @ 150 depth: Display depth.
    form fillColor: Color white.
    pen := Pen newOnForm: form.
```

```
pen roundNib: 1;
    color: Color black.
pen home; down.
pen place: 85 @ 130.
self
    tree2a: length
    angle: angle
    pen: pen.
form asMorph openInWorld
```

Figure 5.12. *A tree obtained by* 7 tree2: 7 angle: 20

The second method is responsible for drawing a branch to the left:

```
tree2a: length angle: angle pen: pen
    pen go: length * 2.
    self
        node: length
        angle: angle
        pen: pen.
    pen go: -2 * length
```

As can be seen, drawing a branch to the left is limited to drawing a branch of length length * 2, launching the drawing of subbranches, after which we will find our turtle at the top of the left branch, and going down our branch to – eventually – clear the way for the drawing of a right branch.

The third method, symmetrical to the method tree2a, is responsible for drawing a branch to the right:

```
tree2b: length angle: angle pen: pen
    pen go: length.
    self
```

```
node: length
angle: angle
pen: pen.
pen go: 0 - length
```

Finally, the fourth method node:angle:pen: which is responsible for relaunching the drawing from the terminal point of a left or right branch, that is this method is responsible for the drawing of the entire tree, is activated in the method tree2a.

```
node: length angle: angle pen: pen
  self = 0
    ifFalse: [pen turn: 0 - angle.
      self - 1
        tree2a: length
        angle: angle
        pen: pen.
      pen turn: 2 * angle.
      self - 1
        tree2b: length
        angle: angle
        pen: pen.
      pen turn: 0 - angle]
```

My favorite fractal is the Sierpinski triangle, discovered by the Polish mathematician Waclaw Franciszek Sierpiski and published for the first time in 1915 [SIE 15]. There are an impressive number of different algorithms for its construction (see [PEI 92]). Obviously, as shown in Figure 5.13, it can be approximated by a continuous curve (in the figure, this curve starts at the bottom right and ends at the left tip).

The most common construction is to start with an equilateral triangle of length l, then to slice the middle triangle[13], then to slice the middle triangle of the remaining three triangles and so on. Figure 5.2 shows this development, the first stage on the left: a triangle with the middle triangle sliced, the second stage at the center and the third stage on the right.

This process of successive slices is the same as starting with an equilateral triangle of length l and copying over in each of its corners a smaller copy half the length of the same triangle. This operation divides the original triangle (of a surface S), into four triangles (each of a surface $\frac{S}{4}$). This process is then repeated for the three triangles that touch the corners, and so on. As the iterations are performed, we get a triangle containing an increasing number of "holes", with one hole of size $\frac{S}{4}$, three holes of

---

13 The triangle is formed by connecting the middle points of the three sides.

size $\frac{S}{16}$, nine holes of size $\frac{S}{64}$ and after n iterations we have sliced the original triangle of surface S into the surfaces:

$$S \times \left(\frac{1}{4} + \frac{3}{16} + \frac{9}{64} + ... + \frac{3^{n-1}}{4^n} \right) = S \times \sum_1^n \frac{3^{n-1}}{4^n}$$

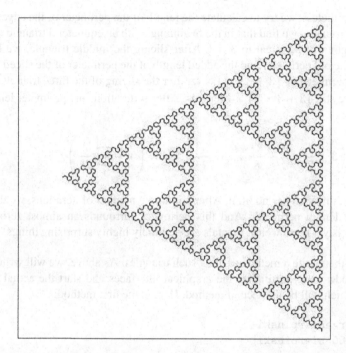

Figure 5.13. *A Sierpinski triangle drawn with a continuous line*

Figure 5.14. *The first three steps in the construction of a Sierpinski triangle by successive divisions*

The sliced triangles, and therefore the remaining triangles too, will be of decreasing sizes, approaching the size of a point. This will give us a triangle with an extremely small surface after n iterations – and after an infinite number of iterations, the remaining surface will be very close to 0: there will be no surface at all, just a cloud of points. It is weird.

If, nevertheless, we try to calculate the length of the perimeter of the edges, of this Sierpinski triangle, we find that in the beginning, with an equilateral triangle of length l, this length will be equal to $3 \times l$. After slicing the middle triangle, we have the length of the old perimeter and the added length of the perimeter of the sliced triangle, so a total perimeter of $\left(3 + 3 \times \frac{1}{2}\right) \times l$. After the slicing of the three triangles of side $\frac{1}{4}$, there are still $\left(3 + 3 \times \frac{1}{4}\right) \times l$ lengths. After n iterations the perimeter lengths are therefore:

$$l \times \left(3 + \frac{3}{2} + \frac{9}{4} + \frac{27}{8} + .. + \frac{3^n}{2^n}\right) = l \times \left(3 + \sum_{1}^{n} \frac{3^n}{2^n}\right)$$

Clearly, this sum has no limit. After an infinite number of iterations, we then have an infinite length perimeter. And this perimeter surrounds an almost zero surface triangle. It is yet more weird. Fractals are definitely highly surprising things.

Let us then write a method to draw such triangles. As above, we will write at least two methods: one to initialize the graphical interfaces and start the actual drawing method which will be the second method. Here is the first method:

```
Number>>sierpinski
    "280 sierpinski"
    | form pen |
    form := Form extent: 300 @ 300 depth: Display depth.
    form fillColor: Color white.
    pen := Pen newOnForm: form.
    pen roundNib: 1;
        color: Color black.

    pen place: 20 @ 290.
    self sierp: pen.
    form asMorph openInWorld
```

The receiver integer will correspond to the length of the side of the Sierpinski triangle. The method sierp: is then responsible for the proper realization of the drawing. Here it is:

```
Number>>sierp: pen
    self < 2
      ifFalse: [3
            timesRepeat: [self / 2 sierp: pen.
                pen go: self;
                    turn: 120]]
```

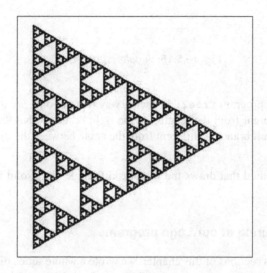

Figure 5.15. *Another Sierpinski triangle*

This method does nothing other than recursively go over the drawing of the three inner triangles. Figure 5.15 shows the Sierpinski triangle obtained by the transmission 280 sierpinski.

5.3. Exercises

The solutions can be found on pages 407 onward.

1) In the example program 5, we have written an "equiangular" spiral with constant angle and variable side length. Write a program that draws an "equilength" spiral with constant length but variable angle.

2) Write a program that draws a colored hexagon as shown in Figure 5.16.

3) Figure 5.9 shows how to construct a Koch curve. Write the method Integer>koch: that draws such curves. The receiver will correspond to the level, or *depth*, of the curve, the argument will correspond to the length of the initial line.

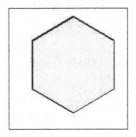

Figure 5.16. *A colored hexagon*

4) Modify the program `tree2`: in such a way that not only are the lengths of the left branches different from the lengths of the right branches, but the angle between the trunk and the left branch is different from the angle between the trunk and the right branch.

5) Write a method that draws the Sierpinski triangle via a solid line as in Figure 5.13 on page 219.

5.4. A restructuring of our Logo programs

In the previous sections of this chapter, we wrote a whole series of small programs and methods for drawing rectangles, circles, spirals, polygons, fractal trees or other structures. Each of these programs was either directly written in a Workspace, or written as a method of the Number class. Each of these programs contained almost identical program parts that could be transfered from one program to the other. Let us try to *refactor* these programs so that the common parts are implemented by specific shared methods.

Let us have a look, for instance, at our program for drawing a Sierpinski triangle on page 220. It starts – as all our other programs – by the declaration of the two temporary variables, form and pen, and their initialization:

```
| form pen |
form := Form extent: 300 @ 300 depth: Display depth.
form fillColor: Color white.
pen := Pen newOnForm: form.
pen roundNib: 1;
    color: Color black.
. . .
```

If we consider the difference in size of the form to be negligible, this series of instructions is clearly identical in all our other Logo-style programs. It is, therefore, a candidate for being extracted from this code to a method shared by all these programs.

A second problem is that our methods have been added to the Number class. This is justified by the fact that each method only works on numbers: the receiver of tree1 is the number of iterations that we want and the receiver of sierpinski is the length of one side of the original triangle. What slightly bothers us is the fact that the methods do other things than just calculations: for instance, initializing a Form and a Pen, as well as displaying the images: two activities that have nothing in common with a numerical calculation. And yet, our methods have been implemented in the Number class, a class designed, as its name indicates, for numerical calculations. We then want to separate the calculation activities from the drawing activities.

For this, we will create our own class for Logo drawings. Let us name it LogoDrawings. Since we know that all the Logo drawings will have a variable named pen and another named form, we can give this class of Logo drawings these two variables as instance variables. This will save us from declaring both variables as temporary variables in each drawing methods. At most, different instance methods will have access to the same values, which leads to the following definition:

```
Object subclass: #LogoDrawings
    instanceVariableNames: 'pen form'
    classVariableNames: ''
    poolDictionaries: ''
    category: 'Course-Smalltalk'
```

It is in this class that we will then implement our drawing methods – while leaving the recursive numerical calculation methods in the Number class.

To realize this let us start by writing a method initializing the instance variables to the appropriate values. This will be the following method initImage:

```
LogoDrawings>>initImage
    form := Form extent: 300@300 depth: Display depth.
    form fillColor: Color white.
    pen := Pen newOnForm: form.
    pen roundNib: 1;
        color: Color black;
        home
```

Let us also immediately write the method displayImage responsible for the display of the calculated drawing:

```
LogoDrawings>>displayImage
    form asMorph openInWorld
```

Then, let us write a `sierpinski` method, also in our new class of objects drawn by the turtle, `LogoDrawings`, as follows:

```
LogoDrawings>>sierpinski
    self initImage.
    long := (FillInTheBlank request: 'Initial length?'
                          initialAnswer: '280') asNumber.
    pen place: 20 @ long + 10.
    long sierp: pen.
    self displayImage
```

Apart from the fact that this method uses the `FillInTheBlank` class that will be presented below, let us note that it does, in the first four lines, nothing else through the activation of the method `initImage` but initialize the instance variables `form` and `pen` and place the turtle in its starting position (through the transmission `pen place: 20 @ long + 10`). Then, in the fifth line, it delegates the actual construction of the Sierpinski triangle to the same method `sierpi:pen:` as the one that has already been used in the initial method `Number>sierpinski`. Through the launch of the method `displayImage`, it ends with the display of the image constructed by the method `sierp:pen:`.

In this way, we managed to put the methods responsible for all the activities concerning drawings in the `LogoDrawings` class, and leave the only method that performs a numerical calculation in the number class[14]. We can generate a drawing with the transmission:

```
LogoDrawings new sierpinski
```

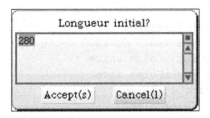

Figure 5.17. *An instance of* `FillInTheBlank`

During the evaluation of this dispatch, SMALLTALK encounters the expression:

---

14 Naturally, we can now remove the `sierpinski` method from the `Number` class: we no longer need it.

```
long := (FillInTheBlank request: 'Initial length?'
            initialAnswer: '280') asNumber.
```

FillInTheBlank is a class, subclass of the StringHolder class[15]. If we dispatch the message request:initialAnswer: it opens at the cursor position, a window with the string given as first argument as the title, and an input window in which the string given as second argument is displayed, as shown in Figure 5.17. The string entered by the user will be the value returned by this method. A single carriage-return will return the default value already in the window. It is just a simple way to interactively obtain values. Since here we prompt for a length, and so a number, we transform the return value into a numerical value with the method asNumber.

Then, the number entered by the user will be the receiver of the message sierp:pen: which makes our turtle draw the drawing on the canvas with the instance variable form. Finally, the method displayImage, as its name suggests, displays the image on the screen.

So far we have not changed the program. We have just slightly reorganized it to better reflect the conceptual separation between image calculation and image display.

Naturally, we can make similar transformations with other drawing methods that we have defined in the Number class.

Thus, our method Number»tree2 can be transformed in the method:

```
LogoDrawings>>tree2
   | long angle level |
   self initImage.
   long := (FillInTheBlank request: 'Initial Length?'
                 initialAnswer: '10') asNumber.
   angle := (FillInTheBlank request: 'angle ?'
                  initialAnswer: '20') asNumber.
   level := (FillInTheBlank request:
                   'Iteration depth?'
                  initialAnswer: '7') asNumber.
   pen place: 150 @ 250.
   level
```

---

15 StringHolder refers to *something that can hold a string*.

```
tree2a: long
angle: angle
pen: pen.
self displayImage
```

while leaving the numerical calculation methods tree2a and tree2b in the Number class.

5.5. A user interface for Logo drawings

In the previous section, we have slightly *refactored* all our Logo programs: we have created a specific class for the drawings (the LogoDrawings class), and we have created drawing methods in this new class, while delegating the necessary calculations for constructing the images to the methods of the Number class.

Each of the drawings can then be generated by transmission to an instance of the LogoDrawings class. Thus, the transmission:

LogoDrawings new sierpinski

yields a window with a drawing of a Sierpinski triangle, and the transmission

LogoDrawings new tree2

displays in another window the drawing of a tree generated by the interaction of the three methods tree2, tree2a and tree2b.

After n Logo drawing launches, we will have n windows on the screen – unless we cancel them, by hand, as and when they are produced.

We would like to have a specific window that will progressively contain each of the different drawings requested. This is what we will do in this section.

We must therefore first create a special window that can display drawings that are successively generated. For this, we need a window that can contain other windows. We already know it: in SQUEAK windows that allow us to drag, enlarge, etc., are *morphs*. All windows that we see in our standard interactions with SQUEAK are morphs.

Morphs[16] are objects that are able to interact with the user, to display on a screen, the Display, to control the positioning and the size of their submorphs.

---

16 The term *morph* is derived from the Greek word for *form* – as in the word *morph*ology.

From the start SQUEAK provides many such structures. Figure 5.19 shows a very small subset. For us, the most important are the SystemWindow, morphs with a titled header and equipped with some icons to reduce/enlarge the windows, to access the inner menu of the window and to destroy the window. In general, our explorers, our Transcripts and Workspaces, are instances of the SystemWindow class.

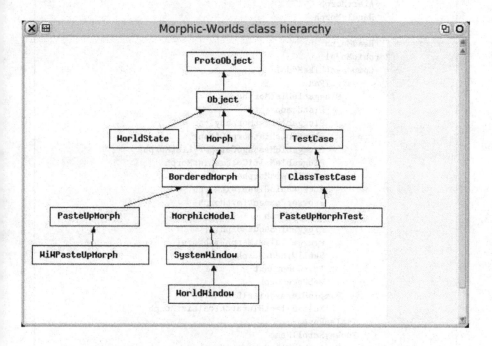

Figure 5.18. *The hierarchy of classes of the* Morphic-Worlds *category*

Other morph types that are of interest here are those of the type AlignmentMorph (to which we will return later) and PasteUpMorph, which, as their names suggest, are able to be "covered" by other morphs. The only PasteUpMorph we have already encountered is the SQUEAK window itself, the window that contains all the other SQUEAK windows. Such windows often play the role of a *morphic world*, of a complete SQUEAK environment. Figure 5.18 shows the hierarchy of SQUEAK classes that are part of the Morphic-Worlds category.

```
ProtoObject
   Object
      Morph
         BackgroundMorph
         BorderedMorph
         BorderedSubpaneDividerMorph
         DoCommandOnceMorph
         EllipseMorph
            AlertMorph
            HandleMorph
               NewHandleMorph
            HeadMorph
         MorphicModel
            ComponentLikeModel
               ScrollPane
                  PluggableListMorph
                     ListComponent
                     PluggableListMorphByItem
                     PluggableListMorphOfMany
                     PluggableMessageCategoryListMorph
                     PluggableMultiColumnListMorph
                  PluggableTextMorph
                     AcceptableCleanTextMorph
                     BrowserCommentTextMorph
                     MethodMorph
                     PluggableShoutMorph
                     PluggableTextMorphWithModel
                     ShellWindowMorph
                     TextComponent
                     WebPageMorph
                  SimpleHierarchicalListMorph
                     MultiSelectHierarchicalListMorph
               TitledPane
               TwoWayScrollPane
                  PluggableTileScriptorMorph
            Slider
               ScrollBar
               SimpleSliderMorph
            SystemWindow
               ArchiveViewer
               PartsWindow
               SystemWindowWithButton
               WorldWindow
         PasteUpMorph
            ComponentLayout
            IndexTabs
            PartsBin
            TextPlusPasteUpMorph
         PolygonMorph
```

Figure 5.19. *A small snippet of the Morphs hierarchy*

Let us then transform our instances of the LogoDrawings class into morphs of type PasteUpMorph. In order to do this, all we need to do is to modify, in the definition of our class,

```
Object subclass: #LogoDrawings
    instanceVariableNames: 'pen form'
    classVariableNames: ''
    poolDictionaries: ''
    category: 'Course-Smalltalk'
```

the first line such that LogoDrawings becomes a subclass of PasteUpMorph, so into the line:

```
PasteUpMorph subclass: #LogoDrawings
```

and to recompile ("Alt+s") this class definition. From now on, our LogoDrawings morphs are operational and can be activated with the message:

```
LogoDrawings new openInWorld
```

For now, such LogoDrawings will be just a small rectangle, with no particular distinction, except that it has a halo (see page 344) as with other morphs. Let us then give it distinctive signs, such as a color, borders and a size. For this, we will first create several methods giving the default values for these features. If we also create an instance initialization method called initialize as:

```
LogoDrawings>>initialize
    super initialize
```

we can delegate the activation of these methods to the superclasses. The writing of the names, and so the selectors, of all our initialization methods is very important, since the initialization methods of the superclasses will activate them with a transmission to the self of exactly these selectors.

To give a color to our instances, we just need to write the following method that returns the default color:

```
LogoDrawings>>defaultColor
    ^ Color gray
```

To give a size to our morphs, we must define its bounds:. Here, we write it as an origin point, the left upper point, and the *extent* point at the bottom right of the rectangle representing the morphic window.

```
LogoDrawings>>defaultBounds
    ^ 0 @ 0 corner: 300 @ 400
```

Let us add a method that defines the width of the border of the rectangle. It is the method `defaultBorderWidth`:

```
LogoDrawings>>defaultBorderWidth
    ^ 2
```

and its color that will be determined by the method `defaultBorderColor`:

```
LogoDrawings>>defaultBorderColor
    ^ Color red
```

If, after defining those few initialization methods, we again activate the transmission `LogoDrawings new openInWorld`, SQUEAK will display a window of size 300 by 400 pixels, with a red border of width 2 pixels surrounding a gray background, as shown in Figure 5.20.

Figure 5.20. *An instance of the* `LogoDrawings` *class*

Let us then add a menu to our morph. For this, we must first tell our morph what type of *event* we want it to respond to. Here the events relate to the behavior of the mouse cursor. The mouse can *enter* or *exit* the display surface of the morph, or it may be on the surface and the user clicks on any of its buttons. It is this kind of event[17]. Let us decide that we want to see the menu by clicking on the yellow button[18] (the button that typically provides the context menu). For this, we need to define the following method:.

```
LogoDrawings>>handlesMouseDown: event
    ^ event yellowButtonPressed
```

No method of `LogoDrawings` will use this method. A bit like our methods giving the default color or size of any instance of our `LogoDrawings` class, which are activated by methods of the superclasses, this method will be activated by the methods of interrupt handling of the `Morph` class (which, itself, uses many interrupt handling routines of SQUEAK core).

Finally, we need to tell our morphs, our instances of the `LogoDrawings` class, what should be done when the yellow button of the mouse has been clicked on. This will be indicated in the method `mouseDown:` [19]. Here we define our menu through an instance of the `MenuMorph` class, subclass of the `AlignementMorph` class. This class is one of the multiple morph classes specialized in the construction and processing of menus. Figure 5.21 shows the hierarchy of classes of the category `Morphic-Menus` that includes such classes.

Below, we give the text of the method `mouseDown:` where we have added line numbers in order to more conveniently comment on it afterward:

---

17 We are talking of *event* here since those are actions outside the control of the program. It is the programmer or the user who moves the mouse and who clicks on one of its buttons. These actions can take place at arbitrary times. For the program to take into account such events, it is necessary that the system (in our case, the SQUEAK system) has a machinery that constantly observes the different peripheral devices, such as the mouse and keyboard, and informs the program when an event has occurred. The part of the system responsible for these observations and information dispatches is called the *interrupt handling system*. We define thereafter the interface methods with this interrupt handling system and for each type of interrupt of interest, we define the methods that the system will activate when such an interrupt occurs. So, our methods relative to the events only enrich the knowledge of the interrupt handling system, which could then, according to the mouse cursor position, activate the specific methods attached to the objects, the morphs, which are in such positions.

18 If you have forgotten the color codes of the mouse buttons, read the footnote on page 6 once again.

19 As the method `handlesMouseDown:`, the method `mouseDown:` will not be activated by an explicit transmission in our program, but by the "interrupt controller" of the superclass `Morph` and the SQUEAK system.

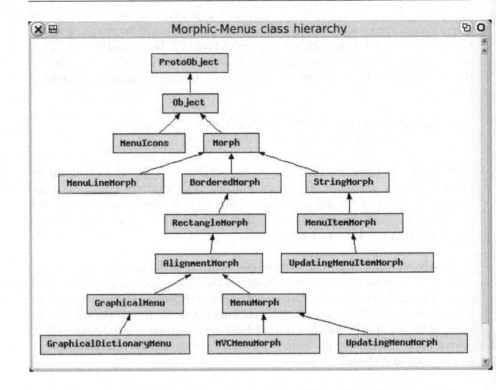

Figure 5.21. *The hierarchy of morphs for menus*

```
1 LogoDrawings>>mouseDown: evt
2   | menu |
3   menu := MenuMorph new defaultTarget: self.
4   menu addTitle: 'Choose a drawing';
5       add: 'Koch curve' action: #koch;
6       add: 'Sierpinski triangle' action: #sierpinski;
7       add: 'polygon' action: #polyferme;
8       add: 'tree' action: #tree2;
9       addLine;
10      add: 'test' action: #tree1;
11      addLine;
12      add: 'inspect' action: #inspect;
13      add: 'suicide' action: #suicide;
14      addStayUpItem;
15      popUpAt: Sensor cursorPoint
16      forHand: evt hand
17           in: self world
```

The method mouseDown: takes an event as an argument. Let us recall that it is the SQUEAK system which determines the event which occurs at a given time in our morph and it is the one which enables this method. Let us explain it:

– Line 3 creates a new instance of the MenuMorph class. The argument defaultTarget: indicates where to send messages attached to each of the menu entries in this instance.

– Line 4 adds a title to our menu with the message addTitle:. Our menu is, therefore, called Choose a drawing.

– Line 5, with the message add:action:, adds a first entry to the menu, a first line that can be selected. This entry is displayed as "Koch Curve". The second argument, the symbol #koch, indicates the selector of the message that it should send to the *target* if the user selects this entry. Since we have defined the menu with the *target* self, and since this mouthdown method is defined in the LogoDrawings class, self will be an instance of this class which will receive the message koch. Naturally, the LogoDrawings class must have an instance method named koch.

– Lines 6–8 define three additional entries, one to launch the drawing of a Sierpinski triangle, one for the drawing of a polygon and one for the drawing of a tree.

– Line 9, with the messageaddLine, inserts a horizontal line in the graphic representation of our menu, separating the previously defined entries from entries to be added afterward.

– Line 10 adds an additional entry called "test" that must activate the method LogoDrawings»tree1.

– Line 11 adds a separation line.

– Line 12 inserts the entry inspect which, if selected, activates the inspect method. Since we have not written a message named inspect in our LogoDrawings class, this method will be inherited from the Object class, the only class which, effectively, implements this method. As can be seen in Figure 5.22, SQUEAK automatically inserts the inspector icon for this entry. This input will allow us to open an inspector on the instance from which we have activated this menu.

– Line 13 launches the suicide method which is:

```
LogoDrawings>>suicide
    self delete
```

a method that sends itself the message delete. The transmission of this message to a morph destroys the morph and all its submorphs. This entry will help us to cleanly exit from a drawing session.

In general, a menu is very volatile: it is displayed until we have selected an entry. Then, it disappears and will only appear again the next time the user clicks on the mouse. If we want that menu to be displayed until it is manually canceled (for instance, by clicking on the ⊠ icon on the top left of the menu), it should be explicitly specified. This is what we do in line 14 where, with the message addStayUpItem, we add an icon in the shape of a pin on the top right of the menu, as shown in Figure 5.22. If the user clicks on this icon, the menu becomes permanent.

– Lines 15–17 show the last message we send to our MenuMorph: the message popUpAt:forHand:in:. This message indicates to the menu:

- the geographic position where it should visually appear – here, it is at the mouse cursor position, Sensor cursorPoint;

- by which it is controlled – here it is the cursor controller attached to the interrupt, the hand of the event hand of the event;

- to what it belongs to – here, it is the world our morph belongs to, and therefore, the whole Display.

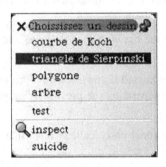

Figure 5.22. *The menu of a LogoDrawings*

If we now create an instance of LogoDrawings and we click on the yellow button of the mouse, we will get this newly created menu, shown in Figure 5.22. If we then select the entry tree and click on it, SQUEAK displays a drawing of a tree, but, unfortunately, on the top left of the screen.

In fact, nowhere have we indicated that the drawing should be a part of our morph. To do this, we will modify our display Image method:

```
LogoDrawings>>displayImage
    form asMorph openInWorld
```

which, for the moment does not say anything else other than to display the image as a form somewhere in the world, our form using canvas for the drawing.

In the new version below, the message addMorphFront: specifies that the form, as a morph, must be added to the current instance of the LogoDrawings class. With the message position: we indicate the position at which our form must be added inside the morph: at the center of the surface with a vertical offset corresponding to the height of our instance. Since we still want to have only one drawing the first dispatch, submorphsDo:, whose argument block eliminates all the submorphs, that could be present ensures that the new drawing is the only drawing present.

```
LogoDrawings>>displayImage
    | temp |
    temp := form asMorph.
    self
        submorphsDo: [:each | each delete].
    self addMorphFront: temp.
    temp position:
            ((self center x - (form width // 2))
                @ (bounds origin y))
```

The message addCenteredAtBottom:offset: allows us to combine the addition of a morph, the message addMorphFront:, with its position, the message position:, which gives the final version of our display method as follows:

```
LogoDrawings>>displayImage
    self
        submorphsDo: [:each | each delete].
    self addCenteredAtBottom: form asMorph
                    offset: bounds origin y
```

Finally, let us modify our method initImage so that the canvas is guaranteed to have the same size (minus the border widths) as our LogoDrawings instance, in order to ensure that the form always has a good size.

```
LogoDrawings>>initImage
        form := Form extent:
                        self extent - (2 * self borderWidth)
                        depth: Display depth.
    form fillColor: Color white.
    pen := Pen newOnForm: form.
    pen roundNib: 1;
        color: Color black;
        home
```

Voila. We have created a first short program displaying a morph which has a context menu and can display Logo drawings. Figure 5.23 shows a snippet of the display of a tree in the instance of LogoDrawings, which can be recognized by its colored frame. We also see the menu that allows us to interact with this instance.

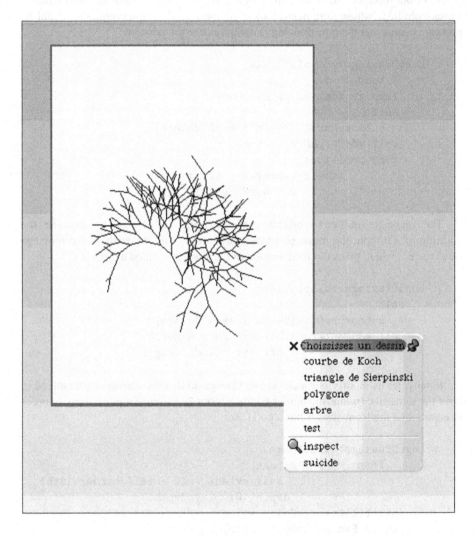

Figure 5.23. *Snippet of* SQUEAK *screen with an instance of* LogoDrawings

NOTE.–It is not always easy to determine which class you want to inherit from.This is particularly true for the choice of a morph superclass. Here, we have chosen to use the `PasteUpMorph` class, mainly because it is one of the most powerful subclasses of `Morph` but it is not at a very high level of abstraction. We could have chosen the `AlignementMorph` class instead, which allows us to easily *align* multiple morphs. If we did not, it is because we only ever wanted one morph to show. But you can change the superclass of the `LogoDrawings` class to be this `AlignmentMorph` class without too much trouble: `addCenteredAtBottom:offset:` is used in the display `Image` method, but is not known to the `AlignmentMorph` class.

Both lines just need to be replaced:

```
self addCenteredAtBottom: form asMorph
              offset: bounds origin y
```

by the line:

```
        self addMorph:  form asMorph
```

which uses the `addMorph:` method known to the `AlignmentMorph` class, and everything behaves in exactly the same way.

5.6. Lindenmayer systems

For all the curves that we have generated with the Logo turtle, the SMALLTALK Pen, the only representations of the curve are either the "Logo" program itself, or the result of its implementation: the drawing. There is no representation that can be manipulated by the program.

If we represent the Logo commands as letters, we can obtain an explicit representation of the curves as follows: let us "F" denote the transmission "pen go: $aLength$", "$-$" the transmission "pen turn: 60" and "$+$" the transmission "pen turn: -60". Then, let us describe a first line with: $D_0 = F$. To transform this line into a Koch curve, we should replace D_0 by $D_1 = D_0 - D_0 + + D_0 - D_0$, and, in general, the nth level of the Koch curve can be expressed as:

$$D_n = D_{n-1} - D_{n-1} + + D_{n-1} - D_{n-1}$$

This is clearly a recursive definition which gives a detailed description of the Koch curve for each level. So, if we slightly change our representation, by giving D_0 as the code for the drawing that we want to obtain at level zero, and F for a Koch curve this is a simple line. We can rewrite our rules as:

$$F$$
$$F \rightarrow F - F + + F - F \qquad [5.1]$$

The operator "$\rightarrow$" tells that the left side can be rewritten as the right side. It is a *rewriting rule*. If there are several rewriting rules, we have a *rewriting system*. Such a system can contain any number of rewriting rules. During each application of a rule, the occurrences of the left side of the rule in the chain undergoing the rewriting are replaced by the right side of the same rule. The characters for which there are no rules (they are the left side of no rule) are rewritten as they are, as if there were implicit rules of the style:

$$c_i \rightarrow c_i$$

Note also that, in our examples, the application of rules always starts with the level 0 chain, the *axiom* of the current rewriting system.

The first three levels of application of the above rewriting rule [5.1] are then:

axiom: F

– First application of the rule:

$$\underbrace{F - F + + F - F}_{replaces\ F\ from\ the\ axiom}$$

– Second application of the rule:

$$\underbrace{F - F + + F - F}_{1^{st}\ F} - \underbrace{F - F + + F - F}_{2^{nd}\ F} + + \underbrace{F - F + + F - F}_{3^{rd}\ F} - \underbrace{F - F + + F - F}_{4^{th}\ F}$$

– Third application of the rule:

$$F - F + + F - F - F - F + + F - F + + F - F + + F - F - F - F$$
$$+ + F - F - F - F + + F - F - F - F + + F - F + + F - F + +$$
$$F - F - F - F + + F - F + + F - F + + F - F - F - F + + F - F$$
$$+ + F - F + + F - F - F - F + + F - F - F - F + + F - F - F -$$
$$F + + F - F + + F - F + + F - F - F - F + + F - F$$

These "abbreviated Logo" chain instructions describe each curve very well. It is clearly shown that at level 0, the Koch curve is reduced to one line: there is only one occurrence of F. At the first level the curve consists of four segments and there are four occurrences of F; at level two, it is composed of 16 segments; and at level three it is composed of 64 segments. At each level, each of the preceding segments is divided into four new segments.

The signs $+$ and $-$ give the angle, to the right and left, of the different segments, respectively. Thus, we have a much more detailed description of the curve than the one we have in the Logo program on page 413 that constructs the same curve. Moreover, the writing of the rewriting rules that are necessary to obtain these descriptions is more compact than writing of the aforementioned Logo program.

This form of rewriting rules, called a *Lindenmayer system* or simply an *L-system*, was invented in the 1960s by the theoretical biologist Aristide Lindenmayer [LIN 68] to model cell and plant growth mechanisms. Such systems are masterfully presented in both books by Przemyslaw Prusinkiewicz ([PRU 89] and [PRU 90]).

5.6.1. *A first interpreter of Lindenmayer systems*

In this section, we will build a SMALLTALK program that is able to interpret the rewriting rules of L-systems and draw the curves obtained.

Let us start then by examining the objects that we need to build an interpreter for Lindenmayer systems:

1) As with our logo drawings, we need a form in which we will draw the L-systems and a morph to properly display them. If we create a subclass of the LogoDrawings class for our future Lindenmayer objects, we will inherit from its two instance variables and all the methods of their initialization and images display.

2) Each L-system is defined with an *axiom*, the zero state of the curve, and a set of rewriting rules. We clearly need at least two corresponding instance variables. Let us name them the axiom and derivationRules.

3) For each generation of a curve, we also need to know up to which level we want to develop the rewritings, we must know the length of a segment to be drawn and the size of the angle that we need to turn every time we encounter a $+$ or $-$ character. This gives us three additional instance variables: angle, level and length.

All of the above, therefore, leads to define the following class[20]:

---

20 Lsystem will then be a sub-subclass of the PasteUpMorph class!

```
LogoDrawings subclass: #Lsystem
   instanceVariableNames: 'level derivationRules
                          axiom angle length'
   classVariableNames: ''
   poolDictionaries: ''
   category: 'Course-Smalltalk'
```

The program should clearly operate as follows:

1) Read the axiom, the rewriting rules, the angle, the requested recursion level and the length of a segment.

2) Rewrite the axiom chain by applying the rewriting rules, apply these same rewriting rules to the result, and so on, until the program has generated `level` times the rewritings.

3) Translate the character string obtained, representing the curve in a drawing.

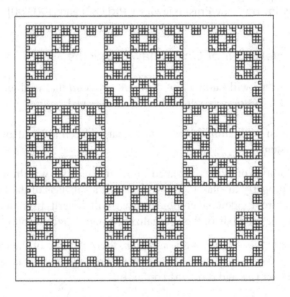

Figure 5.24. *A quadratic Koch curve*

Let us continue to write our program. We naturally need an initialization method for our instances of the Lsystem class. We will call the LogoDrawings class initialize – and for the same reasons: we will use the transmission self initialize present in the superclasses. This initialization must do exactly the same thing as the initialization of our superclass and, in addition, it must provide at least an initial value for our derivationRules variable, which should contain a series of

<keys> <rewriting of the keys> pairs. A dictionary seems to have the right structure for such object pairs. So, here it is our initialization method:

```
Lsystem>>initialize
    super initialize.
    derivationRules := Dictionary new
```

Following this update, let us also change the initial size of our `PasteUpMorph` in a square surface:

```
Lsystem>>defaultBounds
    ^ (0 @ 0 corner: 400 @ 400).
```

Since the menu of the instances of the `LogoDrawings` class contains a `test` entry, activating the method `test` if selected, let us define a `test` method that will handle the drawing of an L-system. It should then initialize all our instance variables, proceed to the rewriting and interpret the resulting string in terms of Logo instructions. Below, as before, we have added numbers to the lines of the method to better comment on it:

```
1  Lsystem>>test
2      self initImage.
3      pen place: 200 @ 390.
4      axiom := FillInTheBlank request: 'axiom?'
                            initialAnswer: 'F'.
5      self getDerivations: 1.
6      angle := (FillInTheBlank request: 'angle?'
                            initialAnswer: '60') asNumber.
7      level := (FillInTheBlank request: 'level?'
                            initialAnswer: '5') asNumber.
8      length := (FillInTheBlank request: 'length?'
                            initialAnswer: '5') asNumber.
9      self
10         automate: (self replace: axiom times: level).
11     self displayImage
```

Comments:

– In line 1, we initialize the form, the canvas of the drawing. The method `initImage` is inherited from the `LogoDrawings` class, being responsible for initializing the instance variables `form` and `Pen`.

– Line 2 places the turtle in a position suitable for drawing – at the bottom middle of the drawing canvas.

– Line 4 prompts the user to enter the character string corresponding to the *axiom* of the current L-system. If the L-system is the one used to build the Koch curve, the axiom is the string F. It is this string which is suggested by default.

– Line 5, the transmission of the message getDerivations with the numeric argument 1, resulting in reading of the rewriting rules. We will implement this method hereafter.

– Lines 6, 7 and 8 prompt for the values of the angle, the level and the length respectively. The program has a default value for each, corresponding to the drawing of a level five Koch curve.

– Lines 9 and 10 launch the construction of the curve with the replace:times: method that will be implemented below. This method must generate the description string of the curve, given as the first argument, up to the level given as the second argument. The first argument is the axiom from which we can develop the curve. This descriptive string of the curve to be constructed is then sent to the automate: method that should interpret it as a sequence of instructions for the turtle in order to generate the drawing of the curve.

– Line 11 is for the transmission, allowing us to effectively *display* the curve. The displayImage method is inherited from the superclass LogoDrawings.

Naturally, before implementing the two main programs, the one that constructs the description string of the curve, replace:times:, and the one interpreting the curve as a series of Logo instructions, automate:, we need to write the getDerivations method, responsible for collecting all the rewriting rules in the variable derivationRules.

This method should read a *<left side of a rule>* *<right side of a rule>* pair and put the corresponding *<right side>* in the derivationRules, dictionary under the key*<left side of a rule>*.

We have decided to syntactically separate the *left side* of a rule from its *right side* by the sign ":". Thus, if the program prompts the user for a rewriting rule, he or she should enter it, for example, as:

$$F : F - F + + F + F$$

We can assume that the left side will always be a *unique* character. This character will be the key. Anything that follows the ":" sign will be on the right side. To allow the user some flexibility in writing (he or she can insert spaces where he or she wants), we will only work on a copy of the input where all instances of the *space* character have been removed[21].

---

[21] We can also choose to leave all the "noise" characters and simply ignore them during the graphic interpretation of this string – but it is not as clean.

Finally, we will prompt the user to enter rules. A blank rule will indicate the end of the rules. All this reasoning gives us the following method[22]:

```
Lsystem>>getDerivations: n
    | tmp |
    tmp := FillInTheBlank
            request: 'derivation ' , n asString , ' ?'
            initialAnswer: 'F:F+F-F+F'.
    tmp := tmp copyWithout: $ .
    tmp = ''
        ifTrue: [^ nil]
        ifFalse: [derivationRules
            at: (tmp at: 1)
            put: (tmp copyFrom: (tmp indexOf: $:)
                            to: tmp size).
        self getDerivations: n + 1]
```

We have finally completed the preparatory work. Let us now tackle the generation of curve description strings. Let us recall that in the variable derivationRules we now have all the rewriting rules and in the variable axiom the string representing the turtle Logo instructions for constructing the initial curve. Let us examine the replace:times: method responsible for generating a string corresponding to the recursion level specified with the instance variable level:

```
Lsystem>>replace: aString times: n
    ^n = 0 ifTrue:[aString]
        ifFalse:[self replace: (self replace: aString)
                        times: n - 1]
```

This method clearly just controls the number of times the rewritings are performed. The rewriting, that is the application of the rewriting rules to each of the characters in the argument string, is delegated to replace: as follows:

```
Lsystem>>replace: aString
    | tmp |
    ^aString inject: '' into:
        [:new :ele |
            (tmp := derivationRules at: ele ifAbsent: nil) isNil
                ifTrue: [new , ele asString]
                ifFalse: [new , tmp]]
```

---

22 Here we use the copyWithout: methods (to remove the space characters) and copyFrom:to: (to write the right side of a rewriting rule) described on pages 90 and 98.

This method constructs a new string where each occurrence of a character that is not on the left side of a rewriting rule is reproduced as it is, and each character that corresponds to the left side of a rewriting rule is replaced by the string representing its right side.

Thus, the `replace:` method yields a string corresponding to the next rewriting level of its argument. The `replace:times:` method applies this rewriting to the successive results obtained by `replace:` as many times as specified with the instance variable `level`. It is this latter string that will be sent to the `automate:` method in order to yield a graphical interpretation.

In fact, this `automate:` method is an *interpreter*, in the same way as the one used on pages 143 onward[23].

To do this, we will use the `perform:` method defined in the `Object` class[24]. This method takes a symbol corresponding to the selector of a method as the argument, and sends this method to its recipient. If the method requires arguments, SQUEAK provides the `perform:with:` methods for two-argument methods: `perform:with:with:` for two-argument methods; and the method `perform:with:with:with:` for one-argument methods. If the method has more then three arguments, we can also use the `perform:withArguments:` method where all the arguments of the method will be send to `perform:` in an array. Below are some usage examples of `perform:`

```
'foo' perform: #size
4 perform: #+ with: 6
Dictionary new perform: #at:put: with: $F with: 'F+F--F+F'
```

The first example does exactly the same as the transmission `'foo' size`. The second example is equivalent to the expression 4 + 6, and the last expression is equivalent to `Dictionary new at: $F put: 'F+F-F+F'`.

Naturally, the use of `perform:`, and its variants, is especially helpful if the selector of the method to be *performed* is the result of a preliminary computation, as in the simplified example below that assumes a variable x containing an integer between 1 and 3:

---

23 Here, the expression will be a string, containing the characters F, $+$ and $-$, whose interpretation will be to read this string, from left to right, and to move the turtle forward each time character F is encountered, to make it turn left $-$, and as right at $+$. This is indeed an *interpretation* of an expression written in a specific language.

24 The `perform:` method is the primitive 83 of SQUEAK system (see Appendix Appendix 4 on page 507).

```
'foo' perform: (#(#size #asUpperCase #asLowercase) at: x)
```

We will be using the method perform: in a similar way in the method automate: below:

```
Lsystem>>automate: aString
    aString
        do: [:ele | ('F+-' indexOf: ele) > 0
                ifTrue:
                [self
                    perform:
                        (#(#forward #plus #minus)
                            at: ('F+-' indexOf: ele))]]
```

Currently our L-systems can contain three graphical interpretation symbols: F, $+$ and $-$. Each time a character is encountered, the method looks to see if it is one of these characters to be interpreted, if so, it sends to the instance of the Lsystem class the first, second or third selector, depending on whether we have encountered the first, second or third character of the 'F+-' string.

For this to work, we therefore need to write the three instance methods: forward, plus and minus that should graphically interpret the characters F, + and -.

Here are these very simple three methods:

```
Lsystem>>forward
    pen go: length

Lsystem>>plus
    pen turn: angle

Lsystem>>minus
    pen turn: 0 - angle
```

Our first version of a Lindenmayer system interpreter is completed. Figure 5.25 gives two curves constructed with the interpreter. The first, a level 5 Koch curve, is the curve that has been directly put in the program with the default values. The second, a Sierpinski triangle, is obtained with the axiom and the two rewriting rules below:

$$FXF - - FF - - FF$$
$$F \rightarrow FF$$
$$X \rightarrow - - FXF + + FXF + + FXF - -$$

The magnificent Peano/Gosper hexagonal curve in Figure 5.26 by Bill Gosper [BEE 72] has also been achieved with this still limited version of our L-system interpreter.

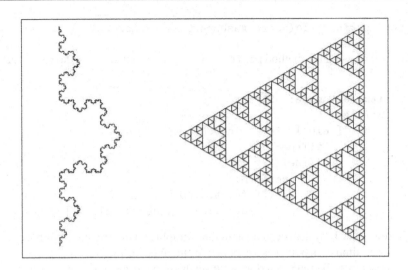

Figure 5.25. *A Koch curve and a Sierpinski triangle obtained with our Lindenmayer system interpreter*

If you have implemented this program and if you have played around with it a little bit, you may have noticed the following limitations and difficulties:

1) As the program is currently written, it is very difficult to find the right length of a line "*F*" and a good starting point for the turtle so it does not draw outside the available canvas and the drawing fits on this canvas. As for determining the starting point of the turtle, whenever we want to change its coordinates we should change the test method.

2) For the moment, the rewriting rules only concern the structures of the drawing, the turtle commands. We would also like to include meta-commands, such as commands to memorize the state of the turtle at a certain time, and to find such memorized states. This would allow the generation of a new class of drawings where it is important to return to previous states. In our Logo programs, we needed such capabilities for the drawings of trees, when the turtle had to return after drawing a branch to the start of this branch in order to draw another, in another direction.

3) The interface is not very satisfactory: each time, we need to give the axiom and the rules, even if we just want to see the curve at some other depth level. Perhaps we should also be able to read the axioms, the rules, angles etc., from files or save them to a file if we have interactively found an interesting L-system.

It is these improvements that we will make to our program in the following sections.

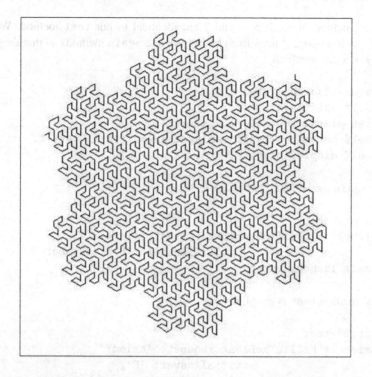

Figure 5.26. *A Gosper curve obtained with our interpreter. Axiom:* XF, *rewriting rules:* $X \to X + YF + + YF - FX - -FXFX - YF+$ *and* $Y \to -FX + YFYF + + YF + FX - -FX - Y$, *level: 4, angle: 60*

5.6.2. *Multiple activations of the same L-system*

Let us start our improvements by adding an `again` entry to our menu. This entry should allow us to obtain a drawing of the current L-system at an interactively specified level. This will facilitate our interactive experiments. The action linked to this entry will mainly do the same thing as the `test` method from the previous section: initialize the form, position the turtle, read the level of recursion and display the image obtained. We just save on the readings of the rewriting rules, the length and the angle. Here is the `again` method:

```
1 Lsystem>>again
2    self initImage.
3    level := (FillInTheBlank request: 'level?'
4                        initialAnswer: '5') asNumber.
5    pen place: 200@390.
6    self automate: (self replace: axiom times: level).
7    self displayImage
```

In this method, rows 2, 5, 6 and 7 are identical to our `test` method. We can, therefore, extract these 7 lines from both `test` and `again` methods so that they form the body of a new method:

```
Lsystem>>launchLsystem
    self initImage.
    pen place: 200@390.
    self automate: (self replace: axiom times: level).
    self displayImage
```

and our `again` method simply becomes:

```
Lsystem>>again
    level := (FillInTheBlank request: 'level?'
                            initialAnswer: '5') asNumber.
    self launchLsystem
```

while the method `test` is simplified as:

```
Lsystem>>test
    axiom := FillInTheBlank request: 'axiom?'
                        initialAnswer: 'F'.
    self getDerivations: 1.
    angle := (FillInTheBlank request: 'angle?'
                        initialAnswer: '60') asNumber.
    length := (FillInTheBlank request: 'length?'
                            initialAnswer: '5') asNumber.
    self again
```

To activate our method `again`, we need to insert the line:

```
    add: 'again' action: #again;
```

in an appropriate place in our `mouseDown:` method of the `LogoDrawings` superclass. In anticipation of the remainder of the program development, even at the cost of a slight duplication of code, I prefer to add a `mouseDown:` method to the `Lsystem` class. This will prevent a user from launching an activity designed for the Lindenmayer systems, from an instance of the `LogoDrawings` class, which cannot know the methods of a subclass. We then have the following modified copy of the `LogoDrawings»mouseDown:` method

```
Lsystem>>mouseDown: evt
    menu := MenuMorph new defaultTarget: self.
    menu addTitle: 'Choose a drawing';
        add: 'Koch curve' action: #koch;
        add: 'Sierpinski triangle' action: #sierpinski;
        add: 'polygon' action: #polyferme;
        add: 'tree' action: #arbre2;
        add: 'duopoly' action: #duoploy;
        addLine;
        add: 'L-System' action: #lSystem;
        add: 'again' action: #again;
        addLine;
        add: 'inspect' action: #inspect;
        add: 'suicide' action: #suicide;
        addStayUpItem;

        popUpAt: Sensor cursorPoint
        forHand: evt hand
        in: self world
```

In the process, we have renamed our test method as lsystem and the entry is
no longer called test but, more correctly L-system. Now, we can redraw the active
L-system with other depths by giving just a depth using the again entry of this new
menu.

5.6.3. *Computing the step size and the initial position*

Too often, while experimenting with our L-systems, we have had problems with
the size of the drawing – either it was too big for the canvas and only a part of it could
be seen or it was too small and a lot of details were hidden. Similarly with the position
and the initial orientation of the turtle: the drawing could be misplaced on the canvas,
or it was drawn only partially or not at all on the canvas. Let us tackle then the problem
about automatically finding a good length for the forward movement of the turtle as
well as a good starting position and orientation.

How can we do this? Since we have, before launching the drawing, a full
description of the drawing, in the form of a string giving all the Logo instructions
for drawing it, we can precede the drawing by a simulation of the activity of drawing
the curve. This *simulation* will allow us to:

1) calculate the *bounding box*;

2) this *bounding box* will allow us both to determine the length of the line that a
simple F should draw so that the whole drawing fits in the canvas, and to determine
the initial position of the turtle.

In order to calculate the bounding box, we will start with a very small rectangle, say of length 0 and height 0. This rectangle will obviously be too small to contain any drawing. We will then assume that the turtle is located at the only and single position that this rectangle allows: the horizontal and vertical position equals to 0. The turtle will have the initial orientation corresponding to the angle 0.

Finally, we will read the description string of the curve, character-by-character, and if we encounter:

– a character "+", we will add the `angle` to the orientation of the turtle;

– a character "−", we will subtract the `angle` from the orientation of the turtle;

– a character F, the horizontal position of the turtle will be increased with the sine of the `angle` and its vertical position will be increased with the cosine of the same angle[25].

Figure 5.27. *A rectangle of origin point* $\alpha\beta$

In order to facilitate our speech, let us suppose that our bounding box is defined with an origin at coordinates (α, β) the diagonally opposite point, the *extent* point, at coordinates (γ, δ), as shown in Figure 5.27. We know that at the start, α, β, γ and δ are all 0.

If after a simulated movement of the turtle, the new horizontal position is smaller than α, the horizontal coordinate of the origin of our bounding box, then this coordinate α will have as a new value the horizontal position of the turtle. If the horizontal position of the turtle is greater than γ, the horizontal coordinate of the *extent* point, then γ will have as a new value the horizontal position of the turtle. We will proceed in a similar manner for the vertical coordinates, β and δ.

If this process is repeated for each of the simulated movements of the turtle, it is obvious that the rectangle will be at every moment exactly of the size of the simulated drawing up to this moment. Naturally, at the end of the simulation, the rectangle will have the size of the final drawing – *if* the latter is drawn with a step length of 1.

25 We could have made the opposite choice: the sine determining the new vertical position, the cosine determining the new horizontal position of the turtle. The result would be the same (or at least symmetrically identical). Let us also note that this calculating approach implies a step length of forward move of 1.

Let us return to the implementation: in order to simulate the movements of the turtles, we need a simulated turtle. The latter is characterized by a vertical and a horizontal position and an orientation. We have the choice to either:

– *create* a new class to represent such a turtle with these three instance variables, one for each of the features;

– *add* those instance variables directly in our Lsystem class.

Let us opt for the second solution and let us add three additional instance variables in our class. These will be the variables sh and sv, to hold the *Horizontal* and *Vertical Position* of the turtle as well as the variable sdir, providing the *direction* of the *s*imulated turtle. We also need an instance variable for the *bounding box*, which will be called box, which gives us the new definition of the Lsystem class as follows[26]:

```
LogoDrawings subclass: #Lsystem
    instanceVariableNames: 'level derivationRules
                            axiom angle length
                            box sh sv sdir'
    classVariableNames: ''
    poolDictionaries: ''
    category: 'Course-Smalltalk'
```

We then need to calculate the bounding box. This should be done after generating the string representing the curve and, obviously, before displaying this curve, which, under the assumption that the method minBox: calculates the bounding box, requires us to change our method launchLsystem in order to obtain the version below:

```
Lsystem>>launchLsystem
    | tmp |
    self initImage.
    pen place: 200@390.
    tmp := self replace: axiom times: level.
    self minBox: tmp.
    self automate: tmp.
    self displayImage
```

In order to calculate the *bounding box*, therefore, to simulate the movements of the turtle, we can take a similar approach to the one we took to perform the drawing: a traversal of the representation of the curve and the activation of a specific method

---

26 We just need to edit the existing definition, that is to add four instance variables and *accept* ("Alt+s") this change.

for each character corresponding to an activity of the turtle. We just need to adjust the method `automate:` to our new needs.

In the adjustment below, we assume the following three methods to be known `forwardS`, `plusS` and `minusS`, which correspond, for our simulation, to the methods `forward`, `plus` and `minus` of our true drawing turtle.

Our method `minBox:` then follows:

```
Lsystem>>minBox: aString
    sh := sv := 0.
    sdir := 0.
    box := Rectangle origin: 0 @ 0 corner: 0 @ 0.
    aString
        do: [:ele | ('F+-' indexOf: ele)
            > 0
            ifTrue: [self
                perform: (#(#forwardS #plusS #minusS)
                    at: ('F+-' indexOf: ele))]]
```

This method is also responsible for initializing the instance variables required for the simulation: the three variables representing the state of the mock turtle are all initialized to 0: the turtle starts at the point 0@0 in the direction 0. The variable box, representing the bounding box, is initialized to an instance of the `Rectangle` class[27]. It is precisely the message `origin: corner:`, sent to the `Rectangle` class that creates the instance. The argument `origin:`, the point 0@0, corresponds to the point $\alpha@\beta$ of Figure 5.27 on page 250. The argument `corner:`, which is here also the point 0@0, corresponds to the point $\gamma@\delta$ of this same figure. It is thus a rectangle reduced to its minimum size.

The three methods of the turtle's movement simulation are then as follows.

```
Lsystem>>plusS
    sdir := sdir + angle
```

---

27 The `Rectangle` class, subclass of the `Object` class, is a relatively abstract class. It is used to factor out the key features found in any rectangular surface and in many methods dealing with the organization of the windows.

```
Lsystem>>minusS
    sdir := sdir - angle

Lsystem>>forwardS
    sh := sh + sdir degreeSin.
    sv := sv + sdir degreeCos.
    self boxUpdate
```

Naturally, the simulation of + and − should just change the orientation of the turtle, through a simple addition or subtraction. On the contrary, the simulation of *F* should both calculate the displacement, it is the calculation of the sine and the cosine,[28] and update the dimensions of our bounding box, which is performed by the method boxUpdate below:

```
Lsystem>>boxUpdate
    sh < box origin x
        ifTrue: [box := box withLeft: sh].
    sh > box corner x
        ifTrue: [box := box withRight: sh].
    sv < box origin y
        ifTrue: [box := Rectangle origin: box origin x @ sv
                                  corner: box corner].
    sv > box corner y
        ifTrue: [box := box withBottom: sv]
```

Knowing that the method withLeft: changes, in our drawing of a rectangle page 250, the value of α, that the method withRight: changes γ and that the method withBottom: changes δ, this method boxUpdate behaves exactly as described above (page 250).

The bounding box being at our disposal, we can − finally − compute the initial position of the turtle as well as the length of one step (of one instruction *F*) so that the drawing fits inside our canvas and that it best fills it. It is this calculation that is performed by the method normalize below:

```
Lsystem>>normalize
1     | stepX stepY step |
2     stepX := box corner x - box origin x.
3     stepY := box corner y - box origin y.
4     step := (form extent x - 20 / stepX)
5                     min: (form extent y - 20 / stepY).
```

---

28 The methods sin and cos calculate the sine and cosine of a numeric argument which represents an angle expressed in *radians*. If the angle is represented in *degrees*, the selectors degreeSin and degreeCos should be used.

```
 6    "rectangle:
 7        origin: starting point of the turtle
 8        corner: length of one step @ 0"
 9    ^ Rectangle origin: form extent x -
10                   (step *
11                       (box origin x + box corner x))
12                   / 2
13                @ (form extent y +
14                   (step *
15                       (box origin y + box corner y))
16                   / 2)
17                corner: step @ 0
```

Comments:

– Line 1: declaration of three temporary variables: stepX will contain the horizontal size of the bounding box, stepY will contain its vertical height and step will contain the value that length should take so that the drawing of the curve fits in the drawing canvas. Let us suppose, as throughout this section, that our bounding box has the origin at the point $\alpha@\beta$ and that the *extent* is given by the point $\gamma@\delta$. Let us note that as we have written the program up to now, $\alpha \in [-\infty, \gamma]$, $\beta \in [-\infty, \delta]$, $\gamma \in [0, +\infty]$ and $\delta \in [0, +\infty]$.

– Line 2: stepX will take as value $-\alpha + \delta$, corresponding to the horizontal size of the bounding box, to the distance of the horizontal coordinates α and γ.

– Line 3: stepY will take as value the vertical size of the bounding box, so the distance between the vertical coordinates of β and δ.

– Lines 4 and 5: until now, we have in stepX and stepY the size of one F for a unit canvas, a canvas whose size is determined such that one F corresponds to a turtle movement of length 1. We should adjust this length to the size of our real canvas, the size of our form. This is what we do in these two lines, where we calculate the size of one F in the drawing covering the canvas, simply by taking the minimum size between the vertical and horizontal size[29]. This size is simply the result of the division of the length (or height) of the real canvas (minus a small constant to prevent border overflows due to rounding errors) and stepX (or stepY).

– Lines 9–17: because we want to return two values: the step size *and* the initial position of the turtle, we return these values in the structure of a rectangle that has the starting position of the turtle as origin and the step size as extensions[30].

---

[29] If we had a guarantee that the drawing canvas is always a square, we would just need to calculate one of the sizes, either horizontal or vertical. As we did it, we guarantee that the drawing will always fit in the canvas, even if it is a very disproportionate rectangle.

[30] We could have taken a two-element collection – this is just an example of the obsession of the programmer: here, we have worked with rectangles, so the rectangle structure was prevailing as the result return structure. Another problem for ergonomists.

```
step * (box origin x + box corner x) / 2
```

The coordinate x of the position of the turtle will then be the middle (hence the division by 2 in the expression above) of the *actual* coordinates (taking into account possible negative values) of α and γ multiplied by the size of the `step`. The coordinate y is calculated in a similar manner with the coordinates β and δ.

If we now perform the adjustments in order to take account of these positioning and step calculations in the rest of the program, we can, without worrying about either the `length` or the initial position of the turtle, draw Lindenmayer systems in windows of any size. Figure 5.28 shows a quadratic Koch curve in a rectangular canvas automatically set to the "right" size and properly positioned in the middle of the rectangle.

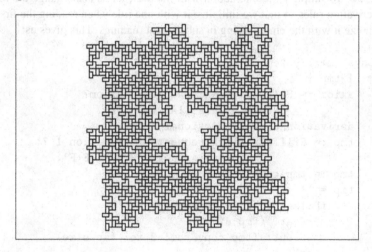

Figure 5.28. *A Koch curve correctly placed on the canvas*

These adjustments are very simple. First, we have to start the computation of the bounding box, initialize the instance variable `length` and place the turtle at the calculated initial coordinates. These activities should take place between the generation of the string corresponding to the description of the curve and its geometric interpretation. This gives us the following new version of the method `launchLsystem`:

```
Lsystem>>launchLsystem
    | tmp tmp1 |
    self initImage.
    tmp := self replace: axiom times: level.
    self minBox: tmp.
    tmp1 := self normalize.
    pen place: tmp1 origin.
    longueur := tmp1 corner x.
    self automate: tmp.
    self displayImage
```

Then, we must eliminate in the method lsystem the interactive reading of a value for the variable length: we do not need it now, it is automatically calculated by normalize. To simplify the interaction with the user, let us also change the reading of the derivation rules so that we initialize it with one rule when reading the first rule, and initialize it with the empty string in subsequent readings. This gives us:

```
Lsystem>>lSystem
    | tmp |
    axiom := FillInTheBlank request: 'axiom?'
                        initialAnswer: 'F'.
    derivationRules := Dictionary new.
    tmp := FillInTheBlank request: 'derivation 1 ?'
                        initialAnswer: 'F:F+F--F+F'.
    tmp := tmp copyWithout: $ .
    tmp = ''
        ifFalse: [derivationRules
                at: (tmp at: 1)
                put: (tmp copyFrom: 3 to: tmp size).
            self
                getDerivations: (tmp = ''
                        ifTrue: [1]
                        ifFalse: [2])].
    angle := (FillInTheBlank request: 'angle?'
                        initialAnswer: '60') asNumber.
    level := 5.
    self again
```

Voila. We have removed the first limitation, mentioned on page 246, of our interpreter of Lindenmayer systems. Let us then tackle the second: allow our rewriting rules to also contain characters corresponding to commands not for plotting but concerning the interpreter itself.

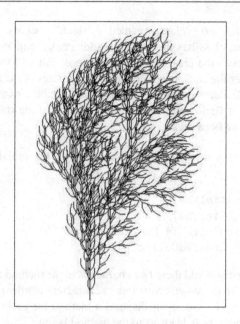

Figure 5.29. *A shrub generated by a bracketed L-system:*
level: 4, angle: 22.5, axiom: F, rule:
F: FF+[+F-F-F]-[-F+F+F]

5.6.4. Bracketed Lindenmayer systems

Bracketed L-systems systems allow two additional characters in the rewriting rules. These are the characters "[" and "]". The opening square bracket, "[", asks the *interpreter* to save the state of the turtle. This state is defined by the position and the orientation of the turtle. The closing square bracket, "]", asks the interpreter to return to the state it had during the last save of its state.

Since this backup and restoration behaves like object stacking, followed by object unstacking, we, computer scientists, talk of *pushing in* and *popping out* the stack, instead of "backing up" and "restoring". We name the place where we push and pop objects a *stack*[31]. It is such an object that we will need here.

_____

31 A stack, and the associated operations of pushing and popping, are ubiquitous in computer science and are part of the basic *data structures*. They are involved in the activation of procedures, interrupts, process management, etc. Its behavior is often described under the acronym *LIFO* for *last in, first out*, which can be translated as *the last thing saved is the first thing restored*.

In SMALLTALK no class named "stack" exists. However, the OrderedCollection class has the methods addFirst: and removeFirst: that well correspond to both the push and pop operations. We will therefore use such a collection to represent the stack in which we save the states of the turtle. This implies that the lsystems feature an additional instance variable, stack that should be initialized to an empty OrderedCollection – because at the start, clearly, no state of the turtle could have been saved.

Let us then add this instance variable and modify the initialization method as follows:

```
Lsystem>>initialize
    super initialize.
    derivationRules := Dictionary new.
    stack := OrderedCollection new.
```

Naturally, we must also add these two characters to the method automate: for our interpreter to recognize these two characters as characters worthy of an interpretation, which, assuming that we have at our disposal a method for pushing the state, push, and another for popping, pop, leads us to the method below:

```
Lsystem>>automate: aString
    aString
        do: [:ele | ('F+-[]' indexOf: ele)
                > 0
            ifTrue: [self
                    perform: (#(#forward #plus #minus
                                    #push #pop)
                        at: ('F+-[]' indexOf: ele))]]
```

Here are both methods to push and pop the state of the turtle:

```
Lsystem>>push
    stack addFirst: pen penDown.
    stack addFirst: pen direction.
    stack addFirst: pen location

Lsystem>>pop
    pen
        location: stack removeFirst
        direction: stack removeFirst
        penDown: stack removeFirst
```

The method `location:direction:penDown:` is a method of the Pen class allowing to force the values of the instance variables (of the Pen class) to the values of the arguments. The methods `direction` and `location` are also methods of the Pen class. They return the values of the instance variables of the same name. We have added to the Pen class the method penDown which provides the value of the instance variable penDown. Thus, we push and pop all the values that distinguish are instance of the Pen from another.

Naturally, we have to make similar adjustments in the methods simulating the movements of the turtle, thus in the method calculating the bounding box. Below are the three corresponding methods:

```
Lsystem>>minBox: aString
    sdir := sh := sv := 0.
    box := Rectangle origin: 0@0 corner: 0@0.
    aString
        do: [:ele | ('F+-[]' indexOf: ele)
                    > 0
                ifTrue: [self
                        perform: (#(#forwardS #plusS #minusS
                                        #pushS #popS)
                            at: ('F+-[]' indexOf: ele))]]

Lsystem>>pushS
    stack addFirst: sdir; addFirst: sv; addFirst: sh

Lsystem>>popS
    sh := stack removeFirst.
    sv := stack removeFirst.
    sdir := stack removeFirst.
```

Figures 5.29 to 5.31 show two drawings obtained with bracketed L-systems. We have corrected the second weakness (see page 246) of our interpreter of Lindemayer systems. There remains only the third: to be able to read a definition of a L-system from a file. This is the subject of the next section.

5.6.5. *Read a L-system from a file*

Before starting programming for the methods required to read a definition of a L-system from a file, let us determine the structure that such a file should have.

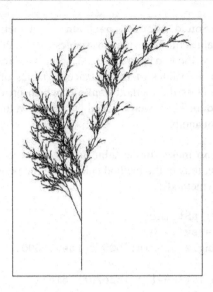

Figure 5.30. *A shrub generated by a bracketed L- system:*
level: 5, angle: 22.5, axiom: X, rules:
X: F-[[X]+X]+F[+FX]-X and F: FF

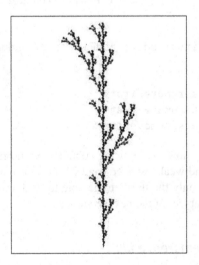

Figure 5.31. *A grass generated by a bracketed L-system:*
level: 5, angle: 25.7, axiom: F, rules:
F: F[+F]F[-F]F

We propose that the files containing definitions of a L-system, have the extension ".1"[32].

Each file defining an L-system should contain in the first line the requested recursion level, in the second line the angle of this, in line 3 its starting axiom, and the remaining lines contain the different rewriting rules, one rule per line. Thus, the file containing the definition shown in Figure 5.29 is as follows:

```
4
22.5
F
F: FF+[+F-F-F]-[-F+F+F]
```

Any definition file must contain at least 4 lines: level angle axiom, rule-1. If there are several rewriting rules, they will be in lines 4, 5, etc.

From this organization of L-systems files, we can start to program their reading. The first thing to do is to find in our default directory[33] all files with the extension ".1". In SMALLTALK, and therefore in SQUEAK too, the FileDirectory class allows the access to directories. The expression:

```
FileDirectory default
```

provides a pointer to the default directory, and the expression:

```
FileDirectory on: '/home/hw/squeak'
```

provides access to the directory /home/hw/suqeak, my default SQUEAK directory.

Every directory understands the message fileNamesMatching: whose argument must be a regular expression[34] and that returns an ordered collection containing all file names described by this regular expression.

---

32 Regardless of the operating system used, files are always organized 1) into a tree structure and 2) their names are composed of a basename and possibly (at least) an extension. The extension is separated from the basename with the character "dot" (.). For instance, if we save our Lsystem class in a file, using the entry fileOut of the context menu in the class browser, SQUEAK creates a file Lsystem.st, a file that has the basename Lsystem and the extension st.

33 The default directory is the directory where the SQUEAK image has been activated.

34 We will not give here a comprehensive description of what a regular expression is. Very briefly: a regular expression is a string possibly enriched with characters having a specific role. The two characters that may be of interest here are the characters "*" and "?". The first character, in a regular expression, indicates any number of arbitrary characters, the second indicates one arbitrary character. The regular expressions are used to describe sets of strings

For our needs, the expression

```
FileDirectory default fileNamesMatching: '*.l'
```

returns an ordered collection containing all file names in the default SQUEAK directory with the extension ".l". Therefore, this transmission gives all the L-system definition files in our SQUEAK directory. It is from this list that we would like to choose the file describing the L-system to display. We should clearly transform this file collection into a menu containing each of these files as entries. The method file below is supposed to do this:

```
Lsystem>>file
1    | menu1 listFic |
2    listFic :=
3        (FileDirectory default fileNamesMatching: '*.l')
4            asSortedCollection.
5    menu1 := MenuMorph new defaultTarget: self.
6    menu1 addTitle: 'L-Systeme Files';
7        position: Sensor cursorPoint.
8    listFic
9        do: [:fic | menu1
10            add: (FileDirectory baseNameFor: fic)
11            selector: #show:
12            argument: fic].
13    menu1 openInWorld
```

Comments:

– Line 1: the declaration of two temporary variables, local to the method file.

– Line 3: built as the ordered collection containing all the file names of the SQUEAK directory with the extension ".l".

– Line 4: transforms this instance of the OrderedCollection class in an instance of the SortedCollection class. Thus, we have the files in alphabetical order.

---

that correspond to the criteria which they describe. Thus, the regular expression f*o., for example, describes any string that starts with a character "f", followed by an any number of arbitrary characters, followed by the two characters "o.", also followed by exactly three arbitrary characters. This expression therefore describes both the string foo.bar and the string f123abcyyeuazyo.aie. These are just two examples of an infinite number of strings matching this description. Naturally, if the expression does not contain any of these *meta-characters* "*" and "?", it describes only the string matching the regular expression itself.

Interested readers will find much more information on regular expressions in any good book on Unix, such as the book Jean-Marie Rifflet [RIF 86].

– Lines 2, 3 and 4: put this sorted collection in the temporary variable listFic.

– Line 5: creates a new instance of a MenuMorph associated with self, therefore, to the current instance of the Lsystem class.

– Line 6: gives a title to this menu.

– Line 7: tells the menu, with the message position:, to appear (when it is asked to appear) at the cursor position.

– Lines 8–12: traverse the SortedCollection, containing all the L-system description files, and add each of the file names[35] to the menu we have just created in line 5. These additions are done with the message add:selector:argument: understood by every instance of the MenuMorph class. We use this message when the method to be launched, after selecting an entry in the menu, needs an argument. Here the method show: of the Lsystem class (we will see it below) clearly needs the name of the selected file as an argument.

– Finally, we display the menu in the wide world of a SQUEAK Display.

We clearly also need a method show: which will be activated if one of the menu entries is selected. For reading the file, we will use the FileStream class. Any instance of this class represents a stream on a file. It should read the L-system from the file and display it. As above, we will first give the method and then comment it.

This is the method show:

```
Lsystem>>show: aFile
1    | fic |
2    fic := (FileStream fileNamed: aFile) contents.
3    fic := fic findTokens:
4             { 10 asCharacter.}.
5    level := (fic at: 1) asNumber.
6    angle := (fic at: 2) asNumber.
7    axiom := (fic at: 3) copyWithout: 32 asCharacter.
8    derivationRules := Dictionary new.
9    4 to: (fic size) do: [:i | | tmp |
10       tmp := (fic at: i) copyWithout: 32 asCharacter.
11       derivationRules at: (tmp at: 1)
```

---

35 File names are composed of a *basename* and an extension (which for our files contain the description of an L-system the string '.l'). The class method baseNameFor: of the FileDirectory class, provides, from a complete file name, the corresponding string to the *basename* part. This will make our menus more readable.

```
12                                   put: (tmp copyFrom: 3
13                                              to: tmp size)].
14    self launchLsystem
```

Comments:

– Line 1: declaration of the temporary variable fic.

– Line 2: this variable takes as a value the string that is the content of the file given as an argument of the method show:. The method fileNamed:, sent to the FileStream class, creates and *opens* the file whose name is given in argument. The method contents returns the contents of the string giving the contents of the file obtained by the transmission FileStream fileNamed: a file as a string[36].

– Lines 3 and 4: put in an OrderedCollection (see the description of the method findTokens: on page 83) the parts of the "file contents" string separated by the *carriage return* character[37]. The temporary variable fic will, therefore, contain the collection of lines of the file read.

– Line 5: the instance variable level takes as value the numeric value of the first line.

– Line 6: the instance variable angle takes as value the numeric value of the second line.

– Line 7: the instance variable derivationRules is reinitialize to an empty instance of the Dictionary class.

– Line 9: the variable i will successively take as a value the indices of lines not yet explored. i will start with the value 4 and end with the value corresponding to the number of lines of the file. Lines 10–13 will be assessed for each of these lines.

– Line 10: the temporary variable of the block do:, tmp, will take as value the ith line of the file after removing all occurrences of the *space* characters (code ASCII: 32).

– Lines 11–13: the first character of the ith line becomes a key in the dictionary derivationRules. With this key is associated the string starting with the 3rd character and ending with the last character of this i^{th} line.

– Line 14: the menu is displayed (at the cursor position).

---

36 This is not always true. It may be that the file is considered as being in *binary*. The default behavior of FileStream is to consider that the file is a text file. In this book, we will not discuss aspects related to binary files.

37 The *carriage return* character (cr) is the line separation character in Unix. In Windows ASCII files, this separator is the *two* characters *carriage return* and *line feed* (lf). The ASCII code of the *line feed* character is 13. We put these as comments for the unfortunate programmers who have to program in this second system.

All that we have left to do is to activate somewhere our method `file` – otherwise, we will never see a menu and we could never choose one of the files from the menu. Let us then insert the contextual menu of our instances of the `lsystem` class, so in the method `mouseDown:` of this class, just after the entry `again`, with the following line:

```
add: 'read file ?' action: #file;
```

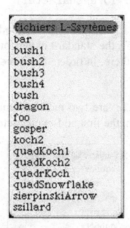

Figure 5.32. *An example of a file menu for the L-systems*

From now on, we can choose, with the entry "`file ?`", to load L-system definition files. Figure 5.32 shows an example of a file selection menu. Naturally, all the examples of Lindenmayer systems seen so far are there.

All that is left to do is add an entry "`save as ?`"in this same menu, with the line:

```
add: 'save as ?' action: #save;
```

that allows us to save an L-system definition file that is currently being worked on. This is accomplished by the method `save` below:

```
Lsystem>>save
    | fic aFile |
    File := FillInTheBlank request: 'file name'
                          initialAnswer: 'foo'.
    fic := (FileStream fileNamed: aFile , '.l').
    fic nextPutAll: level asString;
        nextPut: 10 asCharacter;
        nextPutAll: angle asString;
        nextPut: 10 asCharacter;
```

```
nextPutAll: axiom;
nextPut: 10 asCharacter.
reglesDerivation keysAndValuesDo: [:c :a |
    fic nextPut: c;
        nextPut: $:;
        nextPutAll: a;
        nextPut: 10 asCharacter]
```

Once the user has entered a file name, this method opens a stream on a file of this name and of extension ".1", the standard extension of our Lindenmayer system definition files. Then we write there, in order: the level, the angle, the axiom and the series of rewriting rules.

nextPut: and nextPutAll: are two methods, understood by all streams, that add objects to an opened stream, the first adds a character, the second a string.

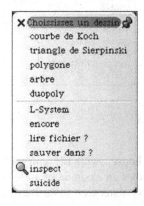

Figure 5.33. *The context menu of L-systems*

Finally, Figure 5.33 shows the menu of our L-systems and Figure 5.34 shows a nice variant of the Koch curve.

5.6.6. *Exercises*

Solutions can be found in section A1.8, pages 423 onwards.

1) Add to our L-systems interpreter, in addition to the commands F, $+$, $-$, [and], the command f that should do the same as the command F, but without leaving a trace. It will be a go: of the turtle, in a state where penDown is false. This command allows us to construct L-systems generating non-continuous drawings, containing holes, such as the one shown in Figure 5.35.

Figure 5.34. *A variant of the Koch curve,*
level: 4, angle: 85, axiom: F, rule: F: F+F–F+F

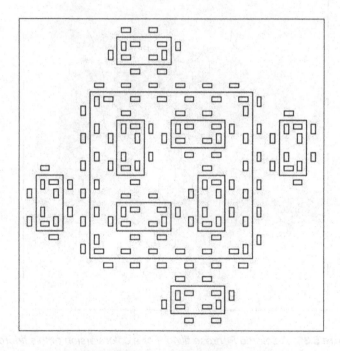

Figure 5.35. *An L-system with holes,*
level: 2, angle: 90, axiom: F-F-F-F, rules:
F:F-f+FF-F-FF-Ff-FF+f-FF+F+FF+Ff+FFF f:ffffff

2) Also add the command *C*, which should give a specific color to the Pen.
This command needs a numeric argument. This argument comes directly after the

command C, as for instance, in the following L-system which models a *Penrose tiling* [GAR 89]:

```
5
36
+WC10F--XC12F---YC12F--ZC10F
W:YC12F++ZC10F----XC12F[-YC12F----WC10F]++
X:+YC12F--ZC10F[---WC10F--XC12F]+
Y:-WC10F++XC12F[+++YC12F++ZC10F]-
Z:--YC12F++++WC10F[+ZC10F++++XC12F]--XC12F
F:
```

which puts the color alternately to the values 10 and 12, a light green and a dark blue. This L-system generates the Penrose tiling in Figure 5.36.

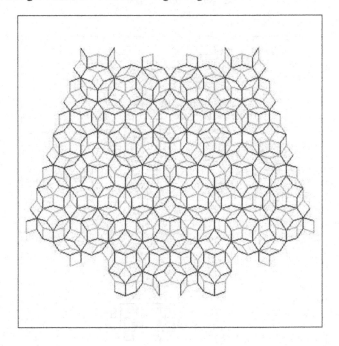

Figure 5.36. *A colored Penrose tiling. For a color version of this figure, see www.iste.co.uk/wertz/smalltalk.zip*

3) Since we are tackling the extension of the graphics capabilities of our L-system, interpreter, add two more commands to control the color of the line: the command > decrements the color of the Pen by the value given as argument, while the command < increments its color by the given value. This allows us to perform color variations

regardless of the numerical values of a specific color. Figure 5.37 shows the result of an L-system where we reduced the color by 1 at each step.

Figure 5.37. *A L-system with a continuous change of color and length level: 13 angle: 7.826 axiom: X rule : X : X>1F+@0.9997X. For a color version of this figure, see www.iste.co.uk/wertz/smalltalk.zip*

4) Figure 5.37, accompanying the previous exercise, presents an L-system that also uses a command @. This command takes as argument a number that determines the new length of a step. This number will be the factor by which length should be multiplied in order to obtain the new length. Thus, in the L-system of Figure 5.37 after each step, the length takes the new value length * 0.9997. Implement then this operator.

5) Our implementation of writing an L-system in a file, the method save, looks very dangerous: there is no test to see if the file where we want to write to already exists. So, if we give the name of an existing file, the latter will be erased and only the new one will remain. Find ways to be more careful.

6) The program *fractint*, freely available on the Internet [WEG 06], also contains a module for drawing L-systems. There also, there is a possibility to read their definitions from files. In contrast to our approach, fractint allows files with several L-system definitions. For this, an L-system in the file can be given as, for instance:

```
Koch2 {
level: 5
angle: 85
axiom: F
rules:
F:F+F--F+F
}
```

Clearly, in this way, a file can contain many definitions; which takes up less space on disk than many small files. Can you adjust our reading system of files written that way?

7) In our Logo programs, we used a random choice of angle or length. Change our interpreter in such a way that we can give *several* rewriting rules sharing the same left side. The interpreter then randomly chooses one of these rules whenever the left side is in the situation of being interpreted.

6

The Dependency Mechanism

In previous chapters, we have encountered a considerable set of salient features of SMALLTALK in general and of SQUEAK in particular. We have seen the mechanisms of message passing, static and dynamic inheritance, graphical interfaces specific to SQUEAK: morphs, and through our example programs, we were able to see that their execution is a series of messages exchanged between objects.

This message passings were always explicitly performed: a well-known object was sending a message to another well-known object. From time to time, it may be interesting to send messages not only to a single object, but also to a whole set of unnamed objects, kinds of implicit receivers, so as to *activate* each of the receiver objects. Such an implicit message passing can be particularly useful:

1) when an object has two aspects, one dependent on the other, and modifying one of the aspects implies modifying the other;

2) when a change of state of an object also requires the change of state of other objects, and those other objects, which need to be changed accordingly, are unknown;

3) when an object should be able to provide information to other objects without knowing exactly these other objects.

In this chapter, we will explore one more of the fundamental features of object-oriented programming proposed in SMALLTALK: the use of a *dependency* mechanism, which is at the basis of message sending to non-explicitly named objects.

This dependency mechanism allows us to express the relationship between a specific object and several other objects in such a way that if the object changes (or we think it has changed), it can – quasi-automatically – notify all the objects that depend on it so that they can be updated accordingly to this change.

This is a beautiful mechanism for the collaboration among multiple objects or actors.

6.1. Basics of the dependency mechanism

Before examining the use cases of this dependency mechanism in programs, let us look at the machinery that SMALLTALK has set up in order to handle them.

Since every object can have other objects dependent on it, its *dependents*, the Object class provides some basic methods to create dependency relationships. They all require a class variable (see section 4.4.7, page 119, which covers class variables) DependentsFields of the Object class. As a reminder, here is the definition of the Object class:

```
ProtoObject subclass: #Object
    instanceVariableNames: ''
    classVariableNames: 'DependentsFields'
    poolDictionaries: ''
    category: 'Kernel-Objects'
```

6.1.1. *Adding and removing dependencies*

This variable DependentsFields is a class variable of the root class Object and is therefore accessible to all classes and class instances of the SQUEAK system (except to the ProtoObject class, unique superclass of Object). It provides access to a dictionary containing the objects having dependents as the key, and the collections of dependents of each of these objects as values. Any object can have access to all of its dependents[1] through the message dependent, which is defined as:

```
Object>>dependents
    ^ self myDependents ifNil: [#()]
```

The method myDependents, activated by the method dependents, searches in the dictionary DependentsFields for the collection of dependents associated with the receiver:

```
Object>>myDependents
    ^ DependentsFields at: self ifAbsent: []
```

The following are two more methods allowing us to either add or remove dependents. To add a dependent, we have the method:

---

1 This set is held in an instance of the DependentsArray class, a subclass of the Array class.

```
Object>>addDependent: anObject
    | dependents |
    dependents := self dependents.
    (dependents includes: anObject) ifFalse:
        [self myDependents:
                (dependents copyWithDependent: anObject)].
    ^ anObject
```

and to remove a dependent, we have the method:

```
Object>>removeDependent: anObject
    | dependents |
    dependents :=
        self dependents
            reject: [:each | each == anObject].
    self myDependents:
            (dependents isEmpty ifFalse: [dependents]).
    ^ anObject
```

Both the latter methods use the method myDependents:, which, like the method myDependents above, accesses the class variable DependentsFields of the Object class:

```
Object>>myDependents: aCollectionOrNil
    aCollectionOrNil
        ifNil:
        [DependentsFields removeKey: self ifAbsent: []]
        ifNotNil:
        [DependentsFields at: self put: aCollectionOrNil]
```

6.1.2. *Dependencies management methods*

As shown in Figure 6.1, a subject-object[2] can be associated with dependent-objects. The subject-object has a state and its state update, its change can be notified to the dependent objects in order to trigger their own updates.

The Object class provides three methods for subject-objects to be able to communicate their state change and two methods for dependent objects to be able to respond to this state change. Everything should happen as if the dependent objects were constantly watching the subject-object on which they depend.

---

2 A subject-object, an object having dependents, is often called *a model*. A *model* can be the subclass of the Object or Model class, a class especially designed for objects with dependencies. It re-implements the methods myDependents and myDependents: by no longer accessing to the class variable DependentsFields but to an instance variable of the Model class, dependents. This greatly accelerates the manipulation of dependents.

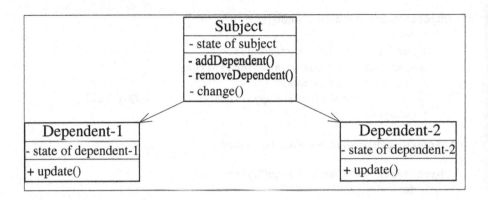

Figure 6.1. *An object with two dependencies*

Since the subject-object does not *a priori* know its dependents, it cannot directly send them information on its state change: it can only send this information to itself while relying on the ability of the SMALLTALK system to be able to dispatch this information to its dependent objects. This is exactly what is achieved by the methods changed, changed: and changed:with: below:

```
Object>>changed
    "The receiver has changed in a global way.
    Let us notify the dependents"
    self changed: self

Object>>changed: anAspect
    "The receiver has changed. This change concerns
    the aspect given as argument. Let us notify the dependents"
    self dependents do:
        [:aDependent | aDependent update: anAspect]

Object>>changed: anAspect with: anObject
    "the receiver has changed. This change
    concerns the aspect given as the first argument.
    Let us notify the dependents. Let us pass anObject
    as additional information"

    self dependents do: [
        :aDependent | aDependent update: anAspect
                                with: anObject]
```

Clearly, each of these messages transforms into the sending of the update messages update: or update:with: to all of its dependents.

The methods for updating the dependents are then as follows:

```
Object>>update: anAspect with: anObject
    "receives a change message of the object whose
    receiver is a dependent. The default behavior
    is to do nothing. The subclasses can change
    this default behavior"

    ^ self update: anAspect

Object>>update: aParameter
    "receives a change message of the object whose receiver
    is a dependent. The default behavior is to do nothing.
    The subclasses can change this default behavior"


    ^ self
```

Figure 6.2 shows the sequence diagram for an example combining a *model* with two *dependents*, corresponding to the methods given above.

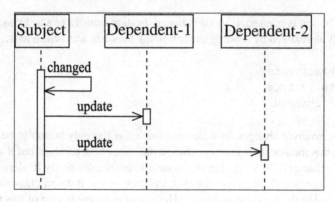

Figure 6.2. *The update sequence of the dependents*

6.1.3. *A first use case of dependencies*

Let us start with a very simple use case: let us write a microprogram that creates five buttons for a TV set (rather like a model of the 1970s). On such a TV, there are five buttons, one button per channel. A channel is selected by pressing the corresponding button. For example, the action of pressing the first button selects the first channel (at the time, it was ORTF-1), which naturally has the effect, almost mechanical, of bringing another button out (corresponding to another previously selected channel). Therefore, selecting a channel is simultaneously deselecting another channel.

In SMALLTALK terms, it means that there is a mutual dependence between all buttons. The state change of a button can influence any other button. This is what we will model.

Let us start by creating a class for the buttons, subclass of the Model class, for the sole reason that in this way the dependents are held in an instance variable, therefore easier to access for inspections. Here is this class definition:

```
Model subclass: #Button
    instanceVariableNames: 'state'
    classVariableNames: ''
    poolDictionaries: ''
    category: 'Course-Smalltalk'
```

Any instance of this class has an instance variable state, which will be true when the instance corresponds to a pressed button, otherwise it will be false.

When a button is pressed, it should change its state from false to true. Pressing a button will be realized by sending the following message activate to it:

```
Button>>activate
    state := true.
    self changed
```

Since the receiver changes its state, and since it is the only button to be aware of this change, this method does not only change the state of the receiver, but it also sends the message changed, indicating to the system to eventually notify its dependents of this state change, which requires that each instance of the Button class also knows how to respond to the message update:. Here is an implementation of this message:

```
Button>>update: aNil
        state := false
```

specifying that when a button receives the message update:, it should put itself in the false state (not pressed).

In order to observe it better, let us also give a method printOn: to each button:

```
Button>>printOn: aStream
            aStream nextPutAll: state printString
```

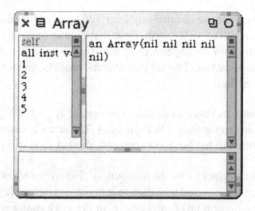

Figure 6.3. *The inspector on the Button array*

So, every time that a button should be displayed, it will be responsible for only outputting its state, `true` or `false`.

Let us suppose then that we have a collection of buttons. For the state of these buttons to be mutually dependent, these dependencies must be initialized. We do this with the following method `initialize::`

```
Button class>>initialize: aCollection
    aCollection
        do: [:b1 | aCollection
                do: [:b2 | b2 == b1
                        ifFalse: [b1 addDependent: b2]]]
```

which takes each element of the argument collection and associates all the other elements of that same collection as dependents.

Our microprogram is completed. We simply need to test it. For this, we define an additional class method of `Button` as follows:

```
Button class>>example
    "Button example"
    | collection |
    collection := Array new: 5.
    1
        to: 5
        do: [:b | collection at: b put: Button new].
    Button initialize: collection.
    collection inspect
```

Very deliberately, we have omitted any interface to this program: we just want to see if the dependencies work as we wish. Note that neither the subject-objects (in this example, there are five) nor the dependent-objects (in this example, there are also five: the same objects) have names. The subject-objects, models, cannot, therefore, know their dependents by name.

When we activate `Button example`, (we select it and we perform a doIt) SQUEAK opens the inspector shown in Figure 6.3. The array is indeed initialized with five buttons. None of them has yet been activated, their state is still undefined, `nil`.

Let us then open an inspector on the first button[3]. Figure 6.4 shows both inspectors, the former on the button array and the latter on `Button-1`, after the first button has been activated by the transmission `self activate`, in the `Workspace` window of the new inspector.

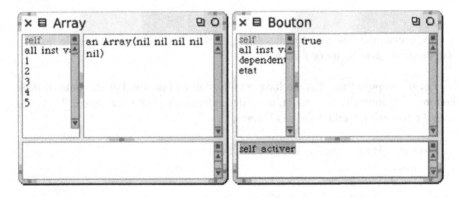

Figure 6.4. *Two inspectors, one on the array, the other on* `Button 1`

In the inspector of `Button-1`, we see that this transmission has changed its state, the value of the instance variable `state` is now `true`. After this transmission, the inspector on the button array, the inspector on the left in Figure 6.4, will have updated *all* the buttons: except the first, which is activated, they are now all in the `false` state. Naturally, this is the result of sending the message `update:` to each of the buttons depending on `Button` number 1. Figure 6.5 shows the sequence of messages sent.

---

3 For this, we click on the left pane of our inspector on the first element of the array and we start an inspector with "Alt+i".

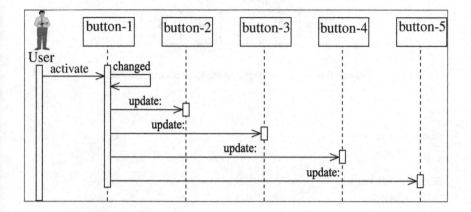

Figure 6.5. *The effect of the activation of the button-1*

6.1.4. A second use case of dependencies

Dependencies are particularly useful in the control of graphical user interfaces: they allow us to clearly separate programs into those parts performing computations and those responsible for the graphical user interface. In SMALLTALK, what is computed is called the *model*. In contrast, what is displayed is called the *view*[4].

To explore a bit more the dependencies, and to see how they are used in graphical user interfaces, let us change our simulation program of the buttons of a TV set so as to be able to interactively change the channel by pressing a button. Figure 6.6 shows the button row with which we would like to interact.

Since each button should display a name, the name of the channel which we access through it, let us start by adding the instance variable, `channel`, to our `Button` class.

```
Model subclass: #Button
    instanceVariableNames: 'state channel'
    classVariableNames: ''
    poolDictionaries: ''
    category: 'Course-Smalltalk'
```

Let us also create the two access methods, `state` and `channel`, and the two methods for modifying these instance variables, `state:` and `channel:`

---

4 SMALLTALK introduces yet another concept: the *controller* which refers to interactive inputs. Thus, in "classic" SMALLTALK programming, we talk of the MVC trilogy, where MVC stands for *model, view, controller*. All the implementation of morphs is based on this trilogy.

Figure 6.6. *The initial row of buttons on our TV set*

```
Button>>state
    ^ state

Button>>channel
    ^ channel

Button>>channel: aNumber
    channel := aNumber

Button>>state: aBool
    state := aBool.
    self changed: #changeLabel
```

We will return later on the transmission of changed: to self in the last line. Let us also update our two methods that change the value of the state of a button, activate and update:, in order to use the method state: that we have just defined:

```
Button>>activate
    self state: true.
    self changed: #button
```

Above, we have also changed the transmission self changed to self changed: #button, just to be absolutely sure, that first *our* update method update: can recognize that it is the one targeted by this state change, second, the other update:s possibly triggered because of a self changed, therefore a changed without argument, avoid taking the latter in account and third, to prevent triggering another update:, not anticipated by us, with our method activate.

Obviously, our method update: below considers this argument:

```
Button>>update: aSymbol
            aSymbol == #button
                ifTrue: [self state: false]
```

Finally, let us return – this time as an instance method – to our method `example`, let us call it `initialize:`, by enriching it with the necessary transmissions to create the graphic representation of our buttons row. Let us also give it as an argument the number of buttons that our TV set has, like this we are no longer limited to five buttons at the time of ORTF, we can have an arbitrary number of channels, each selectable by a specific button:

```
Button>>initialize: n
1    "Button example"
2    | window collection aux |
3    window := AlignmentMorph newRow.
4    window
5        layoutBounds: (0 @ 0 corner: 300 @ 50).
6    collection := Array new: n.
7    1
8       to: n
9       do: [:b |
10          collection at: b put: (aux := Button new).
11          aux state: false;
12              channel: b asString.
13          aux := PluggableButtonMorph
14                 on: aux
15                 getState: #state
16                 action: #activate
17                 label: #changeLabel
18                 menu: #buttonMenu:.
19          aux onColor: Color lightGray
20              offColor: Color white;
21              feedbackColor: Color red;
22              useRoundedCorners;
23              hResizing: #spaceFill;
24              vResizing: #spaceFill.
25          window addMorphBack: aux].
26   Button initialize: collection.
27   window openInWorld
```

Comments:

– Line 1: provides in comment the transmission required to initialize the buttons row. In general, the human code explorer appreciates to find somewhere a starting example of your program. This allows us, without much reflection, to launch our program in order to at least see what it does. So, just do:

```
SystemNavigation new browseAllImplementorsOf:  #example
```

to see all the examples SQUEAK provides in its image. Naturally, for this to work, we need to define the method example in the Button class. There it is:

```
Button class>>example
Button new initialize: 5
```

– Line 2 declares three temporary variables: window, collection and aux.

– Line 3 creates a new instance of AlignmentMorph. The instances of this class are reservoirs that can contain other morphs. They allow us to specify the relative position of morphs placed within, either vertically aligned or horizontally aligned. Here, we create an instance that can align its submorphs horizontally, using the creation instance selector: newRow. If we want to create an AlignmentMorph that aligns its submorph vertically, it should be created with the selector newColumn.

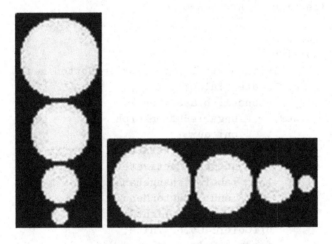

Figure 6.7. *Two AlignmentMorph aligning circular morphs*

Figure 6.7 shows the two example instances of an AlignmentMorph, the one on the left created by program:

```
| x |
x:= AlignmentMorph newColumn.
1 to: 4 do:
   [:y | x addMorph:
          (EllipseMorph new
               extent: y * 10 @ (y * 10))].
x openInWorld
```

vertically aligning four instances of the EllipseMorph class, and the one on the right created by the same program but with an Alignment-Morph where submorphs are horizontally aligned:

```
| x |
x:= AlignmentMorph newRow.
1 to: 4 do:
  [:y | x addMorph:
          (EllipseMorph new
              extent: y * 10 @ (y * 10))].
x openInWorld
```

– Lines 4 and 5: provide the graphical size of the "reservoir" morph: it will fit in a rectangle 300×50 pixels.

– Line 6: as in the method example in the previous section, we create an array with as many elements as there are buttons.

– Lines 7–25: these lines construct the collection of n buttons.

– Lines 7–10: are copies of our previous method example. As the only change we keep in the temporary variable aux the new instance of the Button class created in each iteration.

– Line 11 initializes the new button to the false state: no button will be turned on at the start, as it can well be seen in Figure 6.6.

– Line 12: the name of this button is the string corresponding to the iteration counter b.

– Lines 13–18: creation of an instance of the PluggableButtonMorph class. It is created with the message on:getState:action:label:menu:. A PluggableButtonMorph is a combination between an indicator of a Boolean value and an action button. The Boolean value is a value of the *model* to which this morph is associated. This model is specified to the morph in the argument to on:. Here the argument is aux, therefore, the instance of the Button class we have just created. Each TV's button will be represented by such a morph within our AlignmentMorph. When we speak of *model*, we refer to the model-view-controller trilogy mentioned above, and, even more clearly: a model involves dependencies. The morph we are creating will be a dependent of the button we have just created. This is the result of the transmission on:. From the moment of the implementation of this dependency, the new button sends its requests update: *also* to the PluggableButtonMorph associated with it. This is why we have given, in the method activate, an argument (#button) to the transmission of the message changed: – hoping that the PluggableButtonMorph has no method update: expecting the argument #button. The argument getState: provides the selector of the *model* class that allows us to consult the Boolean value that the morph represents. The method

Button»state, whose selector is given here as an argument, is clearly a method that returns a Boolean value: the value, on or off, of the button. The argument action: provides the selector of the method (of the model) to be triggered when the PluggableButtonMorph is activated by a mouse click. Here, the argument is the selector #activate, our method of the Button class that selects a channel on our virtual TV. The argument label:, #changeLabel, denotes the method of the model to activate in order to obtain the new label to display on the button. Here is this method:

```
Button>>changeLabel
  ^ state
      ifTrue: [self channel , ' turned on']
      ifFalse: [self channel]
```

Depending on the state of the button, its PluggableButtonMorph displays either the channel number or the channel number followed by the sentence turned on. Initially, since no button will be turned on, we will have a row of numbered buttons, as shown in Figure 6.6. As we have seen in the definition of method state, page 280, we use the method changeLabel in the expression:

```
self changed:  #changeLabel
```

Simply put, when a button changes state, it notifies all its dependents that the aspect changeLabel has changed. Since no method update: of the Button class takes this aspect into account, the only dependent for which this information can be of value is its morph. In fact, this mechanism provides the ability to respond to this aspect. It is set up by the argument label: during the definition of aPluggableButtonMorph. Figure 6.8 shows our button row with the fourth button turned on.

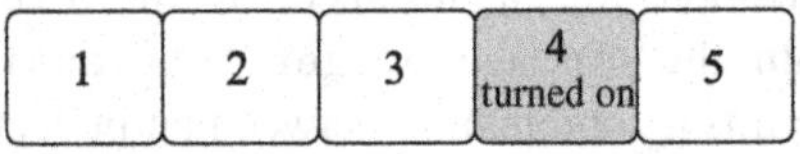

Figure 6.8. *The button row with the channel 4 turned on*

Finally, the argument menu:, #buttonMenu:, provides the method of the model that is able to return the context menu to activate. Our method buttonMenu: allows us to inspect the button located under the mouse cursor and is defined as follows:

```
Button>>buttonMenu: evt
  | menu |
  menu := MenuMorph new defaultTarget: self.
  menu addTitle: 'TV-Menu';
      add: 'inspect' action: #inspect.
  ^ menu
```

Since the method `on:getState:action:label:menu:` expects a lot of arguments which we do not always need, the `PluggableButtonMorph` class also provides the methods:

– `on:getState:action:label:` that does not need a menu;

– `on:getState:action:` that does not require changing a label nor displaying a menu;

– `on:` which expects that the model given as argument has a method `isOn`, providing the model's state, and a method `switch`, implementing the action to perform when the `PluggableButtonMorph` is activated.

– Lines 19 and 20: the method `onColor:offColor:` specifies to the morph the background color to display when the model's state is `true` and when the state is `false`. Here, we have chosen a pale gray background if the button is activated and a white background otherwise. In Figure 6.6, all the buttons are displayed with a white background since they are all off. In Figure 6.8, button number 4 is turned on, therefore displayed with a pale gray background.

– Line 21: the message `feedbackColor:` indicates the morph border color during the mouse click. This is a kind of *feedback* so that the user can see – even if no visible action is associated with the mouse click – that the click is considered.

– Line 22: the message `useRoundedCorners` rounds the corners of the rectangle representing the morph. This message is understood by all subclasses of `RectangleMorph`; the `PluggableButtonMorph` class is indeed one of its subclasses.

– Lines 23 and 24: the messages `hResizing:` and `vResizing:` indicate here to the `Pluggable-Button-Morph`, to any morph in general, how to occupy the space of the owner morph. For our morph, the owner will be the `AlignmentMorph` that has been created in line 3. For both methods, we have given the argument `#spaceFill` which forces the morph(s) to occupy the entire surface of the owner morph. Clearly, if there is only one submorph, and it has this property, it will occupy the entire surface, as shown in the first row of Figure 6.9, if there are two morphs, each takes half of the surface (see the second row of Figure 6.9), and so on. The third row in Figure 6.9 shows 10 submorphs sharing a space always proportional in size.

The fourth row in Figure 6.9 shows the filling without specifying `#spaceFill`. This is the default behavior, it can be forced with the argument `#rigid` to the methods `hResizing:` and `vResizing:`.

In those first four rows in Figure 6.9, we have given the same argument to the two dynamic adjustment methods of morph size. In the last row, we gave the argument `#spaceFill` to the method `hResizing:` and the argument `#rigid` to the method `vResizing:`. Therefore, in this last row of the figure, the morphs fill all the space horizontally, but remain in their default size vertically: `hResizing:` specifies how to fill the surface horizontally, while `vResizing:` specifies the vertical filling.

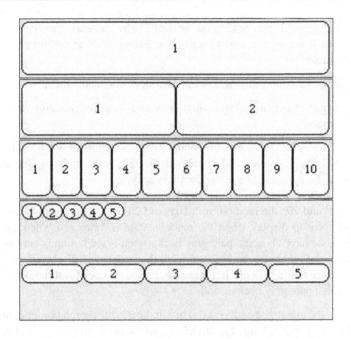

Figure 6.9. *The different ways of filling a surface*

– Line 25: finally we add, with the message `addMorph:`, our new morph as submorph to our `AlignementMorph` that is used as a surface where to place the buttons.

– Line 26: after constructing all the buttons and their visual forms, we can, as in the method `example` of the previous section, build the dependencies between the different buttons. For this, we use the same *class* method, of the `Button` class, `initialize:`, like the one already seen on page 277. We thus have two types of dependencies in our program: the one required to properly operate the buttons, the interdependence among all the buttons, and the one between each button and its morphic representation, necessary for correctly displaying their behavior.

Two classes are responsible for these dependencies: the `Button` class is responsible for dependencies on the calculation (here that is a minimum of computation, nevertheless …) and the `PluggableButtonMorph` class which is responsible for the display dependencies, of the *view*. This is manifested through two implementations of the method `update:`, one in the `Button` class that we have already seen. Here is a reminder:

```
Button>>update: aSymbol
        aSymbol == #button
            ifTrue: [self state: false]
```

and that of the `PluggableButtonMorph` class which we replicate below:

```
PluggableButtonMorph>>update: aParameter
    getLabelSelector ifNotNil: [
        aParameter == getLabelSelector ifTrue: [
            self label: (model perform: getLabelSelector)]].
    self getModelState
        ifTrue: [self color: onColor]
        ifFalse: [self color: offColor].
```

Carefully study this implementation. It starts with looking, with the message `getLabelSelector`, if this morph has a label that is likely to change (it was the argument `label:`, line 17, above). If this is the case, then it looks if the argument sent to `update:` corresponds to this functionality. In our case, it looks if the argument is equal to the symbol `#changeLabel`. If this is also the case, then it changes its label (with the method `label:`) into the string that the model, a specific button, returns in response to the transmission of the message `changeLabel`. It is quite beautiful – and to use it we do not even need to know how this is implemented. But to understand its implementation and admire the beauty of these interactions may be quite hard.

– Line 27: we simply need to open the window containing this button row in order to use it.

We have finished modeling buttons of the channel selection button TV. In order to illustrate the power of this dependency mechanism, we show in Figure 6.10 the sequence diagram for the activities generated by one click on the first button: as it can be seen here, the whole chain of the computations is performed by the dependency mechanism.

A word of warning:

– The dependency mechanism described in this chapter is obviously very powerful and very elegant. Any SMALLTALK programmer uses it constantly in its programs, since it allows us to clearly separate the calculation of ones program from the representations it may require, in SMALLTALK terms: to easily separate the *model* from its *views*. Thus, during representation changes, the *model* part of the program does not need to be touched, and changes to the *model* do not influence the *view* parts of the program.

– Using this mechanism can considerably accelerate the development of programs. For the beginner – and occasionally also for advanced programmers – its use may, however, bring the risk of introducing into ones program *hidden* loops. *Hidden*, because this kind of loop is not expressly transcribed in the text of the program, it is induced by the inadvertent use of the pair `changed` (and its variants) and `update:`.

To give an example, let us suppose that we have defined the method update: not as:

```
Button>>update: aSymbol
   aSymbol == #button
      ifTrue: [self state: false]
```

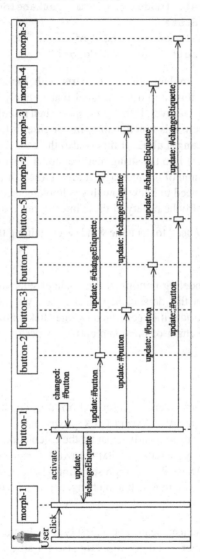

Figure 6.10. *Sequence diagram for an activation of button-1 with a click on the first button*

but simply as:

```
Button>>update: aNil
    self state: false
```

Moreover, that is how we have defined this method in the previous section: let us imagine that here we have just forgotten to take into account the specific aspect of the object that has changed.

With this little change to a previous version, here is then what happens when you click, for instance, on button 1:

1) The morph on which you have clicked sends the message `activate` to the button that it is associated with.

2) The associated button sends the message `state:` with the argument `true`.

3) After putting its instance variable `state` to `true`, button 1 sends the message `changed:` with #change-Label as argument.

The result of this transmission is, we now know, that this button sends to all its dependents the message `update:` with #changeLabel as argument.

4) According to the order in which the button finds its dependents in the dependent array, this update message, `update:`, is first sent to all buttons dependent on it, or first to the morph also dependent on it, – the morph on which we have clicked.

If the message is first sent to a dependent button, then:

1) The dependent button ignores the argument (it is not used in the body of the method `update:` and sends to itself the message `state:` with the argument `false`).

2) Then, in the method `state:`, it sends the message `changed:` with the argument #changeLabel, resulting in the dispatch of the message `update:` with this same argument to all its dependents.

3) According to the order in which the button finds its dependents in the dependent array[5], the dispatch of the message `update:` can be first sent to all buttons dependent on it, or first to the morph also dependent on it – the morph that should change its label and its background color. Below, let us then assume that the message is first sent to dependent buttons.

4) One of these buttons is button 1 whose activation has triggered all this series of message passings. This button 1, therefore, receives the message `update:` with the argument #changeLabel. Its own method of `update:` ignores the argument (as it

---

[5] Figure 6.11 shows an inspector opened on button 1 when the button 4 is turned on. The dependency array contains its `PluggableButtonMorph` and the four dependent buttons.

is not used inside the body of the method) and sends the message `state:` with the argument `false`.

Disaster! Since we have clicked on this button, we wanted to turn it on – we turned it on – but now, we will turn it off again. This is the first bug.

Then, button 1 sets its instance variable `state` to `false` and continues by sending the message `update:` with the argument `#changeLabel`.

Warning! This same message has already been sent to the same object, button 1, in the point 3 above. We will, therefore, repeat the same sequence of transmissions, to then restart again the same sequence of dispatches, etc., and do this endlessly. Our program is looping: it will never end. This is bug number two.

5) If the message is first sent to the dependent morph, the morph on which we have clicked, then:

a) The morph will send to its model, button 1 the message `changeLabel`, which returns the string `1 turned on`. Then, the method `update:` (of the `PluggableButtonMorph` class) replaces the displayed label of the morph and changes its background color.

b) The same message `update:`, always with the same argument, is then sent to all the dependent buttons. Naturally, during these dispatches, the same bug as above will occur: at a specific moment, button 1 will receive the message `state:` with the argument `false`, and the loop will start over.

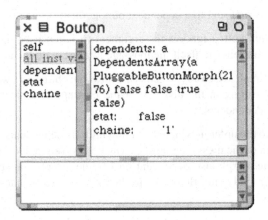

Figure 6.11. *An inspector opened on button 1*

Regardless of the order in which the message update is sent to all dependents, the program will never end. In the first case, the button rows will be frozen on the *feedback* image of button 1 (the button border is displayed in red). In the second case, the button will appear for a brief moment as turned on and will turn off thereafter.

In both cases, the execution of the method `activate` will never reach the line `self changed:    #button`.

This type of bug is very difficult to detect, so always beware when you use the methods `changed` (and its variants) and `update:` (and its variants), so as not to introduce *hidden loops*.

6.2. Programming a calculator

To explore the dependency mechanism and the importance of separating the *model* from the *view* a little more, let us build a small calculator, a simplified version of, for instance `KCalc` (see Figure 6.12), a calculator available on Linux.

Just looking at this figure, we see that such a calculator consists of several button rows and a display screen. In order to build one, the objects that we need are, therefore, the keys and at least one screen.

Figure 6.12. *KCalc: an example of a calculator*

6.2.1. *The keys*

Let us start with the calculator keys. They should not be very different from the buttons we were handling in the previous section: they all have a label and a functionality. Each activation of a key should generate an action from the calculator: if it is a function key, such as the key *C*, the calculator should run the program that performs the action of the key, for instance a reset action, if it is a numeric key, the digit corresponding to the key should be sent to the calculator so that the latter inserts it in the proper place.

The Key class should provide all the necessary methods to operate the calculator keys. Naturally, as we have just learned, we will first define the *model* and when the model will work properly, we will associate the *views*. Here is then the definition of the Key:

```
Model subclass: #Key
    instanceVariableNames: 'label function'
    classVariableNames: ''
    poolDictionaries: ''
    category: 'Course-Smalltalk'
```

with both its instance variables, label, its label and function, the functionality linked to the key.

As always, we define the access and modification methods of those instance variables:

```
Key>>function
    ^ function

Key>>label
    ^ label
```

No key changes label nor functionality. We will, therefore, delegate the assignment of instance variables to a single initialization method:

```
Key>>label: itsLabel function: selector on: aCalc
    label := itsLabel.
    function := selector.
    self addDependent: aCalc
```

Because each key is a key of a calculator, which will be in charge of the interpretation of the activation of a key, let us assimilate the keys as objects dependent to a calculator. This is achieved with the above method addDependent:.

The communication with the calculator will then be through the pair changed: / update:.

The activation of a key is the only functionality we can associate with it. Any other activity generated by this key will be handled by the calculator. This gives us the following method:

```
Key>>activate
        self changed: self
```

For our first minimal version of the keys of a calculator, we have completed their definition. Let us then tackle the core, the engine of the calculator.

6.2.2. The calculator

For a calculator to deliver a result, it should receive two numbers and an operator. Following the order in which it receives these arguments, we will talk of a *postfix*[6] calculator, of an *infix*[7] calculator or of a *prefix*[8] calculator.

6.2.2.1. Development of the calculator model

Let us start by aiming to obtain a postfix calculator.

Any calculator needs a screen, we call it screenBuffer, an accumulator (accu), to hold the results obtained up to now, and an indicator, firstTime, which should be true if we begin to write a new number on the screen, and false when the digit that has just been entered should be concatenated to the partial number already on the screen.

The definition of the Calculator:

```
Model subclass: #Calculator
    instanceVariableNames: 'accu screenBuffer firstTime'
    classVariableNames: ''
    poolDictionaries: ''
    category: 'Course-Smalltalk'
```

and its initialization method:

---

6 Like the famous Hewlett–Packard calculators: first the operands, and then the operation.

7 As most calculators on the market: first, we give an operand, then an operator and then a second operand.

8 This type of calculator is very rare: first, we give the operator, and then both operands.

```
Calculator>>initialize
    accu := 0.
    screenBuffer := accu asString.
    firstTime := true
```

Since the instances of the Key class communicate with the calculator via the message pair changed: and update:, we should determine how to respond to the activation of a key. The easiest way is to trigger the functionality associated with the key. We will associate with the numeric keys the functionality activateNumber:, to the operator keys +, −, × and / the corresponding arithmetic operations using a method activateFunction:, and the key C, for Clear, the functionality activateClear:. This reasoning already gives us the following two methods to reset the calculator, activateClear:, and to handle the numeric keys, activateNumber::

```
Calculator>>activateClear: label
    self initialize
```

```
Calculator>>activateNumber: label
    firstTime
        ifTrue: [firstTime := false.
            screenBuffer := label]
        ifFalse: [screenBuffer size = 1 & ((screenBuffer at: 1)
                = $0)
                    ifTrue: [screenBuffer := ''].
            screenBuffer := screenBuffer , label]
```

The second method distinguishes between the case where one starts writing a number and the other cases. If this is the start of the writing of a number, we initialize the instance variable screenBuffer with the digit corresponding to the key that has been activated and sent in the argument label as a string. Otherwise, after removing the 'zero' that is eventually displayed on the screen, we concatenate this digit to the number already contained in the variable screenBuffer. Thus, the screen will contain a number and, in any case, it is certain that we are out of the state where firstTime is true.

For the implementation of the other functionalities we should make a decision: do we want a postfix or infix calculator? Since in an infix calculator the interpretation of the key =, for instance, involves the start of the previously entered arithmetic operation, while the interpretation of the same key in a postfix calculator can only be the transfer of the contents of screenBuffer to the accumulator, the instance variable accu.

Let us then start by building a postfix calculator: it seems simpler. Nevertheless, in preparation for the subsequent construction of an infix calculator (and why not prefix too?), let us put the methods specific to the calculation approach in a specific subclass. For our postfix calculator we create the subclass `PostfixCalculator`:

```
Calculator subclass: #PostfixCalculator
   instanceVariableNames: ''
   classVariableNames: ''
   poolDictionaries: ''
   category: 'Course-Smalltalk'
```

In this subclass we will define two methods `activateEqual:` and `activateFunction:` as follows:

```
PostfixCalculator>>activateEqual: label
   accu := screenBuffer asNumber.
   firstTime := true
```

The method `activateFunction:` should consider the contents of the two instance variables `accu` and `screenBuffer` as operands of the operator given by the label of the function key that has been activated. Which gives:

```
PostfixCalculator>>activateFunction: label
   accu := accu perform: label asSymbol
                  with: screenBuffer asNumber.
   screenBuffer := accu printString.
   firstTime := true
```

We simply need to write the interface method with the keys, the method `update:`, which should activate the method given in the instance variable `function` of the key, with the label of that same key as argument. Which leads to the following definition:

```
Calculator>>update: aKey
   self perform: aKey function with: aKey label
```

Voila! We have completed writing the core of a postfix calculator, of the *model* of such a calculator.

6.2.2.2. *test of the calculator* model

Before continuing the development of our calculator, we present below a small method for checking the proper functioning of the model:

```
PostfixCalculator class>>example
   "PostfixCalculator example"
   | aCalc t1 tPlus tEqual tCE |
   aCalc := self new.
```

```
t1 := Key new
        label: '1'
        function: #activateNumber:
        on: aCalc.
tPlus := Key new
        label: '+'
        function: #activateFunction:
        on: aCalc.
tEqual := Key new
        label: '='
        function: #activateEqual:
        on: aCalc.
tCE := Key new
        label: 'C'
        function: #activateClear:
        on: aCalc.
self halt
```

Here we proceed as in section 6.1.3: we use a combination of the debugger and inspectors in order to get a first impression of the program correction.

If we activate the expression PostfixCalculator example we will obtain the debugger window given in Figure 6.13. We have access to a numeric key, the key t1, an arithmetic key, the key tPlus, the key tEqual corresponding to the key =, and the key tCE for resetting. In short, we have one key for each of the four possible interpretation methods of the keys. We can then open an inspector on the calculator and inspectors on each of these keys in order to activate them and observe their effects. Figure 6.14 shows on the left an inspector opened on the key t1 and on the right another opened on the key tPlus. The inspector on the left in Figure 6.15 shows the state of our postfix calculator after:

– activating the key t1, through the evaluation of the dispatch self activate in the inspector's interaction window on this key (see the inspector on the left in Figure 6.14);

– activating the key tEqual (not shown in the figures) in the same way, which had led the accumulator accu to take the value 1 (visible in the left inspector on Figure 6.15);

– activating three times the key t1, which had led the variable screenBuffer to take the value '111' (visible in the left inspector on Figure 6.15).

The inspector on the right in Figure 6.15 shows the state of our calculator after activating then the addition key tPlus (visible on the right in Figure 6.14).

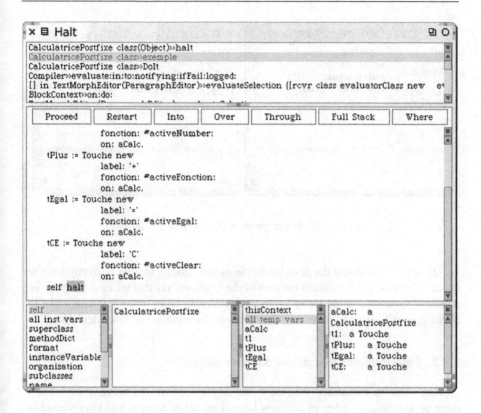

Figure 6.13. *The* `Halt` *exception window opened on a calculator*

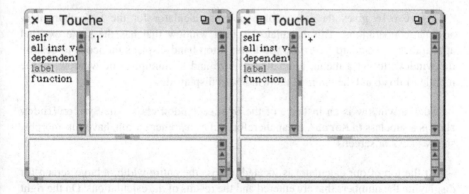

Figure 6.14. *Two inspectors on keys*

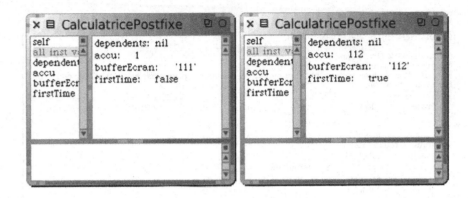

Figure 6.15. *Two inspectors on a postfix calculator*

Obviously, our calculator is on track: the model appears to work correctly because the accumulator `accu` contains the sum of the two numbers that we have entered. We still have to develop some views for this calculator, in order to use it interactively, by clicking on the keys and observing the effects in the windows of this calculator.

6.2.3. *Development of a graphical user interface*

Any calculator consists of at least one display screen, ten numeric keys and a more or less large number of function keys. This set of screens and keys should be integrated visually in a frame and functionally in such a way that each activation of a button changes the display.

Figure 6.16 gives the image of a postfix calculator for the four elementary arithmetic operations. This calculator is in a window that has the same external appearance as standard SQUEAK windows: a top band displays the icons to destroy the window, to get a menu, to change its size and to minimize the window; in the middle of this band the *name* of the window is displayed.

Such a window is an instance of the `SystemWindow` class. The `SystemWindow` class is a subclass of `Morph`[9]. It can therefore, like any other morph, have sub-morphs, such as keys or screens.

At the top of our calculator is located, across the entire width, a large screen for displaying the numbers that are entered and the results of the calculations. On the right

---

9 look for that class in the hierarchy of the `Morph` class on page 228.
In non-morphic SMALLTALK versions, the `SystemWindow` class is the class `StandardSystemView`.

of the calculator is a second screen that displays the history of performed operations and obtained results. Both windows are instances of the `PluggableTextMorph` class, morphs designed for displaying (and possibly editing) text.

The keys are, naturally, instances of the `PluggableButtonMorph` class that we have just seen operating through our TV buttons in the previous section.

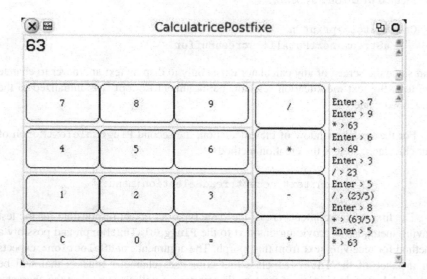

Figure 6.16. *Our first calculator*

Let us return for a moment to the `PluggableTextMorphs`. Such a morph should know at least its *model*, the class, which provides to it the text to display, and the selector of the method allowing us to import this text (this should be a method that returns a string). Often the selector of the method allowing to change the text is also provided to it. Both selectors should refer to the methods of the model class, since the model owns the text and has the access and modification methods of this text.

One of the class methods for creating a `PluggableTextMorph` is `on:text:accept:` that creates such a morph on the class given as an argument to `on:`, with the text access selector given as argument to `text:` and the text modification selector given as argument to `accept:`. Thus, the `PluggableTextMorph` that we should create for the main screen of our calculator is created by the transmission:

```
PluggableTextMorph
    on: self
    text: #printString
    accept: nil.
```

where self designates the instance of the calculator for which we are building a *view*, the selector printString returns the string screenBuffer, since we have redefined the method printOn: as below:

```
Calculator>>printOn: aStream
    aStream nextPutAll: screenBuffer
```

and since the screen of any calculator exists only to display text and never to change the text, the text modification selector, the argument accept:, is initialized to the undefined value.

For the history window of the calculation, the second PluggableTextMorph of our calculator, we use the creation method:

```
on:text:accept:readSelection:menu:
```

The first three arguments are of the same type: an object responsible for the test having methods for providing this text to the PluggableTextMorph and possibly a method for receiving text from this morph. The argument readSelection: expects an instance of the Interval class that comprises character indexes that will be selected during the display of the text. Thereafter we will always select the character that follows the last character of the displayed text. This way we guarantee that the window will always make the last added text visible[10]. Finally, the argument menu: expects a context menu.

Let us start by creating on top of the classes Key, Calculator and PostfixCalculator a Screen class that represents the history screen of our calculator. It has an instance variable, hist, which accumulates all the interactions between the user and the calculator:

```
Model subclass: #Screen
    instanceVariableNames: 'hist'
    classVariableNames: ' '
    poolDictionaries: ' '
    category: 'Course-Smalltalk'
```

---

10 The text in the window rolls from the bottom to the top, always leaving the last line of text in the window visible.

Both the access and modification methods of the instance variable will also serve as interface with the morph responsible for displaying the screen:

```
Screen>>hist
    ^ hist
```

and

```
Screen>>hist: aString
    hist := aString.
```

In order to print an instance of screen, we just need to display the content of the instance variable hist:

```
Screen>>printOn: aStream
    hist printOn: aStream
```

After these preparatory definitions, let us start by setting up the views for each part of our calculator. The views will be built by the method openInWorld and the start of its definition is as follows:

```
Calculator>>openInWorld
1    | window view c l color a1 a2 a3 |
2    window := SystemWindow labelled: self class name.
3    a1 := AlignmentMorph newRow.
4    a2 := AlignmentMorph newRow.
5    a3 := AlignmentMorph newRow.
```

To simplify the work, we first declare some temporary variables:

– window will contain the main morph of the calculator. All the other morphs that we will use will be sub-morphs of window. In line 2 we initialize this variable to an instance of SystemWindow with the class name as a header of the window. At first, the name will be PostfixCalculator, since we will create the calculator through the transmission

```
PostfixCalculator new openInWorld
```

– view will be used to temporarily hold morphs that are in construction;

– c and l are temporary variables that will help us know in which column and in which line of a morph array we are at a given time;

– color is just used to hold once and for all the background color for our sub-morphs;

– a1, a2 and a3 will temporarily hold the AlignmentMorphs as shown in lines 3 to 5 of the above method openInWorld.

Let us examine the remainder of our method:

```
6    view := PluggableTextMorph
7            on: self
8            text: #printString
9            accept: nil.
10   view
11       font: (StrikeFont familyName: 'Atlanta' size: 22).
```

In lines 6-11 we create the display window of the calculator: it is an instance of the `PluggableTextMorph` class with the instance of the calculator we are creating as model. It displays the text that the method `printString` returns when it is sent to the model and it prevents any change of the model text (the argument `accept:` is undefined, `nil`).

This `PluggableTextMorph` displays its text in large print, size 22 pixels, in the `Atlanta` character set. Every morph that can display a text has the attribute `font:` which determines the character set used for the display[11].

Here are the three following lines of the method `Calculator»openInWorld`:

```
12   window
13       addMorph: view
14       frame: (0 @ 0 extent: 1 @ (1 / 5)).
```

With the method `addMorph:frame:` we add the view that has just been built, the screen of the calculator, to the main morph of our calculator. The corresponding rectangle begins at the upper left point (the point 0@0) and will extend horizontally across the entire width and will vertical take $\frac{1}{5}$-th of the main window.

To place sub-morphs at specific locations in a morph, we either use, as we have done previously, the `AlignmentMorphs`, and the positioning will be done proportionally with the method `addMorph:`, or we give, with the method `addMorph:frame:` the positioning with a rectangle where all points are given in relative measures with respect to the size of the receiver morph. The rectangle:

$$0 @ 0 \text{ extent: } 1 @ (1 / 5)$$

can be read as:

$$0 \times receiver\text{-}morph\text{-}width @ (0 \times receiver\text{-}morph\text{-}height)$$
$$\text{extent: } 1 \times receiver\text{-}morph\text{-}width @ (\tfrac{1}{5} \times receiver\text{-}morph\text{-}height)$$

---

11 Those are mainly the instances of: `PluggableListMorph`, `PluggableShoutMorph`, `PluggableTextMorph` and `StringMorph`. Explore these classes and look at the examples provided.

The screen occupies the top of the calculator and a fifth of the height.

Below is the part responsible for setting up the *history* screen of our calculator. This screen, also a PluggableTextMorph, has as model an instance of the Screen class which in turn has the calculator as model. The latter dependency is performed during its creation in the method on: of the Screen as follows:

```
Screen class>>on: aCalc
    | aux |
    aux := Screen new.
    aux hist: ''.
    aux addDependent: aCalc.
    ^ aux
```

But, let us return to the remainder of our method openInWorld:

```
15   view := PluggableTextMorph
16           on: (c := Screen on: self)
17           text: #hist
18           accept: nil
19           readSelection: #selectTextInterval
20           menu: #myMenu:.
21   self addDependent: c.
22   view setTextColor: Color blue.
23   window
24       addMorph: view
25       frame: (4 / 5 @ (1 / 5) extent: 1 / 5 @ (4 / 5)).
```

Let us repeat it: the view of the history screen displays the text obtained by the message hist, therefore the contents of the instance variable hist and does not accept, like the main screen of the calculator, any change: the displayed text will be read-only. To force the morph to roll the text such that its ending is always visible in the window, the method selectTextInterval chooses the ending of the text as the part of the text to be selected, therefore to be displayed.

Here is this method selectTextInterval:

```
Screen>>selectTextInterval
    ^Interval
            from:  hist size + 1
            to: hist size + 1.
```

The argument menu:, in the creation of the PluggableTextMorph, is the selector of a method of the model, therefore, the Screen class here, which returns the menu to activate when the yellow button of the mouse is clicked on. Our method myMenu:

```
Screen>>myMenu: evt
  | menu |
  menu := MenuMorph new.
  menu addTitle: 'Screen-Menu';
     add: 'inspect'
     action: #calculatorInspect.
  ^ menu
```

provides a menu with a single entry: inspect. We naturally want to inspect our calculator and not the PluggableTextMorph from which we can get this menu. For this, we write the new method calculatorInspect that should be added to the Pluggable-Text-Morph class as follows:

```
PluggableTextMorph>>calculatorInspect
  self model dependents
     do:[:obj | (obj isKindOf: Calculator)
              ifTrue:[^obj inspect]]
```

The screen, an instance of the PluggableTextMorph class, has an instance of the Screen class as model. Such an instance has two dependents: the morph which represents it graphically and the calculator from which it is the history screen. In the above method, the transmission self model, therefore, returns the instance of the Screen class associated with the receiver PluggableTextMorph. This instance of the Screen class receives the message dependents that returns the array of its dependents. This array is then traversed, with the message do: till the encounter of an object that is *a kind of* Calculator. The method isKindOf: of the Object class answers true if the receiver is an instance of the class or one of the subclasses of the class given as argument. Here, isKindOf: answers true if the receiver is an instance of Calculator or PostfixCalculator. This instance then receives the standard message inspect.

Lines 15–20 of our method Calculator»openInWorld create this instance of PluggableTextMorph and temporarily hold it in the variable view.

Line 21 of this method adds the newly created instance of the Screen class to the dependents of this calculator. Thus, the calculator will also know its history screen.

The line 22:

```
                view setTextColor:  Color blue
```

specifies that any text displayed in the morph view, the history screen, should be written in blue characters.

Finally, lines 23–25:

```
23   window
24     addMorph: view
25       frame: (4 / 5 @ (1 / 5) extent: 1 / 5 @ (4 / 5)).
```

add our new morph to the main morph of the calculator. Like earlier, the measures for the dimension of this submorph, therefore, for its positioning inside the owner morph, are expressed relative to the measures of the owner morph. The history screen occupies the last fifth of the right part of the calculator, and this throughout the free height under the screen for displaying results. Such a calculator, composed of only two screens, is shown in Figure 6.17.

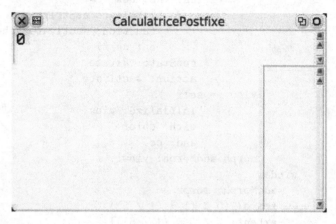

Figure 6.17. *Our calculator at current stage of the program: a screen for displaying the result at the top and a screen for the history on the right*

The addition of the numeric keys is performed in lines 26–49 (shown below) of our method openInWorld. We should create nine keys, therefore, nine instances of the PluggableButtonMorph class aligned into three horizontal rows, each consisting of three keys. Each of these key rows is formed by an AlignmentMorph on which are placed three PluggableButtonMorph. Each keys row, therefore, forms the same structure as our buttons row in the previous section – it is quite natural: a key in the calculator essentially performs the same role as a button of our TV.

In line 26, we initialize the temporary variable 1 to the value 0. It serves as a counter for determining where a key should be inserted on its AlignmentMorph: in the first, second or third position.

Line 27 holds in the temporary variable color the background color of the window representing our calculator. All our keys will have that same color in order to have a single-colored representation of the different keys of our calculator.

```
26    l := 0.
27    color := window color.
28    #(#(9 8 7) #(6 5 4) #(3 2 1) )
29        with: {a1. a2. a3}
30        do: [:ro :morph |
31          l := l + 1.
32          ro
33            do: [:co |
34              view := PluggableButtonMorph
35                    on: (Key new
36                        label: co asString
37                        function: #activateNumber:
38                        on: self)
39                    getState: #state
40                    action: #activate.
41              view := self
42                    initialize: view
43                    with: color
44                    and: co.
45            morph addMorph: view].
46        window
47          addMorph: morph
48          frame: (0 @ (l * (1 / 5))
49          extent: 3 / 5 @ (1 / 5))].
```

The initialization of all the keys takes place in two nested loops: an outer loop, formed by the transmission of the message with:do: going from line 28 to line 49, and an inner loop, formed by the transmission of the message do: and going from line 32 to line 45.

The receiver of the message with:do: is an array composed of three subarrays corresponding to the keys labels of the three keys rows to build (line 28). The argument with: is the array of three AlignmentMorph representing the three keys rows (line 29).

The inner loop goes through the three keys labels of a subarray (lines 32 and 33) in order to create for each of them an instance of PluggableButtonMorph (line 34) associated with a new instance of the Key class (line 35) having the current label (line 36), the function activateNumber: (line 37) is also associated with the same calculator that is being visualized with this method openInWorld (line 38). The new PluggableButtonMorph finds the state of its model, so its key, with the method Key»state (line 39) and will trigger, when it is activated, the method Key»activate (line 40).

Every `PluggableButtonMorph` requires the knowledge of the method yielding the state of the model, either `true` or `false` – even if it should not distinguish between these two possible states. This is why we add to the class `Key` the method `state` as follows:

```
Key>>state
    ^ false
```

Clearly, our key never changes state; that is not necessary. Consequently, the `PluggableButtonMorph` associated with a key always displays the color `offColor`, the one corresponding to the `false` state of its model.

Let us return to our method `openInWorld`: lines 41–44 contribute to the initialization of the newly created `PluggableButtonMorph`. Here is the method `initialize:with:and:` that is responsible for these additional initializations:

```
Calculator>>initialize: view with: color and: co
    ^ view offColor: color;
      borderWidth: 1;
      borderColor: Color black;
      hResizing: #spaceFill;
      vResizing: #spaceFill;
      label: co asString;
      useRoundedCorners;
      yourself
```

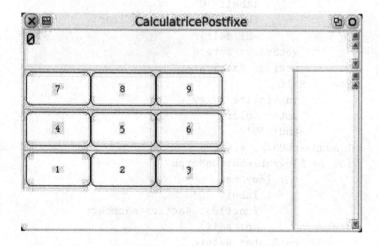

Figure 6.18. *Our calculator at the current stage of the program: two screens and nine numeric keys*

This method initializes the color offColor of the morph to the color of the calculator window, the color of our instance of SystemWindow, gives to the morph a border with a width of one pixel (the sending of the message borderWidth:) a black color (the sending of borderColor:), tells it to occupy all the available horizontal and vertical space (the sendings of hResizing: and vResizing: with the argument #spaceFill), gives a label to the morph (the sending of label:) and indicates to the morph to appear as a rectangle with rounded corners (the sending of useRoundedCorners). This method returns the initialized PluggableButtonMorph (with the transmission yourself).

After these initializations, the PluggableButtonMorph is added (line 45) to the current instance of the three available AlignmentMorphs.

Once the inner loop completed, we have created three key views, the outer loop adds the AlignmentMorph containing these three views to the calculator window (lines 46–49). The temporary variable 1, which is incremented during each iteration, allows us to know the vertical position, $\frac{l}{5}$, of this morph.

As can be seen in Figure 6.18, which shows a view of our calculator at the current moment of its programming, it starts to look like a real calculator. The few remaining keys will be built below.

```
50    a1 := AlignmentMorph newRow.
51    view := PluggableButtonMorph
52             on: (Key new
53                  label: 'C'
54                  function: #activateClear:
55                  on: self)
56             getState: #state
57             action: #activate.
58    view := self
59             initialize: view
60             with: color
61             and: 'C'.
62    a1 addMorphBack: view.
63    view := PluggableButtonMorph
64             on: (Key new
65                  label: '0'
66                  function: #activateNumber:
67                  on: self)
68             getState: #state
69             action: #activate.
70    view := self
```

```
71                    initialize: view
72                    with: color
73                    and: '0'.
74      a1 addMorphBack: view.
75      view := PluggableButtonMorph
76                    on: (Key new
77                        label: '='
78                        function: #activateEqual:
79                        on: self)
80                    getState: #state
81                    action: #activate.
82      view := self
83                    initialize: view
84                    with: color
85                    and: '='.
86      a1 addMorphBack: view.
87      window
88          addMorph: a1
89          frame: (0 @ (4 / 5) extent: 3 / 5 @ (1 / 5)).
```

The snippet from the method Calculator»openInWorld above can be read as a succession of three blocks of 12 lines. Each of these blocks defines the view of a particular key: lines 51–62 define the reset key C, lines 63–74 define the numeric key 0 and lines 75–86 define the enter key =.

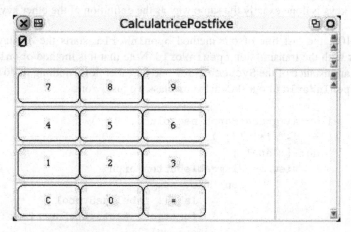

Figure 6.19. *Our calculator at the current stage of the program: two screens, 10 numeric keys and the keys C and =*

The first line, line 50, creates a new instance of the AlignmentMorph class that is used as a container for these three keys. The lines 62, 74 and 86 add each key to this morph. We use here the message addMorphBack: which is identical to addMorph:, with the slight difference that the first adds the argument morph *after* the morphs already in the container morph, while the second adds it before the morphs that are already in the container morph.

Lines 87–89 add the container morph of these three keys, the AlignementMorph created in line 50, to the view of the calculator. Figure 6.19 shows the view of the calculator at the current stage of the program: what is left is a vertical row of arithmetic operator keys.

Let us then finish the view of our calculator by adding these arithmetic operator keys. They will be vertically aligned: we, therefore, use an AlignmentMorph with vertical insertion of submorphs. This is done in line 91 through the creation method newColumn.

Then, as we did for the numeric keys, we will go through an array containing the labels of each of the four operation keys (the keys $+$, $-$, $*$ and $/$, line 91 below) in order to build a new PluggableButtonMorph for each of them. If the instances of the Key class that correspond to the numeric keys have as label: the numeric value and as function: the selector activateNumber:, the instances of the operators have as label: the *symbol* corresponding to their label and as function: the selector activateFunction: (lines 94–97). For the rest, the definition of the views of these operation keys is done exactly the same way as the definition of the other keys.

Line 108, the last line of our method openInWorld, starts the display of our calculator with the transmission openInWorld. Note that this method openInWorld is sent to an instance of the SystemWindow and has, therefore, nothing to do with the method openInWorld of our Calculator class we just wrote.

```
90    a1 := AlignmentMorph newColumn.
91    #('+' '-' '*' '/' )
92        do: [:label |
93            view := PluggableButtonMorph
94                on: (Key new
95                    label: label asSymbol
96                    function: #activateFunction:
97                    on: self)
98                getState: #state
99                action: #activate.
100        view := self
101            initialize: view
102            with: color
```

```
103                      and: label.
104          al addMorph: view].
105   window
106       addMorph: al
107       frame: (3 / 5 @ (1 / 5) extent: 1 / 5 @ (4 / 5)).
108   window openInWorld
```

Clearly, our method openInWorld is too long: 108 lines, which is really too much. Our advice for the SMALLTALK program writing *style* is that a method should not exceed the size of a standard display screen. We leave the factorization which is required here as an exercise.

6.2.4. Construction of the interface between views and models

Up to now, we have written a program that knows how to do the operations of a postfix calculator and we have defined the views necessary for this calculator to be used through a graphical interface. During this phase, we have developed dependency relationships between the calculator and its screen for displaying results, the calculator and the history screen, the calculator and its keys, the history screen and its graphical representation and, finally, the keys and their graphical representations. All these dependencies are illustrated in Figure 6.20.

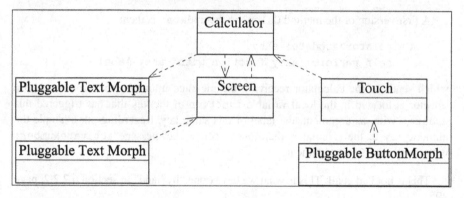

Figure 6.20. *The dependencies between the various objects of the calculator*

What is still missing is an interface between the graphical objects and their respective models. In the previous section, we saw that such an interface between dependent objects from each other is most simply realized with the method pair changed: and update:, by carefully choosing the moments when the model notifies the dependent objects when it has changed state and how the dependent objects should respond to a state change of their model.

Let us start with the interface between the keys and the calculator: the graphical objects corresponding to the keys are PluggableButtonMorph that send to *their* models, instances of the Key class, the message activate. Naturally, each instance of the Key class must transmit its activation to its dependents, since it alone does not really do much apart from knowing its label and its associated functionality. Here is the implementation of the method activate in the Key class:

```
Key>>activate
    self changed: self.
```

This method notifies its dependents that the receiver object has just changed and provides this receiver as argument to the dependent which knows how to interpret this message through a corresponding update:. For instance, if we activate key 9, the instance 9 of the Key class receives the message activate which sends to itself the message changed: with the key 9 itself as argument.

Since every key has the calculator to which it belongs as the one and single dependent, the calculator class should have a method update: that handles this information change of its key 9. Naturally, for the calculator to correctly respond to the information that a key has just been activated, it must know which key has been activated: this is the reason for also providing to update: the key that triggered the start of the method update:.

A first version of the method Calculator»update: is then:

```
Calculator>>update: aKey
    self perform: akey function with: aKey label
```

which sends to the calculator receiving the message update: the message whose selector is located in the local variable function of the key that has triggered this update: with, as argument, the label of this same key. Regarding our example the numeric key 9, the calculator, therefore, receives the message activateNumber: with the string '9' as argument.

This is not bad at all. This is what we have done "by hand" in section 6.2.2.2, page 295.

Let us recall the method activateNumber::

```
Calculator>>activateNumber: label
    firstTime
        ifTrue: [firstTime := false.
        screenBuffer := label]
        ifFalse: [screenBuffer size = 1 & ((screenBuffer at: 1)
            = $0)
            ifTrue: [screenBuffer := ''].
        screenBuffer := screenBuffer , label]
```

There is nothing to change *except* that we should let our graphical dependents know that the value of screenBuffer has just changed. The only graphical dependent that a calculator has is the PluggableTextMorph representing its main screen. It responds to the message update: with as argument the message to be sent to its model in order to obtain the text. Since we have defined the method:

```
Calculator>>printOn: aStream
    aStream nextPutAll: screenBuffer
```

we just need to add at the end of our method activateNumber: the following dispatch

```
self changed: #printString
```

Thus, the PluggableTextMorph dependent of the calculator will use all that is necessary to display the new content of the instance variable screenBuffer and the screen will always be in correspondence with the progress of the input of numbers: after each activation of a numeric key, like the variable screenBuffer, of which it is the graphical representation, it will be updated.

To finalize our calculator, we need to perform similar adjustments for each type of key. Thus, the reset key C has the following functionality activateClear:

```
Calculator>>activateClear: label
    self initialize
```

So we should also adjust the method initialize of the Calculator class, by specifying the change through the dispatch of the message changed: to the receiver in order to notify, with the message update: that follows, the change to the screen:

```
Calculator>>initialize
    accu := 0.
    screenBuffer := accu printString.
    firstTime := true.
    self changed: #printString.
```

The key = acts as a "enter" key in our postfix calculator. The associated method activateEqual: has been defined up to now as:

```
PostfixCalculator>>activateEqual: label
    accu := screenBuffer asNumber.
    firstTime := true
```

When this key is activated there is no need to update the main screen: the value of screenBuffer does not change, it is just transferred to the variable accu. On the contrary, it is the moment to notify the history screen of a change, since the flag firstTime is set to true, the value of screenBuffer will change with the next activation of a key. Let us therefore keep a memory of the current state by sending to the Screen instance, a dependent of the calculator, the information of the change. Which gives the following new version of activateEqual::

```
PostfixCalculator>>activateEqual: label
    self changed: #hist with: 'Enter > ' , screenBuffer.
    accu := screenBuffer asNumber.
    firstTime := true
```

Every calculator has the main screen and a Screen instance as dependent. The main screen responds to the symbol printString, it cannot be triggered by this change notification. Let us then add to our Screen class a method update:with: responsible for the change of the aspect hist:

```
Screen>>update: aText with: aString
    aText == #hist
        ifTrue: [self hist: (hist , '\' , aString) withCRs.
        self changed: #hist]
```

This method adds to the instance variable hist the string provided as the argument of with: and, in turn, it notifies all its dependents that its aspect hist has changed. What are the dependents of an instance of the Screen class? There are two: a PluggableTextMorph, the history screen, which in fact was designed to respond to changes of the aspect hist – that's perfect. But there is also the calculator itself, the one that has just notified the screen that the aspect hist has just changed. Naturally, we do not want to introduce looping in the exchanges changed: / update:. Let us then modify our method Calculator»update:, which is currently implemented as:

```
Calculator>>update: aKey
    self perform: aKey function with: aKey label
```

in the more polished version:

```
Calculator>>update: aKey
    aKey == #hist
        ifFalse: [self perform: aKey function
                      with: aKey label]
```

Thus, the method Calculator»update: will respond to all the update requests *except* those concerning the aspect hist.

In order to complete our implementation of a postfix calculator we just need to modify the method activeFonction: so that it also knows how to notify the main screen and the history display of the changes that it generates. Here is the new version of this method:

```
PostfixCalculator>>activateFunction: label
    self changed: #hist with: 'Enter > ' , screenBuffer.
    accu := accu perform: label asSymbol
                   with: screenBuffer asNumber.
    screenBuffer := accu printString.
    self changed: #hist with: label , ' > ' , screenBuffer.
    self changed: #printString.
    firstTime := true
```

Voila! You can now test the calculator: it is not as sophisticated as that of KCalc, but it is quite identical to the calculators that one can find on the Palm type computers and similar. The extensions will be proposed as exercises.

To see the structure of dependencies and the multitude of morphs that compose our calculator, we show below, in Figure 6.21, an explorer opened on an instance of a postfix calculator as it was obtained with our program.

Let us note that the graphical user interface did not change the algorithms of the model, of the calculator. All we have done is added the messages changed (or changed:, and even changed:with:) in places where a change occurs, then add the corresponding messages update: and write a method, openInWorld, to generate the nice graphical representation. Let us take this as an example of the power of the metaphor $M.V.C$ of object-oriented programming.

6.2.5. *An infix calculator*

Our postfix calculator has two private methods:

– activateEqual:: the method describing the actions of the calculator after activating the key =;

– activateFunction:: the method describing the actions of the calculator after activating an arithmetic operator key.

All the other methods are independent of the order in which the calculator expects the operands and operators. If the design of our calculator is correct, it should be sufficient to redefine only these two methods in order to have a calculator running in infix mode.

Figure 6.21. *An explorer on a postfix calculator*

The main difference between these two calculation approaches, postfix and infix, is that for the postfix order the activation of an operator key can directly start the calculation – since the necessary operands have preceeded the operator – however, in the infix order, the activation of an operator key cannot start the calculation – since an operand is still missing. In infix calculations, we, therefore, have to store the operator in order to activate it only after the input of the second operand.

Let us then create a subclass of Calculator class in order to also have an infix calculator:

```
Calculator subclass: #InfixCalculator
    instanceVariableNames: 'memFunc'
    classVariableNames: ''
    poolDictionaries: ''
    category: 'Course-Smalltalk'
```

Since we have given to the InfixCalculator class an additional instance variable, the variable memFunc that should hold the operator pending the input of the second operand, we need to create an initialization method of this variable:

```
InfixCalculator>>initialize
    super initialize.
    memFunc := nil
```

After these few additional initializations, all the others are inherited from the superclass Calculator, let us look at what should be done if the user activates a key of an arithmetic operator. Several possibilities can occur:

1) The instance variable firstTime (a variable set to false in the method activateNumber: and to true in the methods activateEqual: and activateFunction:) is true and the accumulator accu is different from zero. We then find ourselves in a situation where the user requests a calculation without entering a number. Such a situation can only occur if the previously activated key was also a key implying an operation. In this situation, we can do nothing except returning the control to the user to enter a number.

2) The variable memFunc, the variable used for storing the operator previously entered, is different from nil. This situation can occur if the user is in the middle of a calculation. For instance, when he has entered, as in Figure 6.22, the number 7, then the operator ×, then the second number 9 and now the second operator +, where, he clearly wants to calculate an expression that begins as $7 \times 9 + \ldots$. In this situation, we first should calculate, display on the screen and transfer to the accumulator the result of the multiplication 7×9 and store the second operator +, and then return the control to the user so that he enters the second operand for the addition in progress.

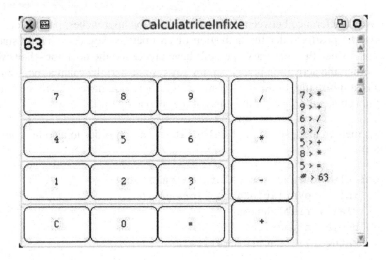

Figure 6.22. *Our infix calculator (compare it with the one given in Figure 6.16, page 299)*

3) The variable `memFunc` is `nil`. So, we are at the beginning of a calculation. In this case, we should just transfer the number displayed on the screen to the accumulator and store the operator.

If we put all these points together, we get the following new method `activateFunction::`

```
InfixCalculator>>activateFunction: label
    (firstTime
            and: [accu ~= 0])
        ifTrue: [^ self].
    memFunc notNil
        ifTrue:
            [accu := accu perform: memFunc
                            with: screenBuffer asNumber]
        ifFalse: [accu := screenBuffer asNumber].
    self changed: #hist
            with: screenBuffer , ' > ' , label.
    memFunc := label asSymbol.
    screenBuffer := accu printString.
    self changed: #printString.
    firstTime := true
```

We still have to decide on the action associated with the key =. This key is used as the key "Enter" in our postfix calculator. In the infix calculator, the input of the first operand ends with the activation of an operator key. The input of the second operand also ends with the activation of an operator key if we find ourselves in a compound calculation. It ends with this key = when we reach the end of the calculation. At this point, it should start the last stored arithmetic operation.

The difference with the activation operator keys is the need to reset the variable memFunc to nil. For the rest, the method activateEqual: looks much like the activateFunction: method

```
InfixCalculator>>activateEqual: label
    firstTime
        ifTrue: [^ self].
    memFunc notNil

        ifTrue:
            [accu := accu perform: memFunc
                            with: screenBuffer asNumber.
                self changed: #hist
                        with: screenBuffer , ' > ' , label]
        ifFalse: [accu := screenBuffer asNumber].
    memFunc := nil.
    screenBuffer := accu printString.
    self changed: #printString.
    firstTime := true.
    self changed: #hist with: '# > ' , screenBuffer
```

We have completed the definition of the infix calculator. In fact, the infix calculator shown in Figure 6.22 was obtained after the addition of these two methods to the InfixCalculator class. Figure 6.23 shows the diagram of all the classes and their relations.

Only for the program esthetic, let us factor out identical parts of both methods that handle operation keys.

Which gives the following method activate::

```
InfixCalculator>>active: label
    memFunc notNil
        ifTrue:
            [accu := accu perform: memFunc
                            with: screenBuffer asNumber]
        ifFalse: [accu := screenBuffer asNumber].
    self changed: #hist
            with: screenBuffer , ' > ' , label.
```

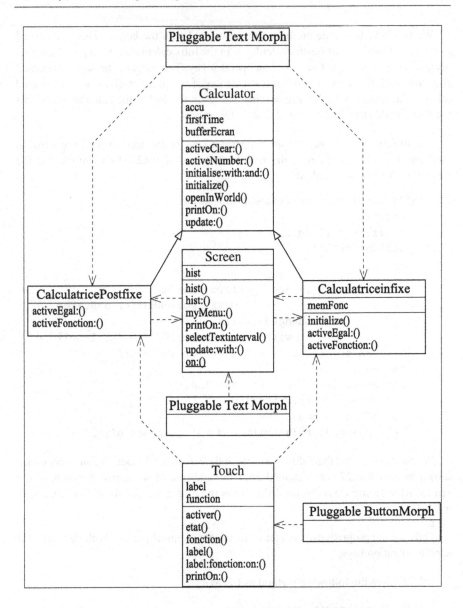

Figure 6.23. *The relations between the classes required
for our calculators. The solid arrows connect a class with its superclass,
the dashed arrows connect instances of a class with instances that
depend on it*

```
      screenBuffer := accu printString.
      self changed: #printString.
      firstTime := true
```

and thereby allows us to simplify both methods as follows:

```
InfixCalculator>>activateFunction: label
    (firstTime
          and: [accu ~= 0])
        ifTrue: [^ self].
    self active: label.
    memFunc := label asSymbol
```

and

```
InfixCalculator>>activateEqual: label
    firstTime
        ifTrue: [^ self].
    self active: label.
    memFunc := nil.
    self changed: #hist with: '# > ' , screenBuffer
```

6.3. Exercises

The solutions can be found in section A1.9.

1) As we have already noted, our method openInWorld is definitely too long with its 108 lines. Refactor this method in order to obtain a version of a reasonable size.

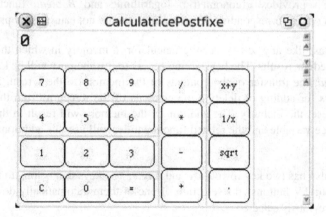

Figure 6.24. *A calculator with an additional keys row*

2) Our calculator allows us to enter only integers, although the results can be fraction numbers. Ordinary calculators have a dot key (.), which allows us to enter real numbers. Add this dot key and change the behavior of the calculator in order to provide real numbers (if necessary) and not fractions.

While doing so, also add the keys x^y, $\frac{1}{x}$ and $\sqrt{}$. Thus, simply add a keys column, as shown in Figure 6.24. Naturally, these extra features should be available both for postfix and infix calculator.

3) Add a PrefixCalculator class allowing us to enter the expressions in a prefix order.

6.4. A KCalc calculator

To conclude this chapter, and to integrate in a program all the characteristics of dependencies and morphs learned in this chapter, let us transform our calculator in one similar to the **KCalc** calculator we saw in Figure 6.12 on page 291 and that we provide again another image in Figure 6.25.

6.4.1. *KCalc description*

This calculator clearly does not have a history screen. We had put it in our calculator mainly for development and computation monitoring reasons. It provides no functionality and to be more in harmony with the appearance of the **KCalc** calculator, we will therefore remove it.

KCalc has considerably more function keys: in addition to standard arithmetic operations, it provides trigonometric, logarithmic and *Boolean* functions. The introduction of the corresponding functionalities should not cause major problems.

It also has, like any self-respecting calculator, a memory in which the user can keep intermediate results. The keys giving access to this memory will be keys MR, for *memory read*, the transfer of the contents of the memory to the screen, M+ and M- the two keys for adding or deleting the contents of the screen to/from the memory and MC to reset the memory. The addition of the memory will result in the addition of an instance variable and the related functionalities will use this additional instance variable.

KCalc also has two key rows *Base* and *Angle*. The keys that belong to these rows behave as our TV buttons: the selection of one of them automatically deselects any other key previously selected.

The keys that belong to the *Base* row indicate the base in which the numbers are entered and displayed. **KCalc** distinguishes the four most common bases in computer science: hexadecimal, decimal, octal and binary. We will add a key allowing us to choose an arbitrary base between base 2 (binary) and base 16 (hexadecimal). The keys A to F are designed for entering the hexadecimal numbers. After selecting a base, the keys corresponding to the digits that are not part of the digits used in the selected base must be disabled. We make the keys inaction visible by coloring them in pale red. Figure 6.26 shows our version of KCalc calculator accepting and displaying numbers in base five. We see that all the numeric keys, except the keys 0–4 are disabled. The number displayed on the screen, 121, is the representation in base 5 of the decimal number 36.

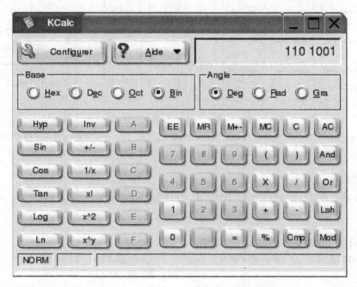

Figure 6.25. *Another view on the KCalc calculator*

The keys belonging to the *Angle* row indicate the format in which we wish to enter the angles for trigonometric calculations: either in degrees or radians or gradiants. The behavior of these keys is the same as the one of the keys in the *Base* row.

The keys specifying the base and the keys specifying the angle format will each add an additional instance variable, the instance variables base and angle, respectively.

6.4.2. *KCalc implementation*

After this brief description of the **KCalc** calculator, we can start our implementation – naturally, starting from the implementation of calculators that we already have.

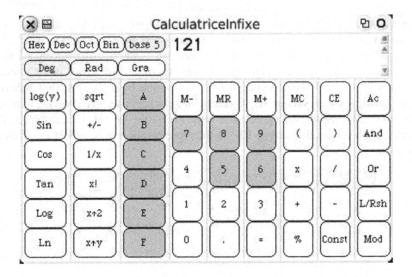

Figure 6.26. *A view on our version of KCalc. For a color version of the figure, see www.iste.co.uk/wertz/smalltalk.zip*

First, the new definition of the Calculator class including the new instance variables:

```
Model subclass: #Calculator
    instanceVariableNames: 'accu screenBuffer firstTime
                            memory base angleIn'
    classVariableNames: 'AllNumericKeys'
    poolDictionaries: ''
    category: 'Course-Smalltalk'
```

The instance variable memory represents, as its name suggests, the working memory of the calculator, the variable base contains at all time the integer corresponding to the base in which we express the calculations and angleIn contains at all time the selector of the conversion method to be applied to a number in order to obtain the equivalent angle in the desired format. Internally, we use the *radians* format, the selector to convert from degrees to radians will be called degreesToRadians, the selector to convert from radians to radians will be called yourself and the selector from gradiants to radians will be called gradiantsToRadiants.

If we take as default base the decimal base and the degrees as default angle format, we have the following additional initialization method:

```
Calculator>>init
   base := 10.
   memory := 0.
   angleIn := #degreesToRadians.
```

and the instance creation method new becomes:

```
Calculator class>>new
   ^super new init; initialize
```

with the method `initialize` of the calculator that we have just defined in the previous sections (and in the solutions to the previous exercises).

Let us continue with the changes on the method openInWorld which defines the external appearance of our calculator and which defines the set of keys available to the user. Since the appearance of KCalc is very different from our calculators, the modifications of this method will be fairly substantial. Here is then our new method openInWorld (we will comment as we progress):

```
   Calculator>>openInWorld
 1    | window view |
 2    window := SystemWindow labelled: self class name.
 3    view := PluggableTextMorph
 4           on: self
 5           text: #printString
 6           accept: nil.
 7    view
 8        font: (StrikeFont familyName: 'Atlanta' size: 22).
 9    window
10        addMorph: view
11        frame: (2 / 5 @ 0 extent: 3 / 5 @ (1 / 5)).
```

Unless the size of the calculator screen (line 11), which has reduced by two fifths in the beginning of this method, nothing has changed from our previous version.

On the contrary, we did not need to create keys that behave like buttons in our old version. The method create CalcButton: for: and: frame: window: etat: was not there. We will examine it later. In this current case, we simply need to know that it takes as first argument the label arrays corresponding to key rows, as second argument the selectors corresponding to the actions of these keys, as third argument the selectors of the activation method for each of the key rows, as fourth argument the AlignmentMorph coordinates where these key rows will be positioned, as fifth argument the window in which the AlignmentMorph will be placed, and finally, as sixth argument, the initial states of each key.

Clearly, create Calc Button:... is a very specific method, written just to create these particular keys that are the keys specifying the number base and the angle format.

```
12    self createCalcButton: #(
                        #('Hex' 'Dec' 'Oct' 'Bin' 'other')
13                      #('Deg' 'Rad' 'Gra') )
14          for: #(
15                      #(#Hex #Dec #Oct #Bin #otherBase)
16                      #(#Deg #Rad #Gra))
17          and:
18                      #(#activateBase:    #activateAngle:)
19          frame:
20                      {0 @ 0 extent: 2 / 5 @ (1 / 10).
21                       0 @ (1 / 10) extent: 2 / 5 @ (1 / 10). }
22          window: window
23          state: #(#(false true false false false)
24                   #(true false false)).
```

The method createKeys: with: and: function: frame: window: is the method that we have implemented in the solutions to the exercises, page 475. It is responsible for initializing keys as we know them so far.

```
25    self
26      createKeys: #(
27                      #('log(y)' 'Sin' 'Cos' 'Tan' 'Log' 'Ln')
28                      #('sqrt' '+/-' '1/x' 'x!' 'x^2' 'x^y')
29                      #('A' 'B' 'C' 'D' 'E' 'F')
30                      #('M-' '7' '4' '1' '0')
31                      #('MR' '8' '5' '2' '.')
32                      #('M+' '9' '6' '3' '=')
33                      #('MC' '(' 'x' '+' '%')
34                      #('CE' ')' '/' '-' 'Const')
35                      #('Ac' 'And' 'Or' 'L/Rsh' 'Mod'))
```

Let us recall thereafter that we took some liberties compared to the original **KCalc** calculator:

1) We have replaced the key Hyp, which calculates the hyperbolic trigonometric functions, with the key Log(y), which calculates the logarithm of the number displayed on the calculator screen, with respect to the base given as second argument.

2) Also, we have replaced the key inv by the key sqrt, the key EE by the key M- and the key Cmp by the key Const that should provide us a choice between many constants, such as e, π and $\frac{\pi}{2}$.

```
36    with: #(
37            #(#log: #Sin #Cos #Tan #log #ln)
38            #( sqrt negated inv factorial squared raisedTo:)
39            #('A' 'B' 'C' 'D' 'E' 'F')
40            #(memSub '7' '4' '1' '0')
41            #(memRead '8' '5' '2' '.')
42            #(memPlus '9' '6' '3' '=')
43            #(memClear '(' * + percent)
44            #('CE' ')' div: - 'Const')
45            #('Ac' bitAnd: bitOr: bitShift: \\))
46    and: {AlignmentMorph newColumn. AlignmentMorph newColumn.
47          AlignmentMorph newColumn. AlignmentMorph newColumn.
48          AlignmentMorph newColumn. AlignmentMorph newColumn.
49          AlignmentMorph newColumn. AlignmentMorph newColumn.
50          AlignmentMorph newColumn. }
51    function: #(
52            #(activateFunction: activateTrigo: activateTrigo:
53              activateTrigo: #activateUnaryFunction:
54              #activateUnaryFunction:)
55            #(activateUnaryFunction: activateUnaryFunction:
56              activateUnaryFunction: activateUnaryFunction:
57              activateUnaryFunction: #activateFunction: )
58            #(activateNumber: activateNumber: activateNumber:
59              activateNumber: activateNumber: activateNumber:)
60            #(#activateMem: #activateNumber: #activateNumber:
61              #activateNumber: #activateNumber:)
62            #(#activateMem: #activateNumber: #activateNumber:
63              #activateNumber: #activeNumberPoint:)
64            #(#activateMem: #activateNumber: #activateNumber:
65              #activateNumber: #activateEqual:)
66            #(activateMem: activateOpening: activateFunction:
67              activateFunction: activateFunction:)
68            #(activateClearScreen: activateClosing:
69              activateFunction: activateFunction:
70              activateConstant:)
71            #(activateClear: activateFunction: activateFunction:
72              activateFunction: activateFunction:))
73      frame: {
74            0 @ (1 / 5) extent: 2 / 15 @ (4 / 5).
75            2/15 @ (1/5) extent: 2/15 @ (4/5).
76            4/15 @ (1/5) extent: 2/15 @ (4/5).
77            6 / 15 @ (1 / 5) extent: 1 / 10 @ (4 / 5).
78            5 / 10 @ (1 /5) extent: 1 / 10 @(4 / 5).
79            6 / 10 @ (1 /5) extent: 1 / 10 @(4 / 5).
80            7 / 10 @ (1 /5) extent: 1 / 10 @(4 / 5).
81            8 / 10 @ (1 /5) extent: 1 / 10 @(4 / 5).
```

```
82              9 / 10 @ (1 /5) extent: 1 / 10 @(4 / 5).}
83    window: window.
84    self initKeys.
85    window openInWorld
```

After the initialization of all the keys, we still activate the method initKeys. It did not exist in previous versions of calculators. It will be used to enable/disable the numeric keys so that the keys that are out of the base are displayed in red and disabled, and the keys corresponding to the digits allowed in the base displayed in white and enabled. This method will also be used by the keys that determine the number base.

To initialize the keys that specify the base and the angle format, we have used the method createCalcButton:for:and:frame:window:state:. Let us return to it for a moment, since this method should initialize the button-keys and ensure the interdependency of each key of a row.

It is a variant of the method createKeys:with:and:function: frame: window:: it traverses in parallel the collection of labels, arithmetic selectors and rectangles defining the position and the states in order to build a new collection containing the interdependent keys. Let us note that it uses a method withOff:andOn:on: defined in the Pluggable-ButtonMorphclass, which differs from the method with:and: only by the positioning of a color "on" different from the color "off" of the keys.

It also uses the method newCalcButton that defines a key in terms of label, functionality and a representation change criterion. The selector changeLabel, imported from our old Button class, serves as a model for the button keys that we are defining. For the reading of its implementation, as given below, please carefully examine the difference between the visualization aspects (temporarily stored in the variable view) and the arithmetic aspects (temporarily stored in the variable button).

To create the interdependencies between the keys in the same row, it also uses the method initialize inherited from our Button class.

Here is the method createCalcButton: for: and: frame: window: state::

```
Calculator>>createCalcButton: tabLabel
                        for: tabSelector
                        and: tabActivF
                     frame: rects
                    window: window
                     state: states
    | view collection views |
```

```
tabLabel
    with: tabSelector
    and: tabActivF
    and: rects
    and: states
    do: [:keys :funs :func :rect :myStates |
        | m button |
        collection := OrderedCollection new.
        views := OrderedCollection new.
        m := AlignmentMorph newRow.
        keys
            with: funs
            and: myStates
            do: [:key :fun :eta |
                view :=
                    (self newCalcButton:
                        (button := fun == #otherBase
                        ifTrue:
                            [CalcButtonLabelVariable new
                                label: fun
                                function: func
                                state: eta
                                on: self]
                        ifFalse:
                            [CalcButton new
                                label: fun
                                function: func
                                state: eta
                                on: self]))
                views addFirst: view.
                self addDependent: button.
                collection addFirst: button].
        CalcButton initialize: collection.
        views
            do: [:tView | m addMorph: tView].
    window addMorph: m frame: rect]
```

The CalcButton class is defined as a subclass of the Key class. The CalcButton LabelVariable class is a subclass of this class CalcButton and has, in the current version, only a single instance, the key "other base", the only key that should change label. This is why the instances of the CalcButtonLabelVariable class have an instance variable, chain, for changing the label if the user decides to define a new base.

Here is the definition of this class:

```
CalcButton subclass:
     #CalcButtonEtiquetteVariable
instanceVariableNames:
'chain'
          classVariableNames:
               poolDictionaries: ''
          category: 'Course-Smalltalk'
```

Upon activation of a button key, of an instance of the CalcButton class, the state of the key becomes true. It notifies the other keys (through a changed: of the aspect #button) and its morph, its graphical representation (through a changed: of the aspect self) as shown below:

```
CalcButton>>activate
    self state: true.
    "for the other buttons :"
    self changed: #button.
    "for the morph :"
    self changed: self
```

Every CalcButton should, therefore, know how to change its aspect #button with a suitable method update::

```
CalcButton>>update: aSymbol
    aSymbol == #button
        ifTrue: [^ self state: false]
```

Where state: is defined as follows:

```
CalcButton>>state: aBool
    state := aBool.
    self changed: #hist
```

The aspect #hist serves only to be an aspect different from other aspects, such as #button and #label. It notifies its morph to change the background color of its representation[12].

---

12 A change of the background color of a Pluggable-Button-Morph is the default action of the method update: defined in this class. In order not to interfere with other aspects that intend to update a morph, we invent a specific aspect, distinct from all others, the aspect #hist. The symbol hist *is* indeed a new symbol, different from all the other symbols representing aspects.

As we have said before, the key `other base` should be able to change its name, its label. Thus, if the user wants to work, for instance, in base 5, this key should be displayed as `base:   5`. The method `newCalcButton:` distinguishes between two types of `PluggableButtonMorph`: morphs that can change label and those that cannot. Given that we have created a single instance of `CalcButtonLabelVariable`, there will exist only one morph able to change its label. In the method, the aspect `#changeLabel` is defined as a symbol allowing us to request its label to a button key:

```
Calculator>>newCalcButton: aFunction
  ^ (aFunction isKindOf: CalcButtonLabelVariable)
        ifTrue: [PluggableButtonMorph
              on: aFunction
              getState: #state
              action: #activate
              label: #changeLabel
              menu: nil]
        ifFalse: [PluggableButtonMorph
              on: aFunction
              getState: #state
              action: #activate]
```

We also need to define a method changeLabel:

```
CalcButtonLabelVariable>>changeLabel
    chain isNil
            ifTrue: ['other base']
            ifFalse: ['base ' , chain]
```

For the label change to be possible, our single and unique button key should also be able to receive from the calculator the information that the label has changed. It needs a second update method responding to this type of information and transmitting to the associated morph the request to change label as:

```
CalcButtonLabelVariable>>update: aSymbol with: aValue
    aSymbol == #label
        ifTrue: [chain := aValue asString.
                 self changed: #changeLabel]
```

Let us continue with the processing of button keys at the top of the calculator. We have defined two keys activation methods: `activateAngle:` and `activateBase:`. The first method is responsible for trigonometric angle format changes, the second method is responsible for numeric base changes. Here they are:

```
Calculator>>activateAngle: label
    label == #Deg
        ifTrue: [angleIn := #degreesToRadians.
            ^ nil].
    label == #Rad
        ifTrue: [angleIn := #yourself.
            ^ nil].
    label == #Gra
        ifTrue: ["This is left as an exercise"
            ^ nil]
```

The calculator works internally with angles represented in radians. The instance variable angleIn contains the selector of the method allowing us to go from the internal representation, radians, to the external representation, radians, degrees or gradiants. To convert an angle expressed in radians to an angle expressed in degrees, SMALLTALK provides the method degreesToRadians. To convert an angle expressed in radians to the same angle expressed in radians, there is obviously nothing to do. This is why we use for this case the method yourself. The conversion of an angle expressed in gradiants to the same angle expressed in radians is here left as an exercise.

```
Calculator>>activeBase: label
    screenBuffer := Number readFrom: screenBuffer base: base.
    base := #(16 10 8 2 )
                at: (#(#Hex #Dec #Oct #Bin ) indexOf: label)
                ifAbsent: [self changeBase].
    self initKeys.
    screenBuffer := screenBuffer printStringBase: base.
    self changed: #printString
```

Comments:

1) readFrom:base: is a method of the Number class allowing us to read a string as a number expressed in a base. Here in the first line, we put in the instance variable screenBuffer the numerical value of the string that is currently on the screen. This string is naturally written in the current base.

2) According to the function associated with the activated key, Hex, Dec, Oct or Bin, we set the instance variable base to the value 16, 10, 8 or 2, respectively. If none of these functions is linked to the key, clearly, the activated key should be the key other base. In this case, we have to prompt the user for the base. This is done by the method changeBase:

```
Calculator>>changeBase
    | x |
    x := FillInTheBlank
                request: 'a base between 2 and 16 :'
                initialAnswer: '3'.
    ((x := x asInteger) between: 2 and: 16)
        ifTrue: [self changed: #label with: x.
            ^ x].
    self changeBase
```

Primarily, this method opens a dialog box prompting for a number between 2 and 16[13]. If the entered number is outside this range, it prompts again for another number. Otherwise, it notifies the key that should change its aspect #label and returns this number which then becomes the new value of the instance variable base.

3) Once the base is determined, we should reset the numeric keys: activate the keys corresponding to allowed digits and disable the others. This is what is done in the method initKeys, which uses the class variable All-Nume-ric-Keys. This class variable contains the array, an instance of the Array class, of all the numeric keys. It is initialized when creating the keys in the method newKey:with: as follows[14]:

```
Calculator>>newKey: co with: function
    | morph key |
    morph := PluggableButtonMorph
                on: (key := Key new
                    label: co
                    function: function
                    on: self)
                getState: #state
                action: #activate.

    (co isSymbol not and: [co size < 2]
        and: [((co at: 1) digitValue between: 0 and: 15)])
                ifTrue:
                    [AllNumericKeys
                        at: (co at: 1) digitValue + 1
                        put: key].
    ^morph
```

---

13 We limit ourselves to these 15 bases since we have only 16 numeric keys on our calculator. The SMALLTALK method readFrom:base: allows arbitrary integer bases. Nevertheless, bases higher than 61 do not make sense, since we are limited by the number of characters that can act as a digit: $\{1 - 9, a - z, A - Z\}$.

14 The method digitValue of the Character class translates the possible numeric characters (see footnote on previous page) into numeric values.

Here, then, is the `initKeys` method that activates the keys corresponding to digits of the base (their state is set to `false`) and disables the other numeric keys (their state becomes `true`). We know that the state changes of a key also generate background color changes of the same key.

```
Calculator>>initKeys
    1
        to: base
        do: [:i |

              (AllNumericKeys at: i)
                  state: false]
    base + 1
        to: 16
        do: [:i |
              (AllNumericKeys at: i)
                  state: true]
```

4) Let us return to our method `activeBase:`. After changing the base and reinitializing all the numeric keys, we should adjust the number displayed on the screen of the calculator in this new base. This is done using the method `printStringBase:` of the Number class. This method is complementary to the method `readFrom:base:`: it translates a number into the string corresponding to its representation in the base given as argument. Once this string is assigned to the variable `screenBufer`, we simply need to notify the morph of the screen that its content has changed, it is the dispatch of `changed:` with `printString` as argument in the last line of the method.

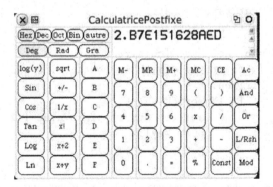

Figure 6.27. *A postfix version of KCalc, the number displayed represents the constant e in the hexadecimal base*

We have completed the description of the main changes required to transform our calculators of the previous section in calculators similar to **KCalc**. Naturally, this new calculator will also exist in prefix, infix and postfix version. Figure 6.27 shows a postfix version of this calculator.

The entire code of this new version of our calculators is available on our Website. In case of doubt, the readers can always consult this Website. Here, we will just give two more indications of the necessary additions and changes for transforming our original calculators in this new version that is considerably more complete.

The conversion of the trigonometric angle format is accomplished in the method `activateTrigo:` as follows:

```
Calculator>>activateTrigo: label
  | x |
  x := ((Number readFrom: screenBuffer base: base)
          perform: angleIn)
          perform: (#(#sin #cos #tan )
              at: (#(#Sin #Cos #Tan )
                  indexOf: label)).
  screenBuffer := x printStringBase: base.
  self changed: #printString.
```

Predefined constants input is achieved through the method `activate-Constant:`. It is easy to add additional constants. For this, we simply add to the Number class the required selectors. If, for instance, you also want to have the constant of fine structure α,[15] you simply need to add the following method `fineStructureConst` to the Number class:

---

[15] For those who are interested: this constant characterizes the strength of the electromagnetic interaction. It was originally introduced in 1916 by the physicist Arnold Sommerfeld as a measure of relativistic deviations relative to the atomic model of Bohr, in the spectral lines of atoms. It was the ratio between the velocity of an electron in the first circular orbit of an atom and the speed of light in vacuum. In quantum electrodynamics theory, it acts as a coupling constant that represents the interaction force between electron and photons. As a set of other physical constants (around 20), its value cannot be obtained theoretically and should be based on the experimental results. This is why, it is considered as an *external parameter* in the standard model.

It can be defined as: $\alpha = \frac{e^2}{2\epsilon_0 hc}$, where h is Planck's constant, c is the speed of light in the ether and ϵ_0 is the permissiveness of the empty space. Its numerical value is $\alpha = 7.297352568 \times 10^{-3} = \frac{1}{137.03599911}$.

```
Number>>fineStructureConst
    ^ 1 / 137.0359991146
```

and insert the selector in the array listConst of the method activateConstant:
below:

```
Calculator>>activateConstant: label
    | menu1 listConst |
    listConst := #(e pi halfPi).
    menu1 := MenuMorph new defaultTarget: self.
    menu1 addTitle: 'Constants';
        position: Sensor cursorPoint.
    listConst
        do: [:c | menu1
                add: c
                selector: #insert:
                argument: c].
    menu1 openInWorld
```

Now, we have reached a respectable version of our calculators, result of our
programming exercise implementing the dependency mechanism. The two simple
exercises below will help you familiarize yourself more with this mechanism.

6.5. Exercises

Solutions can be found in section A1.10, page 486 onwards.

1) Figure 6.28 shows an interactive counter. It consists of a screen which occupies
the upper half, and two keys labeled + and −, which occupy the bottom half. The
activation of the key + increments the counter and the activation of the key −
decrements it. Define the Counter class that implements such a counter.

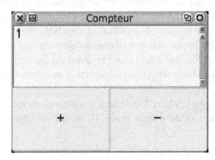

Figure 6.28. *A counter*

2) Figure 6.29 shows an array of five rows and four columns. Each of the 20 rectangles is a `PluggableTextMorph` containing as initial text the string corresponding to its index in the array. Write the program allowing us to construct such arrays of arbitrary dimension. For instance, the array in Figure 6.29 can be created by the transmission (`Array-Of-Text width:    4 height:    5`) `openInWorld`. Naturally, it should be able to change the different texts, i.e. we would like to be able to change them just by clicking in the corresponding rectangle and by editing the text. An "Alt+s" should save the modified text.

⊗🖾	Tableau de Textes		🗗 O
1@1	1@2	1@3	1@4
2@1	2@2	2@3	2@4
3@1	3@2	3@3	3@4
4@1	4@2	4@3	4@4
5@1	5@2	5@3	5@4

Figure 6.29. *An array of texts*

6.6. Concluding remarks

After solving these few exercises, you have finished, not learning this beautiful language SQUEAK (we never stop learning) but this introductory book to its programming. Unfortunately, in order to prevent this book from becoming too large, we left out too many notable aspects, such as the use of *change sets*, which allows us, in case something bad happens, to reconstruct an earlier version of the SQUEAK image. We did not have time to discuss the environment for testing programs (the *unit-tests*) or the meta-programming through the `meta-classes`. We have not seen how to create a reduced image which can be efficiently used in a real production environment, nor the possibility to interface a SQUEAK program with other systems external to SQUEAK, such as a database system. So, there are many areas that still need to be explored.

If this book has made you want to learn all these aspects – especially those I have not mentioned (the list goes on) – then yes, this book will have fully fulfilled its role.

Happy continuation in your exploration of the SQUEAK universe!

PART 3

Appendices

Appendix 1

Solutions to Exercises

A1.1. Exercises from Section 1.3

1) Copy, "Alt+c", copies the selected text; paste, "Alt+v", inserts the most recently copied or deleted text at the cursor's location; cut, "Alt+x", deletes the selected text; undo, "Alt+z", cancels the effect of the last command. Also, note the presence of the paste... command in the context menu. This entry opens a submenu in which we can choose the desired text from the last five which were copied or deleted.

If you have entered the following text This text is the first text entered in Squeak, the selection of the first occurrence of the word text, followed by typing the word test, has the effect of replacing the word text by the word test. The "Alt+j" shortcut, or selecting the do again option from the context menu, will repeat this action, i.e. the second occurrence of the word text is also replaced by the word test. Of course, the do again command can be repeated as many times as we wish. If it cannot be applied to the text (in our case, if there are no more occurrences of the word text to be replaced), then the command has no effect.

2) To open a class browser, we must either click on the Tools tab and select the Browser icon (by clicking on it and, while holding down the left mouse button, dragging it outside the tab), or type the following line into the Workspace:

```
Browser openBrowser
```

and choosing the do it entry in the Workspace context menu (or instead of opening a menu and clicking on the correct entry by simply executing the "Alt+d" shortcut):

– To search for the Integer class in a class browser, position the mouse in the categories pane and type "Alt+f" or open the context menu and select the find class entry. This will open a window, as in Figure A1.1, which asks for the name of the class you want to browse. You can enter just part of the name, SQUEAK then prompts you to choose the class you are looking for from a list of class names containing this part as a substring. Here, the easiest option is to type Integer, as in Figure A1.1, and then click on the accept button or type "Alt+s".

– Once you have selected the Integer class, you can select the show hierarchy entry from the context menu of the classes pane. This will display, in the large subwindow, the inheritance tree of the class (see Figure A1.2).

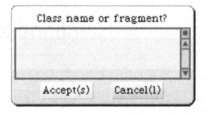

Figure A1.1. *Class name prompt*

browse	senders	implementors	versions	inheritance	hierarchy	inst vars	class vars	source

```
ProtoObject #()
    Object #()
        Magnitude #()
            Number #()

                Integer #()
                    LargePositiveInteger #()
                    LargeNegativeInteger #()
                    SmallInteger #()
```

Figure A1.2. *Hierarchy of the Integer class*

You can also click on the hierarchy button, which is visible in Figure A1.2. This will open a Hierarchy Browser, which is an ordinary class browser, except for the fact that it does not have a categories pane, and that in the classes pane, only the classes which are part of the selected class hierarchy are accessible (in our case, the Integer class hierarchy).

– To see the implementation of the + method, we only need to select the + entry in the methods pane of the class browser centered on the Integer class.

– To see *all* of the implementations of the + method, we simply need to click on the implementors button (visible in Figure A1.2) after having selected the +

method. This opens a menu containing the names of all the selectors contained in the method. Of course, + is one of these. If you select it with a left click, SQUEAK will open an implementor browser like the one shown in Figure A1.3.

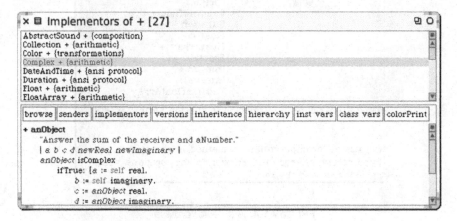

Figure A1.3. *An implementor browser*

The header of the window shows the selector of which we can browse the different implementations (in this case, the + selector) and the number of existing implementations (here, there are 27 different implementations of the + method).

Another method for finding all of the implementations of a selector is to activate a Method Finder from the Tools tab. This will open a selector browser as shown in Figure A1.4. You must then enter the name of the selector for which you are looking for implementations in the top left subwindow and then accept it with "Alt-s". This will bring up, in the subwindow right underneath, the list of all the selectors for which the name contains the string of characters which you have typed. In our example, the selector which we provided was + and the window beneath will only contain this selector, since no other SQUEAK selector contains the "+" character. If there was a *a+b* selector, we would also see this selector in the second subwindow. If you then select the + in this second window, the subwindow on the right will display all of the classes implementing this selector. Clicking on one of these classes will open a class browser with the implementation of the + method of this class.

You could also have used the Message Names tool in the Tools tab. Try this out yourself and find out how it works.

Finally, you could have simply typed the line:

```
SystemNavigation new browseAllImplementorsOf:  #+
```

followed by do it ("Alt+d"). Try this yourself too.

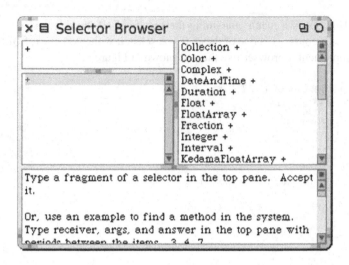

Figure A1.4. *A selector browser*

– In order to browse all of the senders of the + message, as with the implementors, we simply need to select the + method and then click on the `senders` button. This will bring up a *sender browser* as in Figure A1.5. As can be seen, the + message has been used many times: 4,938 times in my SQUEAK image. Of course, one of the senders is found in the `Parrot` class, in our `random` message.

As with the implementor browser, a more direct way would be to directly send to an instance of `SystemNavigation` a message opening such a browser for all of the senders of the + message. A do it, in a `Workspace`, in the expression below:

```
SystemNavigation new browseAllCallsOn:  #+
```

will create the same sender browser.

– In the meantime, after so many operations with the class browser and other browsers, I am sure that at one instant or another, you must have accidentally clicked the wrong mouse button, and seen something similar to Figure A1.6, a set of icons surrounding the browser window like a sort of halo. Each of these icons is a button which corresponds to a particular functionality of the *graphical objects* representing this window. Indeed, a window is also a graphical object. In SQUEAK, we refer to graphical objects as *morph*s. We obtain this halo by positioning the cursor over the window and clicking on the blue button (see the footnote on page 6) of the mouse. If we click on this button again, we obtain the same halo for the subwindow, the submorph, of the cursor. Repeat this again: each window is also a graphical SQUEAK object, and thus a morph. Any morph can be subject to a set of standard graphical transformations: it can change size, be moved, be put into rotation, etc. In order to convince yourself of this, look at the image of the browser in Figure A1.7 where four of the subwindows have undergone graphical transformations: either a rotation (the categories subwindow and that for the source code), a movement, a change in border style and a color change (the class subwindow) or a rotation and increase in scale (the protocol subwindow). Even in this unorthodox state, the class browser is continuing to be functional.

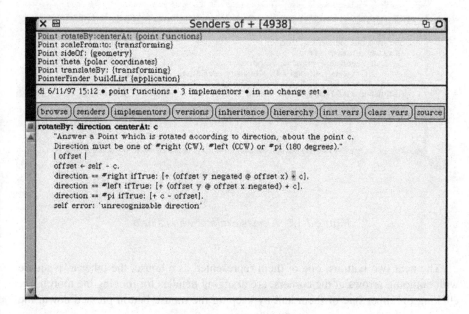

Figure A1.5. *A sender browser*

Let us return to the halo surrounding the morphs and examine these icons, these buttons, which form it. We will start with the top left icon, in the form of a ⊗ and then progressing clockwise around the System Browser window. The first button permits us to close the morph. Functionally, clicking this button has the same effect as the ⊠ button in the top right of every SQUEAK window.

The button to the right of this, represented as a stylized scroll-down menu, displays the morph's menu. In this menu, we can, among other things, *export* the morph in the form of an image file. The majority of the illustrations in this book were produced using this menu option. Other options help to change the background color or the style of the morph's borders, output the morph directly to a Postscript file, etc.

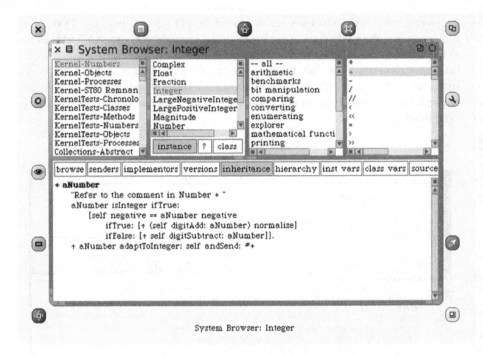

Figure A1.6. *A class explorer with its halo*

The next two buttons, one of them represented as a house, the other as a square with outgoing arrows at the corners, are dragging handles for moving the morph. By clicking on either one of them and by keeping the mouse button pressed down, the morph will follow any movement of the mouse.

The next button, in the top right corner, copies the morph.

The next button, with the icon in the form of a spanner, provides access to the morph's debugging menu, while the following one provides access to a color palette letting us choose a new background color for this morph.

The button in the bottom right corner is for resizing the morph.

Finally, the button in the bottom left corner lets us rotate the morph. Evidently, in order to solve the problem of the class browser image being upside down, we must use this button and perform a rotation of 180 degrees.

Going upward, the next button provides a reduced version of the morph, and the one above that provides a table of parameters and the last one, the icon with the small circle, lets us iconify the morph.

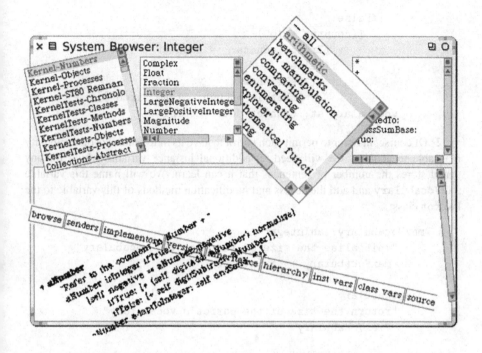

Figure A1.7. *A class browser in an unorthodox state*

We will return to the graphical objects that are morphs in more detail. Morphs do not present the part of the SQUEAK system inherited from prior versions of SMALLTALK, but rather the Self [UNG 87] language (see also the SQUEAK family tree, Figure I.1, page xiii).

A1.2. Exercises from section 2.6

1) It is sufficient to test the value of the counter instance variable. If this variable has a value higher than 100, then no more sentences should be added to the vocabulary. This gives way to the vocabulary: method below:

```
vocabulary: aString
    "add a new sentence to the parrot's
    vocabulary"
    vocabulary isNil
        ifTrue: [counter := 1.
                 random := Random new.
                 vocabulary := Array new: 100]
```

```
        ifFalse:
            [(counter < 100)
                ifTrue: [counter := counter + 1]
                ifFalse:
                    [^self answer:
                        'that is enough - I am tired']].
    vocabulary at: counter put: aString
```

2) Of course, in order to permit each parrot to have its individual size of vocabulary it is able to acquire, we will need an additional instance variable which for any parrot stores the number of sentences that it can learn. We will name this variable maxVocabulary and add the access and modification methods of this variable to the Parrot class:

```
maxVocabulary: anInteger
    "initialise the size of the parrot's vocabulary"
    maxVocabulary := anInteger
```

```
maxVocabulary
    "return the size of the parrot's vocabulary"
    ^maxVocabulary
```

For the purpose of simplification, we will extract from the speak method:

```
speak
    "provide a random sentence from the vocabulary"
    self answer:
        (vocabulary at:
            (self random next * 100 \\ counter)
                truncated + 1)
```

the section computing the index, such that we can rewrite this method as:

```
speak
    "provide a random senctence from the vocabulary"
    self answer:
        (vocabulary at: self random)
```

This implies the addition of the auxiliary method, random. We will take care to replace the 100 constant with a reference to the new instance variable maxVocabulary. This gives:

```
random
    "provides a random integer between
    1 and maxVocabulary"
    ^(random next *
        (self maxVocabulary) \\ counter)
    truncated + 1)
```

All that is left is to update the vocabulary: method, which must now test whether we have surpassed the maximum number of sentences to be learnt, and if so, it must randomly replace a previously learnt sentence by a new one. Here is the new version of the vocabulary: method:

```
vocabulary: aString
    "add a new sentence to the parrot
    vocabulary"
    vocabulary isNil
      ifTrue:
      [counter := 1.
        random := Random new.
        vocabulary := Array new: self maxVocabulary]
      ifFalse:
        [(counter < self maxVocabulary)
            ifTrue: [counter := counter + 1]
            ifFalse:
                [self answer: 'this is enough - I am tired'.
                ^vocabulary at: self random
                        put: aString]].
    vocabulary at: counter put: aString
```

Let us keep in mind that in order to be able to make a parrot do something, it needs values for each of its instance variables: name, maxVocabulary, random and vocabulary. After the creation of such an animal, we must therefore, in one way or another, initialize these different instance variables. One way to do this:

```
Parrot new name: 'Polly'; maxVocabulary: 10;
            vocabulary: 'Polly wants a cracker'
```

or even:

```
Polly := Parrot new.
Polly name: 'Polly'.
Polly maxVocabulary: 10.
Polly vocabulary: 'Polly wants a cracker'
```

and perform a doIt on all of these transmissions.

We could also envision to do these initializations directly at the creation of each Parrot instance. What we would like to have is an *instance creation* method which initializes these instance variables. In a nutshell, at least, something like:

```
Parrot new: 'Polly' "its name"
       with: 10 "its number of maximum sentences"
       andPhrase: 'Polly wants a cracker'
```

Regardless, we can achieve these initializations by adding a *class method* to our Parrot class. For this, we need to change the selection from *instance*, at the bottom of the class pane, to *class*. Then, we need to create a protocol for the class methods, let us call it initialize-release, in which we define and accept the following method (we will return to the possibility of class – not instance – method definitions later on):

```
new: name with: anInteger andPhrase: aString
     "creation of a Parrot instance"
     ^self new name: name;
            maxVocabulary: anInteger;
            vocabulary: aString
```

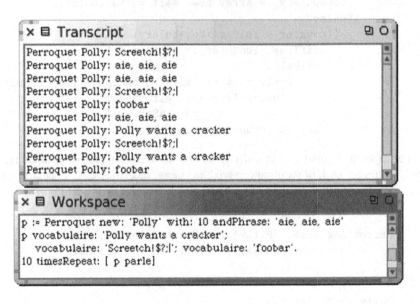

Figure A1.8. *A test for the methods of the* Parrot *class*

Thus, the creation of parrots will initialize all of its instance variables. Figure A1.8 shows a Workspace where a parrot named Polly is created, with the initialization of the instance variables name, maxVocabulary and vocabulary, followed by the learning of a few sentences, followed by 10 requests to speak. The Transcript, in this same figure, shows the result of those 10 transmissions of the speak message.

A1.3. Exercises for section 2.8

1) This is what happens for the different commands in the Workspace containing the two expressions:

```
jenny := Dog new: 'Jenny'
jenny speak
```

– "Alt+i" with the cursor located after the phrase "jenny speak' opens an *inspector* on the result of the phrase preceding the cursor. In this case, it will be an inspector for the jenny object, the instance of the Dog class called Jenny. An *inspector* is a window in which we can see the state of the inspected object. Figure A1.9 shows the obtained inspector. The left window lists the different inspectable aspects of the object. In the figure, we have selected the all inst vars aspect (an abbreviation for "all instance variables"), which is why the right window lists the instance variables and their values.

– "Alt+I", in the same cursor position, opens an *object browser* for the dog Jenny. This kind of browser is similar to an inspector. It differs in the header and in the tree representation of the object to be browsed. Figure A1.10 shows the object browser obtained.

– Pressing "Alt+b" having selected the Dog word opens a class browser for the Dog class.

– "Alt+E" opens a method browser for each method containing the selected string of characters. In this case, having selected the speak selector, and therefore the character string speak, SQUEAK will open a method explorer containing the speak method for the Animal class, the only method for which the body contains an occurrence of the speak string.

– "Alt+n" opens a method browser for all of the methods which send the selected message. In this case, the method browser will open for the speak method of the Dog class, the only method which contains a transmission containing this selector: the "super speak" transmission.

– "Alt+m" opens a method browser on all implementations of the selected method. In this case, the method browser will open for the speak method of the Animal, Dog and Parrot class, the only classes implementing this method.

– "Alt+o" opens a window containing the same thing as the original window. If "Alt+o" is pressed in a Workspace, this will create a copy of the workspace.

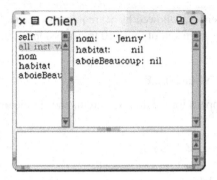

Figure A1.9. *The class inspector for the dog* Jenny

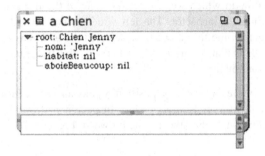

Figure A1.10. *Object browser for the dog* Jenny

– "Alt+w" deletes the word left of the cursor. In our example, this will delete the word speak. "Alt+z" cancels the effect of the last command. In this case, it will make the word speak reappear. Thus, nothing would have changed.

– "Alt+x" deletes the current selection. In this case, we have selected the word speak, which is the word which will be deleted. "Alt+v" inserts, at the cursor's position, the last thing to have been copied or deleted. In this case, "Alt+v" will reintroduce the word speak. "Alt+x" corresponds to the "cut" command of your favorite word processor, while "Alt+v" corresponds to the "paste" command.

– "Shift+←" moves the cursor by one character and selects this character. In this case, three repetitions of this operation will select the last three characters of the word speak.

– "Ctrl+←" will move the cursor by one word to the right. In this case after repeating this operation three times, the cursor will be placed just left of the letter "J" of the word Jenny on the previous line.

– Finally, an "Alt+(" surrounds the selection with a pair of parentheses. In this case, after selecting the string of characters "Dog new: 'Jenny'", the entire line will become:

```
jenny := (Dog new:   'Jenny')
```

If the selected expression is already surrounded by a pair of parentheses, "Alt+(" will remove these parentheses. Repeating this operation will, therefore, restore the line to its initial state.

2) Evidently, the one variable contains an instance of the One class, the two variable contains an instance of the Two class and the three variable contains an instance of the Three class. Sending the a message to an instance of the One class will return the integer 1. This will be the first number displayed, followed by a carriage return.

Sending the same message a to an instance of the Two class will activate the a method of this class. This method says that the integer 2 must be returned. This will be the second number displayed, also followed by a carriage return.

The third transmission is two b. The b method of the Two class says that the result of super a must be returned, and therefore that the a method of the super-class of Two must be activated, therefore the a method of the One method. This method returns the integer 1. This will be the third number displayed.

The fourth transmission is three b. The body of the b method of the Three class says that the value of self a must be returned, and therefore the value obtained after sending the message a to itself (three). The body of the a method of the Three class shows that the integer 3 must be returned. This will be the fourth displayed number.

The fifth transmission three c is simply the transmission super b.Therefore, the b method of the Two class must be activated, this class in turn says that the value of super a must be returned. With the super-class of the Two class being the One class, it is, therefore, the a method of the One class which will be activated.[1] The latter, which we have already seen, returns the 1 integer. It is, therefore, the fifth number to be displayed.

Finally, the last transmission is three d, which can be reduced to super a. The method containing this reference to super, the d method, being a method of the Three class, therefore the a method must be found in the super-class of Three, in other words: in the Two class. This class contains an a method which returns the 2 integer.

---

1 Remember that super designates the object receiving the object, in our case it is the instance of the Three class stored in the three variable. *However*, the search for the method, in our case the a method, starts in the super-class of the class in which we find the method containing the occurrence of the super pseudo-variable to which the selector of the a method is sent.

This will be the last number displayed by this program.

Figure A1.11 shows the `Transcript` with the result of the program for the exercise. For display purposes, we have slightly modified it:[2]

```
| one two three|
one := Onw new. two := Two new. three := Three new.
Transcript show: '(one a): ' , (one a) asString; cr;
          show: '(two a): ' , (two a) asString; cr;
          show: '(two b): ' , (two b) asString; cr;
          show: '(three b): ' , (three b) asString; cr;
          show: '(three c): ' , (three c) asString; cr;
          show: '(three d): ' , (three d) asString; cr
```

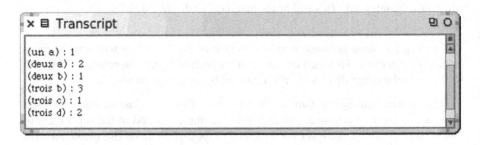

Figure A1.11. *Transcript showing the results
of the different transmissions*

Now, have you understood how `self` and `super` work?

3) We will begin by creating the`AnimalHabitat` class. We have said that it must know the set of animals which inhabit it and that it must have a name. In this case, "know" clearly means that these are the two properties which distinguish one habitat from another. The new `AnimalHabitat` class must, therefore, have two instance variables, one for storing the set of animals which inhabit it, which we will call `animals`, and another for its name. Naturally, the second instance variable will be, as for each of the animals, `name`. Like the `Animal` class, `AnimalHabitat` will be a subclass of the `Object` class, which gives us:

---

2 The first line:

      | one two three |

represents a way of declaring temporary variables. We discuss this in section 4.4.1, page 107.

```
Object subclass: #AnimalHabitat
        instanceVariableNames: 'animals name'
        classVariableNames: ''
        poolDictionaries: ''
        category: 'Smalltalk-Animal-Course'
```

Let us straight away create an `initialize-release` protocol in which we will put the access and modification methods of these two instance variables. This will give:

```
animals
        "return the set of animals inhabiting the
                receiver".
        ^animals

animals: aSet
        "initialize the animals variable"
        animals := aSet

name
        "return the name of the habitat"
        ^name

name: aString
        "give a name to the habitat"
        name := aString
```

In order to create a habitat, as per usual we will use the new message which we will send to the `AnimalHabitat` class, and we will give it a name with the `name:` message, such as:

```
AnimalHabitat new name:  'AtMine'
```

or, in order to access it later, we will store it in a variable, like below:

```
Me := AnimalHabitat new name:  'AtMine'
```

Now, we need to tell `AnimalHabitat` how to let an animal live in the habitat. We know that the message which adds an animal to a habitat will be `add:`. To make Polly the parrot live at mine, the transmission `Me add:  Polly` should suffice. We also know that the addition of an element to a set is done with the message `add:`. Upon the creation of a habitat, there is no set yet, therefore we must pay attention and see whether the `animals` instance variable is defined or not. If it is defined, you only need to send it the `add:` message with the new inhabitant as the argument, otherwise the set must first be created. If we put all of this together, we obtain the method:

```
add: anAnimal
        "adds an animal as an inhabitant"
        self animals isNil
                ifTrue:[self animals: Set new].
        self animals add: anAnimal.
```

With this method, if we perform the transmission:

                    Me add: Polly

the habitat Me initializes its animals instance variable as an empty set, with the Set new transmission, and then adds the parrot Polly to this marvelous habitat that is AtMine. The problem that we have is that the habitat AtMine knows that Polly lives there, while Polly does not know anything. Perhaps, it would be adequate to inform Polly that she has just moved. We, therefore, add the line anAnimal habitat: self at the end of our add: method, which gives:

```
add: anAnimal
        "adds an animal as an inhabitant and
        informs the animal about their habitat"
        self animals isNil
                ifTrue:[self animals: Set new].
        self animals add: anAnimal.
        anAnimal habitat: self
```

and of course this means that we need to add a habitat: method to the animals class. This will again be one of the ways to distinguish one animal from another. We will, therefore, need to add an additional instance variable, to the Animal class. This variable will aptly be called habitat. Here are the two methods habitat and habitat: of the Animal class:

```
habitat
        "this is where the animal lives"
        ^habitat
```

```
habitat: anHabitat
        "the anmial changes habitat"
        habitat := anHabitat
```

We add an additional method to the Animal class which lets us ask an animal where it lives:

```
whereAreYou
        "respond with the habitat"
        Transcript show: self habitat name; cr
```

Our AnimalHabitat class is still missing a method which lets us ask the habitat what resides in it. For this, we would need to display each of the animals in the Transcript, their class and their name.

Note first that any collection can understand the do: message. This message takes a *block* as an argument which must indicate what must be done with each of the elements of the collection. For example, after having added Polly and Lassie to the AtMine habitat, the transmission:

```
Me animals do: [:anAnimal | Transcript show: anAnimal name, '
          ']
```

displays the string 'Polly Lassie' in the Transcript.

We already know that a block is written between square brackets. However, if we take the block

```
[Transcript show:  'Whow!'; cr]
```

and we execute a *do it* (press "Alt+d") on this expression, nothing is displayed. If we had written this block within a Workspace and executed a *print it* (press "Alt+p") on the expression, then there would still not have been anything displayed in the Transcript and the value that the evaluation of this expression returns would be printed to the Workspace:

```
[] in UndefinedObject»DoIt {[Transcript show:  'Whow!'; cr]}
```

This is again one of the non-transparent messages of SQUEAK. It will say that SQUEAK has properly computed the value of this block (within the specific context of UndefinedObject) and that this value is the block itself. A block is a bit like a number: in the same way that the value of a number is this number, the value of a block is this same block. In reality, a block is a piece of code. And to execute this piece of code, the value message must be sent to it, very explicitly. Thus, if we execute a doIt on the expression:

```
[Transcript show:  'Whow!';  cr] value
```

the Transcript will properly display Whow!: the piece of code, the block, has been executed and evaluated.

Every now and then, we will want to pass an argument to a block. In this case, the message to be sent to the block will no longer be value but instead value:, with the argument being the value which we wish to pass to the block. For this, we need a way to indicate *from within the block* that it can receive an argument. As with methods which take arguments, we need a parameter. And similarly to the selector of a method where this fact is indicated by the ":" character, in a block, the parameters are also indicated by the ":" character. Thus, in the transmission:

```
Me animals do: [:anAnimal | Transcript show: anAnimal name, '
    ']
```

anAnimal is the name of a parameter which will take as a value the argument sent with the value: message. In this case, the message do: of the Set class will evaluate this block for each of the elements of the set of animals of the Me habitat. The vertical bar "|" is simply a syntactic way to indicate the end of the list of parameters.

Equipped with this new knowledge, we can add a show method which tells the AnimalHabitat class how to display in the transcript the animals which inhabit it:

```
show
    "show all of the animals which inhabit
    the receiver"
    self animals do:
        [:anAnimal |
            Transcript show: (anAnimal class asString,
                ': ' , anAnimal name; cr)]
```

It will be up to the readers to note the following variation: if we define, in the Animal class, the printString message:

```
printString
            ^self class asString , ': ' , self name
```

we can rewrite the answer: method of the Animal class more simply as:

```
answer: aString
        "print the class and the name of the animal
        in question, followed by the aString argument"
        Transcript show:
            (self asString , ': ' , aString); cr
```

and the show method of the AnimalHabitat class will become:

```
show
    "show all of the animals which inhabit
    the receiver"
    self animals do:
        [:anAnimal |
            Transcript show: anAnimal; cr)]
```

There is still one minor problem with the program in its current state: if we must move an animal from one habitat to another, it becomes ubiquitous, in other words, without knowing it, it will live in both habitats at the same time. If we ask whereAreYou, it will respond correctly with the new habitat, but the old habitat will also have it labeled as one of its inhabitants. Of course, before adding an animal to a new habitat, we must remove the old habitat, with the remove: message. This gives the following add: message:

```
add:    anAnimal
        "add an animal as an inhabitant"
        self animals isNil
            ifTrue:[self animals: Set new].
        anAnimal habitat isNil
            ifFalse:
                [anAnimal habitat animals remove: anAnimal].
        self animals add: anAnimal.
        anAnimal habitat: self
```

This is all for exercise 2.

4) It is up to you to develop the extensions as you see fit. You can always send me your proposals via e-mail (address: hw@ai.univ-paris8.fr), with the subject line: *smalltalk-animals*.

A1.4. Exercises from section 4.3.6

1) operations on numbers:

- 16rFF ↝ 255

- 10/2 ↝ 5

- 11/3 ↝ (11/3)

- 2e5 ↝ 200000

- 1+2 ↝ 3

- 1+2; yourself ↝ 1

- 8r55 ↝ 45

- 8r55e2 ↝ 2880

- 2.5 asInteger ↝ 2

- 2.5 truncated ↝ 2

- -2.5 truncated ↝ -2

- 2.5 rounded ↝ 3

- 2r1010.1010 ↝ 10.625

- 2 + 1.0 ↝ 3.0

- 5 factorial ↝ 120

- 1/12 + (1/6) ↝ (1/4)

- 1/12 + 1/6 ↝ (13/72)

- 1 / 4 / 3 ↝ (1/12)

- 12 squared ↝ 144

- 12 odd ↝ false

- 1.2 odd ↝ true

- (11/3) ceiling ↝ 4

- (11/3) negated ceiling ↝ -3

- 4 asFloat ↝ 4.0

- 4 asFraction ↝ (4/1)

- 4.0 asFraction ↝ 4

- 5 between: 1 and: 10
↝ true

- (1/3) = 0.3333333333
↝ false

- (1/3) = 0.3333333333333333
↝ true

- 1 + 3 * 4 ↝ 16

- (1@6) + (1@5) ↝ (2@11)

- (3.8@7.3) rounded ↝ 4@7

- (3@6) + 5 ↝ 8@11

- (3@6) \\ 5 ↝ 3@1

- 144 sqrt ↝ 12

2) operations on characters:

  – $W asLowercase ↝ $w

  – $e isVowel ↝ true

  – $r asInteger ↝ 114

  – $t < $$ ↝ false

  – $z isAlphabetic ↝ true

  – $2 isAlphabetic ↝ false

  – $2 isDigit ↝ true

  – $a asUppercase ↝ $A

  – $f between: $A and: $z ↝ true

  – $f between: $a and: $Z ↝ false

  – $f = $f ↝ true

  – ($f asInteger + 1) asCharacter ↝ $g

  – $a asciiValue ↝ 97

  – 32 asCharacter isSeparator ↝ true

3) exercises on tables:

  – results from transmissions:

  - #(((1 2 3) 4) 5) first first first ↝ 1

  - #(-1 2 -3 4) detect: [:x | x > 0] ↝ 2

- #(-1 2 -3 4) select: [:x | x > 0] ⤳ #(2 4)
- #(1 ($a $b) 2) at:

    (#(1 ($a $b) 2) indexOf: #($a $b)) ⤳ #($a $b)
- #(1 2 3 (1 2 3) 2 3 (2 3) 3 (3)) copyWithout: 3

    ⤳ #(1 2 #(1 2 3) 2 #(2 3) #(3))

    #(1 2 3) raisedTo: 3 ⤳ #(1 8 27)
- #(1 2 3) * #(4 5 6) ⤳ #(4 10 18)
- #(me you his her ours yours their)

    reject: [:ele | ele size > 2] ⤳ #(#me)

– method definitions:

- to find the element located in the middle of a collection, we add the following method to the SequenceableCollection class:

```
middle
        ^self at: self size // 2 + 1
```

- to swap the ith and jth element of a collection, we add the following method to the SequenceableCollection class:

```
swap: i with: j
    | aux |
    aux := self at: i.
    self at: i put: (self at: j).
    self at: j put: aux
```

- to flip the signs of a collection of numbers, we add the following method to the Collection class:

```
negated
        self collect: [:e | e negated]
```

Note that the receiver of the negated selector inside the block is a number. The method corresponding to negated is, therefore, the one which is found in one of the subclasses of Number and is fundamentally different from the one we are defining in the Collection class;

- to concatenate two tables, we add the following method to the SequenceableCollection class:

```
concat: aCollection
  | newC aCollectionSize |
  newC := self class new:
            self size + aCollection size.
  1 to: self size
    do: [:i | newC at: i
                  put: (self at: i)].
  aCollectionSize := aCollection size.

  1 to: aCollection size
    do: [:i | newC at: i + aCollectionSize
                  put: (aCollection at: i)].
  ^newC
```

- a definition for the inject:into: method, which is valid for all collections, was already given on page 100. It would be difficult to do better;

- to make a copy of a collection, one possibility is given in the following method:

```
copy
      ^self collect: [:e | e]
```

- to make a copy of a SequenceableCollection with an additional element at the head, one possibility is given in the method below:

```
copyWithFirst: unElement
    | newC |
    newC := self class new: self size + 1.
    newC at: 1 put: unElement.
    1 to: self size
      do: [:i | newC at: i + 1
                    put: (self at: i)].
    ^newC
```

- the select: method can be defined, for any collection, as:

```
select: aBlock
      | newC result counter|
      counter := 0.
      newC := self class new: self size.
      1 to: self size
        do: [:i | aBlock value: (self at: i)
                      ifTrue:
                          [counter := counter + 1.
```

```
                    newC at: counter
                        put: (self at: i)]].
        result := self class new: counter.
        1 to: counter
            do: [:i |
                    result at: i
                        put: (newC at: i)].
        ^result
```

- the anySatisfy: method can be defined for any collection as:

```
anySatisfy: aBlock
    self do: [:ele |
                (aBlock value: ele)
                    ifTrue: [^true]].
    ^false
```

- the allSatisfy: method for any collection:

```
allSatisfy: aBlock
    self do: [:ele |
                (aBlock value: ele)
                    ifFalse: [^false]].
    ^true
```

- the before: for a SequenceableCollection:

```
before: ele
    1 to: self size
        do: [:i |
            (self at: i) = ele
              ifTrue:
                [i > 1 ifTrue: [^self at: i - 1]
                    ifFalse: [^nil]]].
    ^nil
```

here, we have chosen to return nil in case the element being sought is not in the collection, or it is the first element and therefore has no predecessor. A better solution would be to throw an error in both of these cases. We will return to this later on;

- the atAll: method:

```
atAll: indexCol
    | newC |
    newC := self class new: (indexCol size).
    1 to: indexCol size
      do: [:i |
          newC at: i
                put: (self at: (indexCol at: i))].
    ^newC
```

- and the complementary atAll:put: method:

```
atAll: indexCol put: anObject
    indexCol do: [:i |
          self at: i
                put: anObject]
```

- and, finally, the complementary atAll:putAll: method:

```
atAll: indexCol putAll: anObjectCol
    indexCol with: anObjectCol
              do: [:i :v |
                    self at: i
                          put: v]
```

which uses the with:do: method of SequenceableCollection given here:

```
with: aCollection do: aBlockWith2Args
    1 to: self size
      do: [:i |
          aBlockWith2Args
              value: (self at: i)
              value: (aCollection at: i)]
```


4) Exercise 4:

– $w asUppercase

– 3.14 * (64 sqrt + 2) (⤳ 31.4)
however: 3.14 * 64 sqrt + 2 ⤳ 27.12

– $b > $E ⤳ true

– Transcript show:
    ((3 raisedTo: 3) even
            ifTrue: ['even']
            ifFalse: ['odd'])

The placement of the parantheses is absolutely necessary.

We could also have written:

```
(3 raisedTo: 3) even
        ifTrue: [Transcript show: 'even']
        ifFalse: [Transcript show: 'odd']
```

However this second form is less tidy: it contains two transmissions of the show: selector to the Transcript object.

– $0 isVowel ⤳ true

– (47 + 50) asCharacter isVowel ⤳ true

– (1/4) / 5 ⤳ (1/20)

– '1a2b3c4d500e' onlyLetters ⤳ 'abcde'

– ='Boom ! Boom !=

The king O and the queen= É are sitting

on their thrones' indexOf: = É   ⤳ 36

Of course, in SMALLTALK you will not have layout problems as we have here: in reality, for the result to be correct, the entire sentence would have to be written on one line, so as to not introduce additional characters.

– In order to write all of the vowels in a text, thus a string of characters, in uppercase, we will need to add a new method to the String class. We will call this new method asUppercaseVowels and add it to the converting protocol. Here is one possible way of writing it:

```
asUppercaseVowels
    "transform the receiver string into one where
    all of the vowels are written in uppercase"
    1 to: self size
      do:
        [:n |
        (self at:n) isVowel
            ifTrue:
                [self at: n
                    put: (self at: n) asUppercase]]
```

This method says: let n be the successive numbers between 1 and the size of the string which we wish to modify. For each value of n we look to see whether the nth character is a vowel. If this is the case, then we change the vowel into an uppercase vowel. When we have finished, we return the modified string. Thus, the transmission:

```
'here is an example text' asUppercaseVowels
```

returns the string hErE Is An ExAmplE tExt. All of the vowels are written in uppercase.

There is just one more small problem: we calculate the expression self at: n twice. As usual, we can factorize this computation, for example by storing the value of this expression into a local variable. This gives:

```
asUppercaseVowels
  "transfoms the receiver string into one where
  all of the vowels are written as uppercase
  characters"
  | x |
  1 to: self size
    do:
    [:n |
      x := self at:n.
      x isVowel
          ifTrue: [self at: n put x asUppercase]]
```

Any method can declare *local variables*. This is done right at the start of the body by writing the one or more local variables between two vertical bars (|). In our method below, we declare a local variable called x. A local variable is a variable which is known only within the *context* where it is declared. In this case, the context is the MethodContext of the asUppercaseVowels method. It is, therefore, known and can be used anywhere within this method. Generally, local variables, as seen here, are used to temporarily store the results of computations.

Since this variable is only used within the inside of a block, we could have also declared it inside this block. It would, therefore, no longer be known outside of this block (in other words, in the other parts of the method which are not a part of this block), only within the BlockContext of this block. This is what we do in the version of asUppercaseVowels below. Examine the vertical bars: the first occurrence is there to indicate that the set of parameters for the block is finished (in this case, there is only one parameter), whereas the next two wrap the local variable declaration.

```
asUppercaseVowels
  "transform the receiver string into one where
  the vowels are written as uppercase
  characters"
  1 to: self size
```

```
do:
    [:n || x |
     x := self at:n.
     x isVowel
        ifTrue: [self at: n put x asUppercase]]
```

5) Before beginning to solve this problem, we will determine how to represent the two nucleotide chains. Even though the structure of such a molecule is very complex (see Figure A1.12), for the problem that we wish to solve, we will choose the simplest solution: a chain of nucleotides, for us, will be a string of characters made up of the letters A, C, G and T.

We will, therefore, write a method which iterates through two strings in parallel and tests to see if we are in the presence of A↔T or C↔G pairs. In the previous exercise, we have already seen how to iterate through a string of characters in order to test each of the characters. Why not do the same here: two variables which successively contain the same corresponding elements from the two strings. This gives us the beginning to our isDNA: method:

```
isDNA: aString
    "test whether two nucleotide chains
     can form a DNA chain,
     here is a possible transmission:"
    "'ACTG' isDna: 'TGAC'"
    1
    to: self size
        do: [:n |
               | x y |
               x := self at: n.
               y := aString at: n.
               .....
            ]
```

Then, we will need to verify that each pair of values for the x and y variables corresponds to a valid nucleotide pair.

We will, therefore, need to check each time: either x is equal to $A and y is equal to $T, or x is equal to $T and y is equal to $A, or x is equal to $C and y is equal to $G, or x is equal to $G and y is equal to $C. If at any point none of these possibilities are seen, then the two chains cannot form a double DNA chain.

Since we have already studied the True and False classes (see section 4.1.2) I am sure that you have seen that there exists, in both classes, an or: method as well as another called and:. These are our two favorite logic operators. The or: operator returns true if the receiver is true, otherwise it returns the value of its argument. The

and: operator returns **false** if the receiver expression has the value **false** otherwise it returns the value of its argument. These are effectively the ∨ and ∧ operators of propositional logic. Below, for recall purposes, are their truth tables: first of **or:**

∨	true false
true	true true
false	true false

then for **and:**

∧	true false
true	true false
false	false false

Also, the **or:** selector as well as the **and:** selector are, therefore, sent to Boolean values, **true** or **false**, with a *block* as argument which must also be a Boolean. Naturally, since a block is a piece of code which is only evaluated on demand, in this case, inside our Boolean operators, for the **or:** operator we need to compute the value of the argument only if the receiver is the **false** object, and for the **and:** operator we only need to compute the argument if the receiver is the **true** object. Thus, SMALLTALK guarantees that we will only proceed with the minimum amount of necessary computation. In order to convince you of this, here are the definitions for the **or:** method in the **True** and **False** classes.

In the **True** class:

```
or: alternativeBlock
    "non-evaluation case
    replies with true since the receiver is true"
    ^true
```

In the **False** class:

```
or: alternativeBlock
    "non-evaluation case
    replies with the value of alternativeBlock"
    ^alternativeBlock value
```

This is the same idea as that used for the implementation of **ifTrue:ifFalse:**. You should, therefore, revisit the classes **Boolean**, **True** and **False**.

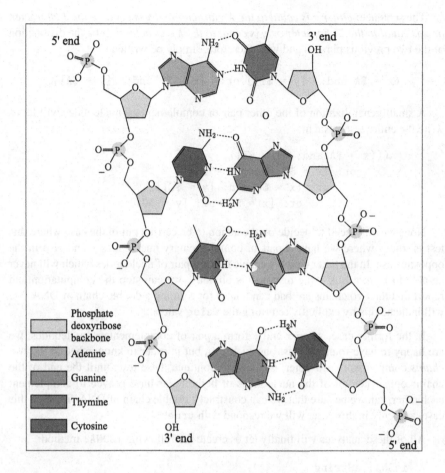

Figure A1.12. *Piece of DNA chain showing the structure of the complementary nucleotide links (according to [WIK 06a])*

Now, equipped with this information, we can begin to write our tests. Clearly: the phrase *x is equal to the A character and y is equal to the T character* can be written in SMALLTALK as:

```
x = $A and: [y = $T]
```

Similarly, *x is equal to the T character and y is equal to the A character* can be written in SMALLTALK as:

```
x = $T and: [y = $A]
```

The sentence: *either x is equal to the A character and y is equal to the T character, or x is equal to the T character or y is equal to the A character* will be the disjunction of the two previous phrases and will, therefore, simply be written as:

```
(x = $A and: [y = $T]) or: [x = $T and: [y = $A]]
```

A small generalization of the other pair of complementary nucleotides will let us write the entire test as such:

```
(((x = $A and: [y = $T])
    or: [x = $T and: [y = $A]])
        or: [x = $G and: [y = $C]])
            or: [x = $C and: [y = $G]]
```

Now, we only need to decide on the action to be carried out in the case where this test is true – where we have a pair of complementary nucleotides – and also in the opposite case. In the latter case – we have found a pair of nucleotides which will never be able to form a link – the response is obvious: we can stop the computation and report that the two chains are bad candidates for forming a double chain of DNA. We will indicate this by explicitly returning the `false` value.

In the former case, when x and y form a pair of complementary nucleotides, we are happy to have found at least one such pair, but in order to know whether the two *chains* complement each other, we need to continue these tests until the end of the chain: only when all of the nucleotides of both chains have proven to complement each other, can we be sure that we can construct a double chain of DNA. Then, in this case, and only in this case, will we respond with `true`.

All of these analyses will finally let us create the following `isDNA:` method:

```
isDNA: aString
    "test whether two chains of nucleotides
    can form a DNA chain,
    here is one possible transmission:"
    "'ACTG' isDna: 'TGAC'"
    1
    to: self size
        do: [:n |
            | x y |
            x := self at: n.
            y := aString at: n.
            ((((x = $A and: [y = $T])
                or: [x = $T and: [y = $A]])
```

```
                    or: [x = $G and: [y = $C]])
                      or: [x = $C and: [y = $G]])
             ifFalse: [^ false]].
     ^true
```

or if we use the with:do: method defined on page 364:

```
isDNA: aString
   "test whether two chains of nucleotides
    can form a DNA chain,
    here is one possible transmission:"
   "'ACTG' isDna: 'TGAC'"
   self with: aString
        do: [:x :y |
            ((((x = $A and: [y = $T])
              or: [x = $T and: [y = $A]])
               or: [x = $G and: [y = $C]])
                or: [x = $C and: [y = $G]])
           ifFalse: [^ false]].
     ^true
```

This is all well and good, providing us with a set of new methods and highly useful programming techniques. There is only one problem with this way of writing: it does not correspond to object-oriented thinking.

Right at the beginning of this book, we stated that the concept of an object-oriented program begins with the definition of the objects which this program must process. In the program, we have so far written the objects are characters and strings of characters. However, in the problem outline, we talked about DNA chains and the nucleotides which form them. We will thus rewrite our program by first creating the objects which the program must manipulate and we will start by creating an abstract Nucleotide class, which collects all of the information common to all nucleotides: in the Nucleotides category

```
Object subclass: #Nucleotide
       instanceVariableNames: 'complement'
       classVariableNames: ''
       poolDictionaries: ''
       category: 'Nucleotides'
```

For each of the nucleotides A, C, G and T, the complementary nucleotide will be indicated in the complement instance variable.

We will now add the two access and modification methods of this instance variable:

```
complement
    ^complement

complement: aNucleotide
    complement := aNucleotide
```

For each type of nucleotide, we will create a subclass of this Nucleotide class, thus ensuring that each nucleotide will know its complementary nucleotide:

```
Nucleotide subclass: #A_nucleotide
        instanceVariableNames: ''
        classVariableNames: ''
        poolDictionaries: ''
        category: 'Nucleotides'

Nucleotide subclass: #T_nucleotide
        instanceVariableNames: ''
        classVariableNames: ''
        poolDictionaries: ''
        category: 'Nucleotides'

Nucleotide subclass: #C_nucleotide
        instanceVariableNames: ''
        classVariableNames: ''
        poolDictionaries: ''
        category: 'Nucleotides'

Nucleotide subclass: #G_nucleotide
        instanceVariableNames: ''
        classVariableNames: ''
        poolDictionaries: ''
        category: 'Nucleotides'
```

To initialize instances, we create for each of the four nucleotide classes an initialization method initialize. For the A_nucleotide class, this method will be:

```
initialiZe
    self complement: T_nucleotide new
```

Similarly, for the other subclasses:

```
T_nucleotide>>initialiZe
    self complement: A_nucleotide new

C_nucleotide>>initialiZe
    self complement: G_nucleotide new

G_nucleotide>>initialiZe
    self complement: C_nucleotide new
```

Now, we have an abstract[3] Nucleotide class which, primarily, only exists to ensure that each of its subclasses has access to a complement instance variable; we have a class for each of the nucleotides and we know how to initialize instances of these classes such that they know their complementary nucleotide.

Since the simplest way to write a DNA chain is to write it as a string of characters, we create, as above, an isDNA: method in the String class. This method should be able to iterate through the two DNA chains (of characters) in parallel in order to verify that there are complementary pairs of nucleotides in each position. To do this, each time it encounters an A, T, C or G character we will, respectively, create an instance of the A_nucleotide, T_nucleotide, C_nucleotide and G_nucleotide. Then, we will only need to compare the object class created for the character in the receiver chain with the complement of the object created for the character corresponding to the argument chain aString. It is only when each pair of characters of these two classes is equal that we would be dealing with a DNA chain. Thus, here is the String»isDNA::

```
isDNA: aString
    "'ACTG' isDNA: 'TGAC'"
    self with: aString
        do: [:n1 :n2 |
            n1 newInstance class
                == n2 newInstance complement class
                ifFalse: [^false]].
    ^true
```

All that remains is to create a class instance creation method depending on the parsed character. This is the Character»newInstance method below:

---

3 Please note that the writing "initialiZe" (and not "initialize") is not a typing error. Remember that the method initialize (with a lower case "z") are launched automatically at each creation of aninstance. So, if we would have used "initialize" as the name of this four methods, the transmission "A_nucleotide new" would have launched "A_nucleotide initialize" which in turn would have launched "T_nucleotide new", which would have launched "T_nucleotide initialize" which in turn would have launched "A nucleotide new". You see: we would have created an infinite loop. Since Smalltalk is case sensitive, this doesn't happen when we use "initialiZe" as a selector.

```
newInstance
    self == $A
        ifTrue:
            [^A_nucleotide new initialiZe].
    self == $T
        ifTrue:
            [^T_nucleotide new initialiZe].

    self == $C
        ifTrue:
            [^C_nucleotide new initialiZe].
    self == $G
        ifTrue:
            [^G_nucleotide new initialiZe]
        ifFalse:
            [self error:
                (self asString,
                    'is not a nucleotide')]
```

This is it. Make sure you study this last version carefully: it is much more in the spirit of *object-oriented programming*

The above version of isDNA: converts the characters iteratively along the sequence of the two chains and the subclasses of Nucleotide. This minimizes computation, since we only proceed with this conversion as long as we have a valid start of two complementary chains.

For better readability of this method, we could also have written a stringToCollection method for the String class which transforms a string of characters into a collection of nucleotides, as below:

```
stringToCollection
    | collection |
    collection := OrderedCollection new.
    self
        do: [:car | collection add: car newInstance].
    ^ collection
```

This method could also be used in isDNA: so as to change the iterating process from a string of characters to a collection of nucleotides. This gives the two modified isDNA: methods here:

```
String>>isDNA: aString
    ^ self stringToCollection
        isDNA: aString stringToCollection
```

```
Collection>>isDNA: aCollection
    self with: aCollection
        do: [:n1 :n2 |
            n1 complement class = n2 class
                ifFalse: [^ false]].
    ^ true
```

This second version is not as good since it not only transforms the set of characters into nucleotides, even if the first characters in the two strings are already not complementary, but it also performs two additional iterations. It is used if we find ourselves in a situation requiring much more manipulation of the two chains of nucleotides than the simple complementary test.

The newInstance method is not very elegant with this cascade of tests in order to know which character has just been read. Ideally, it would be possible to create a subclass of the Character class which only has four instances, the characters $A, $C, $G and $T. Unfortunately, this is not possible in SQUEAK.

Below is a modification of our program which gives a unique role to each of the four characters in order to eliminate this cascade of tests. This modification involves the addition of a class variable to the Nucleotide class, an initialization of this class variable, and a rewrite of the NewInstance method. Here is the modified program, now it is up to you to understand it.

The new definition of the Nucleotide class:

```
Object subclass: #Nucleotide
    instanceVariableNames: 'complement'
    classVariableNames: 'Nucleotides'
    poolDictionaries: ''
    category: 'Nucleotides'
```

An access method for the class variable:

```
Nucleotide class>>nucleotides
    ^Nucleotides
```

The initialization method for the class variable:

```
Nucleotide class>>initialize
    "Nucleotide initialize"
    Nucleotides := Dictionary new.
    Nucleotides
        at: $A put: A_nucleotide;
        at: $T put: T_nucleotide;
        at: $C put: C_nucleotide;
        at: $G put: G_nucleotide
```

Finally, the new version of newInstance:

```
Character>>newInstance
   | nucl |
   nucl := Nucleotide nucleotides
             at: self
             ifAbsent: [nil].
   nucl isNil
       ifTrue: [self
                    error: self asString ,
                        'is not a nucleotide].
       ifFalse: [^ (nucl perform: #new) initialiZe]
```

A1.5. Exercises for section 4.4.9

Program comprehension exercises.

1) The expression:

$$B \text{ new a: } 4; a$$

is clearly a cascade: B new creates a new instance of the B class. For clarity, we will call this instance b_1. This instance receives the message a: 4, which results in the initialization of the instance variable a of the instance b_1. The message a is transmitted through cascade to this same instance.

We recall the implementation of the a method:

```
a
   | x |
   ^super a <= 0
       ifTrue:[1]
       ifFalse:[x := B new.
                x a: super a.
                x a + 1]
```

It declares a temporary variable x; therefore, it creates this variable and returns the value from the evaluation of the test which makes up its body. Let us run the program *by hand*, step-by-step:

i) first, b_1 receives the message a – and since there is the super pseudo-variable, we know that the method to be executed cannot be the a method of the B class above, but it must be and a method of one of the super-classes of B. The first such method is that of the A class which returns the value of the transmission a - 2;

ii) the instance variable a of the b_1 object, therefore, receives the message "$-$" with the argument 2. Given that a is bound to the integer 4, the result will be the integer 2 which;

iiii) itself, receives the <= message with argument 0. The integer 2 knows that it is not less than or equal to 0, and therefore responds with the only and unique instance of the False class: false;

iv) false, therefore, receives the message ifTrue:ifFalse: with the two argument blocks. false transmits, without hesitation (see page 70), the message value to the block:

```
[x := B new. x a:   super a. x a + 1]
```

v) the temporary variable x receives as a new value the result of sending the message new to the B class. We will call this newly created instance of B, b_2. This instance will be the value of x and it receives the message a: with, as argument, the result of the super a transmission;

vi) we have already seen this: super still referring to object b_1, this transmission returns, as above, the integer 2;

vii) with no a: message present in the B class, it will again be the a: message in the A class which will be activated and, as above, it will not do anything other than give a value to the instance variable a of its receiver, which, in this case, is the object b_2. This instance variable a of the b_2 object will, therefore, take the value of the transmission super a which;

viii) as before, returns the integer 2.

ix) x, thus b_2, then receives the message a, corresponding to the same method which we are in the process of executing. It is, therefore, a recursive method. Let us execute it again – but let us not forget that the result of the x a transmission, and therefore the sending of message a to object b_2 will then need to receive the message + with argument 1;

x) the a method starts with the declaration of a new temporary variable x. We, therefore, create this variable, and since there already exists a variable of the same name (we still have not exited the first call to the a method), we call it x_2;

xi) as before, we will start by evaluating the transmission of super a, except that this time super refers to object b_2, for which the instance variable a was initialized to 2. The result of this transmission will, therefore, be $2 - 2$, the integer 0;

xii) the integer 0 receives the message <= with argument 0. It responds with the true object, the one and only instance of the True class;

xiii) `true` receives the `ifTrue:ifFalse:` message with the two blocks as argument;

xiv) `true` sends the message `value` to the first argument, the block `[1]`, which returns the integer 1. This is the last expression to be computed in the a method. We, therefore, exit the current call: x_2 ceases to exist and the returned value is the integer 1;

xv) as we stated in point 1.9 above, this integer receives the + message with argument 1, which delivers the integer 2 as the result of the call to the a method;

xvi) we, therefore, exit the method: x ceases to exist and 2 is the result of the first call to the a method, and therefore the result for the whole expression B `new a:    4;` a.

Figure A1.13, page 379, shows, in Unified Modeling Language (UML)[4], a sequence diagram for this trace. We have kept the same numbering as in the text. The simplification involves the grouping of multiple activities and the decision to not draw all of the method return values: they are implicit.

2) We already know the result of sending the a message to an instance of the B class, for which the instance variable a is initialized to 4, this is the integer 2. Here, we collect the successive results of sending this message to instances of B for which the variables of the instances of a are, respectively, initialized to 1, 2, 3, etc. up to 10. The result is, therefore, the table #(1 1 2 2 3 3 4 4 5 5).

3) The a method of the B class contains two references to the super pseudo-variable. Both times, the same message a is sent to it. Thus, we only need to use a second temporary variable in which the result of this transmission is temporarily stored. This gives us the method below:

```
a
   | x temp |
   temp := super a.
   ^temp <= 0
         ifTrue:[1]
         ifFalse:[x := B new.
               x a: temp.
               x a + 1]
```

4) The b method of the C class contains three references to the super pseudo-variable, all three times with the same message:

---

4 UML is an accronym of "Unified Modeling Language". This modelling language uses pictograms to visualize system architectures or system behaviors.

b

```
| c |
^ super b = 0
        ifTrue: [1]
        ifFalse: [c := C new.
              c b: super b.
              c b + super b + 1]
```

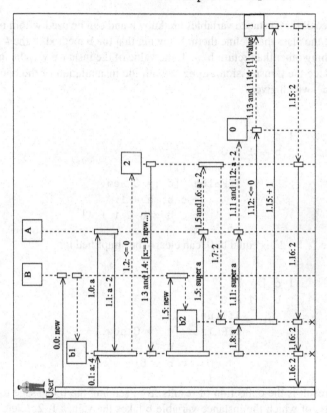

Figure A1.13. *The diagram of the simplified sequence of* B new a: 4

One solution is, therefore, as in the previous exercise, to use an additional temporary variable to store the intermediate results, which gives us the following method:

b

```
| c temp |
temp := super b.
^ temp = 0
```

```
ifTrue: [1]
iffalse: [c := C new.
         c b: temp.
         c b + temp + 1]
```

However, this solution always contains one reference too many to the super pseudo-variable: we do not want any more.

Let us recall that instance variables are known and can be used within methods of instances of the class that define them. Knowing that the b method of the A class does not do anything other than return b - 1, the value of the instance variable minus one, we can replace the transmission super b with the instantiation of the body of the b method of a[5], which gives:

```
b
    | c |
    ^ b - 1 = 0
        ifTrue: [1]
        iffalse: [c := C new.
                 c b: b - 1.
                 c b + b - 1 + 1]
```

which, since "- 1 + 1" is equal to 0, can clearly be simplified to:

```
b
    | c |
    ^ b - 1 = 0
        ifTrue: [1]
        iffalse: [c := C new.
                 c b: b - 1.
                 c b + b]
```

5) The result is the collection of results from sending the b message to instances of the C class of which the instance variable b takes the values 1, 2, 3, etc. up to 10. This is the table #(1 3 6 10 15 21 28 36 45 55). Where is the regularity in this series?

6) Clearly, the a method of the B class provides as a result the division by two of the integer contained in the instance variable a *if* this integer is an odd number. If this integer is an even number n, then the result is $\frac{(n+1)}{2}$.

---

5 The technique of replacing a call to a procedure with the body of this procedure, with the variables replaced by the values received in the call, is referred to as *unfolding*. This is a powerful technique which is useful for the optimization of programs. Here we only see a small example of this. If you are interested in such techniques, see [BUR 77] or [DAR 73].

The b method of the C class computes the sum of the successive numbers from 1 up to the value of the instance variable b, in other words, it computes $\sum_{i=1}^{b} i$.

We could have also defined this method as:

```
b
    (1 to: b) inject: 0
             into: [:c :e | c + e]
```

7) The new definition of b:

```
b
    | c |
    ^ super b = 0
         ifTrue: [1]
         ifFalse: [c := C new.
               c b: super b.
               c b * super b + 1]
```

can, by *unfolding*, be rewritten as[6]:

```
b
    | c |
    ^ b - 1 = 0
         ifTrue: [1]
         ifFalse: [c := C new.
               c b: b - 1.
               c b * (b - 1) + 1]
```

From here, we can deduce that c b, with the instance variable b of the c instance of the C class bound to the integer n, which we write as C_n, can be defined recursively as:

$$C_n = \begin{cases} 1 & n = 1 \\ C_{n-1} \times (n-1) + 1 & n \neq 1 \end{cases}$$

For an instance variable b bound to 3, C_3, the result of sending the message b should, therefore, be: $C_2 * 2 + 1$, where $C_2 = C_1 * 1 + 1$, and C_1, as we know, is equal to 1.

Through instantiation, we can then substitute the value of C_1 into the definition of C_2, which gives $C_2 = 1 * 1 + 1 = 2$. Again, through instantiation, we can use this

---

6 Be careful with the parentheses. The multiplication operation in SMALLTALK has the same priority as the addition operation, in other words: the SMALLTALK expression 1 + 2 * 3 does not compute $1 + (2 * 3)$, but rather $(1 + 2) * 3$.

result in the definition of C_3, which then gives $C_3 = 2 * 2 + 1 = 5$. C_3 is, therefore, equal to 5.

Figure A1.14 shows a Workspace with the first 20 numbers of this series. It is up to you to verify that our definition is correct. Note the surprising growth of this series of numbers.

Figure A1.14. *The first 20 elements of our series obtained with the modified b method*

8) In order to modify the a method of the B class so as to compute the division by 3 of the value of the instance variable a, we only need to see that the division by 2 of the current version is simply the result of calling the a method of the A class. Indeed, the algorithm in the b method works by starting with a number n initially associated with the variable a, and adds 1 to the result obtained from applying the same algorithm to the integer $n - 2$ – in programming terms: by asking a new instance of B, which has its instance variable a initialized to the integer $n - 2$, to provide the result of its division by two to then add 1 to this result, since n contains 2 at least once more than $n - 2$.

We conclude that there is nothing that needs to be changed in the b method, but we just need to modify the a method of class A, since it is the latter which is computing the value $n - 2$. The new version will then be:

```
a
    ^ a - 3
```

and we are done.

9) First we recall the a method of class B:

```
a
    | x |
    ^super a <= 0
        ifTrue:[1]
        ifFalse:[x := B new.
                 x a: super a.
                 x a + 1]
```

Knowing that the division by 3 is completed by the A»a[7] method, we simply need to find the part where we compute the rounded number. Since in this version the number is rounded upward, we just need to modify this part of the program so that it rounds down to the integer below instead.

Of course, there is no explicit calculation of the rounded number, for example with the asInteger, floor or ceiling messages[8]. Computing the rounded number must, therefore, be a side-effect of the algorithm used in the B»a method. The only possible areas are the test super a <= 0 and the parameter of ifTrue:, the block [1].

Indeed, if the value of the instance variable a is less than or equal to 3, then the result of this method will be the integer 1. This is a good response for the value 3, $\frac{3}{3}$ is clearly equal to 1, however, this is no longer a correct response for the integers 1 and 2, since we now want $\frac{2}{3}$ and $\frac{1}{3}$ to return 0.

This reasoning gives us the solution: we only need to change the $\leq$ test into a $<$ test, and, in the case where this test is passed, return 0. This will give the new a method below:

```
a
    | x |
    ^super a < 0
            ifTrue:[0]
            ifFalse:[x := B new.
                     x a: super a.
                     x a + 1]
```

10) After everything we have seen up until now, modifying the b method such that it computes the factorial of the instance variable b should no longer be a problem.

We recall that the nth factorial number, !n, is defined as:

$$!n = \begin{cases} 1 & n = 0 \\ !(n-1) \times n & n > 0 \end{cases}$$

i) The first method:

this very much resembles the definition of our C_n number. We, therefore, only need to take our SMALLTALK definition of C_n, the b method

---

7 We recall that we have introduced compact notation *Foobar»foo* to refer to the *foo* method of the *Foobar* class.

8 floor and ceiling are two methods from the Number class. floor returns the closest integer less than the receiver. ceiling returns the closest integer more than the receiver.

```
b
    | c |
    ^ b - 1 = 0
        ifTrue: [1]
        ifFalse: [c := C new.
                  c b: b - 1.
                  c b * (b - 1) + 1]
```

and replace the b - 1 factor in the multiplication by the new factor b and eliminate the transmission of + 1. This gives us the new b method here:

```
b
    | c |
    ^ b - 1 = 0
        ifTrue: [1]
        ifFalse: [c := C new.
                  c b: b - 1.
                  c b * b]
```

which, in effect, computes the factorial of its instance variable b.

ii) The second method:

knowing that in our program, the variable is not called n but instead b, we can rewrite our definition as:

$$!b = \begin{cases} 1 & b = 0 \\ !(b-1) \times b & b > 0 \end{cases}$$

We can translate this directly as:

```
b
    b = 0
        ifTrue: [1]
        ifFalse: [(C new b: b - 1; b) * b]
```

Now, we recall that any method in which we do not explicitly specify a return value returns the receiver of the message which caused the activation of this method. In this case, the receiver of the message b is always an instance of the C class. It is not this instance which we wish to return, it is the numerical value computed by the method. We, therefore, specify this return value:

```
b
    ^ b = 0
        ifTrue: [1]
        ifFalse: [(C new b: b - 1; b) * b]
```

and that is it, we have another SMALLTALK method which computes the factorial of its instance variable b.

These two methods, one being based on the transformation of a program, the other based on the transformation of a specification, are very different, in the same way that our two transformation approaches were conceptually very different.

It is not always easy to decide whether it is better to transform an existing program to obtain a modified program having to address new constraints, or whether it is better to reconsider – as a kind of reshaping – the specification of the problem and transform it, step-by-step, toward an implementable program. The opinions are split, as you can easily convince yourselves by studying the literature on the transformation of programs: start by reading the summary given by Partsch and Steinbrlggen in [PAR 83], then continue with the excellent PhD Thesis by Nachum Dershowitz [DER 83] or Wossner *et al.'s* course [WOS 78], or the literature on the transformations of specifications, starting with Dijkstra's book [DIJ 76], or even the literature on reverse-engineering, particularly, the annual reverse engineering conferences published by the IEEE Computer Society [IEE 05].

11) First, we must think about where we can store the dictionary. Since it is a dictionary which must store all of the results provided by the C⋗b method, we cannot store it in an instance variable: only the instance has access to its instance variables. We need something more global, such as a global variable, a class variable or a pool variable.

The use of a global variable here is out of the question: some objects only need to know which sums have already been computed, thus there is no need for every object to know everything. We will, therefore, opt for the second solution and use a class variable, which we can store either in the A class, the super-class of the C class where our b method is implemented, or directly in the C class.

The program is written in such a way that all of the instance variables are declared in their super-class. We will also add this dictionary to the A class and, as a result, modify the definition of this class to be:

```
Object subclass: #A
        instanceVariableNames: 'a b'
        classVariableNames: 'Sum'
        poolDictionaries: ''
        category: 'Lesson-Smalltalk-Exercices'
```

and add a class method for initializing this class variable Sum as an empty dictionary:

```
initSum
        Sum := Dictionary new
```

and another to be able to see the contents of the dictionary:

```
sum
    ^Sum
```

We can then initialize or re-initialize this class variable with the following simple transmission:

```
A initSum
```

This initialization must be completed at least once before using the Sum variable, otherwise how would SMALLTALK know that Sum is the name of a dictionary?

With which type of key should we store the results of the b method? If we examine this method:

```
b
    | c |
    ^ super b = 0
            ifTrue: [1]
            ifFalse: [c := C new.
                    c b: super b.
                    c b + super b + 1]
```

and after everything we have seen up to this point, it seems clear that it computes a different value for each different value of the instance variable b. These values seem to act as very suitable keys which we can associate with the corresponding results. Thus, at a certain instant, our Sum dictionary could hold the following key-value pairs:

```
(1->1 2->3 3->6 4->10 5->15)
```

This shows that b has already computed the sums of the first five numbers. We recall that any SMALLTALK object can be a key, and therefore integers as well[9].

Now, we only need to write an additional method which acts as the interface between our b method and the dictionary. Here is the first version of such a method, which we will call sum, in the C class:

---

9 In the case where all keys are integers, instead of a dictionary, we could also have used a table, an instance of the **Array** class. The index of the table would correspond to the key of our dictionary. The problem with tables is that they must be declared with a preset size, and if all of a sudden there are more results to be stored than the size set during the declaration, SMALLTALK will throw an out-of-bounds error for exceeding the indices. A dictionary does not have this limitation: its size is dynamic.

```
sum
      ^ sum includesKey: b
          ifTrue: [Sum at: b]
          ifFalse: [Sum at: b put: self b]
```

It says: each time we ask an instance of the C class to compute its sum, we should start by asking the Sum class variable whether the integer corresponding to the value of its instance variable b exists as a key. If so, then we need to add the key-value pair "value of the instance variable b" -> "return value from sending message b, the method which effectively computes the sum" to the dictionary. This return value will be the result of calling the sum method, since the at:put: method returns the value of its put: parameter.

For esthetic purposes, every indexed SMALLTALK collection not only understands the at: message, but also the at:if-Absent: message. The latter returns the value associated with the at: parameter if the index or the key exists, and returns the value of the block passed as an argument to the ifAbsent: parameter if this index or key does not exist[10]. Thus, our sum method can be written more elegantly as below:

```
sum
      ^ Sum at: b
          ifAbsent: [Sum at: b put: self b]
```

Figure A1.15 shows a Workspace with a few commented examples on the use of our new methods.

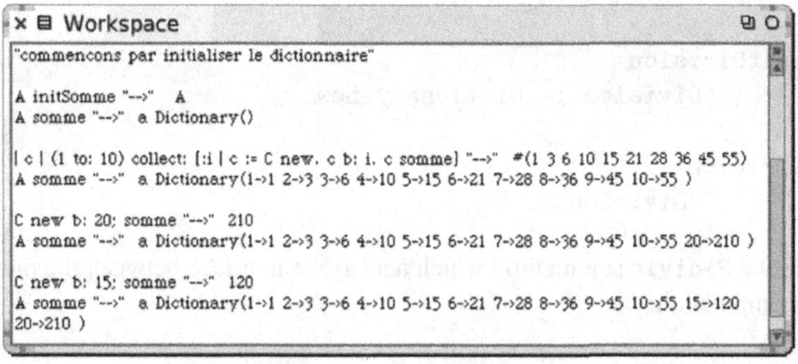

Figure A1.15. *A few examples demonstrating the use of memorizations*

---

10 The at: method returns an error if we try to access a non-existing index or key. Thus, to avoid error messages, instead of "at: *smthng*", we can always write "at: *smthng* ifAbsent: []", knowing that the return value nil of such an expression can both signify the absence of the key and the requested index or that the value of the key is nil.

The technique involving the storage of results of computations, so as to avoid recomputing them later, when performing a later request of the same computation, is often used in the writing of programs which have a lot of recursion and which are likely to lead to a large number of calculations. It plays a similar role to temporary variables. While these variables store the results of intermediary computations, as their name implies, *temporarily*, to be used only within the *current* execution of a program, here we can store complete results for any *future* reuse of the program. The transformation of an ordinary program into a program which recalls its results can be automated (this would make for a good exercise). The routines, functions and methods so obtained are called *memo-routines*, *memo-functions* or *memo-methods*.

12) After having solved the previous exercise, this one should not pose any problems: we need to declare a class variable, which we will call Division; we need initialization and access methods for this class variable, and we also need to create an interface method between the dictionary and the a method.

Here are the small modifications and additions, first the new definition of the A class:

```
Object subclass: #A
        instanceVariableNames: 'a b'
        classVariableNames: 'Somme Division'
        poolDictionaries: ''
        category: 'Lesson-Smalltalk-Exercices'
```

Then, the two class methods for access to the dictionary:

```
initDivision
        Division := Dictionary new

division
        ^Division
```

Then, the B»division method which acts as the interface between the dictionary and the computation:

```
division
        ^ Division at: a
            ifAbsent: [Division at: a put: self a]
```

And this is all. You can see that this transformation is carried out mechanically: there should not be any problem to automate it.

Now, having executed the two transmissions below:

```
A initDivision.
B new a: 10; division
```

the dictionary Division contains the key-value pair (10->5).

Let us imagine then, that we have many more memorizations to be carried out in the subclasses of A. For each of the activities to be memorized, we should create a new class variable containing a dictionary. This is the time to use a pool variable: a variable which will contain all of its dictionaries. For this, we redefine the A class by removing all of the class variables and simply add a pool variable called Dictionaries:

```
Object subclass: #A
        instanceVariableNames: 'a b'
        classVariableNames: '
        poolDictionaries: 'Dictionaries'
        category: 'Lesson-Smalltalk-Exercices'
```

Then, we add a class method for the initialization of our *pool* dictionary and *pool* variables:

```
initDictionaries
    Dictionaries at: #Somme put: Dictionary new;
                 at: #Division put: Dictionary new
```

The transmission

```
A initDictionaries
```

then creates two pool variables, Sum and Division, which are accessible in the same way as our old class variables Sum and Division.

We do not have anything left to change in our program: all of the transmissions which we tested earlier now work, except this time they no longer use class variables but use pool variables instead. And if we need to memorize results from other activities, we simply add the additional pool variables with the A»addDictionary: class method below:

```
addDictionary: newDict
    Dictionaries at: newDict put: Dictionary new.
```

A1.6. Exercises from section 4.8

1) Exercises on collections: the set of these exercises has the aim of helping to better tell the difference between the different types of collections. Let us recall: tables, instances of the Array class are fixed-size collections for which the elements are indexed with integers. The elements of the instances of the Bag class are not ordered and they can contain multiple occurrences of the same element. Sets, instances of the Set class, are not ordered either, however, there cannot be multiple occurrences of the same element. Dictionaries, instances of the Dictionary class, are indexed by some type of object. Intervals, instances of the Interval class, correspond to finite arithmetic progressions. OrderedCollections are tables of non-fixed size, as are SortedCollections. However, as the name implies, the elements of a SortedCollection are sorted. A string of characters, an instance of the String class, is a table of fixed size containing only characters. There also exist the Heap, LinkedList, SharedQueue, Array2D and Text classes. It is up to you to open a class browser and examine these classes in more detail.

1.1) Here are the results for the different conversions:

i) The transformation of the string 'cat' into a sorted collection returns a collection with each of the elements of the string in ascending order. In this case, this will be the SortedCollection ($a $c $t).

ii) This second exercise is also a transformation of one collection into another, this time a string into a Bag (a set with repetitions). The result will, therefore, be the Bag ($f $o $o $b $a $r).

iii) To see the difference between a Bag and a Set, here is the transformation of this same string 'foobar' into a Set (no repetitions): a Set($f $o $r $a $b). Note that the elements of a Bag as well as those of a Set are not in any kind of order.

iv) As in exercise 1.1.i, the **asSortedCollection** method transforms the receiver into a collection of sorted elements, the result of the transmission of messages to the table #(3 1 4 9), therefore, returns the SortedCollection (1 3 4 9).

v) If we send the message asSortedCollection:, the elements will be sorted according to the sorting criteria indicated in the argument block which must contain two variables as arguments. In this case, the argument is the block [:x :y | x > y] which indicates that the sorting must be done in decreasing order since the first argument must be greater than the second argument. The result is, therefore, the SortedCollection (9 4 3 1).

vi) The block which gives the sorting criterion indicates an increasing order, the default for a SortedCollection. The result is, therefore, identical to the result of exercise 1.1.iv.

vii) The temporary variable a will hold the l'OrderedCollection ($a 'cat' 3).

viii) The addAll: method adds each of the elements of the argument to the receiver. The temporary variable a will, therefore, hold the ordered collection ($a 'cat' '3' $f $o $o $b $a $r).

1.2) Here is the state of the data variable after each of the transmissions. We assume, as stated in the question, that it is always the same value of data which acts as the receiver for the successive messages: the sorted collection (3 1 4 9).

i) The remove: method removes the object passed as argument to the receiver. If this object is not a part of the receiver collection, then remove: throws up an error. In this case, the object to be removed, 4, exists and after its deletion, the data variable will be bound to the sorted collection (3 1 9). The removed object is the return value of this transmission.

ii) Here, we are trying to remove an object, the integer 5, from a collection which, of course, does not contain this object. It will, therefore, be the value of the argument block of ifAbsent: which will be returned. This value is nil. The variable data will not change in value.

iii) The removeAll: method transmits each element in the collection passed as an argument, as an argument to a transmission from remove: to self. In other words, removeAll: removes from the receiver all of the elements of the argument collection. In this case, the integers 1 and 9 are removed from the collection (3 1 4 9), which leaves the collection (3 4) in the data variable. Since the removeAll: method uses remove:, if one of the elements of the argument collection has no occurrences in the receiver collection, an error: exception is thrown up.

Here is the Collection»removeAll: method as implemented in the SQUEAK system:

```
removeAll: aCollection
    aCollection do:
        [:ele | self remove: ele].
    ^aCollection
```

iv) The method removeAllFoundIn: is like the removeAll: method except that it uses the remove:ifAbsent: method instead of the remove: method. As such, if one or more of the elements in the argument do not occur in the receiver collection, no exception is thrown: we simply move onto the next element. In our example, 6 is not a part of the receiver, therefore, it is just the integer 1 which will be removed from the receiver. data will, therefore, be bound to the collection (3 4 9).

Here is the implementation of the `Collection»removeAllFoundIn:` method of your SQUEAK interpreter:

```
removeAll: aCollection
    aCollection do:
        [:ele | self remove: ele
            ifAbsent: []].
    ^aCollection
```

v) Finally, the `removeAllSuchThat:` method takes as argument a block which indicates the condition which an element of the receiver must satisfy in order for it to be removed from the collection. In this case, the argument block is [:ele | ele > 3], therefore, it will be all of the elements with a numerical value greater than 3 which will be removed. The data variable will contain the ordered collection (3 1).

Here is a possible implementation of this method in the `Collection` class:

```
Collection>>removeAllSuchThat: aBlock
    self copy do:
        [:ele |
        (aBlock value: ele)
            ifTrue: [self remove: ele]]
```

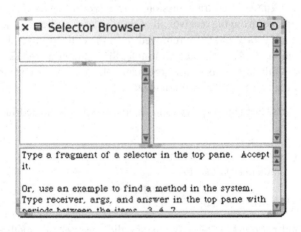

Figure A1.16. *A selector browser window: a* `Method Finder`

How do we find methods in the SQUEAK system?

In case you have forgotten, here is a reminder on how to find all of the implementations of a given method: in the `Tools` tab, to the right of the SQUEAK screen, drag the Method Finder object into the screen. This will open a new selector browser window as shown in Figure A1.16. This kind of window, a Method Finder, is made up of four subwindows: in the top left is an input window where the user can enter the name or part of the name of a selector, below that is a window where SQUEAK responds with the set of selectors corresponding to the input. If we have chosen one of these selectors, the window in the top right displays the set of classes which implement this selector. The selection of one of these classes then opens a class browser on the method in the selected class. The large window at the bottom is – as always – a Workspace window.

Figure A1.17 shows a selector browser open on the remove: method. The window beneath that shows all of the selectors containing the string remove:, from elsewhere without distinguishing from the different classes. We can recognize the remove: selector, as well as all of the other selectors containing the string "remove:", such as remove:from: and filterRemove:. In this figure, the user has selected the remove: method which resulted in the displaying, in the right window, of all of the classes implementing this method.

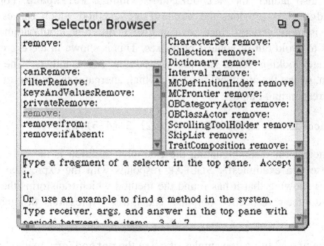

Figure A1.17. *A MethodFinder open on remove:*

As we have just seen, if we know the name, or a substring of the name of a selector, a MethodFinder gives us all of the implementations of the corresponding methods. If we are searching for a method for which we have a very specific example of an input/output (for example, input: 4, output: 24), we would simply need to provide this example in the input window (in the top left) of the *SelectorBrowser*, which will then respond with all of the methods which transform this specific input into this specific output. You will need to end each input with the 'full stop' character. Thus, if we enter "4. 24", after an accept ("Alt+s"), the MethodFinder responds, in the window below, with the line:

4 factorial –> 24

Indeed, the factorial method is the only method which transforms 4 into 24. If we give the two inputs 1 and 2 and the output 3, as "1. 2. 3", the MethodFinder responds with the following three lines:

```
1 + 2 --> 3
1 bitOr: 2 --> 3
1 bitXor: 2 --> 3
```

SQUEAK will thus provide the three methods which, when they take 1 and 2 as input, will return 3 as a result[11]. If we click on one of the lines, implementations of the chosen method will appear in the right subwindow. Figure A1.18 shows the MethodFinder after having selected the line 1 + 2 -> 3.

We can also launch the MethodFinder within a Workspace. For this, the MethodFinder class provides the methodFor: method which carries out these searches. It is more general since we can give it different input/output examples, which helps to avoid out-of-context responses. This is shown in the example above, where we are looking for a method for adding two numbers. The following transmission, where the argument is a table which alternates the inputs (of subtables) with the corresponding outputs:

```
MethodFinder methodFor: #((1 2) 3 (4 5) 9)
```

will be sufficient for disambiguating the example: addition is the only one which satisfies these two examples[12]. SQUEAK responds with the expression "data1 + data2", thus showing that it has found the method which transforms the two input examples into their respective outputs. The $data_i$ expressions designate the ith entries.

Below are two additional examples of using the methodFor: method for finding the methods which are already present for resolving the given examples. Of course,

---

11 Indeed, $1 + 2$ is equal to 3. The bitOr: method will return the result of the logical *or* operation between the binary representation of the receiver and the argument. In this case, the receiver is 1, in binary representation: 01, the argument is 2, in binary representation: 10. If we execute the *or* operation bit-by-bit on these two binary numbers, this will return the binary number 11 which is equivalent to 3 in decimal representation.

The logical *xor* operation corresponds to "either one or the other, but not both at the same time". Therefore, the bit-by-bit *xor* between 1 and 2 also gives 3. This explains the three possibilities.

12 Clearly, this example is looking to replace *what* with a unique selector, in both expressions "1 *what* 2 –> 3" and "4 *what* 5 –> 9".

there can be multiple proposals. We just need to choose the right method.

```
MethodFinder methodFor: #((6 9) 6 (27 3) 0 (13 9) 4)
    '(data1 \\ data2) (data1 rem: data2)'
MethodFinder methodFor: { #(1). true. {2.}. false}
    '(data1 odd)(data1 = 1)(data1 <= 1)(data1 anyMask: 1)
    (data1 allMask: 1)(data1 closeTo: 1)(data1 == 1)'
```

For more information, explore the `MethodFinder` class and – particularly – study the examples given in the `verify` method instance.

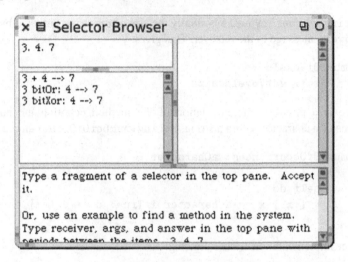

Figure A1.18. A MethodFinder open on example 3. 4. 7

2) Exercises involving enumerative structures:

2.1) In order to find a collection of the same type as the receiver, made up of a subset of elements from the receiver collection, SMALLTALK provides us with the `select:` message. This message takes as argument a block indicating the condition which an element from the collection must satisfy in order to be part of the resulting collection. Here is the `String»getVowels` method:

```
getVowels
    ^ self select: [:ele | ele isVowel]
```

2.2) This second exercise is clearly only a variant of the above exercise: it is simply the condition which changes. Here is a possible `Collection»pair` method:

```
pair
    ^ self select:
        [:ele | ele isNumber and: [ele even]]
```

2.3) In order to write Collection»pairSquared, the easiest way would be to consider that we have just written a method which extracts even numbers from a collection. We just need to take each of these numbers returned by Collection»pair and multiply them by themselves, which is equivalent to squaring them. This gives:

```
pairSquared
    ^ self pair collect: [:ele | ele squared]
```

2.4) String»numberOfVowels is simply the size of the string obtained by sending the getVowels message to the receiver. This gives:

```
numberOfVowels
    ^ self getVowels size
```

2.5) Here is a possible implementation of the method counting the number of occurrences of a character within a string, String»numberOfOccurrences:

```
numberOfOccurrences: aCharacter
    | c |
    ^ self do:
        [:x | x == aCharacter ifTrue: c := c + 1].
    ^c
```

Another implementation is the following:

```
numberOfOccurrences: aCharacter
    ^ self inject: 0
            into: [:c :ele |
                ele == aCharacter
                    ifTrue: [c + 1]
                    ifFalse: [c]]
```

or even:

```
numberOfOccurrences: aCharacter
    ^ (self select: [:ele | ele == aCharacter]) size
```

2.6) In order to create a table containing n repetitions of the elements from the receiver table, we will begin by creating a new table of size $n * $ self $size$. Then, we will need to transfer each of the elements n times to the right indices. For this transfer, we can use the replaceFrom:to:with: method which replaces elements which are found between the indices passed as arguments to replaceFrom: and to: with the elements in the collection passed as an argument to with:. Here is a possible implementation of the times: method of ArrayedCollection:

```
times: n
  | newCollection counter cte |
  cte := self size.
  counter := 0.
  newCollection := self class new: cte * n.
  n timesRepeat:
    [newCollection
        replaceFrom: 1 + (cte * counter)
        to: cte + (cte * counter)
        with: self.
      counter := counter + 1].
  ^newCollection
```

We can write this same method while taking advantage of the conversions between different types of collections: since we know that an OrderedCollection has dynamic sizing, we can successively copy all of the elements into an ordered collection which we will then reconvert within the class of the receiver. This will save us from computing the indices and copying each of the elements individually. The following alternative implementation of the ArrayedCollection»times: method follows these steps exactly:

```
times: n
  | newCollection |
  newCollection := OrderedCollection new.
  n timesRepeat:
    [newCollection addAll: self].
  ^newCollection as: self class
```

We use the addAll: method, present in all dynamically sized collections, which adds all the elements from the collection passed as an argument, to the receiver. The conversion method as: transforms the receiver collection into a collection of the class passed as an argument – of course while keeping the same elements.

2.7) An initial way to solve this problem would be to use a do: as below:

```
Array>>sum
  | s |
  s := 0.
  self do:
        [:ele | s := s + ele.
                Transcript cr;
                          show: 'the sum is ';
                          show: s].
  ^s
```

If we evaluate the transmission: #(1 2 3 4) sum, the method returns the integer 10, the sum of its four numbers, and displays it in the Transcript:

```
the sum is: 1
the sum is: 3
the sum is: 6
the sum is: 10
```

We can also write this method by using the inject:into: such as:

```
Array>>sum
    ^self inject: 0
          into: [:s :ele |
                  Transcript cr;
                             show: 'the sum is ';
                             show: s.
                  s + ele]
```

which will then display:

```
the sum is: 0
the sum is: 1
the sum is: 3
the sum is: 6
```

Instead of also having the final result, 10, this time we have the initial state of the temporary variable s.

Finally, SQUEAK also provides us with the do:separatedBy: method which executes the do: block for each of the elements of the receiver and separates the successive executions of the do: block by evaluating the separatedBy: block, which, for the same exercise, gives us:

```
Array>>sum
    [s|
    s := 0.
    self do: [:ele | s := s + ele]
         separatedBy:
              [Transcript cr;
                         show: 'the sum is ';
                         show: s].
    ^s
```

which, effectively, only displays the intermediary sums:

```
the sum is: 1
the sum is: 3
the sum is: 6
```

2.8) An intersection between two sets is the set containing the elements common to both of these sets. In order to find these common sets, we just need to traverse one of these collections and see for each of the elements if it is also present in the other set. If this is the case, then it is a part of the intersection. In SMALLTALK, the iteration can be done with the select: method and the inclusion test can be performed with the includes: method. This gives us the following method:

```
Collection>>intersection: aCollection
  ^ self select:
      [:ele | aColleection includes: ele]
```

The difference between the two sets is the set of elements which only belong to one of the two sets. In programming terms, we would need to construct a collection obtained by iterating through *both* sets while only keeping the elements which are not a part of the other set. This will give us the following method:

```
Collection>>difference: aCollection
  ^ (self reject:
          [:ele | aCollection includes: ele])
        , (aCollection
          reject: [:ele | self includes: ele]
```

The union of two sets is the set of elements included in both sets. In order to compute the union of the two sets #(1 2 3 4) and #(1 2 6 4), we can start by adding one set to the other, for example with the transmission:

```
#(1 2 3 4)} , #(1 2 6 4)
```

However, this returns the collection #(1 2 3 4 1 2 6 4), a collection with too many elements. We only want a single occurrence of each element. This comes down to transforming this instance into an instance of the Set class which will remove all duplicates. Thus, the transmission:

```
#(1 2 3 4)} , #(1 2 6 4)) asSet
```

returns the set a Set(1 2 3 4 6), a set with a single occurrence of each element. To be sure of always having a sorted set, we can convert this Set into a SortedCollection to then reconvert the obtained collection back into the type of the original receiver, in this case an Array. All of this will give us the following union method below:

```
Collection>>union: aCollection
  ^ (self , aCollection)
        asSet asSortedCollection as: self class
```

2.9) To solve this problem, we will simulate, step-by-step, what a SQUEAK programmer will do interactively when trying to understand a method.

The first transmission of the foo method

```
Transcript show: 'character';
          tab;
          show: 'frequency';
          cr.
```

does not pose any obvious problems. Its effect will be the displaying of two strings on a line of the Transcript, character and frequency, separated by a tabulation[13] character.

The second part starts with the transformation of the receiver, a string of characters, and thus an instance of the String class, into an instance of the Bag class. We recall that a Bag is an unsorted collection of elements which, unlike a Set, can contain multiple occurrences of the same element. If we evaluate the expression:

```
'small is beautiful' asBag
```

SQUEAK will respond with an instance of the Bag class: ($e $f $i $i $ $ $l $l $l $m $s $s $t $u $u $a $a $b), a collection consisting of the set of characters of the receiver string – even the space character is included twice. It is to this collection that the sortedElements message is transmitted.

If you take a MethodFinder and you search for all of the implementations of this method, you will only find one in the Bag class. Here, it is:

```
Bag>>sortedElements
    | elements |
    elements := SortedCollection new.
    contents associationsDo:
            [:assn | elements add: assn].
    ^elements
```

It starts by creating an instance of the *SortedCollection* class, elements, to which it adds *things*, with the transmission elements add: assn. However, what are these *things*? Since the addition of these elements is done within the argument block of associationsDo:, and since this selector contains the "*do*" word, we can hypothesize that the above-mentioned *things* are elements of the receiver, contents, to which we send the message associationsDo:.

Just to be sure, we will reopen our MethodFinder to look for the implementors of the associationsDo: method. There exists one in each of the following classes: Collection, Dictionary, MethodDictionary and UrlArgumentList.

---

13 The tabulation is a by-effect of the transmission of the tabulation message to the Transcript.

Let us look at the implementation in the two classes which we already know:

```
Collection>>associationsDo: aBlock
    "Evaluate aBlock for each of the receiver's
    elements (key/value associations).  If any
    non-association is within, the error is not
    caught now, but later, when a key or value
    message is sent to it."

    self do: aBlock

Dictionary>>associationsDo: aBlock
    "Evaluate aBlock for each of the receiver's
    elements (key/value associations)."

    super do: aBlock
```

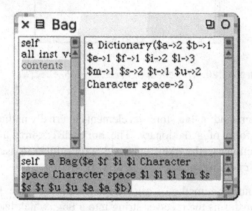

Figure A1.19. *Inspector on 'small is beautiful' asBag*

So, independent of the membership to the receiver, the message associationDo: is simply an ordinary do:: it iterates through a collection. We will note, however, that the two comments talk about <key, value> pairs, therefore, something which strongly resembles a Dictionary. The receiver of the do: message, contents, must, therefore, be an instance of the Dictionary class.

However, where does this content come from? Since it is in a receiver position, and since we have not defined something of this name anywhere, we are led to think that contents must be the name of a variable which the receiver of the sortedElements message must have access to. We will verify this by opening an inspector on the value of the 'small is beautiful' asBag transmission. This will open the inspector shown in Figure A1.19. In its Workspace window, we have executed a `printIt` on `self`, so the inspected object. This is our `Bag` from earlier and – in effect – this `Bag` has an instance variable named `contents`, which contains a dictionary in which the keys are characters and the values are the number of occurrences they have in the `Bag`.

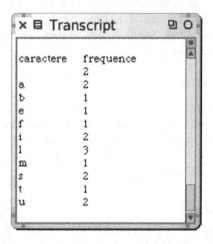

Figure A1.20. *The effect of* `'small is beautiful'` *foo*

Finally, we understand: a Bag stores its elements internally in the instance variable `contents` in the form of a dictionary. The `sortedElements` message sorts the elements of the dictionary (the <key, value>[14] associations) in ascending order and stores them in a `SortedCollection`.

Returning to our `foo` method: after having displayed the line "character frequency", it transforms the receiver string into a Bag, which itself is transformed into a sorted collection and it is this instance of `SortedCollection` which is iterated by the `do:` in order to display, pair-by-pair, separated by three tabs, the keys and their values. The `String»foo` method then prints a statistic on the use of letters in a text. Figure A1.20 shows the `Transcript` after the evaluation of:

```
'small is beautiful' foo
```

Figure A1.21 shows an extract of such statistics, on the distribution of letters for the LATEX file corresponding to this very appendix[15]

---

14 In essence, the elements of a dictionary are instances of the `Association` class which includes `key` and `value` messages for accessing the two parts of an association.

15 These statistics correspond to the file in the French version, from March 2006. The numbers of the occurrences of the different characters in the final version which you are holding in your

We can see as is always the case in texts written in French, that apart from the "space" character which has 873,245 occurrences[16], the letter "e" is the most used.

These statistics were easily obtained by evaluating the expression:

```
(FileStream fileNamed: 'annex1.tex')
                 contentsOfEntireFile foo
```

2.10) Solution to exercises on DNA chains:

i) We recall that a DNA molecule is made up of two chains of nucleotides. In the simplified test, we did not preoccupy ourselves with the actual chains themselves, we just looked at the set of nucleotides which form them to check for equality between the sums of the numbers of nucleotides of a certain type. In short, checking that the equation[17]

$$|\mathcal{A}| + |\mathcal{C}| = |\mathcal{G}| + |\mathcal{T}|$$

is true.

We can, therefore, start by creating a long string resulting from the concatenation of the two nucleotide strings which make up the DNA. Then, we can use, as in the previous exercise, the features of Bags and how they preserve their structure in a dictionary where the element is the key and the number of occurrences of this element is the value. This will give us a starting point:

```
simplifiedDNATest: aDNA
    ...
    (self , aDNA) asBag
    ...
```

Within this Bag, we will need to search for the number of occurrences of the different nucleotides in order to do the two additions which must give the same result for it to be a valid DNA chain. A brief look at the Bag class shows us the instance method occurrencesOf: which returns the number of occurrences of its argument.

---

hands will be different.

16 Not visible in Figure A1.21 which only shows lowercase letters.

17 The "$|\mathcal{X}|$" notation indicates the size of the $\mathcal{X}$ set. Moreover, the falsification of this equality indicates that the two chains are not a double chain of DNA. Its verification only shows that it is possible to construct a double chain of DNA from the set of nucleotides which are present, but this does not let us check that the set of nucleotides *is* a double chain of DNA.

This lets us write the following method which performs the simplified test:

```
String>>simplifiedDNATest: aDNA
    | aux |
    aux := (self , aDNA) asBag.
    ^((aux occurrencesOf: $A)
            + (aux occurrencesOf: $C))
        = ((aux occurrencesOf: $G)
            + (aux occurrencesOf: $T))
```

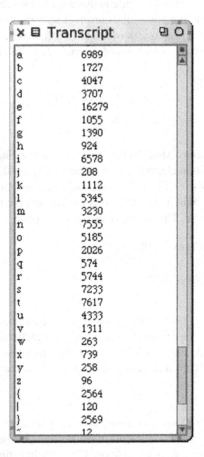

Figure A1.21. *Distribution of lowercase letters in this chapter (from the start, page 341, up to this page)*

ii) Here are the rest of the solutions to the exercises involving genetic engineering. For the time being, we will simplify the PCR process so as to not take into account *primers*, the direction of the reconstruction of chains or the explicit representation of the polymerases and we assume that the solution contains an infinite reserve of nucleotides:

a) In keeping with our representation of a chain of nucleotides as a string of characters, we will then construct a new string with the nucleotides that are complements of the first one.

In exercise 4, page 105, we have already defined the four classes of nucleotides, each one being a subclass of Nucleotide, and a Nucleotide»complement method which returns the nucleotide which is complementary to the receiver. Knowing that we have also defined a newInstance, in the String class, which generates a nucleotide corresponding to a specific letter in the chain (with the letter A generating an instance of the A_nucleotide class, etc.), then if we use these methods, all that we need to do is to create a new chain of the same length as the receiver where each letter is replaced by the letter corresponding to the complementary nucleotide.

If we add the Nucleotide»asCharacter method such as:

```
Nucleotide>>asCharacter
 ^ self class asString at: 1
```

which returns the first character in the chain representing the name of a nucleotide, A_nucleotide, T_nucleotide, etc., the creation of a chain of complementary nucleotides can simply be written as:

```
String>>doPolymerase
 ^ self collect: [:i |
       i newInstance complement asCharacter]
```

b) In order to perform PCR on a double chain, we need to create a polymerase on the component chains.

We will begin by creating a DNA class which is capable of storing the two chains of nucleotides:

```
Object subclass: #DNA
    instanceVariableNames: 'alpha1 alpha2'
    classVariableNames: ''
    poolDictionaries: ''
    category: 'Nucleotides'
```

where the instance variables alpha1 and alpha2 will contain the two nucleotide chains. In order to grant access to these variables, we will also create, as always, access and modification methods for these two variables. Below are the methods for the alpha1 variable. Those for alpha2 are symmetrical.

```
DNA>>alpha1
  ^ alpha1


DNA>>alpha1: aString
  alpha1 := aString
```

Since we already have the method which provides us with the complementary chain given a chain of nucleotides, then we only need to *separate* the double chain into its two component chains to then combine each chain with its complementary chain. This will create two new DNA molecules which are identical to the initial molecule.

Below is the implementation of this method which returns an instance of the Set class, with the two new molecules as elements.

```
DNA>>doPolymerase
  ^ (Set with: alpha1 with: alpha2)
        collect: [:c |
          DNA new
            alpha1: c;
            alpha2: c doPolymerase;
            yourself]
```

c) Now, all we need to do is to write the rest of the necessary methods for iterating this reproductive process of amplification. A first approach would be to create a polymerase on the first DNA molecule and then repeat this again $n - 1$ times, if we want to reach n iterations of the PCR operation:

```
DNA>>doPCR: n
  ^ n < 1
      ifTrue: [self]
      ifFalse: [self doPolymerase
                 doPCR: n - 1]
```

Be careful, this method works very well as long as it only needs to create two copies of a DNA molecule. If we want to create more, we transmit the doPCR: message to the result of the polymerase of self. The result is a Set of DNA molecules, and for the time being a Set does not know how to respond to the doPCR: message.

Thus, here is the missing method:

```
Set>>doPCR: n
  | newSet |
  newSet := Set new.
  ^ n < 1
     ifTrue: [self]
     ifFalse: [self
          do: [:e |
               (e doPolymerase)
                  do: [:c| newSet add: c]].
       newSet doPCR: n - 1]
```

It takes the set of DNA molecules obtained in the previous iteration in order to apply a PCR cycle and collect (with the add: message) each of the obtained DNA molecules into a set representing the test tube. Then, it will execute $n - 1$ more PCR cycles on this new set.

If we also want to proceed with a PCR iteration by starting with a unique string of nucleotides, then we just need to add a doPCR: to the String class, as seen below:

```
String>>doPCR: n
  ^ (DNA new alpha1: self;
       alpha2: self doPolymerase;
       yourself) doPCR: n - 1
```

A1.7. Exercises for section 5.3

1) In order to draw a spiral without changing the length, we need to change the angle. If the two are constants, then the resulting drawing will never be a spiral.

Let us revisit the core of our program which draws an "equiangular" spiral:

```
200 timesRepeat:
     [pen go: (dist := dist * 1.03);
      turn: 13]
```

We can rewrite this by removing the management of the temporary variable dist, as such:

```
1 to: 200 do: [:i |
     [pen go: i * 0.05);
      turn: 13]
```

which will draw the very elegant spiral shown in Figure A1.22.

Figure A1.22. *An elegant spiral with a constant angle of 13 degrees*

If we replace this iteration with the one that keeps the length constant but which modifies the angle, as below:

```
1 to: 200
    do: [:i | pen go: 5.5;
              turn: i * 0.25].
```

then, we will obtain the following program as a possible solution:

```
| form pen |
form := Form extent: 150 @ 150 depth: Display depth.
form fillColor: Color white.
pen := Pen newOnForm: form.
pen roundNib: 1;
    color: Color red.
pen place: 10 @ 90; home.
1
    to: 200
    do: [:i | pen go: 5.5;
              turn: i * 0.25].
form asMorph openInWorld
```

The image on the left in Figure A1.23 is the result of the execution of this program. The image on the right in Figure A1.23 is the result of the execution of this program with the constant changed from 0.25 to -0.25, therefore instead of turning to the right, the turtle will turn left instead. Of course, the two obtained spirals are symmetrical.

It is up to you to play around with this program: modify the constants and look at the results. The result is not always obvious.

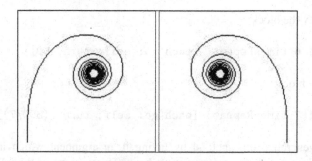

Figure A1.23. *A right and left spiral of constant length*

2) In order to write a program which draws a colored hexagon, we can take inspiration from our program which draws a colored star. The only difference is the angle at which the turtle must turn after drawing each segment. In the drawing our star has five branches, we used an angle of 144 degrees, which lets the turtle create a closed shape after having turned by a total angle of $2 \times 360 = 720$ degrees.

In this case, it is more simple, as we do not want a star, just a regular polygon with six edges. A path of its perimeter will give us a complete 360 degree circuit. The angle between two successive edges will, therefore, be $\frac{360}{6} = 60$ degrees.

Here is a small method Number»hexagon which solves the problem:

```
hexagon
    | form pen |
    form := Form extent: self * 3 @ (self * 3)
                 depth: Display depth.
    form fillColor: Color white.
    pen := Pen newOnForm: form.
    pen roundNib: 1;
        color: Color black.
    pen place: self  / 2 @ (self * 2);
        fill: [:each |
               6 timesRepeat: [each go: self; turn: 60]]
        color: Color yellow.
    form asMorph openInWorld
```

The receiver of this method specifies the length of one edge of the hexagon. We have also used this length to adapt the size of the canvas, which the turtle draws on, to the size of the hexagon.

This method can also be used as a model for creating other methods for drawing specific regular polygons. Thus, in order to draw a polygon with seven sides, we just need to modify the block:

```
[:each | 6 timesRepeat: [each go: self; turn: 60]]
```

to be this new block:

```
[:each | 7 timesRepeat: [each go: self; turn: (360/7)]]
```

We can generalize this method by giving it an argument which indicates the number of edges which the polygon must have. This is done in the closedPoly: method below:

```
Number>>closedPoly: nbC
  | form pen |
  form := Form extent: self * (nbC/2) @ (self * (nbC/2))
                depth: Display depth.
  form fillColor: Color white.
  pen := Pen newOnForm: form.
  pen roundNib: 1
      color: Color black.
  pen place: self  / (nbC/3) @ (self * (nbC/3)).

  pen fill: [:each | nbC timesRepeat:
                     [each go: self; turn: 360 / nbC]]
        color: Color yellow.
  form asMorph openInWorld
```

We can also reverse the situation by drawing a regular closed polygon so that instead of determining the number of edges, we specify the constant angle formed between two edges. The problem here will be that some angles are not dividers of 360, and after completing the circuit the figure will not be closed.

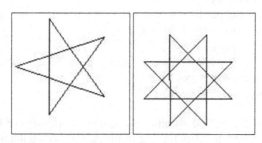

Figure A1.24. *Two drawings obtained with* polygon:, *angles: 144 and 135*

We can solve this problem by storing the total of the angle traveled at each instant and stopping only if this total is a multiple of 360. For an angle of 60 degrees, this condition will be met after one round, however, for an angle of 144 degrees (our famous five branch star), the condition will only be met after two rounds, at an angle of 720 degrees.

Below is a method which draws regular polygons with an angle given through its receiver:

```
Number>>polygon: long
    | form pen total|
    total := 0.
    form := Form extent: long * (360/self) / 2
                        @ (long * (360/self) / 2)
                  depth: Display depth.
    form fillColor: Color white.
    pen := Pen newOnForm: form.

    pen roundNib: 1;
        color: Color black.
    pen place: long  / ((360/self) )
                @ (long * ((360/self) / 2 ) - 10).
    [pen go: long; t
        urn: self.
    ((total := total + self) \\ 360) = 0] whileFalse.
    form asMorph openInWorld
```

Figures A1.24–A1.26 show four drawings with different angles obtained with the polygon: method.

3) Figure 5.9, page 214, and the accompanying text at the start of section 5.2 give us the recursive algorithm for the construction of the Koch curve. We just need to follow this. We will first recall this algorithm:

To draw a Koch curve, we must:

– *level 0:* draw a line of length l;

– *level 1:* split the line into three equal parts of length $\frac{l}{3}$. Remove the middle part, duplicate it and put both of these parts back in the middle, such that the middle forms an equilateral triangle which is open at the base, as seen in the first drawing of Figure 5.9;

– *level 2:* the drawing obtained in the previous level is made up of 4 lines. For each of these lines the operation from the previous level is repeated, in other words: split each line into 3 equal parts of length $\frac{l}{9}$, remove the middle parts and replace them with two copies of length $\frac{l}{9}$ such that each of the middle parts becomes equilateral triangles which are open at the base, as seen in the second drawing of Figure 5.9;

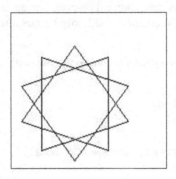

Figure A1.25. *Another drawing obtained with* `polygon:`*, angle: 108*

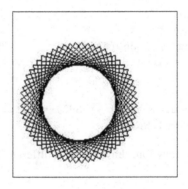

Figure A1.26. *Again another drawing obtained with*
`polygon:`*, angle: 102*

$-$ ...

$-$ *level n:* in the drawing obtained at level $n-1$, take each of the lines (of length $\frac{1}{3^{n-1}}$) which belong to it and to each one of them apply the operations from level 1. The fourth drawing in Figure 5.9 shows the curve obtained at level 5.

Knowing that an equilateral triangle only has *internal* angles of 60 degrees, we can confidently write the drawing method for a Koch curve. We will start with an initialization routine for the drawing environment, then the drawing method:

```
Number>>koch: long
    "4 koch: 280"
    | form pen |
    form := Form extent: long + 20 @ (long / 2)
                      depth: Display depth.
    form fillColor: Color white.
    pen := Pen newOnForm: form.
    pen roundNib: 1;
        color: Color black.
    pen place: 10 @ (long / 2 - 5);
        turn: 90.
    self koch: long pen: pen.
    form asMorph openInWorld


Number>>koch: long pen: pen
    self = 0
        ifTrue: [pen go: long]
        ifFalse: [self - 1 koch: long / 3 pen: pen.
            pen turn: -60.
            self - 1 koch: long / 3 pen: pen.
            pen turn: 120.
            self - 1 koch: long / 3 pen: pen.
            pen turn: -60.
            self - 1 koch: long / 3 pen: pen]
```

4) The tree2 program consists of four methods: the tree2 method which prepares the canvas, the turtle and begins the drawing of the tree with the tree2a method which has the task of drawing a left branch of the tree. Its first call results in the drawing of the tree's trunk. The symmetrical method, tree2b, draws a right branch of the tree. These two methods ask the node method to decide the rest of the drawing once the branch has been drawn.

Below, for recall purposes, are the three methods, starting with the branch drawing methods:

```
tree2a: length angle: angle pen: pen
    pen go: length * 2.
    self
        node: length
        angle: angle
        pen: pen.
    pen go: -2 * length
```

```
tree2b: length angle: angle pen: pen
   pen go: length.
   self
      node: length
      angle: angle
      pen: pen.
   pen go: 0 - length
```

then, the method which supervises the actions carried out at each branch:

```
node: length angle: angle pen: pen
   self = 0
      ifFalse: [pen turn: 0 - angle.
         self - 1
            tree2a: length
            angle: angle
            pen: pen.
         pen turn: 2 * angle.
         self - 1
            tree2b: length
            angle: angle
            pen: pen.
         pen turn: 0 - angle]
```

Given that neither the tree2a method, nor the tree2b method perform a turtle rotation, in order to have different right and left angles, we need to modify the node method, the only method which is responsible for turning the turtle at each new branch. At the start, it turns the turtle toward the left of the angle angle, then in the middle, after drawing the left branch, it turns the turtle toward the right of this same angle, and at the end it puts the turtle back in the position it was before drawing the two branches. So clearly, it is either at the start, or in the middle that the method needs to be modified.

Before even starting to change the node method, we will simplify the program by combining the tree2a and tree2b methods into a new method: drawBranch so as to let the node method compute the difference in length, which gives:

```
drawBranch: length angle: angle ind: ind pen: pen
   pen go: length.
   self
      node: (ind ifTrue: [length / 2]
                  ifFalse: [length])
      angle: angle
      pen: pen.
   pen go: 0 - length
```

and the node method becomes:

```
node: length angle: angle pen: pen
   self = 0
      ifFalse: [pen turn: 0 - angle.
         self - 1
            drawBranch: 2 * length
            angle: angle
            ind: true
            pen: pen.
         pen turn: 2 * angle.
         self - 1
            drawBranch: length
            angle: angle
            ind: false
            pen: pen.
         pen turn: 0 - angle]
```

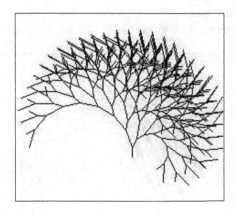

Figure A1.27. *A tree with a left angle of 20 and a right angle of 29*

Let us return to our task of giving two different values to the left and right angles. The most simple solution would be to introduce an additional argument in the node method. This argument will specify the right angle and the old angle argument, angle will specify the left angle. Here is the new method:

```
node: long angleL: angleL angleR: angleR pen: pen
   "8 tree2: 10 angleL: 20 angleR:   29"
   self = 0
      ifFalse: [pen turn: 0 - angleL.
         self - 1
            drawBranch: 2 * long
            angleL: angleL
            angleR: angleR

            ind: true
            pen: pen.
         pen turn: angleL;
            turn: angleR.
         self - 1
            drawBranch: long
            angleL: angleL
            angleR: angleR
            ind: false
            pen: pen.
         pen turn: 0 - angleR]
```

Figure A1.28. *A branch of a weeping willow,
left angle: 20 and right angle: –25*

Of course, we will also need to modify our method which draws a branch so that it accepts these additional arguments. Moreover, our main `tree2:angle:` method must become `tree2:angleL:angleR:` and the initial call of the

```
drawBranch:angle:ind:pen:
```

method must be changed into a call to our new method:

```
drawBranch:angleL:angleR:ind:pen:.
```

After having done all of this, we can test the behavior of these new methods. Figures A1.27 and A1.28, respectively, show the results of the following transmissions:

```
8 tree2:   10 angleL: 20 angleR: 29
7 tree2:   10 angleL: 20 angleR: -25
```

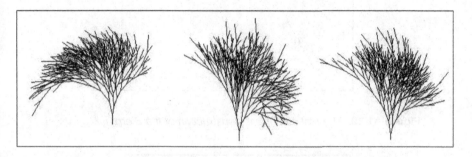

Figure A1.29. *Three trees with variable angles and branch lengths*

Finally, in order to make the trees seem a bit more natural, less regular, we can always introduce additional variations to our program, for example, by having the angles pick their values from a specified interval. Figure A1.29 shows a few trees which were obtained by making the angles and branch lengths variable.

5) The Sierpinski curve is constructed with a constant angle of 60 degrees. Its construction requires that we start with a line $\overline{AB}$, which we replace by three segments x_1, x_2 and x_3 which link the initial point A on the line with its final point B. The segment x_1 forms an angle of 60 degrees with the line, the segment x_2 forms an angle of 120 degrees (in turtle language, this is the same as taking an angle of –60 degrees) with x_1 and the line x_3 forms another angle of 60 degrees with the line x_2, as shown in Figure A1.30.

Naturally, seeing as all of our drawings are recursive, this curve is also constructed recursively. We will, therefore, take each of these segments x_1, x_2 and x_3, and replace each of them by three more segments having the same open trapezium shape as the one obtained in the first step shown in Figure A1.30. The "catch" is that we need to alternate between replacing the segments, once to the left and once to the right[18], which will give something like the curve shown in Figure A1.31, where we have

18 Or alternatively, once toward the interior, once toward the exterior.

circled the transformation of line x_1. We can see that the next three lines, resulting from the transformations of segment x_2 at the first level, are done in the opposite direction to the transformation applied to segment x_1 and the one applied to segment x_3.

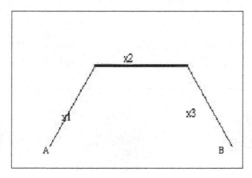

Figure A1.30. *The first step in the construction of the Sierpinski curve*

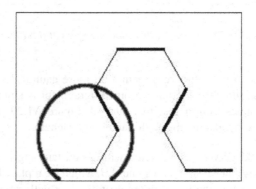

Figure A1.31. *The second step in the construction*
of the Sierpinski curve

Figure A1.32 shows the state of the curve after the third level of recursion: we can begin to see the shape of a triangle. This form becomes more evident after the fourth level shown in Figure A1.33.

Before we look at the implementation of a SMALLTALK program for drawing the just mentioned curve, try to write it yourselves. You will surely come up with an original solution.

Now, equipped with our analysis, we can begin to create this program. We will break it down into three methods: a first method called `sierpinskiLine:` which will be responsible for the initialization of the turtle and the canvas and which will call the two remaining methods. The second method will be responsible for sierpLeft:pen: drawing the trapezoids toward the left and the third method, which will be symmetrical to the latter, sierpRight:pen: will be responsible for drawing the trapezoids toward the right. They will alternate between calling each other.

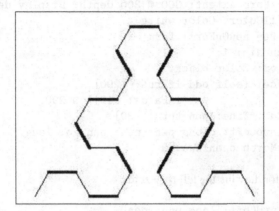

Figure A1.32. *The third stage of the Sierpinski curve*

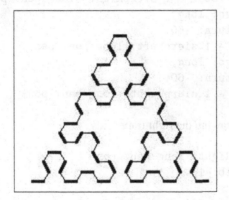

Figure A1.33. *The fourth stage of the Sierpinski curve*

Within these methods, we will dynamically change the thickness of the pen's tip in order to see which method draws which line. This is the reason for the thicker width on some of the lines in the curves in Figures A1.30–A1.33.

Thus, here is the initial startup routine:

```
Number>>sierpinskiLine: long
  "4 sierpinskiLine: 12"
  | form pen |
  form := Form extent: 300 @ 300 depth: Display depth.
  form fillColor: Color white.
  pen := Pen newOnForm: form.
  pen roundNib: 1;
      color: Color black.
  pen place: (self odd ifTrue: [290]
                       ifFalse: [10]) @ 290.
  self odd ifTrue:[pen turn: -30].
  self sierpLeft: long pen: pen. pen go: long.
  form asMorph openInWorld
```

The method for drawing the left trapezoids:

```
Number>>sierpLeft: long pen: pen
  pen roundNib: 3.
  self > 0
     ifTrue: [self - 1 sierpRight: long pen: pen.
        pen go: long;
           turn: -60.
        self - 1 sierpLeft: long pen: pen.
        pen go: long;
           turn: -60.
        self - 1 sierpRight: long pen: pen]
```

and the method for drawing the right trapezoids:

```
Number>>sierpRight: long pen: pen
  pen roundNib: 1.
  self > 0
     ifTrue: [self - 1 sierpLeft: long pen: pen.
        pen go: long;
           turn: 60.
        self - 1 sierpRight: long pen: pen.
        pen go: long;
           turn: 60.
        self - 1 sierpLeft: long pen: pen]
```

When you ran this program, did you notice that our algorithm begins to draw a horizontal line and then the drawing progresses from the bottom left corner of the canvas toward the top left corner if the initial level is an even number, but that it starts with a line moving progressing upward from right to left if the initial level is an odd number? This is one of the reasons why, in the sierpinskiLineprogram, we initially placed the turtle in a different position depending on the parity of the receiver, the initial level.

If we want the drawing to always keep the same orientation (as shown in Figures A1.30–A1.33), with the start and end of the curve on the same horizontal level at the bottom of the figure, we can modify the initial positioning *and* the initial subprocedure which is called. This gives:

```
Number>>sierpinskiLine: long
   "4 sierpinskiLine: 12"
   | form pen |
   form := Form extent: 300 @ 300 depth: Display depth.
   form fillColor: Color white.
   pen := Pen newOnForm: form.
   pen roundNib: 1;
       color: Color black.
   pen place: (self odd ifTrue: [290]
                         ifFalse:[10]) @ 290.
   self odd
      ifTrue: [pen turn: -30.
         self sierpLeft: long pen: pen]
      ifFalse: [pen turn: 90.
         self sierpRight: long pen: pen].
      pen go: long.
   form asMorph openInWorld
```

where the names of the methods containing the words *left* or *right* are now completely unjustified: sierpLeft will make the drawing progress from right to left and sierpRight will make it progress from left to right. If the readers are bothered by this, they can always switch the names[19].

Finally, our two methods sierpLeft and sierpRight are very, very similar. The only difference is that in one of the methods the turtle turns to the left at an angle of 60 degrees and in the other method the turtle turns to the right at this same angle. We can combine these two methods into the new sierpAuxiliary method, which will take an additional argument, angle:, which will let us alternate between the angles 60 and –60. Here is this method:

---

19 Computer scientists do not like to say *change the name*. In computer science, this is referred to as *making an α-conversion*. This sounds much more knowledgeable.

```
Number>>sierpAuxiliary: long angle: angle pen: pen
  pen
    roundNib: (angle > 0
         ifTrue: [1]
         ifFalse: [2]).
  self > 0
    ifTrue: [self - 1
         sierpAuxiliary: long
         angle: -1 * angle
         pen: pen.
       pen go: long;
         turn: 60 * angle.
       self - 1
         sierpAuxiliary: long
         angle: angle
         pen: pen.
       pen go: long;
         turn: 60 * angle.
       self - 1
         sierpAuxiliary: long
         angle: -1 * angle
         pen: pen]
```

Of course, in order to run this program, we will also need to change, in the
sierpinskiLine: method, the lines:

```
self odd
    ifTrue: [pen turn: -30.
       self sierpLeft: long pen: pen]
    ifFalse: [pen turn: 90.
       self sierpRight: long pen: pen].
```

to:

```
self odd
    ifTrue: [pen turn: -30]
    ifFalse: [pen turn: 90].
self
    sierpAuxiliary: long
    angle: (self odd
         ifTrue: [-1]
         ifFalse: [1])
    pen: pen.
```

A1.8. Exercises for section 5.6.6

1) The first exercise, which asks us to add the f command to be able to move the turtle by a certain length *without* leaving traces of the movement, will require three changes in our program:

– we will need to recognize this character as a key command, both in the graphical interpretation of the generated L-system string and in the calculation of the bounding box;

– we will need a method which will be responsible for graphically interpreting the f command. We will call this method move f, which is analogous with our move method which will be in charge of the graphical interpretation of the F command;

– finally, we will need another method for simulating this movement during the construction of the bounding box.

Let us never forget that any command can have two interpretations: one for creating the drawing associated with an L-system and one for simulating the graphical effect of this command if it intervenes in the calculation of the size of the drawing.

The first point implies that we will need to modify our automate: method in order for it to recognize this new command and call the move f method:

```
1 Lsystem>>automate: aString
2    aString
3       do: [:ele | ('Ff+-[]' indexOf: ele)
4          > 0
5             ifTrue: [self
6                perform: (#(#move #movef #plus
7                            #minus  #push #pop)
8                      at: ('Ff+-[]' indexOf: ele))]]
```

Do not forget to insert the f command both in line 3, where we look to see if the the current character has an interpretation, and in line 8, where we determine the method corresponding to this command which was recognized in line 3.

To speed up the computation and render the method more readable, we will store the index found in line 3 in a temporary variable which we will then use in line 8. This will avoid us repeating the same calculation. This will give us the version below:

```
Lsystem>>automate: aString
   | x |
   aString
      do: [:ele | (x := ('Ff+-[]' indexOf: ele))
            > 0
```

```
        ifTrue: [self
            perform: (#(#move #movef #plus
                        #minus  #push #pop)
                      at: x)]]
```

We will now write the movef method. It is simple: we only need to wrap the go:
command in the move method with a disabling and a re-enabling of the turtle's pen:

```
Lsystem>>movef
    pen up; go: length; down
```

We will then perform the analogous operations in the boxMin: method which are
responsible for computing the bounding box of the drawing:

```
Lsystem>>boxMin: aString
    | x |
    sdir := sh := sv := 0.
    box := Rectangle origin: 0@0 corner: 0@0.
    aString
        do: [:ele | (x := ('Ff+-[]' indexOf: ele))
                    > 0
                ifTrue: [self
                        perform: (#(#moveS #moveS #plusS
                                    #minusS #pushS #popS)
                                  at: x)]]
```

It is not an error if this method calls the same method moveS for the simulation
of the F command and the f command. The *size* of the drawing only depends on the
movement, whether the turtle traces the movement or not does not matter. It is for this
reason that we will use the same method in both cases.

All that remains for us is to test our program with, for example, the L-system given
in Figure 5.35, page 267.

2) Our second exercise is slightly more difficult: we must write a command which
has a numerical argument in order to extract the string representing the curve of the
L-system so as to send it to the method processing this command.

However, after the previous exercise, we know that a color change does not
intervene on the same level as the calculation of the bounding box: there is no need
to change the boxMin method which computes this rectangle.

Therefore, as above, we will start by changing the automate: method so that our
interpreter recognizes this new C command. We cannot treat it like the other
commands since it requires an argument. We will, therefore, separate the recognition

of letter-commands, and operators, into two distinct parts: one which recognizes commands without arguments, and one which recognizes commands with arguments. The recognition of the former will activate the method which interprets them using the perform: method as we have done with all of the commands which we have encountered up until now, whereas the recognition of operators with arguments will activate interpreter methods with the perform:with: method (see section 5.6.1, page 244), where the with: argument will be the next numerical value, in the string of characters, following the letter-operator.

For the extraction of the numerical argument from the string of characters describing the curve of the L-system, we will use asNumber[20] which, like the asInteger[21] extracts in the form of a number the first set of characters, which correspond to a representation of a number, from the receiver string. The difference is that asInteger returns an integer, whereas asNumber can also return a float. Therefore, here is our modified automate: method:

```
Lsystem>>automate: aString
   | x c |
   c := 1
   aString
       do: [:ele | c := C + 1.
            (x := ('Ff+-[]' indexOf: ele))
              > 0
            ifTrue: [self
                perform: (#(#move #movef #plus
                            #minus  #push #pop)
                    at: x)]

            ifFalse: [(x := ('C' indexOf: ele))
                > 0
              ifTrue: [self
                   perform: (#(#color:)
                       at: x)
                   with: (aString copyFrom: c
                              to: aString size)
                   asNumber]]]
```

In this method, we introduced a second temporary variable, c. This variable counts how many characters in the curve's description string, the aString argument, we have already processed. Thus, when we encounter a character C, the variable c will contain

---

20 We have already encountered this method, the first time was in section 4.3.3, page 82. We have also used it in our Logo and L-system programs, each time the user needed to enter a *number*. Look at our uses of FillInTheBlank in these two programs.

21 The asInteger method is described in section 4.3.3, page 82.

the index of the next character to be analyzed. This lets us (this will be the argument of with:) create a copy of the string, from the cth character, which we will extract, due to the transmission of the asNumber message to this copy, of the number from where it starts.

Also note that we have chosen to write 'C' indexOf: ele), instead of doing a simple equality test. The reason for this is simply because we are predicting the addition of other commands as arguments, which can then be added as simply as the f command in the previous exercise.

To finish this exercise solution, we just need to write the color: method which must interpret, and therefore *do*, the color change. Here, it is below:

```
Lsystem>>color: aNumber
    pen color: aNumber
```

Figure A1.34 shows a Sierpinski triangle colored due to the three uses of the C command, as well as the definition of the corresponding L-system.

3) This exercise, which is similar to the previous one, should not pose any particular problems. We will need, as in the previous exercise, to recognize new commands, > and <, with arguments. This time also, the new operators only involve the display of colors, therefore, they do not intervene at the level of the calculation of the bounding box.

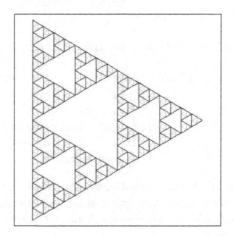

Figure A1.34. *A colored Sierpinski triangle, level: 6 angle: 60 axiom: X rules: X: ++ C6FXF ++ C8FXF ++ C10FXF F:FF. For color version of this figure, see www.iste.co.in/wertz/smalltalk.zip*

The problem lies instead with the change of colors. How do we do this?

We will first adopt the simplest solution (it is up to you to find more elegant solutions which respect the colors better): an integer represents the default color. Since this default color must be accessible in multiple places, we will create an additional instance variable, the coLor variable[22]. This will give us the new definition of the Lsystem class below:

```
LogoDrawings subclass: #Lsystem
    instanceVariableNames: 'level rulesDerivation
                            axiom angle length
                            box sh sv sdir coLor'
    classVariableNames: ''
    poolDictionaries: ''
    category: 'Lesson-Smalltalk'
```

We initialize this new instance variable to 1 which corresponds to an extremely dark blue, which is almost black[23]. We also initialize the color of the pen to the color corresponding to this integer. These initializations are carried out in the runLsystem method in order to guarantee that for each new creation of a curve we will find ourselves with the same coLor configuration. This will give us the modified version of the runLsystem: method:

```
Lsystem>>runLsystem
    | tmp tmp1 |
    self initImage.
    coLor := 1.
    tmp := self replace: axiom times: level.
    self boxMin: tmp.
    tmp1 := self normalize.
    pen place: tmp1 origin;
        coLor: (color asColorOfDepth: Display depth)
                asNontranslucentCoLor.
    length := tmp1 corner x.
    self automate: tmp.
    self afficheImage
```

The asColorOfDepth: message, which we send to the color method, is defined in the Integer class. It creates a new color based on the receiver, and considers this

---

22 We cannot name this variable color, since the Lsystem class already inherits an instance variable with the name coLor from the Morph class.

23 Normally, the value 0 corresponds to the color black. In SQUEAK, this color does not exist, since for SQUEAK when the lowest bit of a color is set to 0, this corresponds to a translucent color.

integer as the numerical value corresponding to a pixel on a canvas of a certain depth[24]. If we also send the `asNontranslucentColor` message to this new color, this new instance of the `Color` class, it is only to be absolutely sure that the color is genuinely very dark[25], it is not absolutely necessary.

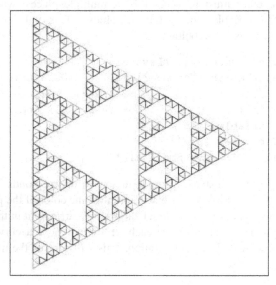

Figure A1.35. *A Sierpinski triangle colored differently, level: 6 axiom: X rules: X: ++ FXF++FXF++FXF>1 F:FF. For color version of this figure, see www.iste.co.in/wertz/smalltalk.zip*

As in the previous exercise, we must also modify the `automate:` method so that it recognizes the two new commands < and >:

```
Lsystem>>automate: aString
  | x c |
  c := 1
  aString
    do: [:ele | c := c + 1.
      (x := ('Ff+-[]' indexOf: ele))
        > 0
      ifTrue: [self
```

---

24 The depth of a canvas provides us with the number of available colors for this canvas. SQUEAK allows canvases of depths 1, 2, 8, 16 and 32 (expressed in the number of bits). This allows for pixels able to display 2, 4, 16, 256, 32,768 and 16 million colors.

25 For computer scientists who are well versed in graphics programming: this message imposes a maximum α value for this color.

```
           perform: (#(#move #movef #plus
                       #minus  #push #pop)
                     at: x)]
        iffalse: [(x := ('C<>' indexOf: ele))
                    > 0
                 ifTrue: [self
                    perform: (#(#color: #decrColor:
                                #incrColor:)
                              at: x)
                    with: (aString copyFrom: c
                                   to: aString size)
                          asNumber]]]
```

All that remains is for us to write the two methods decrColor: and incrColor::

```
Lsystem>>incrColor: aNumber
   pen color: (color := color + aNumber)
```

```
Lsystem>>decrColor: aNumber
   self incrColor: 0 - aNumber
```

Figure A1.35 gives us a version of the Sierpinski triangle which is colored in by this color changing method.

The use of the incrColor: method inside this decrColor: method is completely intentional: it allows us to only modify the incrColor: method if we want to change the way in which the pen color is changed.

Let us change this behavior right now. The Color class provides us with the following methods:

lightShades: which, when it is transmitted to a color with an integer n as argument, will return a table of n colors, from *white* up to the receiver color.

darkShades: is similar to the lightShades: method, but instead it returns a table of n colors from *black* up to the receiver color.

wheel: which, when it is sent a color with an argument n, will return a table of n colors, chosen from the wheel containing all of the colors. The colorwheel starts with the color of the receiver of the message and ends with the color just before the receiver's.

These three methods, therefore, provide a table of n colors, spaced out in a regular manner, which we can then access with the access method at: of the Object class, the atPin: method of the SequenceableCollection class and the atWrap: method of the Array class.

The difference between these methods resides in their behavior when the argument n, which is considered as an index for the table, is outside the boundaries of the table:

at: throws an error: exception (see section 4.7.1, page 176) if the n argument is not a valid index of the table.

atPin: will return the first element of the receiver table if the argument n is less than 1 and will return the last element of the table if the argument n is superior to its upper bound. For values lying within the interval $[1, size\ of\ table]$, atPin: behaves the same as the at: method.

atWrap: considers the table as a circular structure (a colorwheel): values smaller than n go in the anticlockwise direction of the wheel, whereas values larger than n go in the clockwise direction of the wheel.

Now with the ability to create a palette of colors accessible through one of these three methods, we can modify our processing of colors as such:

1) First, we will introduce an additional instance variable, we will call it colorMap, and initialize it as a palette of colors. This introduces the following line to our Lsystem» initialize method:

```
colorMap := Color blue wheel:  256
```

which creates a palette of 256 colors and stores it in the colorMap instance variable.

2) We will modify our incrColor method so that it chooses, after having updated the color instance variable, a color in our color palette colorMap. This gives us the following new method:

```
Lsystem>>incrColor: aNumber
    pen color:
    (colorMap atWrap:
        (color := color + aNumber))
```

And this is it. We have finished the modification to the color processing.

Nonetheless, we will add, so that the users can change palettes (or at least the number of colors), an additional entry to our menu, by inserting the following line in an appropriate location within the Lsystem»mouseDown: method:

```
    add:  'how many colors?'  action:  #setColor;
```

and we will add the following setColor: method:

```
Lsystem>>setColor
    colorMap :=
    Color red wheel:
            (FillInTheBlank request: 'level?'
                        initialAnswer: 256 asString)
        asNumber.
```

Figure A1.36. *An L-system using 256 colors*
level: 14 angle: 7.826 axiom: X rule: X: X>1F+@0.9997X. For color
version of this figure, see www.iste.co.in/wertz/smalltalk.zip

Figure A1.36 shows the L-system which we have already seen on page 269, however, this time it uses our new way of managing colors. In this case, we are using a palette of 256 colors. Figure A1.37 shows this same L-system using only two colors. It is up to you to see the differences and also explore the variations which are obtained by simply changing the number of colors.

3) In this exercise, we will look at an L-system operator which can change the length of the turtle's step. This is an operator for which the effect can be seen, naturally, in the graphical representation of the L-system which uses it *and* which has an influence on the size of the image. As opposed to our operators acting on the color, this one requires changing the automate: and boxMin: methods.

We will begin with a method which changes the size of the turtle's step, which will, therefore, change the value of the instance variable length:

```
Lsystem>>changeLineLength: aNumber
    length := aNumber * length
```

Figure A1.37. *The same L-system using only two colors*
level: 14 angle: 7.826 axiom: X rule: X: X>1F+@0.9997X. For color
version of this figure, see www.iste.co.in/wertz/smalltalk.zip

This method will need to be called by boxMin: each time a @ character is encountered in the string resulting from the edits in the derivation rules.

We will, therefore, adapt the boxMin: method to this new constraint. The necessary changes will be analoguous to the modifications which we have made to the automate: method in the exercise below: we will add a specific clause for the methods requiring an argument. Here is the new version of boxMin::

```
Lsystem>>boxMin: aString
    | c x |
    c := 1.
    sdir := sh := sv := 0.
    length := 1.
    box := Rectangl origin: 0 @ 0 corner: 0 @ 0.
    aString
        do: [:ele |
            c := c + 1.
```

```
((x:= 'Ff+-[]||!' indexOf: ele))
    > 0
ifTrue: [self
    perform: (#(#moveS #moveS #plusS
                #minus #pushS #popS)
        at: x)]
ifFalse: [(x := ('@' indexOf: ele))
    > 0
    ifTrue: [self
        perform: (#(#lineLenS:)
        at: x )
        with: (aString
            copyFrom: c
            to: aString size)
            asNumber]]]
```

In the automate: method, we must also insert the recognition of this new operator, which will change the lines:

```
ifFalse: [(x := ('C<>' indexOf: ele))
    > 0
ifTrue: [self
        perform: (#(#color: #decrColor:
                #incrColor:)
        at: x)
    with: (aString copyFrom: c
                to: aString size)
        asNumber]]]
```

into the lines

```
ifFalse: [(x := ('C<>@' indexOf: ele))
    > 0
ifTrue: [self
            perform: (#(#color: #decrColor:
                    #incrColor:
                    #changeLineLength:)
            at: x)
    with: (aString copyFrom: c
                to: aString size)]]]
```

At this point, the exercise is almost finished and the interpreter should function correctly with this new @ operator in most cases – however, not in all of them. Why? What are these cases in which this program will not work correctly?

Before continuing onto the rest of the proposed solution, stop and take a moment to think of the answer yourselves.

Answer: up until now, during each interpretation of an L-system, the step, length, was a constant. Now, with the @ operator, it is no longer a constant, but a variable value. As such, given the direction of the turtle, its coordinates and its "drawing" state, the length will be one of the values which will need to be stored each time a [operator is encountered, and then restored to the saved value when the] operator is encountered. We will, therefore, need to update the push and pop methods. Here are the new versions of these two methods:

```
Lsystem>>push
    stack addFirst: pen penDown;
        addFirst: pen direction;
        addFirst: pen location;
        addFirst: length

Lsystem>>pop
    longueur := stack removeFirst.
    pen
        location: stack removeFirst
        direction: stack removeFirst
        penDown: stack removeFirst
```

Now we can use @ operator without any fears.

We will recall the commands which our Lindenmayer system can recognize:

F   move forward by one step while tracing a line
f   move forward by one step without tracing a line
+   increase the angle of angle
-   reduce the angle of angle
Cn   change the color of the line to the color n
> n change the color of the line to the color color + n
< n change the color of the line to the color color - n
@n change the length of the step to length * n
[save the state of the turtle
]   restore the state of the turtle

Since we have operators which change the colors, another which change the length, we will add, for symmetry, two other operators which change the angle. Below, we will provide the necessary modifications so as to have access to the / operator as well as \. The two operators will be followed by a numerical argument which indicates the angle by which it will need to turn to the right (\) or to the left (/). Below, we give the required changes to the `automate:` method; the readers could make analogous changes to the `boxMin:` method.

We will start by recognizing these two operators in the `automate:` method. For this, we will need to once again change the following lines:

```
ifFalse: [(x := ('C<>@' indexOf: ele))
            > 0
      ifTrue: [self
               perform: (#(#color: #decrColor:

                           #incrColor:
                           #changeLineLength:)
                         at: x)
               with: (aString copyFrom: c
                              to: aString size)]]]
```

into the following lines:

```
ifFalse: [(x := ('C<>@\/' indexOf: ele))
            > 0
      ifTrue: [self
               perform: (#(#color: #decrColor:
                           #incrColor:
                           #changeLineLength:
                           #increase
                           #decrease)
                         at: x)
               with: (aString copyFrom: c
                              to: aString size)]]]
```

the increase and decrease methods must only turn the turtle by the angle specified in the argument:

```
Lsystem>>increase: aNumber
    pen turn: aNumber

Lsystem>>decrease: aNumber
    pen turn: 0 - aNumber
```

The methods corresponding to the calculation of the bounding box (the `boxMin:` method is tasked with this calculation) will be the methods `increaseS:` and `decreaseS:` below:

```
Lsystem>>increaseS: aNumber
        sdir := sdir + aNumber
```

```
Lsystem>>decreaseS: aNumber
    sdir := (sdir - aNumber)
```

Figure A1.38. *Two curves requiring the / and/or \ operators*

Now, we can make complex L-systems such as the ones shown in Figure A1.38, the left one of which, a double Cesaro curve, is simply defined as[26]:

```
10
90
F+F+F+F+
F:\42!F!/84!F!\42
```

and the right one as[27]:

```
3
12
\84.1A\96@4.783386117f@0.20905692/96A
A:X+X+X+X+X+X+X+X+X+X+X+X+X+X+X+Z
```

---

26 It is not this simple. We use the additional ! operator. This operator flips the direction of the +, −, \ and / operators in the interpretation of the string of characters representing the curve. It is up to you to implement this operator. We will not discuss it here. However the methods and changes necessary for their implementation are in the corresponding file on the author's Website.

27 The rules for rewriting are written here over several lines. This is done due to the lack of space on the page and does not equate to any changes in the rule-parsing algorithm.

```
X: [F\78F\46.37236@3.393427F@0.29468734/46.37236F\114[
   \168X\24Y]F\78F\46.37236@3.393427F@0.20905692
   /46.37236F/78F]
Y: [F\78F\46.37236@3.393427F@0.2905692/46.37236F/78F\168
   [\192Y]F\78F\46.37236@3.393427F@0.20905692/46.37236F]
Z: [F\78F\46.37236@3.393427F@0.20905692/46.37236F\114F
   \78F\46.37236@3.393427F@0.20905692/46.37236F/78F]
```

4) This exercise aims to help you explore the FileDirectory and FileStream. If you have not yet done so, now would be a good time. These two classes are the most important ones for the interface between the SQUEAK system and the file system of the computer on which SQUEAK is running. As the names imply, the first one implements the methods involving directories and files, the second one implements the methods involving the contents of individual files.

Here, we will mostly focus our attention on the FileDirectory class which offers class methods for navigating through directories, for example the root method, which returns the root of the file tree, our default method which returns the SQUEAK directory by default or even the splitName:to: method which takes two arguments, a directory name (for example, /usr/home/hw/.xemacs/init.el) and a block with two arguments. This block receives the directory of the file (in this case: /usr/home/hw/.xemacs/) as the first argument and the local name of the file (in this case: init.el) as the second argument.

The most important instance methods of the FileDirectory class are:

i) containingDirectory which returns the directory containing the directory receiving the message.

This message, the on: message and directoryContentsFor:, is sufficient for exploring the file system of your computer.

ii) copyFileNamed:toFileNamed: which copies the contents of the file given as the first argument into a file of which the name is given in the second argument. The two files are assumed to be in the directory receiving this message.

iii) createDirectory: which creates, in the directory receiving the message, a subdirectory with the name passed as the argument.

iv) deleteDirectory: which removes the subdirectory with the name given as argument to the directory receiving the message.

v) deleteFileNamed: which removes the file given as argument to the receiving directory.

vi) directoryContentsFor: returns the table (an instance of the Array class) of all the files in the directory given as argument. If the argument is the empty string, this method returns the table containing all of the files in the receiver directory – which we can obtain more simply by transmitting the `entries` message to the receiver directory.

vii) `directoryExists:` responds with `true` if the directory given as argument exists.

viii) `directoryNamed:` returns the subdirectory with the name given as an argument. This method lets us create directories.

ix) `directoryNames` returns a table containing the set of subdirectories of the receiver directory.

x `fileExists:` responds with `true` if the file given as argument exists. The argument can either be a complete path to a file, or simply be the name of a file in the receiver directory. There is also a `fileOrDirectoryExists:` method which checks if either an ordinary file, or a directory with the name given as the argument exists.

xi) `fileNamed:` opens the file given as argument for writing. This file must be in the receiver directory.

xii) `fileNames` returns a table containing all of the files (but not the subdirectories) of the receiving directory.

xiii) `forceNewFileNamed:` opens the file given as argument for writing. If this file already exists, its contents will be erased.

xiv) `keysDo:` which takes as argument a block and applies it to each of the files or subdirectories of the receiver directory.

xv) `newFileNamed:` creates the file with the name given as argument in the current directory.

– `on:` grants access to the directory given as argument. This is exactly the same method as the class method which is also called `on:`.

So as to not bloat this text, we will let the readers construct an equivalent list for the important methods in the `FileStream` class: for this, you will just need to open a file browser and examine the class and instance methods of `FileStream`.

Let us return to our exercise: we need to modify the writing to a file such that the system notifies us when we want to write to an existing file. For this, we can precede the opening of a file with a test for its existence with the `fileExists:` method (see the list of methods above).

The save method will, therefore, be:

```
Lsystem>>save
  | aFile |
    aFile := FillInTheBlank request: 'file name'
                    initialAnswer: 'foo'.
```

```
(FileDirectory default fileExists: aFile , '.1')
    ifTrue: [self otherFile: aFile]
    ifFalse: [self save1: aFile]
```

It begins, like the version seen on page 265, by reading the base name of the file in which we wish to save the current L-system. Then, it tests to see if a file of the same name and the ".1" extension exists already. If yes, then it will call the otherFile: method, otherwise it will call the save1: method. For both methods, the filename read is passed as an argument.

Clearly, the save1: method will need to do the same thing as we did with the old version of save: after reading the name of the file, we need to write the definition of the current L-system to this file. Below is this same computation performed in the save1: method:

```
Lsystem>>save1: aFile
    | fic |
    self.
    fic := FileStream forceNewFileNamed: aFile , '.1'.
    fic nextPutAll: level asString;
        nextPut: 10 asCharacter;
        nextPutAll: angle asString;
        nextPut: 10 asCharacter;
        nextPutAll: axiom;
        nextPut: 10 asCharacter.
    rulesDerivation
        keysAndValuesDo: [:c :a | fic nextPut: c;
            nextPut: $:;
            nextPutAll: a;
            nextPut: 10 asCharacter]
```

This method is effectively a copy of the old save method, except that we have replaced the fileNamed: method, which does not take into account whether the file already exists or not, with the new method forceNewFileNamed: in order to be sure that we will write into an entirely new empty file[28].

---

[28] The fileNamed: method creates a file and opens it for writing, as long as the file does not exist. If it already exists, if opens it for writing. The behavior of the forceNewFileNamed: method is identical in the case of a new file. However, if this file already exists, then it begins by removing it in order to re-create it. Thus, by using this method we can be sure that we will never find *remains* of the old contents of the file which we wish to write to.

The old version of the save method, page 265, is essentially buggy: when we re-use a file which already exists and which contains more lines than those which we will write to it, the writing of each line erases the contents of this line, but the lines over which nothing is written will preserve their old contents.

All that remains is to manage the case where the user enters the name of an already existing file. One solution which is frequently adopted is to open a menu informing the user of the fact that the file already exists and giving him (or her) the choice between confirming the use of this file, or entering a new file name. In the latter case, naturally, the program will need to re-verify whether the file already exists, re-inform the user, etc.

The otherFile: method implements these tasks:

```
Lsystem>>otherFile: name
    | menu1 |
    menu1 := MenuMorph new defaultTarget: self.
    menu1 addTitle: (name , '.l ' , '\already exists')
                    withCRs;
        position: Sensor cursorPoint;

        add: 'delete this file ?'
        selector: #save1:
        argument: name;
        add: 'new name ?' action: #save;
        add: 'abort ?' action: #yourself.
    menu1 openInWorld
```

Within this method we have added, on top of the usual entries, the "abort ?" entry to the menu. If the user chooses this entry, then they do not need to do anything further. This *do nothing* entry is achieved through the use of the yourself method in this case, which – in effect – does not do anything (see the footnotes on page 30 and page 85).

5) Figure A1.39 provides us with an example of a file containing multiple definitions of Lindenmayer systems which represent plants. The definitions of each of these L-systems are written slightly differently in order to show the flexibility in the writing that we like. Nevertheless, it is mandatory to finish a definition with the list of rewriting rules due to the restriction of one line per rule. In this exercise we need to make our program able to read in such files.

Since we already have a set of other files, which only contain a single definition, we will add the ability to read these new files. This will make the system able to read two types of files definitions. We will distinguish them using the extension of the file names. Given that the names of the files written up until now end with the ".1" (1 for L-system), we will give these new files the .11 extension (two "l"s since these files can contain more than one definition of an L-system). Thus, our example file from figure A1.39 is called plants.11.

```
bush1 {
level: 4
angle: 22.5
axiom: F
rules:
F: FF+[+F-F-F]-[-F+F+F]
}

bush2 {
angle: 22.5
level: 5
axiom: X
rules:
X: F-[[X]+X]+F[+FX]-X
F: FF
}
bush3{
level:7
angle:20
axiom:X
rules:
X: F[+X]F[-X]+X
F: FF}
bush4 {
level: 6
angle: 25.7
axiom: Y
rules:
Y: YFX[+Y][-Y]
X: X[-FFF][+FFF]FX
}

bush5 {
level:5
angle:25.7
axiom:F
rules:
F:F[+F]F[-F]F
}
```

Figure A1.39. *A file containing five different L-system definitions*

This means that if the user selects the read a file ? entry, then the file method, which is called in this case, must show both the files with the .1 extension along with those with the .11 extension. This is not difficult, the expression:

```
(FileDirectory default fileNamesMatching: '*.11')
    , (FileDirectory default fileNamesMatching: '*.1')
```

will return the collection of all the file names with these two extensions, simply by concatenating the two collections. It is therefore this kind of expression which we must introduce into the file method. This is the only change which we need to make to the file method, given that nothing changes in the rest of this method: we must, as before, construct a menu for the set of available files, which will let the user select one of them. This method then becomes:

```
Lsystem>>file
  | menu1 listFic |
  listFic :=
    ((FileDirectory default fileNamesMatching: '*.11')
      , (FileDirectory default fileNamesMatching: '*.1'))
    asSortedCollection.
  menu1 := MenuMorph new defaultTarget: self.
  menu1 addTitle: 'L-system files';
      position: Sensor cursorPoint.
  listFic
    do: [:fic | menu1
        add: fic
        selector: #show:
        argument: fic].
  menu1 openInWorld
```

Then, in the show: method we need to make a distinction between the two types of files (those with the .1 extension and those with the .11 extension) in order to call the methods for reading the different L-system definitions, which depend of course on these extensions. Here is the modified method:

```
Lsystem>>show: aFile
  (FileDirectory extensionFor: aFile)
      = '11'
      ifTrue: [self showMultiples: aFile]
      ifFalse: [self showUnique: aFile]
```

Knowing that the `extensionFor:` method, a method from the `FileDirectory`[29] class, returns the extension of the name of the file passed as an argument (without the full separator character); the `show:` method therefore does not do anything other than call either the `showUnique:` method in the case where the selected file has the `.l` extension, or the `showMultiples:` method in the other case.

The `showUnique:` method must do exactly the same thing as our old `show:` method, initialize the current instance of the `Lsystem` with the values read in the file given as an argument and activate the creation of the associated drawing:

```
Lsystem>>showUnique: aFile
  | fic |
  fic := (FileStream fileNamed: aFile) contents.
  fic := fic findTokens: {10 asCharacter}.
  level := (fic at: 1) asNumber.
  angle := (fic at: 2) asNumber.
  axiom := (fic at: 3)
            copyWithout: 32 asCharacter.
  derivationRules := Dictionary new.
  4
      to: fic size
      do: [:i |
          | tmp |
          tmp := (fic at: i)
                        copyWithout: 32 asCharacter.
          rulesDerivation
              at: (tmp at: 1)
              put: (tmp copyFrom: 3 to: tmp size)].
      self runLsystem
```

The `showMultiples:` method is more difficult to write. Given that the file that it receives as an argument can contain multiple L-system definitions, it must first give the user a new choice: this time not a file to read, but an L-system to extract from this file:

```
Lsystem>>showMultiples: aFile
1    | listfic menu1 |
2    listfic := (FileStream fileNamed: aFile)
3                    contents findTokens: $}.
```

---

[29] As we have seen before, the `FileDirectory` class provides the set of methods which process files as entities of the file system of your operating system. The `FileStream` class offers methods for processing the *content* of an individual file.

```
4    menu1 := MenuMorph new defaultTarget: self.
5    menu1 addTitle: 'Lindenmayer\systems' withCRs;
6        position: Sensor cursorPoint.
7    listfic
8        do: [:fic |
9            | tmp |
10           tmp := fic findTokens: {10 asCharacter}.
11           tmp size < 2
12               ifFalse: [menu1
13                   add: ((tmp at: 1)
14                       copyWithout: ${)
15                   selector: #LoadAndShow:
16                   argument: tmp]].
17   menu1 openInWorld
```

COMMENTS.–

– Lines 1 and 2: reading of the file given as argument and creation of a collection containing as elements the character strings delimited by the } character. The collection therefore has as many elements as there are L-system definitions in the file.

– Lines 4 to 6: preparation for the creation of the menu where the user will be able to select their L-system.

– Lines 7 and 8: the method takes one element at a time from the collection in lines 1 and 2 and allocates it to the block's parameter, fic. For our example file, figure A1.39, the first value of fic will be the character string[30]:

```
bush1 {<10>level: 4<10>angle:22.5<10>
    axiom: F<10>rules:<10>F: FF+[+F-F-F]-[-F+F+F]
```

This character string clearly corresponds[31] to the first L-system defined in this file.

– Line 10: the temporary variable of the block, tmp, takes the value of a collection containing as elements the character strings of fic which are separated by the ASCII character 10, the *carriage return* character. tmp therefore contains, for the above fic value, the collection of the following six elements:

```
OrderedCollection('bush1 {' 'level: 4' 'angle: 22.5'
    'axiom: F' 'rules:' 'F: FF+[+F-F-F]-[-F+F+F]')
```

---

30 We have introduced the invisible ASCII character 10, in the form of the string <10>, to the points in the string where it occurs.

31 With the only difference that we have represented *carriage return* characters by their ASCII code.

– Lines 11 and 12: do not do anything if the number of elements in this collection is less than two. This test exists here to avoid interpreting empty lines.

– Lines 12 to 16: this is the code for creating a new entry in the L-systems menu: the menu entry displays the first element of the tmp collection from which the occurrences of the } character were removed. For our example, this will be the string bush1. The loadAndShow: method is associated with this entry, which will, once the entry is selected, receive tmp as an argument.

– Line 17: after having created the menu containing each of the L-system names defined in the file, the menu opens so that the user can choose one of these names.

Now we just need to write the loadAndShow method which must initialize the instance variables of our L-system and run the code which will lead to the displaying of the curve which graphically represents this L-system.

We recall that the contents of our collections alternate between strings ending in the : sign and other strings. Those that end with a : character correspond to the names of our instance variables which we wish to initialize. Thus, if in the above example we find the string 'angle: 22.5', we can translate this as: *the instance variable* angle *must take the value* 22.5.

Unfortunately, allocation (:= or ←) is not, as we mentioned in the Introduction, a method. It is an operator which runs at virtual machine level. Nonetheless, in order to write these rules in an arbitrary order (except for the rewriting rules which must always end in a Lindenmayer system definition), we could consider the first sub-string as a variable, and the second as its future value. This is exactly what we do in the loadAndShow: method below:

```
Lsystem>>loadAndShow: anLsys
1    | ind |
2    ind := true.
3    derivationRules := Dictionary new.
4    anLsys removeFirst.
5    anLsys
6        do: [:ligne |
7            | tmp |
8            tmp := (ligne copyWithout: 32 asCharacter)
9                        findTokens: #($: $= ).
10           ind
```

```
11                  ifTrue: [(tmp at: 1) asSymbol caseOf: {
12                      [#axiom] -> [axiom := tmp at: 2].
13                      [#angle] -> [angle := (tmp at: 2)
14                                    asNumber].
15                      [#level] -> [level := (tmp at: 2)
16                                    asInteger].
17                      [#rules] -> [ind := false]}]
18                  ifFalse: [rulesDerivation
19                      at: (tmp at: 1) asCharacter
20                      put: (tmp at: 2 ifAbsent: '')]].
21      self runLsystem
```

COMMENTS.–

– Line 2: the temporary variable ind serves as an indicator in order to know if we are reading rewriting rules – ind will therefore take the value false – or if we read other parts of the L-system definition – ind will instead have the value true.

– Line 4: we remove the name of the L-system from the collection which describes it.

– Lines 5 to 20: analysis of the definition of the L-system.

– Lines 5 and 6: we take an element from the collection given as argument, therefore from the description of the L-system to be interpreted, and we bind it temporarily to the line variable.

– Lines 8 and 9: we remove all of the space characters from the element and transform it into a collection with two elements. The first element of this collection, temporarily stored in the tmp variable, is the character string preceding the : character, the second element is the string which follows this character. In our example: if the user has selected the entry bush1, then the first value of line is the character string 'level:4', and tmp contains the collection ('level' '4').

– Lines 10, 11 and 18: they depend on the value of ind (normal reading or reading of rules) which we continue on line 10 or on line 18.

We will continue the analysis of our bush1 example: ind has the true value, and we continue on line 10, with the transformation of the first element of the tmp collection into a symbol. For our example, this will be the #level symbol. This symbol is the receiver of a caseOf: message.

caseOf: is a message understood by any object[32]. The argument of caseOf: is a table of associations between blocks, of the style $block1_i$ -> $block2_i$. The caseOf: method searches, one association at a time, until it finds an association where the

---

32 Look at the definition of the caseOf: method in the Object class.

receiver is equal to the value of $block1_i$. In this case, caseOf: responds with the value of $block2_i$. If in the whole table no association satisfying this condition is found, then caseOf: throws an error: exception. If we wish to catch this error, then we can use the caseOf:otherwise: method. In our method, the argument of caseOf: is the table:

```
{
[#axiom] -> [axiom := tmp at: 2].
[#angle] -> [angle := (tmp at: 2) asNumber].
[#level] -> [level := (tmp at: 2) asInteger].
[#rules] -> [ind := false]
}
```

and the receiver of caseOf: is (tmp at: 1) asSymbol, and thus the symbol, in our example, corresponding to the string level: #level. The evaluation of caseOf:, therefore, chooses the association:

```
[#level] -> [level := (tmp at: 2) asInteger]
```

since the receiver symbol of the message is equal to the value of *block1* of the association, and returns the value of *block2*, the integer 4, *after having evaluated it*, thus after having assigned the integer 4 to the level instance variable.

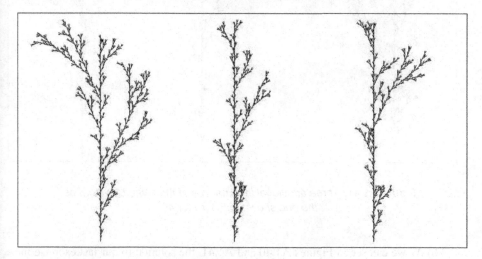

Figure A1.40. *Three incarnations of a stochastic L-system: level: 5, angle: 25.7, axiom: F, rules: F:F[+F]F[-F]F, F:F[+F]F, F:F[-F]F*

This type of operation will be executed line by line of our L-system definition, up until we reach the line containing the `rules` string where we will change the value of the temporary variable `ind` to `false`.

– Lines 18–20: when the variable `ind` is `fasle`, in other words, when we have already read a line containing the `rules` string, we know that the remaining lines will be rewriting lines. We, therefore, instead of assigning instance variables, add the entries to the `derivationRules` dictionary, with the first element of `tmp` as the key (converted into a character) and the second element of `tmp` as the value.

– Line 21: Once the analysis of the definitinon and the initialization of the four instance variables `level`, `angle`, `axiom` and `derivationRules` is finished, we need to activate the interpretation of the newly created L-system.

Finally, from this moment on, our program can read both files containing only one unique L-system definition, the files which have been used up until now with the `.1` file extension, as well as files containing a whole set of L-system definitions, using the `.11` extension, to then be able to choose a specific L-system.

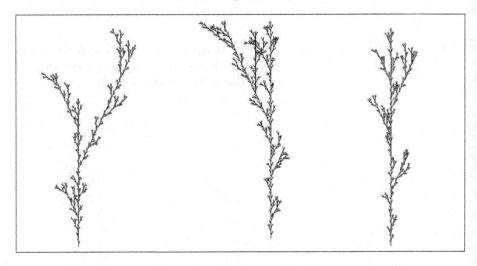

Figure A1.41. *Three additional incarnations of the same L-system as the one shown in Figure A1.40*

6) As we can see in Figures A1.40 and A1.41, the solution to our last exercise in this chapter significantly increases the capabilities of our interpreter of Lindenmayer systems.

What do we need to adapt our interpreter to stochastic L-systems?

First, we will need to change the ways of reading the rewriting rules, since in a stochastic system there can be multiple rewritings for the same letter. Although up until now it was enough to simply associate, in our dictionary derivationRules, the character keys to the rewriting strings, in the case where there is a choice between multiple rewritings, we must associate with it the *collection* of all the possible rewritings. Of course, for deterministic L-systems, the old associations should still be valid. Moreover, we must also adapt our methods responsible for saving an L-system to this new system.

For the purpose of enjoying the exercise, we propose creating a subclass of the Lsystem class which we will call StochasticLsystem. We will have the constraint that the Lsystem class must be able to continue in the same way as it has up until now, but that the new class must be able to interpret both stochastic and deterministic systems.

What do we need to do?

Naturally, during the generation of the character string, which corresponds to the description of the graphical representation of the L-system, we must take into account the fact that multiple ways of rewriting are possible. If this is the case, then we must choose a random outcome.

Thankfully, we do not need to change anything pertaining to the computation of the bounding box, or the graphical interpretation of the character string, since no new command character is introduced.

We will start with preparatory changes to the Lsystem class. First, we will modify the showUnique: method and the loadAndShow: method so as to delegate the saving of a rule to an auxiliary method. Here is the new version of showUnique::

```
Lsystem>>showUnique: aFile
    | fic |
    fic := (FileStream fileNamed: aFile) contents.
    fic := fic findTokens: {10 asCharacter}.
    "13 asCharacter"
    level := (fic at: 1) asNumber.
    angle := (fic at: 2) asNumber.
    axiom := (fic at: 3)
             copyWithout: 32 asCharacter.
    derivationRules := Dictionary new.
    4
        to: fic size
        do: [:i |
            | tmp |
            tmp := (fic at: i)
                   copyWithout: 32 asCharacter.
```

```
      self
         oneOrMultiple: (tmp at: 1)
         values: (tmp copyFrom: 3 to: tmp size)].
   self runLsystem
```

The only change is the transmission to itself of the oneOrMultiple:values: method where in the previous version we had the direct reading of *one* rewriting rule. Below, we give the two versions of this method for the Lsystem class:

```
Lsystem>>oneOrMultiple: key values: values
   derivationRules at: key put: values.
```

```
Lsystem>>oneOrMultiple: key values: values
   | aux |
   aux := derivationRules at: key ifAbsent: nil.
   aux isNil
      ifTrue: [derivationRules at: key put: values].
```

These two versions behave identically if there is only one rewriting rule for a given character. However, if there is more than one, then the first method will only keep the last rule of the rewriting, whereas the second method will only keep the first. This method must of course also be defined in the StochasticLsystem class where it must keep the *collection* of possible rewritings.

As we mentioned earlier, we must make a similar change to the loadAndShow: method (see page 446), which gives:

```
Lsystem>>loadAndShow: anLsys
   | ind |
   ind := true.
   derivationRules := Dictionary new.
   anLsys removeFirst.
   anLsys
      do: [:line |
         | tmp |
         tmp := (ligne copyWithout: 32 asCharacter)
                 findTokens: #($: $= ).
      ind
         ifTrue: [(tmp at: 1) asSymbol caseOf: {
            [#axiom] ->
                  [axiom := tmp at: 2].
            [#angle] ->
```

```
                        [angle := (tmp at: 2) asNumber].
            [#level] ->
                        [level := (tmp at: 2) asInteger].
            [#rules] -> [ind := false]}]
        ifFalse: [self
            oneOrMultiple: (tmp at: 1) asCharacter
            values: (tmp at: 2 ifAbsent: '')]].
    self runLsystem
```

Up until now, we have not done anything other than let an instance of the Lsystem class take into account the files of the definitions containing multiple right parts for a single left part of a rewriting rule. We will arbitrarily choose the second variant of the oneOrMultiple:valeurs: method.

Therefore, we will define our StochasticLsystem class as a subclass of the Lsystem class:

```
Lsystem subclass: #StochasticLsystem
    instanceVariableNames: 'randomNumberGenerator'
    classVariableNames: ''
    poolDictionaries: ''
    category: 'Lesson-Smalltalk'
```

It has an instance variable, called randomNumberGenerator, which must be intialized to be a random number generator, an instance of the Random class. This generator will help us choose a random rewriting in the case where such a choice is needed.

Below is the initialization method of instances of the StochasticLsystem class:

```
StochasticLsystem>>initialize
    super initialize.
    randomNumberGenerator := Random new
```

We will now also write the oneOrMultiple:values: method for this new class. In contrast to this same method in the Lsystem class, here we will need to store the *set* of possible rewritings if such an opportunity presents itself:

```
StochasticLsystem>>oneOrMultiple: key values: values
1   | aux c |
2   aux := derivationRules at: clef ifAbsent: nil.
3   aux isNil
4       ifTrue: [derivationRules at: key put: values]
5       ifFalse: [aux isString
```

```
6                    ifTrue: [ c:= OrderedCollection new.
7                        c add: aux;
8                          add: values.
9                        derivationRules at: clef
10                                     put: c]
11                   ifFalse: [aux add: values]].
```

COMMENTS.–

– Line 2: the temporary variable aux takes as a value either the value associated with the key character in the rulesDerivation dictionary, if such a value exists, the nil value if no association for the key exists.

– Line 4: no association exists, we just need to add the key -> values association to the dictionary of rewriting rules.

– Lines 6–10: an association exists and it is a character string, corresponding to the rewriting of the key character given as the first argument to the method. This string is the value of the temporary variable aux – we stored it there in line 2. We will, therefore, create a new sorted collection (line 6), to which we will add the rewriting stored in the aux variable (line 7) and also the rewriting given in the second argument of this method (line 8). This new collection then becomes the values associated with the key character in the rulesDerivation dictionary (lines 9 and 10). However, if there was already a collection associated with the key – there, therefore, already exist multiple rewriting rules for this same key –, then we just need to add the new rewriting to this collection (line 11).

Now that we can be sure that our interpreter, at least when it is called from the StochasticLsystem,[33] class, will behave like the instances of our old Lsystem and – as well – it will know how to store multiple rewriting rules for the same character. However, it does not yet know how to interpret them.

In the Lsystem class, it is the replace: method which performs the replacement of characters in a string through the rewritings given in the rules. For our class, we will redefine this method so that it also takes into account the choice between the different rewriting possibilities. Below, we have the new definition:

```
StochasticLsystem>>replace: aString
1    | tmp |
2    ^ aString
3        inject: ''
4        into: [:new :ele |
```

---

33 Through a DoIt on the expression StochasticLsystem new opneInWorld.

```
5              (tmp :=
6                 derivationRules at: ele ifAbsent: nil)
7              isNil
8                 ifTrue: [new , ele asString]
9                 ifFalse: [new
10                       , (self getRule: tmp)]]
```

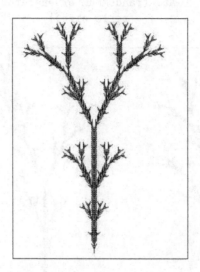

Figure A1.42. *A deterministic plant obtained with the L-system: level: 6, angle: 25.7, axiom: Y, rules: Y: YFX[+Y][-Y], X: X[-FFF][+FFF]FX*

The expression:

```
(rulesDerivation at:  ele ifAbsent:  nil))
```

returns the (one or more) rewriting(s) corresponding to the `ele` character or `nil` if no rewriting is found. This value is stored in the temporary variable `tmp` (lines 5 and 6).

Just like the `Lsystem` class, the characters which are not keys, in the dictionary of rewriting rules, are rewritten as they are (line 8).

In the case where an association with `ele` was found in the `derivationRules` dictionary, the result of calling this method will be the concatenation of the string constructed up until this point and the string returned by the `getRule:` method by transmitting the `tmp` value to it, thus the rewriting associated with the `ele` character (lines 9 and 10).

The `getRule:` method must either return the single and unique rewriting chain, if there only exists one, or a random choice from the set of rewritings, if there exist more than one:

```
StochasticLsystem>>getRule: Rule
    ^ regle isString
        ifTrue: [regle]
        ifFalse: [regle
                    at: (randomNumberGenerator nextInt:
                          regle size)]
```

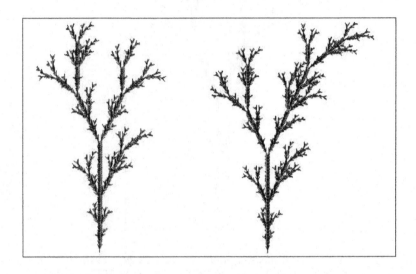

Figure A1.43. *Two incarnations of the previous L-system now made stochastic through the L-system: level: 6, angle: 25.7, axiom: Y, Y: YFX[+Y][-Y], Y: YFX[+YY][-Y], X: X[-FFF][+FFF]FX, X: X[-FF][+FFF]FX*

We have finished processing stochastic L-systems. Figure A1.42 shows a plant obtained with a deterministic L-system and Figure A1.43 shows two variations of this plant obtained by giving two rewriting rules for each of the rewriting rules of the original L-system. As you can see, although the changes in the rules are minimal, the effect is quite spectacular: the stochastic plants seem much more natural.

To finish (for now) our interpreter of LindenMayer systems, we still need to update our methods for saving L-systems, so that we can also save stochastic L-systems and so that we can save them either in individual files, files with the .1 extension or in collective files, those with the .11 extension.

In the following methods, we have made the choice that an unknown file name results in the creation of a new individual file. We can only write into a collective file when at the end of an already existing file.

The first method which we need to modify is the save method. Here is the new version:

```
Lsystem>>save
   | aFile |
   aFile := FillInTheBlank request: 'file name'.
                         initialAnswer: 'foo'.
   (FileDirectory default fileExists: aFile , '.ll')
        ifTrue: [self add: aFile]
        ifFalse: [
            (FileDirectory default
                fileExists: aFile , '.l')
             ifTrue: [self otherFile: aFile]
             ifFalse: [self save1: aFile]]
```

As before, this method begins by asking for the name of a save file. If a file of this name already exists and if it has the .ll extension, the saving process is delegated to the add: method. Otherwise, the method proceeds in exactly the same way as its older version from page 438: either it asks for another file name, since the one that was given already exists with the .l extension and risks being erased, or it asks the auxiliary save1: method to take responsibility for the saving process.

Let us examine the new version of hte save1: method:

```
Lsystem>>save1: aFile
1    | fic |
2    fic :=
3        FileStream forceNewFileNamed: aFile , '.l'.
4      fic nextPutAll: level asString;
5         nextPut: 10 asCharacter;
6         nextPutAll: angle asString;
7         nextPut: 10 asCharacter;
8         nextPutAll: axiom;
9         nextPut: 10 asCharacter.
10    derivationRules
11      keysAndValuesDo: [:c :a | a isString
12            ifTrue: [fic nextPut: c;
13                nextPut: $:;
14                nextPutAll: a;
15                nextPut: 10 asCharacter]
16          ifFalse: [a
17              do: [:r | fic nextPut: c;
18                  nextPut: $:;

19                  nextPutAll: r;
20                  nextPut: 10 asCharacter]]]
```

Lines 1–9 are no different from the version of save1 which we developed on page 439, it writes the values of the instance variables which define the level by default, the angle and the initial axiom of the L-system to be saved. Lines 10 to 15 are also nearly identical to the old version, the only differnce being that writing only takes place if the character to be rewritten is associated with a string of characters. This is essentially the case with all deterministic L-systems.

It is, therefore, on lines 16–20 that we see changes. This is for a reason: it is where we process the case of stochastic L-systems. In such systems, there can be, as we have seen, a character which has several ways in which it can be rewritten: it is, therefore, associated with a collection of rewritings. Lines 16 to 20 iterate through this collection and for each of the elements will write a line containing the character or string to be rewritten, a colon character and the current element of collection (which is a character string). This line ends with a *carriage return* character, the ASCII 10 character.

With this save1 method, the L-system given in Figure A1.43, page 454 will be saved in a file as shown below:

```
6
25.7
Y
X:X[-FFF][+FFF]FX
X:X[-FF][+FFF]FX
Y:YFX[+Y][-Y]
Y:YFX[+YY][-Y]
```

For the sole purpose of making save1 more readable, we will extract the part corresponding to lines 10–20 in order to create the new method writeRules::

```
Lsystem>>writeRules: fic
    derivationRules
        keysAndValuesDo: [:c :a | a isString
            ifTrue: [fic nextPut: c;
                nextPut: $:;
                nextPutAll: a;
                nextPut: 10 asCharacter]
            ifFalse: [a
                do: [:r | fic nextPut: c;
                    nextPut: $:;
                    nextPutAll: r;
                    nextPut: 10 asCharacter]]]
```

Which will finally give the following save1 method here:

```
Lsystem>>save1: aFile
    | fic |
```

```
fic := FileStream forceNewFileNamed: aFile , '.l'.
fic nextPutAll: level asString;
    nextPut: 10 asCharacter;
    nextPutAll: angle asString;
    nextPut: 10 asCharacter;
    nextPutAll: axiom;
    nextPut: 10 asCharacter.
  self writeRules: fic
```

Now, we just need to write the add: method which is responsible for adding the definition of the current L-system to an existing file, with a .ll extension.

For this, we need to open an already existing file. The `oldFileNamed:` method of the `FileStream` class opens, with read and write access, an already existing file[34], and is therefore perfect for using here.

Then, we need to position the writing point to the right location. A file is like a sheet of paper: we can write at the part, or the *position* that we want, be it at the top, the bottom or anywhere between these two extremities. The `position:` method of the `FileStream`[35] class lets us position, within the receiver file, a *virtual* cursor at the point which we wish to read or write. More specifically, the `position:` method changes the value of the descriptor of the file which indicates where its access point currently lies.

To insert text at the end of the file *file*, we can position this virtual cursor with the transmission "*file* position: self size" or more simply with the transmission "*file* setToEnd". setToEnd is a method of the `StandardFileStream` class which positions the virtual cursor of the file at its end.

After these preliminary remarks, we finally have our add: method below (note the use of our `writeRules` method):

```
Lsystem>>add: aFile
  | fic |
  fic := FileStream oldFileNamed: aFile , '.ll'.
  fic setToEnd;
    nextPutAll:
      (FillInTheBlank request: 'name of the L-system?'
              initialAnswer: 'foo');
    nextPutAll: ' {';
    nextPut: 10 asCharacter;
```

---

34 The difference between `fileNamed:` and `oldFileNamed:` resides in the fact that the first one creates a file with the name given as an argument when this file does not exist, while the second one opens an error window in this situtation.

35 In reality, `FileStream` is an abstract class, it will be one of its more concrete subclasses, for example `StandardFileStream` which actually implements this method.

```
      nextPutAll: 'level:';
      nextPutAll: level asString;
      nextPut: 10 asCharacter;
      nextPutAll: 'angle:';
      nextPutAll: angle asString;
      nextPut: 10 asCharacter;
      nextPutAll: 'axiom:';
      nextPutAll: axiom;
      nextPut: 10 asCharacter;
      nextPutAll: 'rules:';
      nextPut: 10 asCharacter.
  self writeRules: fic.
  fic nextPut: $}; nextPut: 10 asCharacter.
```

After this method, whilst saving the current L-system, after having provided as a name the string bush4Alea, the following lines will be added to the file of which the name has been given in the save method:

```
bush4Alea {
level:6
angle:25.7
axiom:Y
rules:
X:X[-FFF][+FFF]FX
X:X[-FF][+FFF]FX
Y:YFX[+Y][-Y]
Y:YFX[+YY][-Y]
}
```

If you wish to continue developing L-system interpreters, you could look into adapting them for three dimensional modeling as done by Fares Belhadj, who has generously provided us with the image of a palm tree (see figure A1.44) which was produced with his three dimensional L-systems interpreter. The production rules used are:

```
Palmier3D { /* By Fares BELHADJ */
  axiom @2.0FF@i2.0SLFFF
  S=[++Z][-Z]TS
  Z=+H[-/^Z]L
  H=-Z[+/^H]L
  T=T/L
  L=[-FFF][+FFF]F
  angle 20 /* rotation angle */
  step 6 /* step size */
  gen 6 /* number of generations */
  random /* insertion of noise to the rotation angle */
}
```

where the additional characters, which control the movements of the turtle in the three dimensional space (following the U, L and H axes), are:

$+$: the turtle turns to the left of the angle α specified around the U axis. The corresponding rotation matrix is:

$$R_U(\alpha) = \begin{bmatrix} cos(\alpha) & sin(\alpha) & 0 \\ -sin(\alpha) & cos(\alpha) & 0 \\ 0 & 0 & 1 \end{bmatrix}$$

$-$: the turtle turns to the right of the angle α. The corresponding rotation matrix is $R_U(-\alpha)$.

$\&$: the turtle turns toward the bottom of the angle α around the L axis. The corresponding rotation matrix is:

$$R_L(\alpha) = \begin{bmatrix} cos(\alpha) & 0 & -sin(\alpha) \\ 0 & 1 & 0 \\ sin(\alpha) & 0 & cos(\alpha) \end{bmatrix}$$

$\wedge$: the turtle turns toward the top of the angle α around the L axis. The corresponding rotation matrix is:

$\backslash$: the turtle turns to the left of the angle α around the H axis. The corrsponding rotation matrix is:

$$R_H(\alpha) = \begin{bmatrix} 1 & 0 & 0 \\ 0 & cos(\alpha) & -sin(\alpha) \\ 0 & sin(\alpha) & cos(\alpha) \end{bmatrix}$$

$/$: the turtle turns to the right of the angle α around the L axis. The corresponding rotation matrix is $R_H(-\alpha)$.

Finally, the i symbol directly after the @ symbol indicates that we must take the inverse of the next number.

A1.9. Exercises for section 6.3

1) The initialization of graphical interfaces is always troublesome: we must define the size, placement and interface with the rest of the program for each of the graphical objects. It is always a long listing of each of the elements which make it up. Nevertheless, we can recognize *patterns*, structures which repeat themselves. Thus, the expression:

Figure A1.44. *A palm tree obtained with a three-dimensional L-system by Farid Belhadj. For color version of this figure, see www.iste.co.in/wertz/smalltalk.zip*

```
PluggableButtonMorph
    on: (Key new
            label: xxx
            function: yyy
            on: self)
    getState: #state
    action: #active.
```

repeats itself five times in the current version of our *openInWorld* method. A first change would, therefore, be to replace all of the occurrences of this expression with:

```
self newKey: xxx with: yyy
```

after having added the `newKey:with:` method below:

```
Calculator>>newKey: label with: function
   ^PluggableButtonMorph on:
      (Key new
         label: label asString
         function: function
         on: self)
      getState: #state
      action: #activate
```

Now, we have five occurrences of the structure:

```
view := self newKey: xxx avec: yyy.
view := self initialise: view with: color and: xxx.
```

Clearly, we can combine these two expressions into a single one like below:

```
view := (self newKey: xxx with: yyy)
                  with: color and: xxx.
```

This requires replacing the initialise:with:and: method from the Calculator class with an with:and: method, however, this time it is defined in the PluggableButtonMorph class, since it is an instance of this class which was the value for view in the initialise:with:and: method and it is of course view which receives the whole stream of messages in this method. To assure ourselves of this, here is its implementation:

```
Calculator>>initalise: view with: color and: co
   ^ view offColor: color;
      borderWidth: 1;
      borderColor: Color black;
      hResizing: #spaceFill;
      vResizing: #spaceFill;
      label: co asString;
      useRoundedCorners;
      yourself
```

We will, therefore, create a protocol calculator in the *PluggableButtonMorph* class and in it we will define the following with:and: method:

```
PluggableButtonMorph>>with: color and: co
   ^ self offColor: color;
      borderWidth: 1;
      borderColor: Color black;
```

```
            vResizing: #spaceFill;
            hResizing: #spaceFill;
            useRoundedCorners;
            label: co asString;
            yourself
```

This is an exact copy of our `initialise:with:and:` method.

In order to reduce the size of the `openInWorld` method, we also replace the three successive creations of the C, 0 and $=$ buttons with:

```
    self
        createKeys: #('C' '0' '=' )
        with: #(#activeClear: #activeNumber: #activeEgal:)
        and: window.
```

which requires the creation of the `createKeys:with:and:` method below:

```
Calculator>>createKeys: tab1 with: tab2 and: window
    | view a1 |
    a1 := AlignmentMorph newRow.
    tab1 with: tab2
        do: [:ro :fonc |
            view := (self
                        newKey: ro
                        with: fonc)
                            with: window color
                            and: ro.
            a1 addMorphBack: view].
        window
            addMorph: a1
            frame: (0 @ (4 / 5) extent: 3 / 5 @ (1 / 5)).
```

The `createKeys:with:and:function:frame:extent:` will allow us to simplify the initialization of the nine numerical keys and the four operator keys:

```
Calculator>>createKeys: tab1 with: tab2 and: window
            function: function frame: fra extent: ext
    | l c view |
    c := l := 0.
    tab1 with: tab2
            do: [:ro :morph |
                l := l + 1.
                ro
                    do: [:co |
                        c := c + 1.
```

```
                  view := (self
                        newKey: co asString
                        with: function)
                        with: window color
                        and: co.
                  morph addMorph: view].
            window
               addMorph: morph
               frame: (fra x @ (1 * (fra y)) extent: ext)].
```

With these changes, our openInWorld method has been reduced from 108 lines down to 43 lines and none of the additional auxiliary methods are much larger than 20 lines. Therefore, here is the new version of openInWorld:

```
Calculator>>openInWorld
   | window view c |
   window := SystemWindow labelled: self class name.
   view := PluggableTextMorph
           on: self
           text: #printString
           accept: nil.
   view
       font: (StrikeFont familyName: 'Atlanta' size: 22).
   window
      addMorph: view
      frame: (0 @ 0 extent: 1 @ (1 / 5)).
   view := PluggableTextMorph
           on: (c := Screen on: self)
           text: #hist
           accept: nil
           readSelection: #selectTextInterval
           menu: #myMenu:.
   self addDependent: c.
   view setTextColor: Color blue.
   window
      addMorph: view
      frame: (4 / 5 @ (1 / 5) extent: 1 / 5 @ (4 / 5)).
   self
      createKeys: #(#(9 8 7) #(6 5 4) #(3 2 1) )
      with: {AlignmentMorph newRow. AlignmentMorph newRow.
            AlignmentMorph newRow}
      and: window
```

```
        function: #activeNumber:
        frame: 0 @ (1 / 5)
        extent: 3 / 5 @ (1 / 5).
   self
        createKeys: #('C' '0' '=' )
        with: #(#activeClear: #activeNumber: #activeEqual:)
        and: window.
   self
        createKeys: #(#('+' '-' '*' '/') )
        with: {AlignmentMorph newColumn}
        and: window
        function: #activeFunction:
        frame: 3 / 5 @ (1 / 5)
        extent: 1 / 5 @ (4 / 5).
   window openInWorld
```

2) In this exercise, we need to define a few additional keys and insert them into the graphical representation. We will start with the definitions of the keys.

The first key, the *dot* key, has no calculation associated with it: it is only used for entering a real number. As with the keys with numbers, its activation must, therefore, call the `activeNumber:` method which, as we recall, must first distinguish between the case where the entered number is the start of a new number and the case where it is the rest of a number which is already on the screen, and then it must eliminate the non-significant 0 at the start of the number, in order to make reading easier.

The elimination of a 0 at the head does not make sense for the activation of the *dot* key: the 0 becomes significant. We will, therefore, create an additional activation method, responsible for the insertion of the dot character:

```
Calculator>>activeNumberDot: label
        firstTime := false.
        bufferScreen := bufferScreen , label.
        self changed: #printString
```

This will let us enter numbers such as 0.06598803584 or even the famous number 22.4591577. The asNumber method will know, as with character strings corresponding to integers, how to transform such strings into numbers.

The second key, x↑y, is an operator key like our other +, −, × and / keys. Well, not entirely: while the operator keys which we have implemented up until now correspond to binary operators, the selector of which is the sybmol which we display on the key, the SMALLTALK method which computes x^y is called `raisedTo:` and this is surely not a string which we wish to display. We will want this key to display x↑y and compute `raisedTo:`.

This implies that for our implementation of this operator, the `createKeys:with:`... methods, like the expression in (see previous page):

```
self
    createKeys: #(#('+' '-' '*' '/') )
    with: {AlignmentMorph newColumn}
    and: window
    function: #activeFunction:
    frame: 3 / 5 @ (1 / 5)
    extent: 1 / 5 @ (4 / 5).
```

must have as an additional argument, the character string displayed on the key. We will then have a transmission corresponding to the structure below:

```
self
    createKeys: #(#('+' '-' '*' '/')
                  #('x^y' 'sqrt' '1/x' '.'))
    with: #(#(#+ #- #* #/)
              #(#raisedTo: #sqrt #inv '.'))
    with: {AlignmentMorph newColumn.
           AlignmentMorph newColumn}
    and: window
    function: #(#(#activeFunction: .... ))
    frame: {(3 / 5 @ (1 / 5)
              extent: 1 / 5 @ (4 / 5). ...}
```

which gives as argument, for the creation of the keys, both the label to be displayed in the graphical representation and the selector of the method which enables the evaluation of the operation associated with the activated key. There will no longer be any equivalence between these two aspects.

It also allows for the initialization of multiple rows of keys at the same time.

We will, therefore, define this initialization method (up to the number of arguments):

```
1 Calculatrice>>createKeys: tabLabel
2                     with: tabSelector
3                     and: tabMorphs
4                function: tabActivF
5                   frame: rects
6                  window: window
7     | view a1 r |
8     tabLabel
```

```
9       with: tabSelector
10      and: tabMorphs
11      and: tabActivF
12      and: rects
13      do: [:keys :funs :m :funcs :rect |
14          keys with: funcs
15              and: funs
16              do: [:key  :func :fun |
17                  r:= rect.
18                  view := (self
19                      newKey: fun
20                      with: func)
21                      with: window color
22                      and: key.
23                  m addMorph: view. a1 := m].
24      window
25          addMorph:a1
26          frame: r].
```

COMMENTS.–

i) Lines 1 – 6: the method waits for six arguments:

   – tabLabels is a table contating subtables with the labels of a line or column of keys.

   – tabSelector is the table of selectors corresponding to the keys.

   – tabMorph contains the AlignmentMorphs for each of these rows of keys.

   – tabActivF contains, for each key, the selector of the method to be transmitted to the calculator so that it can run the computation associated with a key.

   – rects contains the rectangle in which we will need to position each of the AlignmentMorphs.

   – window is the SystemWindow instance of our calculator.

ii) Line 7: declares three temporary variables, a1 and m trasmit the morph and the rectangle which were calculated in the inner loop to the outer loop.

iii) Lines 8–13: initialize the parallel run through of the receiver table, the table of labels and the four tables given as arguments: the arithmetic selectors, morphs, launch selectors and positioning rectangles. The block arguments are, therefore, in order: the labels of a row of keys, the selectors corresponding to these labels, the morph for this row, the launch selectors for these keys and the placement rectangle for this range of keys.

iv) Lines 14–23: for each of these labels, we create an instance of the Key class with the corrsponding selector such as `label` and the launch selector such as `function`. Each of these labels is added to the `PluggableButtonMorph` of the key, which is added to the current `AlignmentMorph`.

v) Lines 24–26: each `AlignmentMorph` in the inner loop is added to the graphical representation of the calculator at the location indicated by the positioning rectangle.

This method for creating rows of keys uses two auxiliary methods `with:and:do:` and `with:and:and:and:do:` for the parallel processing of three and five *sequenceable* collections, respectively, such as:

```
SequenceableCollection>>with: otherCollection
                      and: yetOtherCollection
                       do: threeArgBlock
    1 to: self size do:
      [:index |
      threeArgBlock value: (self at: index)
            value: (otherCollection at: index)
            value: (yetOtherCollection at: index)]

SequenceableCollection>>with: otherCollection
                      and: yetOtherCollection
                      and: fourthCol
                      and: fifthCol
                       do: fiveArgBlock
    1 to: self size do:
      [:index |
      fiveArgBlock value: (self at: index)
            value: (otherCollection at: index)
            value: (yetOtherCollection at: index)
            value: (fourthCol at: index)
            value: (fifthCol at: index)]
```

The latter method requires the use of a block with five arguments. SQUEAK has not anticipated for the use of such a block. We will, therefore, add the `value:value:value:value:value:` message to the `BlockContext` class:

```
BlockContext>>value: arg1 value: arg2 value: arg3
           value: arg4 value: arg5
    ^self valueWithArguments:
```

```
(Array
    with: arg1
    with: arg2
    with: arg3
    with: arg4
    with: arg5)
```

Before updating our openInWorld method in order to better integrate these changes, we will examine the two additional keys which we still need to define: the sqrt and 1/x keys. The difference with all of the other operator keys which we have implemented up until now is that these two operators are *unary*: they only require one argument. We, therefore, cannot activate the callFunction: method, since it expects two arguments.

We will, therefore, define a method which is responsible for calling unary operators. Let us define two versions: one for the postfix calculator and one for the infix calculator.

Let us start with the postfix calculator. Fundamentally, calling a unary operator will not be very different from a binary operator. For the activation of a binary operator, the first argument is in the accumulator accu and the second argument, in the form of a character string on screen, is therefore the bufferScreen variable. For the call to a unary operator, the single unique argument must be the number which is seen on the screen, the last number entered. We just need to transmit the selector associated with the key to this number, and, for the rest, do exactly the same thing as we did with binary operators. We recall the callFunction: method which is responsible for calling binary operators (taken from page 315):

```
PolishCalculator>>callFunction: label
    self changed: #hist
            with: 'Enter > ' , bufferScreen.
    accu := accu perform: label asSymbol
                    with: bufferScreen asNumber.
    bufferScreen := accu printString.
    self changed: #hist
            with: label , ' > ' , bufferScreen.
    self changed: #printString.
    firstTime := true
```

Its simple adaptation to taking a single argument gives us the following method:

```
PolishCalculator>>callUnaryFunction: label
    self changed: #hist with: 'Enter > ' , bufferScreen.
    accu := bufferScreen asNumber perform: label asSymbol.
    bufferScreen := accu printString.
```

```
    self changed: #hist
            with: label , ' > ' , bufferScreen.
    self changed: #printString.
    firstTime := true
```

These two methods have so many transmissions in common that a refactorization becomes necessary. We will first extract the two parts in common and create the new method call::

```
PostfixCalculator>>call: label
    self changed: #hist with: 'Enter > ' , bufferScreen.
    bufferScreen := accu printString.
    self changed: #hist with: label , ' > ' , bufferScreen.
    self changed: #printString.
    firstTime := true
```

then we will simplify the two calling methods:

```
PostfixCalculator>>callFunction: label
    accu := accu perform: label
                    with: bufferScreen asNumber.
    self call: label
```

and

```
PostFixCalculator>>callUnaryFunction: label
    accu :=  bufferScreen asNumber perform: label.
    self call: label
```

In order to finish the adaptation of our postfix calculator to the changes induced from the addition of these few keys, we still need to modify the openInWorld method. Given the version on page 463, it will only be the sections pertaining to the initialization of the rows of keys conataining the operator keys which we need to modify:

```
Calculator>>openInWorld
    | window view c |
    window := SystemWindow labelled: self class name.
    view := PluggableTextMorph
                on: self
                text: #printString
                accept: nil.
    view
        font: (StrikeFont familyName: 'Atlanta' size: 22).
```

```
window
    addMorph: view
    frame: (0 @ 0 extent: 1 @ (1 / 5)).
view := PluggableTextMorph
        on: (c := Screen on: self)
        text: #hist
        accept: nil
        readSelection: #selectTextInterval
        menu: #myMenu:.
self addDependent: c.
view setTextColor: Color blue.
window
    addMorph: view
    frame: (4 / 5 @ (1 / 5) extent: 1 / 5 @ (4 / 5)).
 self
    createKeys: #(#(9 8 7) #(6 5 4) #(3 2 1) )
    with: {AlignmentMorph newRow.
            AlignmentMorph newRow.
            AlignmentMorph newRow}
    and: window
    function: #callNumber:
    frame: 0 @ (1 / 5)
    extent: 12 / 25  @ (1 / 5).
self
    createKeys: #(#('=' '0' 'C')
                  #('+' '-' '*' '/')
                  #('.' 'sqrt' '1/x' 'x^y' ))
    with: #(#('=' '0' 'C')
            #(#+ #- #* #div:)
            #('.' #sqrt #inv #raisedTo: ))

    and: {AlignmentMorph newRow.
            AlignmentMorph newColumn.
            AlignmentMorph newColumn}
    function:
      #(#(#(#callEqual:  #callNumber: #callClear:)
          #(#callFunction: #callFunction:
            #CallFunction: #callFunction:)
          #(#callFunction:  #callUnaryFunction:
            #callUnaryFunction: #callFunction:))
    frame: {0 @ (4 / 5) extent: 12 / 25 @ (1 / 5).
            12 / 25 @ (1 / 5) extent: 4 / 25 @ (4 / 5).
            16 / 25 @ (1 / 5) extent: 4 / 25 @(4 / 5).}
    window: window.
window openInWorld
```

So as to not obtain fractional results, we have also added the inv method to the Number class:

```
Number>>inv
    ^self reciprocal asFloat
```

Finally, we have a Polish calculator which allows for both unary and binary operations on integers and real numbers. Below is the callUnaryFunction: method for the infix calculator. After the changes which we have made above to the Calculator class, this will be the only modification required for allowing these keys in the InfixCalculator class.

```
InfixCalculator>>callUnaryFunction: label
    self changed: #hist with:  ' > ' , bufferScreen.
    memFunc notNil
        ifTrue: [accu := accu perform: memFunc
                                    with: bufferScreen asNumber.
                 bufferScreen := accu asString].
    accu := bufferScreen asNumber perform: label.
    self changed: #hist with: label , ' > ' , bufferScreen.
    bufferScreen := accu printString.
    self changed: #printString.
    memFunc := nil.
```

Even if we stop the development of our postfix calculator for now, we can still continue to improve it. A good intermediary goal would be to also include the ability to compute subexpressions. For example, the postfix expression:

$$30\ 3\ 4\ 5 + \times -$$

should display the result 3, with the infix of the expression being $30 - (3 \times (4 + 5))$, and the expression:

$$30\ 3\ 4 + 5 \times -$$

should return -5, with the infix of the expression being $30 - ((3 + 4) \times 5)$.

For the infix calculator, the calculation of subexpressions requires the addition of parentheses, i.e. the (and) keys. Can you program them?

Let us check to see if you have found the same solutions as the ones proposed below. We will begin, as always, with the postfix calculator.

In order to calculate the expression $30\ 3\ 4\ 5 + \times -$ with our calculator, we should first enter the four numbers, thus store them, and then apply the $+$ operator to the two last numbers which were stored. This calculation should replace the two operands, 4 and 5, with the result of their addition, 9. Now, the situation will then be as if we had stored the three numbers 30, 3 and 9, and then we would need to apply the × operator to the last two stored numbers. This results in the storage of just two numbers, 30 and 27 (the result of the multiplication of 3 by 9). Finally, the subtraction operation removes the two numbers and replaces them by the result of the subtraction, 3.

Our accumulator accu, must therefore not only store a unique value, but eventually also store a collection of values. In short, it must behave like a stack, just like our L-systems with the square brackets (see page 257 onwards). And as with our L-systems, we will use an OrderedCollection to implement the stack and the push operation will be implemented with the addFirst method, the pop method implemented with the removeFirst method and the peek operation will be acheived using the first method. All these methods are defined in the class OrderedCollection.

We will begin with the addition of an initialize method to our postfix calculator:

```
PostfixCalculator>>initialize
    super initialize.
    accu := OrderedCollection new
```

and, so that we can continue to use infix calculators, we will also adapt their initialization method:

```
InfixCalculator>>initialize
    super initialize.
    memFunc := nil.
    accu := 0
```

These two changes mean that we will also need to modify the initialize method in the Calculator super-class, by removing the initialization of the accu variable:

```
Calculator>>initialize
    bufferScreen := '0'.
    firstTime := true.
    self changed: #printString
```

Then, we will look for methods where accu is still used in the PostfixCalculator class, in order to adapt it to the new stack behavior. There are five of them: the initialize method, which we have just written, and the method callFunction:, which calls an operator with two arguments, callUnaryFunction:, which calls an operator with one argument, callEqual:, which terminates the input of a number and call: which factorizes the common parts for processing operators. We need to modify each one of them.

In the `callEqual:` method, we just need to change the simple allocation of the accu instance variable from the numerical value written on the screen to a stack with this same number in the accu ordered collection, which gives us the following new version:

```
PostfixCalculator>>callEqual: label
    self changed: #hist with: 'Enter > ' , bufferScreen.
    accu addFirst: bufferScreen asNumber.
    firstTime := true
```

The `call:` method uses the accumulator for displaying its contents on the calculator's screen. Of course, we will now display the *top of the stack*, therefore, the first element of accu:

```
PostfixCalculator>>call: label
    self changed: #hist with: 'Enter > ' , bufferScreen.
    bufferScreen := accu first printString.
    self changed: #hist with: label , ' > ' , bufferScreen.
    self changed: #printString.
    firstTime := true
```

The `callFunction:` method must always use at least one of the elements from the stack as an operator. If the stack only has one element, then this element will be the first operand and the numerical value on screen will be the second operand. If the stack has at least two elements, then the second element will be the first operand and the first element will be the second operand. The method must also push the result of the operation onto the stack. This is the exact algorithm which the new version of callFunction below will implement:

```
PostfixCalculator>>callFunction: label
    | x y |
    x := accu removeFirst.
    accu isEmpty
        ifTrue: [y := x.
                 x := bufferScreen asNumber]
        ifFalse: [y := accu removeFirst].
    accu
        addFirst: (y perform: label with: x).
    self activer: label
```

The `callUnaryFunction:` method is equivalent to the above method, except that the associated operation only requires a single argument. This argument either will be at the top of the stack accu, or the result on screen if the stack is empty. Of course, the result of the operation will then need to be pushed onto the stack. Here is its new implementation:

```
PostfixCalculator>>callUnaryFunction: label
    accu
        addFirst:
            ((accu isEmpty
                ifTrue: [bufferScreen asNumber]
                ifFalse: [accu removeFirst])
                perform: label).
    self activer: label
```

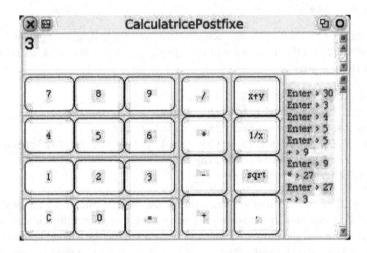

Figure A1.45. *A postfix calculator after the calculation of* $30\ 3\ 4\ 5 + \times -$

Figure A1.45 shows a postfix calculator where we can spot the calculation of $30\ 3\ 4\ 5 + \times -$ in the history window, thus equivalent to $30 - (3 \times (4 + 5))$. This calculator lets us calculate subexpressions without using parentheses, since the order of input of the operators is enough to determine the sub-expressions.

However, to be able to group sub-expressions in an infix calculator we will need the *opening parenthesis* operator, corresponding to the *start of a sub-expression*, and *closing parenthesis*, which corresponds to the *end of a sub-expression*.

In order to develop our infix calculator into one which knows how to process parentheses, the first thing to do is to determine the placement of these two keys. If we reduce the history screen in height a bit, then we can insert the two small keys (and) to the bottom right of the calculator, as shown in Figure A1.46.

After the changes which were made in the previous section to the Calculator»openInWorld method, the insertion of these two keys should not pose a problem. We will need to reduce the vertical height of the history window by one fifth of the height, thus we will need to change the lines where we place the `PluggableTextMorph` on the screen: the argument `'extent:'` $\frac{1}{5}@\frac{4}{5}$ will become $\frac{1}{5}@\frac{3}{5}$, which gives us the lines:

```
window
    addMorph: view
    frame: (4 / 5 @ (1 / 5) extent: 1 / 5 @ (3 / 5)).
```

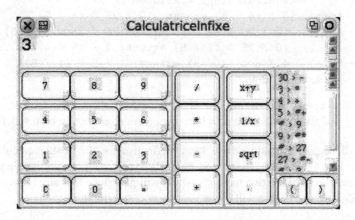

Figure A1.46. *An infix calculator after calculating* $30 - (3 \times (4 + 5))$

In order to insert the two additional keys, we just need to insert their specifications into the argument tables in the last transmission of `createKeys:with:...`, which will give us the new version of this transmission below (we have marked the lines which have been freshly inserted with the `"->"` comment):

```
self
    createKeys: #(#('=' '0' 'C')
                  #('+' '-' '*' '/')
                  #('.' 'sqrt' '1/x' 'x^y' )
"  --> "          #(')' '('))
         with: #(#('=' '0' 'C')
                  #(#+ #- #* #div:)
                  #('.' #sqrt #inv #raisedTo: )
"  --> "          #(')' '('))
         and: {AlignmentMorph newRow.
               AlignmentMorph newColumn.
               AlignmentMorph newColumn.
"  --> "       AlignmentMorph newRow}
```

```
        function:
         #(#(#callEqual:   #callNumber: #callClear:)
            #(#callFunction: #callFunction:
              #callFunction: #callFunction:)
            #(#callNumber:   #callUnaryFunction:
              #callUnaryFunction: #callFunction:)
" --> "     #(#callClosing: #callOpening:))
         frame: {0 @ (4 / 5) extent: 12 / 25 @ (1 / 5).
                 12 / 25 @ (1 / 5) extent: 4 / 25 @ (4 / 5).
                 16 / 25 @ (1 / 5) extent: 4 / 25 @(4 / 5).
" --> "          4 / 5 @ (4 / 5) extent: 1 / 5 @ (1 / 5)}
         window: window.
```

Since the `openInWorld` method is a method of the super-class of our two calculators, postfix and infix, we now have the parentheses keys in both subclasses.

We will begin by making these keys ineffective for the postfix calculator, by simply defining the `callOpening` and `callClosing:` methods so that they do not do anything. Here are the two methods which will guarantee that any instance of the `PostfixCalculator` class will know how to process parantheses:

```
PostfixCalculator>>callOpening: label
```

```
PostfixCalculator>>callClosing: label
```

In order to do nothing, they do nothing: their bodies are empty. This controls the behavior of the paranthesis keys for the postfix calculator.

For the infix calculator, we can take inspiration from the changes which made our postfix calculator able to process sub-expressions. We have transformed our accumulator `accu` into a stack. We will probably need to do the same thing here: upon entering a sub-expression, therefore upon encountering an opening parenthesis, we will need to store the current value of the accumulator in order to restart as if we were calculating an independent expression. Upon leaving a sub-expression, thus upon encountering a closing parenthesis, we will need to (1) calculate the value of the sub-expression and (2) use this value as the second operand of ... well, what exactly? The operator for which the sub-expression was the second operand. However, we no longer have this operator, it was in the `memFunc` instance variable before entering the sub-expression. Since this entry into the sub-expression started a new calculation, the `memFunc` variable changed values during this new calculation. We will, therefore, need to transform the `memFunc` instance variable into a stack, to be able to retrieve the operator which required the value of the sub-expression as the second operand.

We will begin by changing the `initialize` method of the super-class of our calculators so that it always initializes the `accu` variable to a new ordered collection.

We will also remove this same initialization from the initialize method in the PostfixCalculator class, which is the same as completely removing this method:

```
Calculator>>initialize
    bufferScreen := '0'.
    firstTime := true.
    accu := OrderedCollection new.
    self changed: #printString.
```

Then, we will create two additional instance variables for the infix calculators, which act as indicators, which will let us know if one of the two parenthesis keys has just been activated. We will definitely need to make use of them. This gives us the new definition:

```
Calculator subclass: #InfixCalculator
    instanceVariableNames: 'memFunc openPar closePar'
    classVariableNames: ''
    poolDictionaries: ''
    category: 'Lesson-Smalltalk'
```

We will also modify the initialize method so that it gives the correct initial values to these three instance variables:

```
InfixCalculator>>initialize
    super initialize.
    closePar := openPar := true.
    memFunc := OrderedCollection new.
    accu addFirst: 0
```

We already know what we need to do upon encountering an opening parenthesis: store the state of the calculation and act as if we were starting a new calculation. Since we have an instance variable which indicates the encounter of a new opening parenthesis, we will also change its value, which gives us the following callOpening: method:

```
InfixCalculator>>callOpening: label
    memFunc isEmpty
        ifTrue:
            [^ self changed: #hist
                    with: '( > ' , accu first printString]
        ifFalse: [accu addFirst: 0.
                  openPar:=false]
```

The test which looks to see if an operator has already been entered is our way of verifying if we are handling a sub-expression which is acting as the second operand of an operator. If this is not the case, a small indication is displayed on the history screen.

However, let us suppose that we have already entered the number 30 and the "−" operator. The accumulator, therefore, contains the collection #(30) and changes its value after the activation of the (key to become the collection #(0 30). This activation also changes the value of the openPar variable to false. Since the activation of the parenthesis key took place after the activation of the − operator key, we know that the callFunction method positions the memFunc variable. This variable has now acquired the behavior of a stack, therefore, we need to change its current allocation, memFunc := label to an expression which pushes the operator onto the stack, which gives us:

```
InfixCalculator>>callFunction: label
    (firstTime
            and: [accu first = 0])
        ifTrue: [^ self].
    self active: label.
    memFunc addFirst: label
```

We have changed the expression accu = 0, which worked as long as accu was a simple instance variable, into accu first = 0, to take into account its transformation into a stack.

We will continue the rest of the calculation of "30 - ('' and then assume that the user pushes the 3 key followed by the × key which will call the callFunction method, which itself will call the call method. We have changed it so that it takes the two stacks into account as well as the state of the openPar variable:

```
InfixCalculator>>active: label
1     (memFunc isEmpty not and: [openPar])
2       ifTrue:
3       [accu addFirst:
4           (accu removeFirst
5               perform: memFunc first
6                   with: bufferScreen asNumber)]
7       ifFalse:
8       [accu removeFirst.
9           accu addFirst: bufferScreen asNumber.
10          openPar := true].
11    self changed: #hist
12              with: bufferScreen , ' > ' , label.
13    bufferScreen := accu first printString.
14    self changed: #printString.
15    firstTime := true
```

COMMENTS.–

i) Lines 1–6: verify that an operation has been stored *and* that we find ourselves at the start of a new calculation initiated through an opening parenthesis. For our calculation of the expression 30 − (3 ×, openPar will have just been assigned to false. This condition is, therefore, not met and we advance to line 8.

When openPar is true, i.e. the normal case, the condition is met and the method starts by swapping the first element in the collection accu, therefore, the top of the stack of the accu values, with the result of the stored operator applied to both the number at the top of the stack accu and the number displayed on the screen.

ii) Lines 7–10: we only reach line 8 if the condition on line 1 is not met, in other words: if there is no operator and/or a sub-calculation has started since an opening parenthesis has already been enetered.

For our example, in calculating the expression 30 − (3 ×, we find ourselves at the start of a sub-expression. We, therefore, need to replace the top of the stack accu, which is currently the number 0, with the number displayed on the screen. accu then takes the value #(3 30). In any case, we need to set the value of openPar back to true, its default value.

iii) Lines 11 and 12: they send the character string consisting of the number on the screen and the encountered operation, to the dependencies which can recognize the aspect #hist. We know, in our case, that the history screen will display 3 > *.

iv) Lines 13 and 14: the screen displays the top of the stack accu. In our example, this does not change anything, however, if we had executed lines 3–6, the number displayed on the screen would be the result of the calculation performed in these lines.

v) Line 15: indicates that a new number must be entered.

Upon returning from the active: method, callFunction: stores the encountered operator by pushing it onto memFunc. Figure A1.47 shows an inspector which is open on our calculator right when it performs the calculation which we have just described. We recognize both stacks and the text of the bufferScreen variable which is displayed on the history screen.

We will continue our simulation and enter the number 2 followed by a closing parenthesis. Now, we have a complete expression, the expression "3 × 2", for which the closing parenthesis must act as a callEqual: (the input of an ordinary number into an ordinary calculator), which either transfers the number which was just entered to the accumulator, or computes the expression formed with this number acting as a second operand. We find ourselves in the second case here. Once this expression is calculated, since it itself forms the second operand of another waiting operation, we need to start the new calculation of another expression. In our case, after having calculated 3 × 2, which returns the value 6, we still need to calculate the expression

30 – 6. This is exactly what these modified callClosing: and callEqual: methods do:

```
InfixCalculator>>callClosing: label
   memFunc isEmpty
      ifTrue:
         [^ self changed: #hist
                     with: ') > ' , accu first printString]
      ifFalse:
         [self callEqual: memFunc first printString.
          closePar := false.
          accu removeFirst.
          self callEqual: memFunc first printString.
          closePar := true]

InfixCalculator>>callEqual: label
   (firstTime
         and: [closePar])
      ifTrue: [^ self].
   self active: label.
   memFunc isEmpty
      ifFalse: [memFunc removeFirst].
   self changed: #hist with: '# > ' , bufferScreen
```

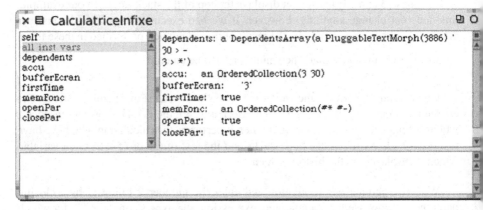

Figure A1.47. *An inspector on the infix calculator after computing* $30 - (3 \times$

We have finished (for now) writing the postfix and infix calculators which understand the $+$, $-$, $\times$, $/$, x^y, $\frac{1}{x}$ and $\sqrt{}$ operators and which know how to correctly calculate sub-expressions. Of course, the program works *if* the inputs are formed correctly. In order to transform it into a real program to be used not just by us, programmers who understand its strengths and weaknesses, but also by other people, i.e. users who just need to use a calculator, a lot of fine tuning still needs to be done.

A commercial program cannot allow itself to return a system error, from where the program was written, when an unexpected situation arises. If we want to make our infix calculator compute an expression such as $30 - (3)$, an error will occur, simply because we have written the program for users who think like us. Who would put parentheses around a number? We only put partentheses around complete and correctly formed expressions. Is this not always the case? Yet, the expression $30 - (3)$ is a perfectly valid arithmetic expression and does not produce any errors on any respectable calculator.

To create a "distributable" program, we need to predict all of the possible use cases, and not just our own cases. This is a good exercise. However, we will not, within the context of this book, address questions about how to make programs more robust and less vulnerable. This task is up to you.

3) In this last exercise, the addition of a prefix calculator should test the reliablilty of our abstract `Calculator` class. For it to be correct, we should not be forced to define the three activation methods: the one for = and the other two for unary and binary operations. The rest of the behavior should be inherited, as it is for postfix and infix calculators, from the `Calculator` super-class.

Prefix expressions, as postfix expressions, do not require parentheses for computing sub-expressions. Thus, our expression $30 - (3 \times (4 + 5))$, which is written in postfix notation as $30\ 3\ 4\ 5\ + \times -$, is written in prefix notation as $-30 \times 3 + 4\ 5$. On a prefix calculator, we need to enter this expression in exactly this order.

Since we will have two calculators which ignore the opening and closing parentheses (and only one, the infix calculator, which requires them), we will start by transferring the two methods `callOpening:` and `callClosing:` from the `PostfixCalculator` class to the `Calculator` class. Thus, any calculator which needs these two keys can redefine their two corresponding methods, with the others inheriting the specific behavior of ignoring them.

In order to make the abstract characteristic of the `Calculator` class more clear, and to inform any future programmers that the activation methods for the = key and binary and unary operations must be defined in subclasses, we will also define these methods in the `Calculator` class here:

```
Calculator>>callEqual: label
    self subclassResponsibility
```

```
Calculator>>callUnaryFunction: label
    self subclassResponsibility
```

and

```
Calculator>>callFunction: label
    self subclassResponsibility
```

We will analyze the calculation of a prefix expression. As an example we will use:

$$\times + 2\,3 + 5\,5$$

– After the activation of the $\times$ key, we cannot calulate anything: we still need two operands.

– The same comment is valid for the activation of the $+$ key.

– Inputting number 2 returns the first operand from the $+$ operation. We need an additional operand.

– Inputting number 3 returns this second operand. Now, we can calculate the sum of the two numbers. The arithmetic operation $+$ is finished. The result, 5, represents the first operand of the $\times$ operator. We once again need a second operand.

– Upon activating the $+$ key, we will wait for two more operands.

– Inputting number 5 will return the first.

– Entering the next number 5 will return the second. Now, we can calculate the sum. The addition operation is finished. The result, the integer 10, represents the second operand of the multiplication operation which is currently waiting. Now, we can compute the product. There are no more waiting operations. The result of the whole expression is, therefore, the integer 50.

Clearly, during the calculation of such an expression we must always store in memory the operations which are waiting for arguments, the number of arguments each of these operations takes and the number of operands which are still waiting for each of these operations.

To implement this storing procedure, the easiest solution is obviously to use three stacks:

1) the memFunc stack for operators;

2) the numArgs stack for the number of arguments for the operators;

3) the counter stack for knowing how many arguments have been computed for each of the stored operators.

This reasoning brings us to the definition of `PrefixCalculator`, the class for prefix calculators, as well as the definition of its initialization method:

```
Calculator subclass: #PrefixCalculator
    instanceVariableNames: 'memFunc numArgs counter'
    classVariableNames: ''
    poolDictionaries: ''
    category: 'Lesson-Smalltalk'

PrefixCalculator>>initialize
    super initialize.
    memFunc := OrderedCollection new.
    numArgs := OrderedCollection new.
    counter := OrderedCollection new.
    accu addFirst: 0
```

The definitions of the `callFunction:` and `callUnaryFunction:` methods also seem very simple. For the most part, they only need to store the operator, the number of arguments and the number of arguments that are still waiting, which gives us the following `callFunction` method:

```
PrefixCalculator>>callFunction: label
    memFunc addFirst: label.
    counter
        addFirst: (numArgs addFirst: 2).
    self call: label
```

where the `call:` method is a sub-routine which is responsible, as with the other types of calculators, for updating the graphical representation of our calculator:

```
PrefixCalculator>>call: label
    bufferScreen := accu first printString.
    self changed: #hist with: label , ' > ' , bufferScreen.
    self changed: #printString.
    firstTime := true
```

For the case where we activate an operator key *after* the end of another calculation, therefore when a new calculation starts and the display is still showing the result of the previous calculation, we introduce the transmission of the `deactivate` message at the start of the `callFunction:` method. Its role will be limited to reinitializing the accumulator `accu`:

```
PrefixCalculator>>deactivate
    counter isEmpty
        ifTrue: [accu removeFirst.
            accu addFirst: 0]
```

The new version of our `callFunction:` method is then:

```
PrefixCalculator>>callFunction: label
    self deactivate.
    memFunc addFirst: label.
    counter
        addFirst: (numArgs addFirst: 2).
    self call: label
```

The `callUnaryFunction:` method is the same for unary operators:

```
PrefixCalculator>>callUnaryFunction: label
    self deactivate.
    memFunc addFirst: label.
    numArgs
        addFirst: (counter addFirst: 1).
    self call: label
```

The latter two methods are so similar that we should factorize them. If we define an auxiliary method with the name `callFunctions:aNargs:` such as:

```
PrefixCalculator>>callFunctions: label aNargs: n
    self deactivate.
    memFunc addFirst: label.
    numArgs
        addFirst: (counter addFirst: n).
    self call: label
```

we can simplify the two operator activation methods as below:

```
PrefixCalculator>>callUnaryFunction: label
    self callFunctions: label aNargs: 1
```

and

```
PrefixCalulator>>callFunction: label
    self callFunctions: label aNargs: 2
```

The method which must carry out the most work is, therefore, the `callEqual:` method. It is activated by the = key, so for the input of a number. Here is what it must do:

– Start by informing the history screen that a number has been entered.

– Place this number at the head of the stack `accu`.

– Decrement the current argument counter.

– See if the counter is equal to zero.

– If this is not the case, the current operator needs additional arguments in order to do the calculation. We, therefore, simply need to put the calculator into a state which waits for the input of a new operator: we need to set the firstTime instance variable to true.

– If the counter is at zero, then we need to calculate the result of the transmission of the waiting operator to the two arguments which are at the top of the stack accu. This result must then be pushed onto this same stack. The operator must be popped from the operator stack, the current counter must be popped from the counter stack.

– If the counter stack is empty, then the calculation is finished. Otherwise, the obtained result acts as the operand of an operator which is still on the stack and we can *enter* this result. In short, the calculation continues with a recursive transmission of the callEqual: method to the calculator, which guarantees the execution of the operators which are still on the stack.

The callEqual: method below implements this algorithm.

```
PrefixCalculator>>callEqual: label
   self changed: #hist
           with: 'Enter > ' , bufferScreen.
   accu addFirst: bufferScreen asNumber.
   (counter addFirst: counter removeFirst - 1)
       = 0
     ifTrue: [| x |
        counter removeFirst.
        x := accu removeFirst.
        numArgs removeFirst = 1
           ifTrue:
           [accu
               addFirst:
                  (x perform: memFunc removeFirst)]
           ifFalse:
           [accu
               addFirst:
                  (accu removeFirst
                     perform: memFunc removeFirst
                     with: x)].
        self call: label.
        counter isEmpty not
           ifTrue:
              [bufferScreen := accu removeFirst asString.
               self callEqual: label]]
     ifFalse: [firstTime := true]
```

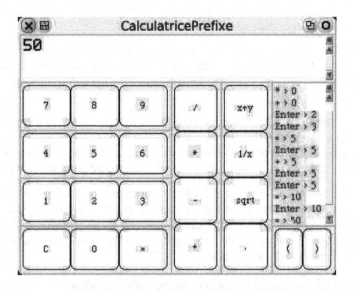

Figure A1.48. *A prefix calculator after having calculated* $* + 2\,3 + 5\,5$

Figure A1.48 shows our prefix calculator after having calculated $* + 2\,3 + 5\,5$. As we can see, adding an additional calculator was straightforward and easy to do: for the most part, we only needed to redefine the three main methods in the calculation: the method for entering a number, `callEqual:` and the other two arithmetic activation methods, `callFunction:` and `callUnaryFunction:`. No change was required to the display methods or the interface between the calculator and its graphical representation.

This is where the power of using dependencies comes in.

A1.10. Exercises for section 6.5

1) Creation of a counter. The *model* of a counter is simple: any variable which can contain an integer will work. Our counter class, `Counter`, therefore requires at least one instance variable. This will give us the class definition here:

```
Object subclass: #Counter
    instanceVariableNames: 'counter'
    classVariableNames: ''
    poolDictionaries: ''
    category: 'Lesson-Smalltalk'
```

Before any calculation, the counter must be initialized:

```
Counter>>initialize
    super intialize
    counter := 0
```

As with the majority of other classes which we have encountered, we will also define the method which specifies how an instance variable from the Counter class must be printed. A good solution would be to print just the value of the counter. This gives us the following printOn: method:

```
Counter>>printOn: aStream
    aStream nextPutAll: counter printString
```

After these preparatory methods, we will define the two methods which act on our counter, the method for decrementing:

```
Counter>>decrement
    self add: -1
```

and the method for incrementing:

```
Counter>>increment
    self add: 1
```

The previous two methods use the auxiliary method add: shown here:

```
Calculator>>add: aNumber
    counter := counter + aNumber.
```

We verify that these few methods will be sufficient for completely defining the counter *model*. For this, we will open an inspector on the Counter class. As we can see in Figure A1.49, where we have executed two doIts on the self increment expression, our counter functions perfectly. Now, we just need to define the graphical user interface.

As with our calculators, the display screen can be defined by a Pluggable-Text-Morph and the two keys for incrementation and decrementation can be defined by a Pluggable-Button-Morph on the Counter model. The morph containing these three objects can be a SystemWindow.

We will, therefore, write an openInWorld method which puts all of the morphs together:

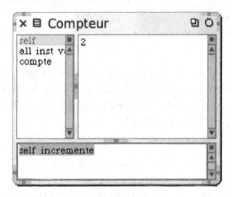

Figure A1.49. *An inspector open on the counter model*

```
Counter>>openInWorld
    | window buttonIncrement buttonDecrement screen |
    window := SystemWindow labelled: 'Counter'.
    window model: self.
    buttonIncrement :=
        PluggableButtonMorph new model: self;
            action: #increment;
            label: '+';
            borderWidth: 2.
    buttonDecrement :=
        PluggableButtonMorph new model: self;
            action: #decrement;
            label: '-';
            borderWidth: 2.

    screen := PluggableTextMorph
            on: self
            text: #printString
            accept: nil.
    window
        addMorph: screen
        frame: (0 @ 0 extent: 1 @ 0.5).
    window
        addMorph: buttonIncrement
        frame: (0 @ 0.5 extent: 0.5 @ 0.5).
    window
        addMorph: buttonDecrement
        frame: (0.5 @ 0.5 extent: 0.5 @ 0.5).
    window openInWorld
```

With this definition of our interface, the transmission `Counter new openInWorld` will display a counter as we had wanted, but the display on the counter does not change – as shown in Figure A1.50, where the inspector says that the counter has the value 9 (we have clicked on the + key nine times), but the screen of the counter still displays 0. Why?

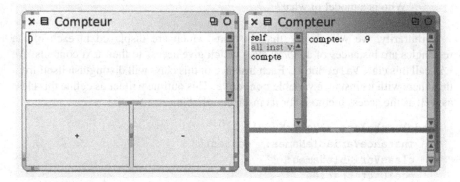

Figure A1.50. *A contradiction between the* model *and the* view

Here, the problem is that we have a graphical representation of the screen *without* the *dynamic* link with its model. We already have the *static* links: the counter was declared as a model of the `Pluggable-Text-Morph` representing the screen, since the model of the keys is also a counter. If this was not the case, clicking the + key would not have incremeneted the counter. However, for the keys, which are `Pluggable-Button-Morphs`, the *dynamic* link goes from the morphs: each click of a morph sends an (`increment` or `decrement`) message to its model. The screen is not an object which we, the users, act upon. It can only be the model which acts on the screen. And, it is the model which must send a message to the screen each time the screen needs to be updated. The dynamic links are not bidirectional – this was the reason for which the history screen of our first calculators had the calculator as a dependent object and the calculator had the screen as a dependency, which is how we obtained bidirectional dependency links.

We will, therefore, modify our `add:` method so that it informs the dependencies of the fact that it has just changed the value of the counter:

```
Counter>>add: aNumber
    counter := counter + aNumber.
    self changed: #printString
```

Now, for each modification of the counter, the screen will be informed of this and will be updated with this new value.

2) This exercise is much less trivial than it seems. Before starting to program, we will need to answer the following three questions:

- What structure do we need to use for this two-dimensional table?

- Where do we put the texts for each of these elements of the table?

- Who is a model of what?

Arbitrarily, we will decide that the texts which are displayed in each of the rectangles are instances of a *model* class which give access to their text contents. We will call this class ValueModel. Each instance of this class will distinguish itself from the others with its instance variable contents. This outline will let us define this class as well as the access methods for its instance variable:

```
Model subclass: #ValueModel
    instanceVariableNames: 'contents'
    classVariableNames: ''
    poolDictionaries: ''
    category: 'Lesson-Smalltalk'

ValueModel>>contents
    ^contents

contents: aValue
    contents:= aValue.
```

In order to implement the two-dimentional table, we can use the Matrix class of the SQUEAK system.

A matrix can be created with the rows:columns: message where the rows: argument specifies the number of rows and the columns: argument specifies the number of columns.

For accessing the elements of a matrix, SQUEAK offers the at:at: method where the first argument is the index of the line and the second argument is the index of the column of a particular element. Changing an element is achieved with the at:at:put: method. Of course, as with any collection – Matrix is the subclass of the Collection class – matrices offer the do: and indicesDo: methods for iterating through the set of these elements, the collect: method for constructing a new matrix with each of the elements obtained by applying the block argument to the elements of the receiver matrix, as well as a whole variety of methods which check for the presence of a particular object in the matrix: includes:, includes:AnyOf: and includes:AllOf:. The rowCount and columnCount methods, respectively, return the number of rows and the number of columns in the matrix.

We can then create the TextTable class which must be able to contain an instance of the Matrix class where each of its elements must be an instance of the

ValueModel class which contains a character string which must be displayed in the box corresponding to this element. This string of values is drawn in Figure A1.51.

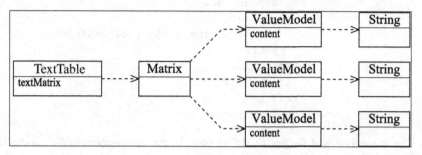

Figure A1.51. *The string of values from instances of* TextTable

We will, therefore, continue programming our text table by defining the TextTable class:

```
Object subclass: #TextTable
    instanceVariableNames: 'textMatrix'
    classVariableNames: ''
    poolDictionaries: ''
    category: 'Lesson-Smalltalk'
```

and its initialization method:

```
TextTable class>>width: x height: y
    ^ self new setMatrixWidth: y height: x
```

This method transmits the setMatrixWidth:height: message to the newly created instance of the TextTable class. This method must initialize the textMatrix instance variable to a matrix with x rows and y columns.

It must also initialize each element in the matrix to an instance of the ValueModel class, for which the contents instance variable will take as value the character string corresponding to a Point with the coordinates being the indices of the matrix element which it belongs to. Here is the method which performs these initializations:

```
TextTable>>setMatrixWidth: x height: y
    | value |
    textMatrix := Matrix rows: x columns: y.
    1
    to: x
    do: [:ro | 1
        to: y
```

```
do: [:co |
  value :=
    ValueModel new
      contents:
        ro asString , '@' , co asString;
      yourself.
  textMatrix
    at: ro
    at: co
    put: value]]
```

The transmission of the yourself message to the new instance of Value-Model (in the 14th line) is crucial: the elements of the matrix must not contain the text, they must contain the model of the text.

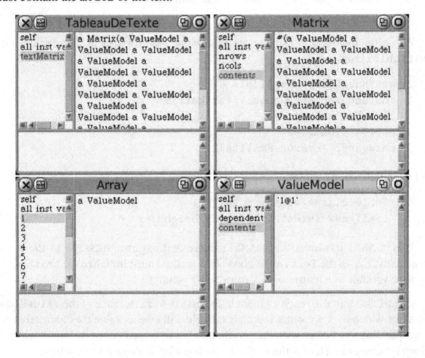

Figure A1.52. *The string of values seen through inspectors*

As always, we will verify that the program works properly by inspecting an instance of our class. Figure A1.52 shows a set of inspectors which will recount the same set of values as those shown in Figure A1.51. In the top left of the figure, we find the inspector on the instance of the TextTable class created by the transmission TextTable width: 5 height: 4. textMatrix, its instance variable, contains an instance of the Matrix class. The inspector on this instance is in the top right of the figure. The contents instance variable of the Matrix class, the variable containing the set of its elements, does contain a collection of instances of the ValueModel class. The inspector which is in the bottom left of the figure, an inspector on the contents variable, shows that the matrix is internally implemented as a table, as an instance of the Array class. We have run an inspector on the first element, which is, as shown in the inspector in the bottom right of the figure, an instance of the ValueModel class for which its contents instance variable contains the character string '1@1'. This is a Point for which its x coordinate is the row number and the y coordinate is the column number of this element in the matrix.

We will now turn our attention to programming the graphical user interface. For this, we will first need to create a view for each of the elements in the textMatrix. Each view will be a Pluggable-Text-Morph. Its size will be determined through a simple calculation on the number of rows and columns of the matrix: relative to the height of the main window, its height will be $\frac{1}{number\ of\ rows}$ and its width will be $\frac{1}{number\ of\ columns}$.

Here is our openInWorld method for instances of the TextTable class:

```
TextTable>>openInWorld
    | window textView testViewRectangle |
    window := SystemWindow labelled: 'Text Table'.
    window model: self.
    1
        to: textMatrix rowCount
        do: [:ro | 1
                to: textMatrix columnCount
                do: [:co |
                    textView :=
                        self textViewOnRow: ro
                                    column: co.
                    testViewRectangle :=
                        self rectangleForRow: ro
                                    column: co.
                    window addMorph: textView

                            frame: testViewRectangle]].
    window openInWorld
```

It creates, with the textViewOnRow:column: method, as we will see later, a Text-Morph for each element in the matrix, and calculates, with the rectangle-ForRow:-column: method, the rectangle in which we will need to insert this morph within the main morph, an instance of SystemWindow. Here is the definition of these two auxiliary methods:

```
TextTable>>textViewOnRow: row column: column
   | model textView |
   model := textMatrix at: row at: column.
   textView := PluggableTextMorph
           on: model
           text: #contents
           accept: #contents:.
   ^ textView
```

```
TextTable>>rectangleForRow: row column: column
   | width height extent left top |
   height := 1 / textMatrix rowCount.
   width := 1 / textMatrix columnCount.
   extent := width @ height.
   left := width * (column - 1).
   top := height * (row - 1).
   ^ left @ top extent: extent
```

If we now call the transmission: (TextTable width: 5 height: 4) openInWorld, we will obtain the view in Figure A1.53 where each subwindow of text has its own scroll bar.

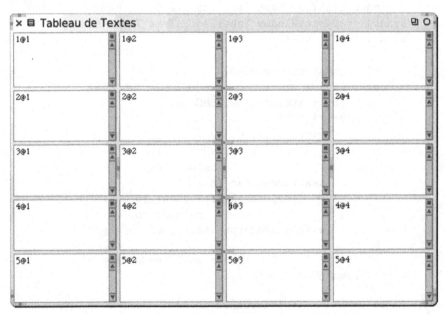

Figure A1.53. *An instance of* TextTable *with scroll bars*

If we do not want any scroll bars, as in Figure 6.29 (page 337), we just need to send to the `Pluggable-Text-Morph`, which represents these subwindows, the message `hide-Scroll-Bar-Indefinitely`. For example, we can insert the line `textView hideScrollBarIndefinitely` as the penultimate line in the `textViewOnRow:column:` method.

When we position the mouse over one of the morphs and we click it, a text cursor (represented as a vertical bar) will appear at the start of the text. We can then insert additional text, modify the text which is already there, or even delete it completely.

As soon as you modify the text in some way, a border will appear around the subwindow which has been modified. You have surely seen the appearance of such a border when editing methods. Any `PluggableTextMorph` indicates in this manner that its text has changed *and* that this change has not yet been saved. Thus, the border surrounding the subwindow containing the text of a method which you have modified disappears as soon as you save your changes (with an "Alt+s").

Any `PluggableTextMorph` provides – without you even having to ask – access to the Squeak text editor. This is very useful. However, if we try it with one of our texts, as shown in Figure A1.54:

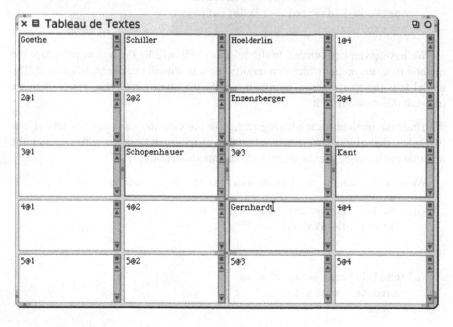

Figure A1.54. *An instance of* `TextTable` *with edited texts*

we can modify these texts, but after an "Alt+s" the border does not disappear. Thus (it is difficult to see this in the figure), all of the subwindows which were edited in Figure A1.54 retain their border.

This means that the texts are not editable. Only the view of the text can be modified. For the text itself to be editable, we need the instance of the ValueModel class which contains this text to provide write access. Otherwise, the text will only be accessible for reading and and not for writing.

Fo a PluggableTextMorph to have write access for the text that it displays, during its creation we need the selector of a method of the model to be given accept: as an argument. We will revisit our morph creation method:

```
TextTable>>textViewOnRow: row column: column
    | model textView |
    model := textMatrix at: row at: column.
    textView := PluggableTextMorph
                    on: model
                    text: #contents
                    accept: #contents:.
    textView hideScrollBarIndefinitely.
    ^ textView
```

We have given contents: to the selector. This will let the morph recognize the method from the *model* which *can* modify the text with the contents: method. The model tells the morph that it *wants* to modify the text by returning true when we transmit this message to it.

Thus, the method for modifying text, is in our case the contents: method, has two roles: that of modifying its text *and* that of telling the morphs with views on the text that the instance does or does not accept modifications.

We must now change the definition of the contents: method from:

```
ValueModel>>contents: aValue
    contents := aValue.
```

to:

```
ValueModel>>contents: aValue
    contents := aValue.
    ^ true
```

so that the modifications made by the editor are taken into account by the model.

We note that a PluggableTextMorph stores the texts which it displays in the form of a *text*, so as an instance of the Text class. These instances contain on top of the character strings which form the text itself, information about its style, the formatting, etc. If the model wishes to extract just the character string corresponding to the text, it must make a conversion, as below:

```
ValueModel>>contents: aValue
    contents := aValue asString.
    ^ true
```

Digression

Throughout this book, we have used *pluggable* morphs. As the name implies, this term comes from the word *plug* as a reference to the detachable connectors, which are connected to a conductor and used to establish contact through insertion of the piece into a socket. *Pluggable* morphs fulfill this role to a certain extent in SQUEAK: they exist and only make sense once they are connected to a model.

Of course, there are also non-pluggable morphs, in other words: morphs which do not have, from their creation, parts which enable an interface between them and a model. Pluggable-Button-Morph, therefore, has the corresponding Simple-Button-Morph and the String-Button-Morph. The Pluggabe-Text-Morph has as a matching non-pluggable TextMorph. The latter has a few characteristics of note, such as the ability to communicate with other TextMorphs, *predecessor* and *successor* morphs, the fact that it can adapt to any form of its parent morph, that it can generate representations of itself in postscript format and that it can provide access to the SQUEAK text editor.

Figure A1.55 shows a TextMorph put inside an EllipseMorph. Its successor is the TextMorph to its left. This means that the entered text which does not fit in the morph in the ellipse is automatically transmitted to its successor. The two texts which we can see in the image are actually one text: the beginning is found in the ellipse and the parts of the text which do not fit are transmitted to the second morph, positioned to its left. This set of morphs was obtained through the sequence of transmissions (in a Workspace) which we will develop below:

1) We will begin by creating a TextMorph and an EllipseMorph with the two transmissions:

```
textA := TextMorph new.
ellipse := EllipseMorph new.
```

2) We insert textA into the ellipse:

```
ellipse addMorph: textA.
```

3) Let us tell the morph textA, with the message fillingOnOff, that it must fit the contours of its parent morph – in this case, the ellipse.

```
textA fillingOnOff.
```

4) Let us enter some text into the `textA` morph:

```
textA contentsWrapped: 'Eine Urteilskraft die diale...'
```

5) We will play around with the editor in order to selectively change the set of characters:

```
(textA editor)
    selectFrom: (textA text string
                findString: 'aesthetischen')
          to: 1071;
    setEmphasis: #bold;
    selectFrom: 62 to: 74; setEmphasis: #underlined.
```

Dialektik des Geschmacks aus: weil niemand sein Urtheil zur allgemeinen Regel zu machen gedenkt. Es bleibt also kein Begriff von einer Dialektik übrig, welche den Geschmack angehenkönnte, als der einer Dialektik der Kritik des Geschmacks (nicht des Geschmacks selbst) in Ansehung ihrer Principien: da nämlich über den Grund der Möglichkeit der **Geschmacksurtheile** überhaupt einander widerstreitende Begriffe natürlicher und unvermeidlicher Weise auftreten. Transscendentale Kritik des Geschmacks wird also nur sofern einen Theil enthalten, der den Namen einer Dialektik der ästhetischen Urtheilskraft führen kann, wenn sich eine Antinomie der Principien dieses Vermögens findet, welche die Gesetzmäßigkeit desselben, mithin auch seine innere Möglichkeit zweifelhaft macht.

Eine Urtheilskraft, die dialektisch sein soll, muß zuvörderst <u>vernünfteln</u> sein; d. i. die Urtheile derselben müssen auf Allgemeinheit und zwar a priori Anspruch machen: denn in solcher Urtheile Entgegensetzung besteht die Dialektik. Daher ist die Unvereinbarkeit ästhetischer Sinnesurtheile (über das Angenehme und Unangenehme) nicht dialektisch. Auch der Widerstreit der Geschmacksurtheile, sofern sich ein jeder bloß auf seinen eignen Geschmack beruft, macht keine

(a) Two connected `TextMorph`s

Figure A1.55. A `TextMorph` in an `EllipseMorph` interconnected with another `TextMorph`: the text which does not fit in the ellipse is automatically pushed to the second morph

In Figure A1.55, we can clearly see the effect of these four transmissions: two words appear in bold characters and another word is underlined.

6) We will create a second `TextMorph` which will be the successor to `textA`:

```
textB := TextMorph new setPredecessor: textA.
```

7) We also need to say this to the morph textA:

```
textA setSuccessor: textB;  recomposeChain.
```

8) Finally, we open our morphs, so that they become visible:

```
ellipse openInWorld. textB openInWorld.
```

After these transmissions if you increase the size of the ellipse, you will be able to see the second morph shrink while the text returns, along with the size increase, into the ellipse, and if you shrink the ellipse, the second morph will fill with more of the text which no longer fits inside the reduced ellipse. Delightful, is it not?

You can also edit the two texts – insert the rest of Kant's thoughts or remove some of them – with the same effect on the fluctuations between the two TextMorphs.

Appendix 2

List of Keyboard Shortcuts

A2.1. Editing shortcuts

Alt+a	select all
Alt+c	copy
Alt+e	swap the contents of the current selection with that of the previous selection
Alt+j	again (repeat the last editing operation)
Alt+v	paste
Alt+w	delete the previous word
Alt+y	swap either the two selected characters, or, if no character is selected, the two characters either side of the cursor
Alt+z	undo
Alt+x	cut
Alt+H	move the cursor to the top of the file
Alt+J	repeat the last editing command up until the end of the text
Backspace	delete the character on the left side of the cursor
Delete	delete the character on the right side of the cursor
Shift+Bksp	delete the word to the left of the cursor
Shift+Delete	delete the word to the right of the cursor
Esc	show the main menu
End	move the cursor to the end of the line
Alt+End	move the cursor to the end of the text
arrow keys ↑, ↓, ←, →	move the cursor one line up, down, one character left, right
Ctrl+←	move the cursor one word to the left
Ctrl+→	move the cursor one word to the right
Ctrl+↑, PgUp	move the cursor one page up
Ctrl+↓, PgDown	move the cursor one page down

A2.2. Search shortcuts

Alt+f search   Alt+g search again
Alt+h the current selection becomes Alt+A positions the cursor on the
     the search string   argument   following   the
                          method selector, or at the end
                          if there are no arguments

A2.3. Cancel/accept shortcuts

Alt+z cancel   Alt+s accept (save) changes

A2.4. Browser, inspector and explorer shortcuts

Alt+b open a class browser on the selection

Alt+d do it : execute the selected Smalltalk expression; if nothing is selected, the expression is the current line

Alt+i inspect it : open an inspector on the result of the evaluation of the selected expression

Alt+m open a method browser on the *implementors* of the selector of the selected method

Alt+n open a method browser on the *senders* of the selector of the selected method

Alt+o open a new window containing the same method as the current window (spawn)

Alt+p print it: evaluate the selected expressions and print the result

Alt+E open a method browser on the methods for which the source contains the selected string

Alt+G read the selected file

Alt+I open an object browser on the result of the evaluation of the selected expression

Alt+O open a browser on the selected method

Alt+W open a browser on the methods where the selector includes the selection as a sub-string

A2.5. Shortcuts for parentheses, square brackets, curly brackets

Alt+(surround the selection with parentheses, or, if they exist already, remove them

Alt+[surround the selection with square brackets, or, if they exist already, remove them

Alt+{ surround the selection with curly brackets, or, if they exist already, remove them

Alt+< surround the selection with chevrons, or, if they exist already, remove them

Alt+' surround the selection with single quotes, or, if they exist already, remove them

Alt+" surround the selection with double quotes, or, if they exist already, remove them

A2.6. Conversion shortcuts

Alt+C open a *workspace* which shows the comparison between the selection and the contents of the clipboard

Alt+U convert line breaks in the selection into carriage returns

Alt+X convert the selection to lowercase

Alt+Y convert the selection to uppercase

Alt+Z capitalize the selected words

A2.7. Code completion shortcuts

Alt+q	auto-completion: proposes a valid selection (new proposition at reach repetition of <Alt+q>)
Alt+r	run SQUEAK's character recognition system
Alt+F	insert ifFalse:
Alt+T	insert ifTrue:
Alt+V	insert the initials of the author
Alt+L	remove indent (left tab)
Alt+R	add indent (right tab)
Shift+Ctrl+Enter	insert a carriage return followed by the number of tabs in the previous line
Shift+Delete	delete the next word or expression

A2.8. Formatting shortcuts

The following shortcuts do no work on all platforms.

Alt+k	specify the font
Alt+u	align
Alt+K	define the syle
Capslock+Alt+1	10-point font size
Capslock+Alt+2	12-point font size
Capslock+Alt+3	18-point font size
Capslock+Alt+4	24-point font size
Capslock+Alt+5	36-point font size
Capslock+Alt+6	open a menu for specifying the color, a link to a class comment, to a method, to a URL...Use Alt-0 to cancel the created links
Capslock+Alt+7	bold
Capslock+Alt+8	italic
Capslock+Alt+9	thin
Capslock+Alt+0	cancel all properties
Alt+-	(hyphen) underline
Alt+=	strike through
Alt+_	thinner
Alt++	wider

Appendix 3

SMALLTALK Syntax Specification

A3.1. Base characters

```
digit             ::= 0 | 1 | 2 | 3 | 4 | 5 | 6 | 7 | 8 | 9
digitSequence     ::= digit+
number            ::= {digitSequence r} {−} digitSequence
                        {. digitSequence} {e {−} digitSequence}
letter            ::= A | ... | Z | a | ... | z
special character ::= + | / | \ | * | ~ | < | > | = | @ | % | | & | ? | !
character         ::= [ | ] | { | } | ( | ) | ← | ↑ | . | ; | $ | # | : | digit |
                        letter | special character
```

A3.2. Constants

```
identifier        ::= letter {{letter}{digit}}+
symbol            ::= identifier | BinarySelector | keyWord+
symbolConstant    ::= # symbol
characterConstant ::= $ {character | ' | " }
string            ::= ' {character | ' ' | " }* '
comment           ::= " {character | " " | ' }* "
constantArray     ::= # table
table             ::= ( {number | symbol | string |
                          characterConstant | table}* )
literal           ::= number | symbolConstant |
                        characterConstant | string |
                        constantArray
```

```
variableName    ::= identifier
unarySelector   ::= identifier
binarySelector  ::= − I special character special character
keyWord         ::= identifier :
primaryThing    ::= variableName I literal I block I
                        ( expression )
```

A3.3. Expressions

```
unaryObjectDescription   ::= primaryThing I unaryExpression
binaryObjectDescription  ::= unaryObjectDescription I
                                 binaryExpression
unaryExpression          ::= unaryObjectDescription unarySelector
binaryExpression         ::= unaryObjectDescription binarySelector
                                 unaryObjectDescription
keyWordExpression        ::= binaryObjectDescription
                                 { keyWord binaryObjectDescription}+
message                  ::= unaryExpression I binaryExpression
                                 I keyWordExpression
cascade                  ::= message {; unarySelector I
                                 binarySelector unaryObjectDescriptionI
                                 {keyWord binaryObjectDescription}+ }
expression1              ::= {variableName :=}+
                                 {primaryThing I message I stream }
expression2              ::= {{expression1 .}* I ↑ expression1}+
block                    ::= [ {: variableName}* I expression2* ]
temporaryVariables       ::= I variableName* I
messageFormat            ::= unarySelector I binarySelector I
                                 {keyWord variableName}+
method                   ::= messageFormat temporaryVariables* expressions2*
```

Appendix 4

List of SQUEAK Primitives

The primitives which are necessary for the system are written in bold. The other primitives are optional and only exist to accelerate the computation.

A4.1. Arithmetic and logic primitives

A4.1.1. *From the* SmallInteger *class*

1	+	**2**	−
3	<	**4**	>
5	<=	**6**	>=
7	=	**8**	~=
9	*	**10**	/
11	\\	**12**	//
13	quo:	**14**	bitAnd:
15	bitOr:	**16**	bitXor:
17	bitShift	**40**	asFloat

A4.1.2. *From the* Number *class*

18 @

A4.1.3. *From the stkLargePositiveInteger class*

21	+	**22**	−
23	<	**24**	>
25	<=	**26**	>=

7 =   8 ~=
29 *   30 /
31 \\   32 //
33 quo: 14 bitAnd:
15 bitOr: 16 bitXor:
17 bitShift

A4.1.4. *From the* Float *class*

41 +   42 −
43 <   44 >
45 <=   46 >=
47 =   48 ~=
49 *   50 /
51 truncated 52 fractionPart
53 exponent   54 timesTwoPower:
55 sqrt   56 sin
57 arcTan   58 ln
59 exp

A4.2. Access primitives

60 LargeNegativeInteger»digitAt:,
   LargePositiveInteger»digitAt:, Object»at:, Object»basicAt:
   Array»atWrap:, B3DPrimitiveVertex»wordAt:,
   B3DFloatArray»wordAt:, ByteArray»byteAt:, String»byteAt:
61 LargeNegativeInteger»digitAt:put:,
   LargePositiveInteger»digitAt:put:, Object»at:put:,
   Object»basicAt:put:, Array»atWrap:put:,
   B3DPrimitiveVertex»B3DFloatArray»wordAt:put:,
   ByteArray»byteAt:put:, String»byteAt:put:
62 ArrayedCollection»size, LargeNegativeInteger»digitLength,
   LargePositiveInteger»digitLength, Object»basicSize,
   Object»size, String»size
63 String»at:
64 String»at:put:

65 ReadStream»next, ReadWriteStream»next,
CompressedSourceStream»next, InflateStream»next,
ReadWriteStream»next, ReadStream»next
66 WriteStream»nextPut:, WordArray»nextPut:,
ZipEncoder»nextBytePut:
67 PositionableStream»atEnd
68 CompiledMethod»objectAt:
69 CompiledMethod»objectAt:put:

A4.3. Object creation primitives

70 Behaviour»basicNew, Behaviour»new, Interval class»new
71 Behaviour»new:, Behaviour»basicNew:
72 Array»elementsForwardIdentityTo:
73 Object»instVarAt:, IslandVMTweaksTestCase»instVarOf:at:,
ObjectOut»xxxInstVarAt:
74 Object»instVarAt:put:, ObjectOut»xxxInstVarAt:put:,
IslandVMTweaksTestCase»instVarOf:at:put:
75 Object»asOop, ProtoObject»identityHash
76 ContextPart»stackp:
77 Behaviour»someInstance,
IslandVMTweaksTestCase»someInstanceOf:
78 ProtoObject»nextInstance,
IslandVMTweaksTestCase»nextInstanceAfter:
79 CompiledMethodClass» newMethod:header:

A4.4. Execution primitives

80 ContextPart»blockCopy:
81 BlockContext»value:value:value:, BlockContext:value,
BlockContext»value:, BlockContext»value:value:
82 BlockContext»valueWithArguments:
83 Object»perform:with:with:with:, Object»perform:with:with:,
Object»perform:with:, Object»perform:
84 Object»perform:withArguments:

A4.5. Process management primitives

19 BlockContext»newProcess, BlockContext»newProcessWith:,
ContextPart»doPrimitive:method:receiver:args:,
ControlManager»activeController:,
ControlManager»scheduleActive:,
Debugger»openContext:label:contents:,
Debugger»openInterrupt:onProcess:, SyntaxError»open:
85 Semaphore»signal
86 Semaphore»wait
87 Process»primitiveResume
88 Process»primitiveSuspend
89 Behaviour»flushCache
90 InputSensor»primMousePt
91 DisplayScreen»supportsDisplayDepth:,
InputSensor»primCursorLocPut:,
InputSensor»primCursorLocPutAgain:
92 DisplayScreen»depth:width:height:fullscreen:
93 EventSensor»primSetInputSemaphore:
94 EventSensor»primGetNextEvent:
97 SystemDictionary»snapshotPrimitive,
SmalltalkImage»snapshotPrimitive
98 ImageSegment»storeSegmentFor:into:outPointers:
99 ImageSegment»loadSegmentFrom:outPointers:
100 Object»perform:withArguments:inSuperclass:

A4.6. Input/output primitives

101 Cursor»beCursor, Cursor»beCursorWithMask:
102 Display»beDisplay
103 CharacterScanner»
primScanCharactersFrom:to:in:rightX:stopConditions:kern:,
CharacterScanner»
scanCharactersFrom:to:in:rightX:stopConditions:kern:
106 DisplayScreen»actualScreenSize
107 InputSensor»primMouseButtons
108 InputSensor»primKbdNext
109 InputSensor»primKbdPeek

A4.7. Search and replace primitives

105 ByteArray»privateReplaceFrom:to:with:startingAt:, also for the
classes: ByteArray, B3DPrimitiveVertex,
B3DPrimitiveVertexArray, B3DInplaceArray,
ArrayedCollection»replaceFrom:to:with:startingAt:, also for
the classes: Array, B3DIndexedQuad, B3DIndexedTriangle,
B3DPrimitiveRasterizerData, Bitmap, FloatArray,
LargePositiveInteger, FloatArray, String, WordArray

A4.8. And the others

110 Character»=, ProtoObject»==
111 Object»class, ImageSegmentRootStub»xxxClass,
ObjectOut»xxxClass, IslandVMTweaksTestCase»classOf:
anObject
112 SystemDictionary»bytesLeft:, ystemDictionary»primBytesLeft
113 SystemDictionary»quitPrimitive,
SmalltalkImage»quitPrimitive
114 SystemDictionary»exitToDebugger,
SmalltalkImage»exitToDebugger
115 Object»primitiveChangeClassTo:
116 CompiledMethod»flushCache
118 ProtoObject»tryPrimitive:withArgs:
119 Symbol»flushCache
121 SmalltalkImage»imageName, SmalltalkImage»imageName:
123 BlockContext»
ifProperUnwindSupportedElseSignalAboutToReturn
124 SystemDictionary»primLowSpaceSemaphore:
125 SystemDictionary»primSignalAtBytesLeft:
126 DisplayScreen»primitiveDeferUpdates:
127 DisplayScreen»primRetryShowRectLeft:right:top:bottom:,
DisplayScreen»primShowRectLeft:right:top:bottom:
128 Array»elementsExchangeIdentityWith:
129 SystemDictionary»specialObjectsArray
130 SystemDictionary»snapshotEmbeddedPrimitive
131 SystemDictionary»garbageCollectMost
132 CompiledMethod»hasLiteral:, ProtoObject»pointsTo:
133 InputSensor»primSetInterruptKey:
134 InputSensor»primInterruptSemaphore:
135 Time class»millisecondClockValue, Time
class»primMillisecondClock

136 Delay class»primSignal:atMilliseconds:
137 Time class»primSecondsClock
138 Object»someObject, IslandVMTweaksTestCase»someObject
139 ProtoObject»nextObject,
    IslandVMTweaksTestCase»nextObjectAfter:,
    PseudoContext»nextObject
140 Beeper class»primitiveBeep
141 Clipboard»primitiveClipboardText,
    Clipboard»primitiveClipboardText:
142 SmalltalkImage»vmPath
143 SoundBuffer»at:, ShortIntegerArray»at:,
    ShortIntegerArray»pvtAt:, ShortRunArray»pvtAt:
144 SoundBuffer»at:put:, ShortIntegerArray»at:put:,
    ShortIntegerArray»pvtAt:put:, ShortRunArray»pvtAt:put:
145 ByteArray»atAllPut:, IntegerArray»primFill:,
    SoundBuffer»primFill:, WordArray»atAllPut:,
    B3DColor4Array»fillWith:, Bitmap»atAllPut:,
    Bitmap»primFill:
148 Object»clone, Object»shallowCopy, ObjectOut»xxxClone,
    ThirtyTwoBitRegister»»copy
149 SmalltalkImage»getSystemAttribute:
165 IntegerArray»at:, B3DPrimitiveRasterizerData»integerAt:,
    B3DPrimitiveVertex»integerAt:, Bitmap»integerAt:
166 Bitmap»integerAt:put:, B3DPrimitiveVertex»integerAt:put:,
    IntegerArray»at:put:
167 ProcessorScheduler»yield
168 Object»copyFrom:
188 Object»withArgs:executeMethod:
195 ContextPart»findNextUnwindContextUpTo:
196 ContextPart»terminateTo:
197 ContextPart»findNextHandlerContextStarting
198 BlockContext»ensure:, BlockContext»ifCurtailed:
199 BlockContext»on:do:
230 ProcessorScheduler
    class»relinquishProcessorForMicroseconds:
231 DisplayScreen»forceDisplayUpdate
232 Form»primPrintHScale:vScale:landscape:
233 DisplayScreen»fullScreenMode:
247 SmalltalkImage»snapshotEmbeddedPrimitive,
    SystemDictionary»snapshotEmbeddedPrimitive
249 Array»elementsForwardIdentityTo:copyHash:
250 SmalltalkImage»clearProfile
251 SmalltalkImage»dumpProfile

Bibliography

[ABE 81] ABELSON H., DISESSA A.A., *Turtle Geometry: the Computer as a Medium for Exploring Mathematics*, The MIT Press, Cambridge, MA, 1981.

[AGH 97] AGHA G., HEWITT C.E., "Actors: a conceptual foundation for concurrent object-oriented programming", in SHRIVER B., WEGNER P. (eds), *Research Directions in Object Oriented Programming*, MIT Press, Cambridge, MA, pp. 49–74, 1997.

[ALB 84] ALBERT P., "KOOL at a glance", *Proceedings of the 6th European Conference on Artificial Intelligence (ECAI)*, Pisa, Italy, p. 345, 1984.

[ALB 88] ALBERT P., "Kool: Merging Object Frames and Rules", in DEMANGEOT J. , HERVÉ T. , ROCHE C. (eds), *Artificial Intelligence and Cognitive Sciences*, Manchester University Press, Manchester, England, pp. 15–21. 1988.

[BAR 93] BARNSLEY M.F., *Fractals Everywhere*, Academic Press, London, England, 1993.

[BAU 80] BAUDELAIRE C., *Les Fleurs Du Mal*, Robert Laffont, Paris, 1980 (based on the 2nd editon of 1861).

[BEE 72] BEELER M., GOSPER W.R., Schroeppel R.H., "Hakmen", *AI Memo 239*, MIT AI Lab, Cambridge, MA, 1972.

[BOB 86] BOBROW D.G., KAHN K., KICZALES G. *et al.*, "CommonLoops: merging Lisp and object-oriented programming", *Proceedings of the ACM Conference on Object-Oriented Systems, Languages and Applications (OOPSLA)*, 1986.

[BOB 88] BOBROW D.G., DEMICHIEL L.G., GABRIEL R.P. *et al.*, Common Lisp object system specification, Technical Report X3J13 Document 88-002R, Xerox PARC, Palo Alto, CA, 1988.

[BOO 72] BOOLE G., *An Investigation of the Laws of Thought*, Macmillan, London, England, 1872 (republished by Dover Publications in 1985).

[BRI 87] BRIOT J.P., COINTE P., "A uniform model for object-oriented languages using the class abstraction", *Proceedings International Joint Conference on Artificial Intelligence*, Paris, France, pp. 40–43, 1987.

[BÜC 39] BÜCKER M.C., GEIDEL J., LACHMANN M.F., *Objectword®\Smalltalk für Anfänger*, Springer-Verlag, Berlin Heidelberg, New York, 1939.

[BUD 88] BUDD T.A., *A Little Smalltalk*, Addison-Wesley, Reading, MA, 1988.

[BUR 77] BURSTALL R.M., DARLINGTON J., "A transformation system for developing recursive programs", *Journal of the ACM*, vol. 24, no. 1, January 1977.

[CAN 82] CANNON H.I., Flavors: a non-hierarchical approach to object-oriented programming, Technical report, Symbolics, Inc., Cambridge, MA, 1982.

[CHA 96] CHAPIN N., *Standard Object-Oriented Cobol*, John Wiley & Sons, New York, NY, 1996.

[CHU 41] CHURCH A., *The Calculi of Lambda Conversion*, Princeton University Press, Princeton, NJ, 1941.

[COX 87] COX B.J., *Object Oriented Programming: An Evolutionary Approach*, Addison-Wesley, Reading, MA, 1987.

[CRO 08] CROS C., *Le collier des griffes*, P. V. Stock, Paris, 1908.

[DAH 67] DAHL O., NYGAARD K., Simula begin, Technical report, Norsk Regnesentral, Norwegian Computing Center, Oslo, Norway, 1967.

[DAR 73] DARLINGTON J., BURSTALL R.M., "A system which automatically improves programs", *Proceedings of the 2nd International Joint Conference on Artificial Intelligence*, Stanford, CA, 1973.

[DER 83] DERSHOWITZ N., *The Evolution of Programs*, Birkhäuser, Boston, Basel, Stuttgart, 1983.

[DIJ 76] DIJKSTRA E.W., *A Discipline of Programming*, Prentice Hall, Englewood Cliffs, NJ, 1976.

[DOD 83] DOD, Reference manual for the Ada programming language, Ansi/mil-std-1815 a, Department of Defense, Washington, DC, 1983.

[DUG 88] DUGERDIL P., OBJLOG II, guide d'utilisation, Technical report, Groupe Représentation et Traîtement de Connaissances, University of Aix-Marseille, Marseille, France, 1988.

[ELL 94] ELLIS T.M.R., PHILIPS I.V.R., LAHEY T.M., *Fortran 90 Programming*, Addison-Wesley, Reading, MA, 1994.

[FOW 97] FOWLER M., SCOTT K., *UML Distilled, Applying the Standard Object Modeling Language*, Addison-Wesley, Reading, MA, 1997.

[GAR 89] GARDNER M., "Penros tilings to Trapdoor Ciphers: and the return of Dr Matrix" *Penrose Tilings and Trapdoor Ciphers*, W. H. Freeman, New York, NY, 1989.

[GIA 85] GIANNESINI F., KANOUI H., PASERO R. *et al.*, *Prolog*, InterEditions, Paris, France, 1985.

[GOL 83] GOLDBERG A., ROBSON D., *Smalltalk-80: the Language and its Implementation*, Addison-Wesley, Reading, MA, 1983.

[GOL 84] GOLDBERG A., *Smalltalk-80: the Interactive Programming Environment*, Addison-Wesley, Reading, MA, 1984.

[GUZ 06] GUZDIAL M., Multimedia nuts-and-bolts, available at www-static.cc.gatech.edu/classes/AY2004/cs2340_summer/13-MultimediaNuts&Bolts.ppt, April 2006.

[HUL 83] HULLOT J.M., "A multiformalism programming environment", in MASON R.E.A. (ed.), *Information Processing 83, Proceedings of the IFIP 9th World Computer Congress*, Paris, France, pp. 223–227, 19-23 September 1983.

[HUL 85] HULLOT J.M., ALCYONE, la boîte à outils objets, Research report, INRIA, Rocquencourt, France, 1985.

[IEE 05] IEEE, Working conference on reverse engineering, available at www.computer.org/portals/site/ieeecs/, 2005.

[ILI 87] ILINE H., KANOUI H., "Extending logic programming to object programming: the system LAP", *Proceedings of the 10th International Joint Conference on Artificial Intelligence*, Milan, Italy, pp. 34–39, 1987.

[ING 97] INGALLS D., KAEHLER T., MALONEY J. *et al.*, "Back to the future: the story of Squeak, a practical Smalltalk written in itself", *OOPSLA'97 Conference Proceedings*, ACM, Atlanta, GA, pp. 318–326, 1997.

[JAC 87] JACKY J.P., KALET I.J., "An object-oriented programming discipline for standard Pascal", *Communications of the ACM*, vol. 30, no. 9, pp. 772–776, September 1987.

[JEN 75] JENSEN K., WIRTH N., *Pascal: User Manual and Report*, Springer-Verlag, New York, Heidelberg, Berlin, 1975.

[KAN 93] KANT I., *Kritik der Urteilskraft*, Lagarde, Berlin, 1793.

[KAY 68] KAY A.C., The reactive engine, Doctoral dissertation, University of Utah, 1968.

[KAY 93] KAY A.C., "The early history of Smalltalk", *History of Programming Languages, HOPL-II*, ACM-Sigplan Notices, vol. 15, no. 3, pp. 69–95, March 1993.

[KER 88] KERNIGHAM B.W., RITCHIE D.M., *The C Programming Language*, Prentice Hall, Upper Saddle River, NJ, 1988.

[KNU 67] KNUTH D.E., BENDIX P.B., "Simple word problems in universal algebras", in LEECH J. (ed.), *Proceedings of the Conference on Computational Problems in Abstract Algebra*, Pergamon Press, Oxford, England, pp. 263–297, 1967.

[LAN 64] LANDIN P.J., "The mechanical evaluation of expressions", *The Computer Journal*, vol. 9, no. 4, pp. 308–320, 1964.

[LER 07] LEROY X., DOLIGEZ D., GARRIGUE J. *et al.*, The objective Caml system, documentation and user's manual, Technical Report release 3.10, INRIA, Rocquencourt, France, May 2007.

[LIN 68] LINDENMAYER A., "Mathematical models for cellular interaction in development, parts i and ii", *Journal of Theoretical Biology*, vol. 18, pp. 280–315, 1968.

[LIS 77] LISKOV B., SNYDER A., ATKINSON R. *et al.*, "Abstraction mechanisms in CLU", *Communications of the ACM*, vol. 20, no. 8, pp. 772–776, August 1977.

[LUK 29] LUKASIEWICZ J., *Elementy logiki mathematycnej, Script autoryzowany*, Warsaw, Poland, 1929 (English translation: *Elements of mathematical logic*, Pergamon Press, Oxford, 1966).

[MAN 77] MANDELBROT B.B., *The Fractal Geometry of Nature*, W. H. Freeman and Company, New York, NY, 1977.

[MAT 01] MATSUMOTO Y., *Ruby in a Nutshell*, O'Reilly, Sebastopol, CA, 2001.

[MCC 62] MCCARTHY J., ABRAHAMS P., EDWARDS D.J. *et al.*, *LISP 1.5 Programmer's Manual*, MIT Press, Cambridge, MA, 1962.

[MEY 86] MEYER B., *Eiffel: un langage et une méthode pour le génie logiciel*, Interactive Software Engineering, Inc., Santa Barbara, CA, 1986.

[MIN 85] MINSKY M., "A framework for representing knowledge", in WINSTON P.H. (ed.), *The Psychology of Computer Vision*, McGraw-Hill, New York, NY, pp. 211–227, 1985.

[MOO 80] MOON D., WEINREB D., FLAVORS: message passing in the LISP machine, AI memo 602, Artificial Intelligence Laboratory, MIT, Cambridge, MA, 1980.

[MUL 98] MULLIS K., *Dancing Naked in the Mind Field*, Vintage Books, New York, NY, 1998.

[NAU 63] NAUR P., "Revised report on the algorithmic language ALGOL-60", *Communications of the ACM*, vol. 6, no. 1, pp. 1–17, 1963.

[PAP 80] PAPERT S., *Mindstorms: Children, Computers and Powerful Ideas*, Basic Books, New York, NY, 1980.

[PAP 05] PAPERT S., Logo, available at www.papert.org/, 2005.

[PAR 83] PARTSCH H.A., STEINBRÜGGEN R., "Program transformation systems", *Computing Surveys*, vol. 15, no. 3, pp. 199 – 236, September 1983.

[PEI 92] PEITGEN H.O., JÜRGENS H., SAUPE D., *Chaos and Fractals: New Frontiers of Science*, Springer-Verlag, New York, Berlin, Heidelberg, 1992.

[PER 59] PERLIS A.J., SAMELSON K., "Report on the algorithmic language ALGOL by the ACM committee on programming languages and the GAMM committee on programming", *Numerische Mathematik*, vol. 1, pp. 41–60, 1959.

[PLO 81] PLOTKIN G.D., A structural approach to operational semantics, Technical Report Tech. Rep. DAIM FN-19, Computer Science Department, Aarhus University, Aarhus, Denmark, 1981.

[POP 98] POPE S.T., The do-it-yourself guide to Squeak primitives, available at http://users.ipa.net/dwighth/squeak/diy_sq_prims.html, April 1998.

[POU 87] POUTAIN R., *Object-Oriented Forth*, Academic Press, London, England, 1987.

[PRU 89] PRUSINKIEWICZ P., HANAN J., *Lindemayer Systems, Fractals, and Plants*, Lecture Notes in Biomathematics, Springer-Verlag, Berlin, Germany, 1989.

[PRU 90] PRUSINKIEWICZ P., LINDENMAYER A., *The Algorithmic Beauty of Plants*, Springer Verlag, Berlin, Germany, 1990.

[REE 91] REESE D.S., LUKE E., "Object oriented Fortran for development of portable programs", *Proceedings of the 3rd IEEE Symposium on Parallel Distributed Processing*, Dallas, TX, pp. 608–615, December 1991.

[REY 87] REYNOLDS C.W., "Flocks, herds, and schools: a distributed behavioral model", *ACM SIGGRAPH Computer Graphics*, vol. 21, no. 4, pp. 25–34, July 1987.

[RIF 86] RIFFLET J.M., *La programmation sous Unix*, Ediscience, Paris, France, 1986.

[SAN 77] SANDEWALL E., "Some observations in conceptual programming", in ELCOCK 2E.W., MICHIE D. (eds), *Machine Intelligence 8*, John Wiley & Sons, New York, NY, pp. 223–365, 1977.

[SAN 78] SANDEWALL E., "Programming in an interactive environment: the 'LISP' experience", *Computing Surveys*, vol. 18, no. 1, pp. 35–71, 1978.

[SCH 86] SCHMUCKER K.J., *Object-Oriented Languages for the Macintosh*, Hayden Book Company, Hasbrouck Heights, NJ, 1986.

[SCO 70] SCOTT D.S., "Outline of a mathematical theory of computation", *Programming Research Group, Oxford University Computing Laboratory*, Oxford University Computing Laboratory, Programming Research Group, available at https://books.google.fr/books?id=LxpmQgAACAAJ, 1970.

[SHA 37] SHANNON C.E., A symbolic analysis of relay and switching circuits, Master Thesis, MIT, Department of Electrical Engineering, 1937.

[SIE 15] SIERPISKI W.F., "Sur une courbe dont tout point est une ramification", *Comptes Rendus de l'Académie des Sciences, Paris*, no. 160 vol. 302, 1915.

[STR 87] STROUSTROUP B., *The C++ Programming Language*, Addison-Wesley, Reading, MA, 1987.

[SUT 63] SUTHERLAND I.E., "Sketchpad: a man-machine graphical communication system", *Proceedings of the AFIPS Spring Computer Conference*, Detroit, Michigan, pp. 329–346, May 1963.

[TAK 83] TAKEUCHI I., OKUNO H., OHSATO N., "TAO: a harmonic mean of LISP, Prolog and Smalltalk", *ACM SIGPLAN Notices*, vol. 18, no. 7, pp. 65–74, July 1983.

[UNG 87] UNGAR D., SMITH R.B., "Self: the power of simplicity", *OOPSLA'87 Conference Proceedings on Object-oriented Programming Systems, Languages and Applications*, Orlando, FA, pp. 227 – 242, 1987.

[VAN 04] VAN KOCH H., "Sur une courbe continue sans tangente, obtenue par une construction gométrique élémentaire", *Archiv för Matermat*, vol. 1, pp. 681–702, 1904.

[VAN 95] VAN ROSSUM G., Python reference manual, Technical Report CS-R9525, CWI, Amsterdam, Netherlands, 1995.

[VIS 05] VISUALWORKS, Cincom, available at: www.smalltalk.cincom.com/, 2005.

[WEG 06] WEGNER T., Fractint, available at: www.fractint.org/, 2006.

[WER 80] WERTZ H., "L'utilisation de l'outil informatique: Pilotage et programmation", in SIMON J.C. (ed.), *l'éducation et l'informatisation de la société (Rapport au Président de la République)*, volume annexes 1: Les voies de développement, Contributions des groupes de travail, La Documentation Française, pp. 177–194, 1980.

[WER 89] WERTZ H., *LISP: une Introduction à la Programmation*, Manuels Informatiques Masson, Paris, 1989.

[WIK 06a] WIKIPEDIA, Deoxyribonucleic acid, available at www.wikipedia.org/ wiki/DNA, 2006.

[WIK 06b] WIKIPEDIA, Le bogue original, available at www.wikipedia.org/wiki/ Software_bug, 2006.

[WOS 78] WOSSNER H., PEPPER P., PARTSCH H.A. *et al.*, "Special transformation techniques", *Proceedings of International Summer School on Program Construction*, GMD, Marktoberdorf, Germany, 1978.

Index

Printed in the United States
By Bookmasters